THE SQUIRES OF SPRINGFIELD

THE SQUIRES
of SPRINGFIELD

by

Katherine Wooten Springs

WILLIAM LOFTIN, *Publisher*
Charlotte, North Carolina

MANUFACTURED IN THE UNITED STATES OF AMERICA
BY HERITAGE PRINTERS, INC., CHARLOTTE, NORTH CAROLINA

To
my husband
ELI

PREFACE

A leather trunk, generations old, stood unopened in my attic for thirty years. One day I untied the rope that bound it securely and lifted the lid. Gazing down into the trunk I saw hundreds of letters, all tied in neat little packages.

Somewhat indifferently, I pulled a letter from one bundle. It was signed "John Springs." He was my husband's great-grandfather. I read the first page. John was writing in 1808 of his love for his wife, his "dearest Mary." How beautifully it was expressed! With more enthusiasm I pulled another letter from its resting place. This one too was from John, written to his son, Baxter Springs, in 1844. The next letter I read was dated 1798.

By this time, I was sneezing from the mustiness of the old paper, but my curiosity prompted me to select still another letter, and another. With great fascination, I read for hours and then for days, because these letters were like voices from the past which amused and intrigued me. Then I saw that the letters should be catalogued according to date. When this was done a sudden realization came over me. Those voices from the past were telling a simple but astounding story. It was not just a story of the Springs family. It was the story of the United States of America as told through the personal experiences of this one family.

I remembered the inscription on the National Archives Building in Washington, D. C., which reads: "The heritage of the past is the seed that brings forth the harvest of the future." This I had never really appreciated before. Now, in cataloguing the Springs letters by date, I could see how each generation influenced the next. The same familiar little phrases were passed down from father to son to grandson. I could see how the grandson's actions were influenced by his father, and he in turn by his father. It was like a human chain.

After reading more than a thousand letters, I came to the conclusion that they should be read by others. They were too important and too good to be locked up again. And so I began to write this story.

The Springs story probably is extraordinary in one respect. Each generation had a mania for saving records, letters, historical data, and even receipted bills. Therefore, each generation has told and documented its story in its own way. All I have done is put it together. I have been fortunate to possess the whole story of three centuries of American living where they, as individuals, could only know a few chapters. Now I pass it on for future generations who will thrill to little intimate details that no academic history book could ever give them.

K. W. S.

Charlotte, N. C.
November, 1964

CONTENTS

ILLUSTRATIONS

Illustration sections will be found between pages 116 and 117 and between pages 276 and 277.

Part One

THE BEGINNING

CHAPTER ONE

MOST COLONIAL AMERICAN FAMILIES were led across the Atlantic by a pioneering male. In many instances the father ventured first and sent for his wife and children later. The Springsteen or Springs family, however, made a different approach. The senior member to cross the ocean was a courageous widow, Gertrude Springsteen. With her were her daughter Barbara and three sons, Johannes, Melchior, and Caspar.

The family originally lived in the Province of Groeningen, Holland. There the father, Caspar Springsteen, died in 1650. That same year the Hollanders revolted against ruling Spain for the second time in a century. A "golden age" of literature, art, learning, and commerce ended in bitter warfare. Surely those trying times influenced the Springsteens in their decision to migrate to America. This they did in 1652.

New Netherlands was a thriving colony under the guidance of the sturdy, indomitable Peter Stuyvesant, governor from 1647 to 1664, when the Springsteens arrived at its capital of New Amsterdam, now New York City. Stuyvesant had settled a boundary dispute with the English in Connecticut, taken control of the Swedish colony of New Sweden on the Delaware, and, what was more important, maintained friendly relations with the Indians. Thus the Springsteens arrived under auspicious circumstances. Being practical people, Gertrude must have brought her household furnishings and her sons their farming implements and seed.

Seeds to plant in America! Those seeds could have been likened to the Springsteen boys' desires, their intentions, their dreams, their hopes. Just as they planted the seeds laboriously and watched them sprout into a noble harvest, they themselves ripened into men of understanding, tolerance, leadership, and learning.

The Springsteens received their first grant of land from the Dutch Crown in what is now Brooklyn and Queens. But they felt the pangs of land hunger, like most new arrivals, and they had a shrewd realization that the vast empty acres would someday fill with people and rise in value. So they bought other land on Long Island from the Indians. Then, still not satisfied, by 1661 they had acquired holdings as far up the Hudson River valley as Schenectady and Albany. The monetary value of their land was not great. After all, Peter Minuit supposedly had purchased the 22,000 acres of Manhattan Island or Manna-hata only 35 years earlier from the Indians for the equivalent of $24. But the Springsteens and the other Dutch settlers sensed the importance of acquiring land. Not even in their wildest imaginings, however, could the Springsteens have envisioned the day in 1929 when only four acres of their vast holdings would bring their descendants nearly $1,000,000.*

The Springsteens did not cringe from perils or back-breaking toils. Indians lurked beyond the Hudson Palisades. Rough seas beset their little boats on Long Island Sound and in the Hell Gate or Gaat. The icy cold of the North American winters penetrated their inadequate houses. Always there was land to clear of the forest and virgin soil to break with the plow. Every acre they owned had to be battled into submission to agriculture.

The Springsteen men dressed and looked like most other burghers of New Netherlands. They wore broad-brimmed hats, breeches full at the knees and caught up with silver buckles, long coats of linsey-woolsey which flared out below broad leather belts, hose, and buckled shoes. In appearance they were stocky, solid, determined and, although often rough-voiced, they were at heart gentle and kindly people.

One trait has been dominant in the family from the earliest time to the present. The men of each generation were of strong opinion. They were masters of their own minds, and those minds were intelligent. They had a keen sense of right and wrong, and would not compromise on moral issues. The first Springsteens in America, puffing away on their pipes, were like that. Their descendants are like that today.

*Mrs. David Springsteen sold in 1929 the four-acre Springsteen estate near Forest Hills, Queens, granted by the Dutch crown, and which had passed from Caspar J. Springsteen in a direct line for seven generations. This property was bounded by Queens Boulevard and Ascan Avenue.

Because they adopted New World forms of living and did not cling to past customs, the Springsteens demonstrated early that they could be unbiased and unprejudiced. Although Dutch to the core, their off-spring were not fed a diet of "Holland." While some customs and ceremonies persisted, they gradually lost all Dutch flavor. A descendant, writing in 1814, explained: "The family must have been among the first settlers of New York, but it could not be known from their appearance or language."

The Springsteens prospered. They made good providers and good husbands in a solid burgher tradition. Their flaxen-haired children married and intermarried with other Dutch families, the De Groots, Vanderbilts, Schermerhorns, Van Tassels, Onderdonks, and Van Bleekers. Washington Irving had this to say of these families:

"I cannot but look back with reverence to the early planting of the Dutch families, which have taken such vigorous root, and branched out so luxuriantly. The blood which has flowed down uncontaminated through a succession of steady, virtuous generations since the times of the Communipaw, the first organized settlement on 'Manahata,' must certainly be pure and worthy and, if so, there are the Van Rensselaers, Van Zants, De Groots, Van Tassels, Schermerhorns, Springsteens, Onderdonks, and other allied families, legitimate nobility and real lords of the soil."

On June 10, 1663, Caspar, one of the original Springsteen brothers, married Catherine Lothie, daughter of Abraham Lothie. The Dutch girls of that time dressed brightly in short skirts and numerous petticoats. When these charming, laughing young blondes danced, their skirts stood out showing the many layers and bright colors of their petticoats. And they liked to dance. At Christmas and New Year's everyone kissed everyone else. So against this background of gaiety and amiability, it is easy to assume that the marriage of Caspar and Catherine was a happy one. Their children included a son, Caspar Joosten, who grew up on Long Island. On August 9, 1693, he married Maria, daughter of Derick Storm, at "Castle Philipse," an interesting house in Sleepy Hollow, Tarrytown, New York.* Caspar Joosten and Maria Storm Springsteen lived for a while in Bushwick, Kings County, and then in Westchester County. In 1714 they moved again, to Newton, Long Island. Their son Derick C. (or Frederick) Springsteen served in the militia company of Captain Nathaniel Hazard in Queens

Castle Philipse is now a historical landmark under the National Park Service.

County, Long Island, and married a local girl named Gertrude.

Derick Springsteen made two major moves, one in name and one in geography. He and Gertrude took their children and migrated to Kent County, Delaware. There the family name became Springs, the name borne by the Southern branch of the family ever since. The Northern branch remained Springsteen.

Derick and his family lived for a short time at Bombay Hook on Delaware Bay and then moved to Jones Neck, near Dover, Delaware. One may ask, why did he choose Delaware? Early history reveals the logic of his choice. The area had been claimed by the Dutch West Indies Company since 1621. A Dutch attempt at colonization in 1631 failed. The Swedes moved in, founding "Christianaham" after their Queen Christiana, now the city of Wilmington. In 1655 the redoubtable Peter Stuyvesant took over "New Sweden" in the name of New Netherlands. Thus there were many Dutch in Delaware in the 1700's. The area was easily reached by water from Long Island, moreover, and so the Springsteens were not isolated from their kin. They were merely venturing a little farther along the paths of colonization with the restless spirit that typified early America, a nation of men on the move, seeking new places to build and new ways to create.

Among Derick and Gertrude Springs' children was a son, John, born about 1717 at Newton before they left Long Island. John grew to manhood in Delaware and wed Sophia Gassaway, a descendant of Colonel Nicholas Gassaway and Hester Bessen, both from prominent families of South River, Maryland, who arrived in America as early as 1650. The old colonel left a noteworthy record as a militia officer and mayor, and a tremendous amount of land. But the broad expanse of Springs and Gassaway land was not enough to still John's pioneering spirit.

John and Sophia Springs grew restless in Delaware and dreamed of pioneering elsewhere. Their friends, the Shelbys and the Alexanders, enthusiastically described a beautiful and promising section of North Carolina called Mecklenburg. In 1766, the Springses packed and moved south with their five children: sons John Jr., 15, and Richard, 12, and three daughters.

In Mecklenburg they found some 5,000 settlers, mostly Scotch-Irish Presbyterians plus a few French and Germans. Mecklenburg County, which then embraced what are now Cabarrus, Gaston, Lincoln, and part of Union counties, took its name from the Duchy of Mecklenburg-Strelitz, home of Queen Charlotte, King George III's German-born consort. There were small communities dotting the county. The Springses could have chosen Rocky River, Clear Creek, Sugar Creek, Hopewell, Waxhaw or others, but they selected a section called Providence because a Presbyterian church was being established there. As it happened, they located about nine miles southeast of the little community which later became the city of Charlotte.

The year before the Springs family arrived, Henry Eustace Mc-Culloh, acting as agent for Lord Augustus Selwyn, donated a tract of 360 acres in trust to the county as a site for a courthouse, prison, and stocks. To forestall a move to build the courthouse some miles to the north, near Rocky River, the Charlotte settlers raised a rude log courthouse at what is now the intersection of Trade and Tryon Streets in Charlotte. Charlotte was incorporated as a town in 1768, two years after the Springses moved into the section. Two hundred half-acre lots were laid off with a stipulation that each must have a house erected on it within three years, or be forfeited.

The history of these lots is fascinating and indicative of how land values soared. Lot No. 13, next to the northeast corner of what is now Charlotte's town square, was bought for 49 pounds on January 15, 1767, by Adam Alexander, a close friend of John Springs and later the father-in-law of John Springs, Jr. Adam transferred the land to Isaac Alexander in 1792. Isaac sold it to the son of John Springs, Jr., in 1807. Springs, Jr., meanwhile, had bought Lots Nos. 9, 10, and 14. This gave the Springs family half of the block running north on Tryon Street from the square and half of the block running east of the square on Trade Street. To this day, the corner is known as "the Springs Corner." Part of it is still owned by descendants of the original John Springs.

John, having forsaken Delaware, meanwhile shrewdly selected land near Providence that lay close to the road. Once an Indian trading path, this muddy highway led south to Camden and Charlestowne, South Carolina. There John's farm products could be sent for sale. He brought up slaves from Charlestowne to work his fields. Clearing the land of oak, hickory, scalybark, elm, gum, pine, cedar, and maple trees, he planted the higher soil in barley and rye. In the bottom lands along the creek he grew corn. He stocked his farm with horses, cows, sheep, and hogs.

In a grove of oaks and elms on high ground, John Springs built his home. There, when the day was done, he could sit on his stoop and smoke his pipe while his children grew up around him. It was a good life for the Springs family. A description of John and Sophia in those days has been left to us in the family Bible by a grandson. John, he wrote, "was a man of common stature, or perhaps what would have been called in his day rather a small man. He was a very neat farmer and was deemed a correct, honest citizen." John's wife Sophia "was a large woman and their children, Hannah Dempsey, Eleanor Henderson, John Springs, Jr., Richard Springs, and Sophia Black, were all large, stout people of good constitutions, none having died under 70 years of age except John, who died at 67."

After a few years, John Springs began to win his great battle against nature. His house and barns were erected, his fields cleared and planted, his slaves trained to their duties. So John found more time to think about politics. He debated the wisdom and justice of paying taxes to the British Crown without representation in Parliament. During interludes in the all-day church services on Sundays, he argued against it. When the Massachusetts colonists rose up and a wagon-train of grain was sent north to Boston to aid them, John contributed. He knew full well what the penalty for "treason" was, but he did not waver. Undoubtedly John and his sons were at the log courthouse in Charlotte on May 19, 1775, when delegates from the nine militia districts met to discuss the crisis. News of the Battle of Lexington electrified the gathering. There was no turning back now.

The men of Mecklenburg faced up squarely to the situation. In many parts of Britain's American colonies, there were timid or reserved people who could not conceive of America as a free country. They regarded it as treason to throw off the yoke of the British Crown. But the leaders in Mecklenburg viewed this drastic move as inevitable and desirable. The delegates at the little log courthouse instructed Dr. Ephraim Brevard, Colonel William Kennon, and the Reverend Hezekiah J. Balch to draft a resolution to this effect. It was after midnight when the three completed their task. By candlelight, the secretary read the important document. It declared Mecklenburg County free and independent of Great Britain. At 2 o'clock in the morning, the delegates, including Adam Alexander, stepped forward and affixed their names.

The Mecklenburg Declaration of Independence was the first resolve of its kind in the American colonies. The delegates sent Captain James Jack to Philadelphia, riding hard along the muddy roads, to present their decision to the Continental Congress meeting there. Jack arrived to find the Congress debating sending a message to the King repudiating the idea of a free America. Political pressure was exerted to keep the Mecklenburg Declaration from being read. Not until years later did the nation come to recognize that little Mecklenburg County, North Carolina, declared its independence a year before the Continental Congress in Philadelphia made its declaration.

The realistic-minded citizens of Mecklenburg, the Springses among them, pioneered in the nation's political policy just as they had in its rugged forests.

CHAPTER TWO

TWO FOURTH-GENERATION DESCENDANTS of the pioneer Caspar Spring-steen were commissioned as Captains of North Carolina units in the Revolutionary War. John Springs, Jr., had just turned twenty-five at the start of hostilities. His brother, Richard, was three years younger.

The first campaign took the Springs boys into western North Carolina where the Cherokee Indians, incited by British agents, had taken the warpath. By May, 1777, they were subdued and signed a peace treaty. The Springses returned home, and a happy event took place. John Springs, Jr., and Sarah Alexander, daughter of John Sr.'s good friend Colonel Adam Alexander, were married. Later that year the Mecklenburg troops were ordered north.

The aging John Springs and his wife, Sophia, could only hope, pray, and wait. From their farm they saw history in the making. At times their boys came home and reassured them. Then the summer of 1780 brought crisis. That July, Richard, the younger son, received a special commission. It read: "July 21st, 1780. I hereby certify that I appoint Richard Springs Capt. of a Company of Foot in the present Expedition." And the appointment was signed by Griffith Rutherford, B.G.M.

The expedition led directly to the Battle of Hanging Rock sixteen days later. Although a relatively small engagement, it was furiously contested. Richard came through unscathed, but further hard fighting lay ahead.

Within a few days, Captains Richard and John Springs, Jr., and their troops were ordered to join the American army at Camden, South

Carolina, under General Horatio Gates. This was the largest force in the South, hastily assembled to halt the army of Cornwallis. Gates, who took command from the German Baron DeKalb, was reckoned second only to George Washington as a skilled military leader. The two young captains, swords at their sides and hats cocked jauntily, felt confidence in their general as they rode across the dusty countryside.

On August 13 the Mecklenburg contingent reported to Gates at Claremont, Rugely's Mill, an evacuated British post about thirteen miles north of Camden on the main highway from Charlotte. The British under Cornwallis garrisoned Camden itself.

The Springs sons found disheartening disorder in Gates' camp. Instead of the 5,000 troops whom Gates expected, there were only some 3,600. The Virginia and Maryland regulars of the Continental Line had arrived by forced marches. They were short of food and near exhaustion. Two-thirds of the little force consisted of raw militia from the southeastern states. Disease was widespread and undermined many.

If Cornwallis had given Gates time to rest and reorganize his army, the result might have been different. But Cornwallis, well informed of his opponent's weakness, struck at once. Approaching the American encampment, he formed his well-trained regulars for battle. His front line ran from a swamp on one flank to a slight ravine on the other. He grouped his reserve infantry behind each wing. Colonel Lord Rawdon commanded on the left, Lt. Colonel Webster on the right. Tarleton's dreaded dragoons held the main highway near the center. In the front line were four light field pieces, with two more in reserve. The Redcoats moved with precision.

In Gates' camp there was confusion. Most of the American officers were aghast at what their general proposed but only DeKalb spoke out. He said Gates' elaborate plan, involving column maneuvers by night, was too complicated for the untried militia. But Gates insisted and issued his orders.

The Second Maryland Brigade and the Delaware Regiment under General Gist formed the right, commanded by DeKalb. The North Carolina militia under Caswell constituted the center. Virginia militia under Stevens formed the left. General Gates took a good position between these front line troops and the reserve, which consisted of the

First Maryland Brigade under General Smallwood. In this brigade was Gassoway Watkins, a cousin of the two Springs captains.

The British attacked fiercely at dawn. Soon the untested Virginia militia broke. Their commander, Stevens, tried vainly to halt and regroup them. The North Carolina militia held under a hail of musketry but faltered and gave way when the British attacked with the bayonet. Only those North Carolinians under General Gregory and Colonel Dixon stood fast—a dwindling little group around Baron De-Kalb.

Gates threw himself into the fray to rally his troops, but it was too late. Six hundred lay dead in the blood-specked dust. Another thousand threw down their arms and sought mercy. The British roped them into a line of march and goaded them toward Charlestowne as prisoners.

Among the captives was Lieutenant Andrew Baxter, Jr., a neighbor and close friend of the Springses. The Baxter family had moved south from Lancaster, Pennsylvania, about 1760. Andrew, Sr., received a grant of land from the Crown including 159 acres on Swearing John's Branch of McAlpine's Creek and 95 acres on McMichael's Creek. But when the colonists took up arms, old Andrew proved himself a true Whig and patriot. It was to cost him his life, and his son's freedom.

An account of young Andrew's fate has come down to us in the volume, *The Family of John Springs, III*. It says:

"He was carried to Charlestowne. Passing down the streets, his extreme youth and fine appearance attracted the notice of a Whig gentleman of that city, who managed secretly to relieve his necessities by supplying him with clothing and otherwise mitigating the evils which military usages imposed upon prisoners of war, until he was released, when he immediately re-entered the army."

The war raged on unabated. After the catastrophe at Camden, Generals Gates and Caswell had hastened to Charlotte and Hillsboro. Captains John and Richard Springs marched their depleted companies dejectedly through the mud to Waxhaw. The men were weary and heartsick. The absent faces of their dead haunted them. Their wounded moaned and groaned in jolting wagons that followed their little column.

The American forces prepared to rally beside McAlpine's Creek at Providence, almost in the back yard of old John and Sophia Springs. A few of the better horsemen under Colonel William R. Davie stayed behind at Waxhaw as an outpost against the British. When Cornwallis moved toward Waxhaw and Charlotte on September 8, this little force harassed his vanguard.

General William Davidson meanwhile supplanted General Rutherford, whom the British had captured at Camden, as the Mecklenburg County militia leader. Davidson assembled every available volunteer. Morale rose high. The patriots were fighting on their home ground, in defense of families and property.

The test soon came. On September 24, Cornwallis moved up from Waxhaw to Providence—almost onto the doorstep of old John and Sophia. The thundering hooves of cavalry and the tramp of marching infantry must have sickened all those who remained on the Springs plantation. Too, they knew that Captains John and Richard Springs would soon be in battle.

General Davidson had withdrawn his main force to Rocky Creek, five miles north of Charlotte. But he left Colonel Davie and a detachment, including the Springs brothers, at Charlotte to delay the British as long as possible. Taking positions behind the courthouse and fences at the crossroads, these troops waited. Tarleton, brandishing his saber, formed his British cavalry for a charge just 300 yards away. The British were halted by a barrage of bullets. Two other charges were repulsed. Then Cornwallis himself rode up and urged his men forward. His infantry advanced steadily and doggedly with the bayonet. The outnumbered Americans recognized that it was time to withdraw.

Cornwallis held Charlotte for sixteen aggravating days. He was infuriated because the Mecklenburgers refused to yield their arms and pledge allegiance to the Crown. Davidson's small detachments harassed his outposts, shot his foragers, and intercepted his communications. The whole countryside boiled over at the Redcoats. Tarleton afterward wrote that Mecklenburg and Rowan counties were the most hostile in all America.

To crush resistance, Cornwallis sent out a Loyalist force under Colonel Patrick Ferguson. American militia armed with long rifles and led in part by General Evan Shelby, uncle of the Springs boys, attacked Ferguson's men at Kings Mountain on October 7 and inflicted an overwhelming defeat. Cornwallis declared Charlotte and the back country a veritable "hornet's nest." He withdrew to Winnsboro, South Carolina. The two young Springs captains and their men dogged his steps.

After wintering in South Carolina, Cornwallis started north again. General Nathaniel Greene now commanded the Americans instead of Gates. Cornwallis, avoiding Charlotte after his painful experience there, went up the west side of the Catawba River to Cowan's Ford, northwest of the town, and crossed there on February 1, 1781. General Davidson, the Springses' good friend, was killed in trying to block the crossing with his men.

Gassaway Watkins, the Maryland cousin of Sophia Springs and a veteran of the Battles of Long Island, White Plains, Germantown, and Monmouth, concluded an account of his war experience with the details of the fateful day when General Davidson was killed:

"I left camp [in the North] the last of April for the South, and was in the Battle of Camden. Was sent to a house by General Greene for information; was pursued by Tarleton's horse, jumped a fence eleven logs high, and was two nights and days without eating and without seeing anyone and slept in the woods. Rejoined General Smallwood at Elizabethtown. Was sent by General Smallwood in September with special dispatches to General Marion. Joined the General at Hillsborough. Left Hillsborough under the command of Colonels Howard and Morgan. Commanded a company at the Battle of the Cowpens in 1781.

"In February, the day General Davidson was killed, I left camp with orders for General Greene and was with the retreating militia, two miles from the battle ground. At twelve o'clock that night, I stopped at a house on the road, cold, wet and hungry, but got nothing to eat. There were at least 100 persons in the house. My dress [uniform] was noticed by an old man of the country, who asked to speak in private with me. He told me that there were enemies as well as friends in the house, and offered his services to me. I started in a few moments after, and told him what I wanted. He was faithful.

"We rode all night and got to the ford about 10 o'clock next morning. The trees came tumbling one after the other down the Yadkin. The old man said it was impossible to cross. I was satisfied there was nothing to stop the enemy and the wish of my general to bring his troops to a point near action, so I immediately pulled off my coat and boots, put the dispatches in the crown of my hat, tied it on my head, took leave of my friend, who, with tears in his eyes, wished me well, and with difficulty crossed the river. My guide and friend expressed his joy by throwing up his hat. . . . About seven o'clock I got to headquarters and was received by Generals Greene and Morgan."

General Davidson's death meanwhile spread gloom over Mecklenburg County. John and Richard Springs took part in the burial of their beloved commander by torchlight in Hopewell Cemetery.

Soon romance reared itself despite the war. Captain Richard Springs proposed to Jean Baxter, a sister of his good friend, Lieutenant Andrew Baxter, Jr., who had been captured at Camden. Jean, daughter of Andrew and Frances Baxter, accepted. They were married June 7, 1781.

Tragedy struck a little less than three months later. Andrew Baxter, Sr., the bride's father, was a true Whig and patriot. He did his best to foil the Tories and British. In reprisal, a Tory band murdered him at his own gate September 4.

The senseless slaughter that cut down Baxter, Sr., was typical of the strife between Whigs and Tories. The Tories spied on patriots and scouted for British troops. In one instance when British raiders approached Waxhaw, the Whigs barricaded themselves in the Waxhaw Presbyterian Church to await reinforcements. Tories alerted the British and, in farmers' clothes like Whigs, screened the Redcoat advance. The Whigs in the church mistook them for friends until the British opened fire at close range.

Some managed to flee but many were captured, and among the prisoners were two brothers, Robert and Andrew Jackson. Taken to Camden, both fell sick. Their mother's personal appeal to Lord Rawdon won their release. Elizabeth Jackson mounted her son Robert, ill with smallpox, on a horse. She rode a pony. Andy, also ill, walked. When they arrived in Waxhaw, Robert was dying and Andy was delirious with fever. Two days later, Mrs. Jackson had only one son left. Fate spared young Andy for greater things.

CHAPTER THREE

EVEN BEFORE THE STORM of the Revolution ceased in 1781, the Springs brothers planned ahead for peace. John, Jr., arranged to farm his aging father's land. Richard then bought John, Jr.'s plantation. After hostilities ended, however, Richard decided to settle on Big Sugar Creek in Lancaster District, which would eventually be surveyed as part of South Carolina. It lay near Providence and Charlotte. The brothers continued their close connection. They shared business ventures and oftentimes borrowed money from each other. Eventually, one of John, Jr.'s daughters was to marry one of Richard's sons.

The discovery of gold in increasing quantities added to the Springs prosperity. They became the first in North Carolina to coin gold with Government consent. Old letters mention their ownership of a mine, but no one today knows where it was. Traces of the precious metal were found early in creek bottoms and small surface veins. When John, Jr., purchased his land in 1772, he bought the mineral rights to "half of all gold and silver mines" underlying it. Gold in some quantity was discovered in Mecklenburg County in 1790. Then the St. Catherine mine was opened in 1825, followed by the Capps mine, and the Rudisill mine in 1830. By 1837, gold mining was of sufficient importance for the Federal Government to establish a United States Mint in Charlotte.

On March 31, 1790, John Springs, Sr., the seventy-four-year-old patriarch and guiding hand of the family, passed away at his home in Providence. He died wealthy for his times, but he died as he had lived, an humble man. Only the previous year, in writing out a disposition of "my worldly affairs and goods which it hath pleased God to bless me with," he directed, "my burial I desire may be without pomp, to be managed at the direction of my dear wife and my executors, my beloved sons, John Springs and Richard Springs."

Sophia, the "beloved wife" of John Springs, Sr., outlived him by a little more than three years. She died August 10, 1793, at the age of seventy. She and her John lie in the Providence Presbyterian Church cemetery twelve miles southeast of Charlotte on Providence Road.

By this time a new generation of Springses was well established. John, Jr., and his Sarah had six children: Mary, Sarah, Adam, John B., Sophia and William. Richard and his wife Jean also had six: John III, Cynthia, Andrew Baxter, Richard, Jane and Eli, with four more, Sophia, Margaret, Baxter, and Harriet, to come in future years.

John, Jr., and Richard carried on the family work and tradition. They acquired more and more land and attained leadership in social, political, and religious circles as well as in business. Their opportunities broadened with the times. Banks and stores were opening. The brothers invested widely.

Richard bought bank stocks, particularly the United States Bank, and lent money at interest. John, Jr., in addition to operating his plantation on Providence Road, bought three plantations in Lincoln County, North Carolina. He also acquired hundreds of acres on Sugar and Steele Creeks. In addition, he purchased real estate around the Square in Charlotte and in what is now the Myers Park section of that city.

Owning as much farm land as they did, both brothers held large numbers of slaves to till the soil. The production of cotton required two things, land and slaves. The Springses possessed both. Tradition has it that one could travel from Providence, southeast of Charlotte, to McAdenville, North Carolina, west of Charlotte, without leaving Springs land. This was the age of landed aristocracy. The slaves performed the labor. Overseers directed their tasks. It remained only for the master to ride over his land, supervise generally, and then to sell his cotton at a favorable price. These duties left him ample time to use his talents elsewhere, and his eyes turned to investments and politics. Naturally he was much occupied with tariffs, slavery, and cotton marketing.

The cotton market slumped in 1804. Napoleon's unrelenting war against England halted trade. The bales piled up at home. This situation soon passed, but it caused concern for a time. In a letter to Adam Springs, a son of Captain John Springs, a John Faires explained from Charleston, South Carolina, in February of 1804: "Cotton is selling for 14½ to 15 Dols cash and 15½ may be had on credit of 60 days. I do not think it will be higher soon unless we receive accounts of some settlement in Europe; there are ships in this harbour who have been waiting 3 months for freight and have not got any yet. Shippers are afraid to send cotton least England should be invaded before it could arrive which makes trade of all kinds very dull. Tobacco I think will be higher. It is from 5½ to 6 Dols per hundred."

Despite their preoccupation with farming and commerce, the busy brothers found time for their many children. They saw to it that each received an excellent education. How, in the countryside in those days, was that possible?

A look at early Mecklenburg history will explain. The county was primarily a Scotch-Irish Presbyterian community. Next to religion, its people believed in education. In Providence and many other places, the clergymen conducted schools. Elsewhere the master of the house hired a private tutor or joined neighbors in paying a teacher for a local "field school"—so called because it usually occupied a field left unplanted under crop rotation. A 1789 deed of the Black family, in-laws of the Springses on McAlpine Creek, mentions "the school house." At Third and Tryon Streets in Charlotte there stood a pre-Revolutionary school, Liberty Hall Academy,* staffed by a Presbyterian clergyman and four tutors. Schools for young ladies, paying "particular attention to manners and conduct," were opened in 1807 and 1812.

Captain John Springs sent his sons to the University of North Carolina. His oldest son, Adam, was a member of the first graduating class and received his diploma on July 4, 1798.†

Mrs. Richard Springs died on May 27, 1804, at the age of forty-four. Two years later, Richard married a widow, Mrs. Mary McBride Craig. They had one son, Richard Clark Springs.

To all their children, Captains John and Richard Springs gave a political concept. They were great admirers of Thomas Jefferson, who became President in 1801, and they shared his belief in local government over centralized government. So they trained their children to believe in "states' rights."

Of all the children, we are most concerned here with the oldest of each set, Mary, daughter of John, and John III, son of Richard, for around them our story centers.‡

---

*Cornwallis placed some of his wounded in Liberty Hall Academy while holding Charlotte, and those who died were buried on the grounds.
†The University of North Carolina is the oldest state university in the United States.
‡Mary L. Springs was born April 3, 1778. John Springs III was born December 24, 1782.

Part Two

SPRINGFIELD

Springfield, York County, South Carolina, built circa *1805.*

CHAPTER FOUR

THE ROMANCE THAT GAVE RISE to Springfield, most gracious of the family homes, sprang up between John Springs, III, and his charming cousin Mary. The young lady, four years John's senior, grew up in the seclusion of her father's Providence plantation. Her lively beauty soon attracted friends and suitors. It was an age of happy marriages. Mary Warren wrote enthusiastically to Mary Springs in 1800 from the Davidsons' plantation at Hopewell, "I am so engaged in frolicking for there is nothing here among us but quiltings and weddings. . . ." A month later, Mary Warren wrote: "I have just returned from another wedding. Young Mr. Davidson is married to Miss Sally Brevard in Center."*

A second friend, Peg H. Alexander, wrote Mary Springs: "There have been very gay times lately on the big Creek. We have the General on all occasions.† I expect some of the ladies will be very much impressed. I believe he says matrimony to some and you have no idea of his gallantry. He looks as if he had just stepped out of the Beaumonde. I have a number of funny circumstances to tell you that I dare not write."

Amid this atmosphere of gaiety and sociability, John Springs, III, suddenly became aware that his cousin Mary was the girl he most desired. He had little time to lose. In 1805, a rival who signed himself simply "M. R. A." wrote Mary that he intended to ask her father for her hand: "My heart is full of anxiety to see you and present my inquiries to your father."

*Jack Davidson, who married Sally Brevard, would eventually have a son, Brevard Davidson, who would in 1836 marry a daughter of Mary and John Springs III.
†This General was probably William R. Davie, who was a widower about that time.

Whether John knew of this rival we cannot say, but on January 9, 1806, he and Mary were married. He was twenty-three and she was twenty-seven. John had begun building a mansion, as it was called in those days, four miles from his father Richard's home. He named the place Springfield* and soon made it a showplace for the countryside.

The two-story white frame house with its tall columns stood at the end of an avenue of stately trees that towered like sentinels. The avenue circled invitingly in front of the house.

On entering, one found a large hall running from front to rear and a cross hall from side to side, allowing breezes to circulate freely. To the front of the entrance hall on each side were parlors with double doors which opened to give a feeling of great space. At the far side of each parlor, mirrors extended from mantel to ceiling. When the parlor doors were open, one could stand in the hall and see himself reflected in both mirrors. Toward the rear on one side was the library. Back of this was the bedroom of John and Mary. Across the hall were the large dining room and pantries. A stairway from the cross hall led to second-floor bedrooms.

The house was furnished in the best style. The parlors held mahogany card and side tables, sofas and chairs upholstered in silk, portraits and paintings. A mahogany sideboard with silver and glass dominated one side of the dining room. A large open fireplace with huge brass andirons warmed those around the mahogany dining table.

The outside surroundings were equally lovely. "A lofty tree throwing its shade over the well to protect it from the rays of the mid-summer sun, swayed to and fro, as if beckoning to the traveler a welcome to quench his thirst. The sound of clanging horse-hoofs or rumbling wheels not only attracted a pack of hounds, but the peacocks immediately spread their gorgeous plumage and with loud, shrill voices proclaimed the approach of visitors.

"Immediately in front of the piazza were fancy flower beds interspersed with mignonette, anemones, roses and other flowers. On one side a bed of Lily of the Valley wafted its sweet perfume abroad, while to the front and sides nearer the road stood the most artistically trimmed evergreens, some of which had been brought from the White Mountains of Massachusetts; also handsome magnolias whose white blossoms filled the air with fragrance, and two large oaks affording a

*Springfield is located 17 miles south of Charlotte, between Pineville, North Carolina and Fort Mill, South Carolina. It was restored in 1947 by Colonel Elliottt White Springs. The long avenue has been separated from the house by a state highway.

grateful shade in summer. In the rear was a large and well kept vegetable garden and behind that was a little village of brick Negro cabins, which was kept scrupulously clean and orderly."*

Keeping the "little village of brick Negro cabins" populated became a prime problem of plantation life. Only a few weeks after John and Mary were married, he left his bride to go buy slaves in Maryland. From there he wrote to Mary: "I have perused the contents of your letter with sensations of pleasure not to be expressed on paper. . . . The fatigue of body I have undergone and have yet to go through, I leave with you, my dear, to judge; you whom I've always found in possession of those tender endearing dispositions, that would pity and sympathize with one in distress and also to animate his pleasure in joy."

Half a year later John made another buying trip. He hated every moment away from his wife. He thought constantly of her. While in his lonely lodging he could picture her as she braided her shining hair by soft candlelight, smiling tenderly at him. He dreamed of their late-afternoon walks when they inspected their newly laid out gardens. He hungered to be in Mary's arms and listen to her words of love, but he could not put those thoughts on paper, so what he really wrote from Princess Anne, Maryland, was: "My dear, when I see societies of people enjoying themselves, men with their wives, young men with their mistresses, etc. and reflect back on the few happy days and hours we spent together, and the distance we are now separated, I feel myself miserable; but when I again look forward with the pleasing expectation that we may again be restored to the mutual enjoyment of each other, I've no doubt of being amply rewarded for all the disagreeable sensations I at present undergo, and I am not unmindful of the lonesome, anxious and disagreeable situation you are placed in."

Mary was expecting a baby. Certainly she was overjoyed at John's return in the fall, because the child, Richard Austin Springs, was born on January 19, 1807. A short time afterwards, John, away from Springfield for a few days, wrote: "Be assured, my dear Mary, that much of my time is spent in thinking of you, my dear little Austin, our business and affairs at home. Accept the assurance of my most anxious wishes for your peace and happiness."

By the following August, John, realizing he needed more field hands, mounted his good horse Dolphin and journeyed again in quest

*From *The Family of John Springs III.*

of slaves. He rode to Norfolk, Virginia, and boarded the "Packett" or fast sailing ship across the broad mouth of the Chesapeake. In light summer breezes, the passage took two days. John wrote Mary on September 5, 1807: "As soon as I got to Princess Ann I was violently attacked and was two or three days very ill. Indeed I applied to a Phisician and he bled and phisiched me severely. That together with the complaint weakened me as much as I ever was for the length of time. I appear now to be recovering my health very fast, have a keen appetite and hope in a few days to be better than I have been this three months. But, my dear, I leave you to judge my feelings to be taken down in this unhealthy country so far distant from you and my dear little son, removed from everything that is near and dear to me, not knowing what way my fate might terminate. Quite insensible too of what complaints and difficulties you may be labouring under which causes me many an anxious and uneasy thought."

But John was not as well as he thought he was. In two weeks time he came down with "the influensy, a complaint that affects the head and breast similar to a bad cold." The disease was remarkably prevalent. After John left his bed, he had a sad experience. "This day at 12 o'clock," he wrote, "I am going to attend the funeral of a brother traveler, a Gentleman from the state of Georgia with whom I contracted a small acquaintance. He was in purchasing Negroes. He was a healthy, hearty looking man and died of a few days illness. . . . One thing mortifies me much. When he took death to himself he sent for me two or three times and no one knew where I was. Poor stranger, never was in this place before, not one friend or acquaintance to sympathize with him in his last distress, or know when he is no more, to drop for him one tear of compassion unless I should take on myself that friendly part. Though no doubt he has a respectable connection to deplore his loss. Oh, my Dear, had this been my situation what would the world have been to me, and know not on my return but I may be deprived of you or my little son, the only objects that render life desirable.

"Negroes are not to be had at any reasonable price. There have been so many purchasers in this summer that they have picked up all that was for sale. I have only purchased four and have only two of them in possession. I have several others in view, but my purchasing them is quite uncertain. But I think in the course of two or three weeks I shall put out for home. I cannot reconcile the idea of being absent from you."

The following summer, a little daughter was born to John and Mary. She was named Sarah Delia. Two months later John went to an adjoining county on business. One evening he was stunned when he received a tear stained letter from Mary: "Oh! My Love, imagine to yourself the scene when I tell you: Your dear little Infant you left smiling in my arms is now no more. The Almighty giver of all things has seen cause to remove her from us and place her in the Mansions of Eternity and we must submit to his Divine will. If you recollect a few days before you went away we thought she was unwell with a cold. After I discovered she was very sick and her cough still increasing on Sunday I sent for my Mother, and when she came our poor baby began to whoop. . . . Then she was taken with strong convulsions. I can not here describe her suffering. Oh! My Dearest Love, you will have an idea of my feelings when you receive this. I have often thought I had known what distress was before, but I now confess I never did until I followed our dear innocent baby to the silent tomb and laid her at the feet of your honored Mother. . . ."

John must have ridden the endless miles home in a daze of sorrow and exhaustion, finally to give way to his own grief while wrapped in the arms of his sobbing wife who cried, "You are the only one to whom I can disclose my grief without reserve."

By the following spring, John was off on his travels again. This time he went to Philadelphia in May to purchase goods for the family store in Charlotte, then a community of some seventy families, in which he, his brother Eli and his brother-in-law Adam held an interest. The trip from Charleston by packet ship took eleven days of rough coastwise sailing.

"I am in hopes I shall be able to buy goods low as trade appears to be rather dull," he wrote Mary. "Money is said to be scarce, a number of people pushed, and several failures and a good many more expected. . . . I laid out all my money in Charleston for drafts on this place on which I made from 9 to 10 per cent." Then John added in his usual affectionate way, "My interest, my affection and all are incontrovertably with you and our lovely offspring."

John hastened home to avoid leaving Mary alone. She would soon have a baby. On August 28th, little Jane was born to them.

That fall, he returned to Philadelphia and found goods "much higher" than he expected. So he headed for New York, where "goods were much more plentiful and on better terms."

The cause of rising prices was, of course, the Napoleonic War in Europe. British restrictions to cut off commerce with France led to United States retaliation with the Embargo Act, later modified to the Non-Intercourse Act. All of it hampered trade and ultimately ushered in the War of 1812.

An old bill gives prices in 1812-1813 as $1 for 16 yards of coarse cotton cloth, $1.17 for 14 yards of "striped cotton," $1 for 8 yards of "Nigro cloth," and $1 for 6 yards of diaper cloth.

In letters and bills of sale, there ran a constant undertone of slavery: buying slaves, working slaves, clothing and nursing slaves, training slaves. The relationship was a peculiar one, with absolute mastery on one side and absolute subjection on the other, but there was an interdependence among whites and Negroes which often involved much real affection. They shared problems and each toiled in his way at solving them. The responsibilities lay heaviest on the master and mistress of Springfield and every like plantation. An old verse sums it up:

> A nigger never dared to die
> Nor marry on our place
> Widout old Mistus helt his han
> Er sed de word o' grace.
> Dat old plantation, hit was run
> On 'rangements bout like dis.
> Der place hit belong'd to Marster,
> Old Marster belong'd to Mis.

The family responsibilities of John and Mary also grew apace. Baby Leroy arrived in 1811. Mary Laura was born in 1813, Jack Lawrence in 1815, Sergeant Jasper—named after the Revolutionary hero—in 1817, Andrew Baxter in 1819, and Sophia in 1821.

John and Mary adored their children and lavished tender care on them. But tenderness, in the absence of medical safeguards against scarlet fever, whooping cough, typhoid, pneumonia, and many other sicknesses, could not ward off illness and sometimes death.

Little Jane, who delighted in throwing herself into John's arms and rubbing her soft yellow curls against his cheeks, died at the age of seven. Two-year-old Jack, always smiling and toddling after his father with unquenchable curiosity, was too handsome to die, but a sudden fever swept him away. Each time John and Mary lost a child, they seemed to die a little themselves, but also they seemed to depend more and more on each other.

Both John and Mary eased their sorrows by keeping enormously busy. She supervised a vast household endeavor that included "preserving, pickling, drying fruits, sewing, carding and spinning and weaving." A contemporary described her as "presiding at her husband's table with a dignified and queenly grace." John meanwhile rose in wealth and prominence. He improved his land, bred fine cattle and hogs, developed his business in Charlotte, and lent considerable sums of money at interest.

In the yard at Springfield stood a brick cottage. John used this as an office to transact business. Here he interviewed his shoemakers, carpenters, wheelwrights, blacksmiths, overseers, and other helpers. Upstairs in the cottage were two bedchambers for overnight guests when the "big house" was filled.

The Springs family usually dined bountifully at two o'clock in the afternoon. After dark a light supper was served. During the winter evenings, John and Mary would gather their children around them before a log fire in the parlor. "Wheeler, we are ready now," John would say. In would come the faithful coachman bearing an iron oven which he put before the fireplace. Behind him would come a Negro girl, Nancy, with a basket of select chestnuts. Wheeler would then fetch a long cane with a hook at one end. This was a contrivance of John's to stir the nuts. While the children recited their day's activities, John would roast chestnuts for them.

When the roasted nuts were eaten and the little heads were nodding "Mammy," a large colored woman, would take the children off to bed. Then John would settle back in his chair and talk to Mary while she embroidered. As he had said so many times before, she made "life most desirable."

Christmas was another exciting event at Springfield. This was the time for the family reunion and for St. Nicholas, patron saint of the Dutch of old. The house was thrown open for a reception. All the kin who could possibly travel to Springfield attended. The bedchambers were filled and the children slept on pallets made down on the floor. It was a time of merriment not only because it was Christmas but because it was John's birthday as well. It was a custom of John's to awaken his house guests early on Christmas morning and hand them his silver "loving cup" of eggnog, from which everyone was expected to take a sip. He had his own special recipe for eggnog and took great pleasure in mixing it. One of the family wrote of Christmas at Springfield:

"At the break of day the whole plantation was astir, and the slaves, big and little, with their voices buzzing like so many bees, crowded at the doors with their greeting of 'Christmas Giff, Christmas Giff' to the inmates of the house and waited in happy anticipation for their packages, which, with their master's customary system, were carefully selected and labeled for them. After receiving their packages the older Negroes still lingered and when questioned by their master, who understood them perfectly, why they waited, the spokesman with a low bow which would have done credit to a courtier, would answer, ' 'Scuse me Massa, but you knows what de Good Book says 'bout a lettle sperits for de stomach's sake, an' mos' specially pon dis happy an' slubrious 'casion does we needs it to drink to de health of Massa, Missus, and all de young misses and gentlemans what's here, yes sah!' To this John would repond and present them with their annual treat."

Another gala event for all was the corn shucking by moonlight at the end of the harvest. Corn was stacked high in a long pile with a dividing rail through the center. Two Negro captains and teams were chosen. Then at a signal the Negroes would start at opposite ends of the pile and shuck frantically to see which team would reach the rail first. Excitement ran high as the several hundred Negroes worked with a frenzy. "Their bodies swayed under the nervous tension, and as each shuck flew to the rear the hands clapped, keeping time to the music of their deep bass voices, led by the high falsetto of the women to the accompaniment of throbbing banjos and rattling bones. At times they would become exhausted and the music almost cease, when losing control of themselves, they would begin a tattoo with their feet, which growing louder and louder would end in some leaping into the air. The singing would then begin again." When finally the goal was reached, the victorious side would seize their captain and carry him off to a seat of honor at the table. A feast of chicken and dumplings for all, followed by singing and dancing, made for gaiety long past midnight. Then a horn would signal an end to the fun and the Negroes would drift off, singing "who laid dat rail?"

Church-going was an important part of plantation life. The Springs family attended Unity Presbyterian Church, which was a gathering place for them and their neighbors to meet and discuss everything from weather to crops. The crowd would gather a couple of hours before the preacher was ready to begin his sermon. The rough log benches were uncomfortable and in cold weather there was no heat, but all the same the hum of voices could be heard a hundred yards off. A neighbor, A. S. White, recorded: "In one of these gatherings before preaching, I remember seeing John Springs stand for more than an hour without moving his feet from their position and talk of the simple practical affairs of the life of the country. I well remember his trim, medium sized, well dressed figure, small shiney boots and brown broadcloth suit, with a tall silk hat. All that time the crowd listened with close attention. Nobody wanted to interrupt. His voice was not loud, but strong and distinct, with a musical timbre peculiar to himself."

On June 25, 1818, Mary lost her father, Captain John Springs. Although only sixty-seven, he had been in poor health for some time. As the end approached, Mary and her John stood beside the dying captain's bed, grieving over the thin, spent body which once had wielded a sword so heroically that Cornwallis had likened him and his comrades to hornets. When the old man closed his eyes, Mary and John walked into the garden together and wept.

The following year, John, ever mindful of business expansion, traveled to Montgomery County in the newly formed state of Alabama, to buy land in the section which the Creek Indians had ceded after their defeat in 1814 by General Jackson. Faithfully he wrote Mary of his trip: "We entered the Creek Nation at Fork Hawkins, crossed the Chattahoochee at Fort Mitchell and arrived at this place [Line Creek] about one o'clock today, having now entered the State of Alabama. We expect to go from here to the Farm of Alabama and from there to Cohaba, where the sale of land comes on Monday next."

John had also added acreage to his South Carolina plantation. Why? Because Eli Whitney's invention of the gin had caused a steady rise in the price of cotton. The demand for land and slaves rose accordingly. By 1820, a good field hand brought $700 to $1,100. Therefore, when John went to Maryland in search of slaves in 1824, he expected to pay up for them. In buying additional slaves, John was doing what other planters did. As a result, Negroes soon outnumbered the whites in South Carolina.

From Princess Anne, Maryland, John wrote his "Dear Mary": "I bargained for ten Negroes since I wrote home last week. I sent out for two of them, and the man sent me word he must have more for them than we had agreed on but that he would see me again on Saturday, but did not come. Eight were to have been delivered on Saturday, but they have not come and I know not the reason. I have only five in possession. I have been more disappointed, perplexed and fretted than I am accustomed to. This, combined with the fact that my crops were destroyed by the rain freshet, which all letters corroborate, makes me set this down as one of my unlucky hits, and misfortunes rarely come alone. I shall think myself favored to get home again without sustaining any other particular losses."

Yes, John was right. "Misfortunes rarely come alone." Their young son, Jasper, died that year at the age of seven.

Fortunately for John, in such times of sorrow there was usually some new endeavor to distract him. This time it was politics. The national government increased the tariff on imports in 1824. The Southern planters felt that this aided Northern industrialists at their expense. South Carolina talked more and more of states' rights as opposed to centralization, and attacked the constitutionality of the tariff. The State pinned her presidential hopes on Andrew Jackson, but he lost to John Quincy Adams. John C. Calhoun became Vice President.

Cotton dropped from 25 cents a pound to 11 cents during the following year. South Carolina's economy suffered a serious blow. Although several factors caused the slump, most South Carolinians blamed the tariff. John became more and more involved in grave discussions with political overtones. He considered running for the South Carolina House of Representatives.

In the midst of the argument against excessive power in Washington there came the nation's fiftieth anniversary, July 4, 1826. People forgot their differences and celebrated. An elaborate observance was planned at Yorkville. John and Mary rode over in their carriage the previous day and visited their Moore kin.*

On the morning of the "glorious Fourth," a "discharge of artillery and musketry" awakened them. Beside a Liberty pole erected for the

---

*John Springs' sister Harriet married Dr. William Moore and John's sister Sophia married James Moore.

occasion, they watched a parade form. The surviving Revolutionary War soldiers of York District mustered bravely but shakily, along with Captain Fleming's artillery company, Captain Hill's and George's light infantry units, Captain Goore's (Moore's?) militia company and Captain Dennis' cavalry troop, all under the command of Colonel Dogers and Lieutenant-Colonel Wright. The citizens formed ranks behind the troops. At eleven o'clock "the whole marched in fine order to a stand erected in the midst of a pleasant grove of oaks to the north of the village." The Declaration of Independence was read, a speaker orated on its significance to mankind, and then "twenty-four toasts were read from the stand, each of which was succeeded by a discharge of artillery and musketry."

The assemblage next returned to the Liberty pole and formed two open ranks. The Revolutionary veterans marched slowly between the ranks, saluted by both military and citizens. "After this tribute of respect, all repaired to a cool retreat and partook of a dinner. After the cloth was removed a number of volunteer toasts were drunk."

At the dinner, John Springs stepped into some eminence with a very special and timely toast. He raised his glass "To South Carolina—may she long be distinguished by love of country, by a fearless independence of opinion, and a marked adherence to her own rights with a due respect for those of others."

The toast accurately reflected John's political feelings and pride in his State. He was a states' righter, but he thought that the southern States should form a solid front at a convention and together demand redress from the North. On the "half century anniversary," he privately felt that the future looked dark for both South Carolina and the nation.

The ominous word "nullification" was beginning to be heard widely over the State. The Nullifier contended that any individual State had the right, as never having surrendered it in the general compact, to declare any act of Congress, so far as that individual State was concerned in the operation of the law, null and void.

When Andrew Jackson was elected President in 1828, the South Carolinians placed their hope in him to see that Federal authority did not interfere with the economy of the State. That was the year John Springs was elected to the South Carolina Legislature.

Congress soon raised the tariff again, and South Carolina questioned its right to pass such discriminatory laws. John C. Calhoun wrote his famous "South Carolina Exposition" on the issue, charging that the tariff was unconstitutional. It was introduced in the Legislature as a committee report. John gravely heard it read.

Never the type of person to be swayed too much by fiery and impetuous speeches, he weighed the issues carefully and reached his own conclusion calmly. His father had fought to help create the Union of these United States. John felt a responsibility to his father, to his own conscience, and to his sons for their future. He decided that states' rights within the Union was the answer.

As part of the attack on the tariff, patriotic Southerners were urged not to buy and use imported items on which a tariff had to be paid. Several publications of the day reported that John Springs, in an ardent nullification stand, asked the ladies of his family to wear homespun instead of imported fabrics and, if homespun were lacking, to make dresses of their white homemade counterpanes. The reports were probably well-founded. Certainly John was a loyal South Carolinian who stood with his State in attempting to reduce excessive tariffs. But he clearly did not favor any move for South Carolina, alone, to withdraw from the Union. There was a rising sentiment for this.

In the fall of 1829, John took his seat in the Legislature again in time to hear Governor Stephen D. Miller open the session with actual mention of the possibility of a civil war. Miller said in part:

"We live under a Government, theoretically the most perfect on earth; whether its actual benefits shall correspond with its theory, or give rise to Tyranny, Disunion and Civil War, depends upon an honest and fair exposition of its powers.

"If the pretension lately set up by Congress, to pass laws to bind the States 'in all cases whatever,' or what is the same thing, to do whatever the General welfare requires, be sustained, then, this Government, instead of being one in which liberty is enjoyed and the right of property protected, is a hateful despotism. Let the consequences be what they may, those must answer for them, who present the alternative of servile submission, or Constitutional resistance, to usurped power. The manufacturers press their claim upon the bounty of Government in a manner unparalleled in the history of legislation. The direct interest of individuals, or of particular sections of the country, is made the basis of a system sapping the foundation of the honest labor and constitutional rights of other sections. It is entirely obvious, that those States owning slaves, have a distinct and separate interest from such as have none.

"With this difference in our institutions we jointly achieved the Revolution; with this difference we formed our present Constitution; we came into the Union with our slaves—And now the selfish sons of chivalrous parents would, directly or indirectly, deprive us of the use of them. Whether this shall be so is the issue. . . ."

South Carolina newspapers immediately echoed the governor's edged words. One editorialized, "The spirit of South Carolina is aroused. Nullification is the order of the day." John Springs read many newspapers and considered all views.

The New York *Courier and Enquirer* commented: "Whatever extremity South Carolina may proceed to in relation to the tariff, we feel satisfied that Virginia, Georgia and North Carolina will not join her in the violent crusade she is meditating."

The Salisbury (North Carolina) *Journal* was very outspoken when its editor wrote: "The Nullifiers in South Carolina are busy in the unholy work of sapping the foundation of the Union."

The Fayetteville (North Carolina) *Journal* stated: "We are sorry to see several newspapers in South Carolina teeming with articles on the subject of the dissolution of the Union."

CHAPTER FIVE

JOHN SPRINGS ALWAYS FOUND TIME from politics and business to guide the education and recreation of his five children. In 1828 his nine-year-old son, Baxter, explained:

"I am growing so big Father has nicknamed me the Big Warrior. I have a nice fat squirrel and a fine cage for him to turn. I have been going to school this year to Mr. Fowler Williams. Cousin Richard Dinkings, Cousin Cynthia Springs, sister Mary and Sophia go with me. Pa calls Richard *Tecumcey* and Leroy the *Little Prince*."

But what impressed young Baxter most was that his father, always a smart dresser, "has got a fine new suit of clothes and in Charlotte they call him the *Dandy*."

That January, Austin, the oldest son, entered the University of Virginia. Like every other venture in those days of epidemics and sudden death, college education was fraught with perils. Within a year, cholera swept the campus at Charlottesville. On April 2, 1829, John Springs received a letter from one Eli Hoyle, whose brother attended Virginia with Austin. Hoyle reported that cholera had killed his brother and eight other students and had left the campus "quite deserted." He acknowledged a "lasting obligation to your Son for the kind attention he paid to my Brother during his illness," and reported that Austin was "in perfect health, which blessing he enjoyed all the time the malady prevailed."

Leroy, the second child, was in school in Charlotte, but not applying himself as his father thought he should. So in the fall, John Springs sent Leroy to Charleston to try his wings there. Leroy wrote home on November 4, 1828:

"Dear Father: I arrived in Charleston last Sunday knight in good health. . . . When you sent me here I know you had no other expectation than I have a home. Mr. Roberson has not yet found any place for me. I understood from you that if Mr. Roberson did not get me a home he would take me himself, but he sais know. . . . He says there is a holesale Merchant at New York which he expects on in a few days. He sais he thinks he can get me in with him. I am now bording at Mr. Thomas Johnsons at an expense of one Dollar pr. Day which I know that you did not calculate on when you sent me here. Mr. Roberson has never invited me home with him. . . . I intend if Mr. Roberson does not prove successful in getting me in to get him to give Recammedations & try myself over town . . . as I know that my Parents wish and desire to see us all Industrious & interprising in Business. . . . I have nothing more to Relate at present but still remain your affectionate son.—Leroy Springs."

Leroy's brush with the cold realities of the business world in Charleston evidently prompted him to think better of continuing his education. By the following year he enrolled at Mount Zion Academy at Winnsboro, S. C. From there he wrote:

"I acknowledge that I was not in the habit of studying hard when I was home but I have studied as hard as a student could do since I came here as I am getting old enough to see the folly of my inattentiveness to my studies."

Leroy returned to the academy at Winnsboro the following year, but soon grew restless. He yearned to travel. On September 11, 1830, he wrote to his father: "As to myself I can say that since my recollection I do not think that I have ever enjoyed as good health as I have done since I have been here. I have not given out the notion of going to France if it is possible to get your consent and which I hope you will give me. You may probably think that I am tired of going to school or dissatisfied with this place or some of my teachers or something, but I can assure you that it is not. If I did not think it best for me to go there I certainly would not ask this with the numberless other favors which you have bestowed upon me, but will say nothing more at present about it as you have said nothing concerning it in my answer to my last. I am aware that it is a long trip and you will probably think too long for one as young as me but I would willingly undertake it if I could get your consent. I should like for you to hear my teacher, Mr. Leroy, give a description of the manner and friendship which the

French treat an American when he goes there. He says there is no ball or gathering in the town he is in but what he is invited to and the ladies are very jealous of each other who shall dance with him first.

"This week we all walked eight miles to a barbecue to hear the members of this District declare their sentiments to the public. All of them spoke in favor of a convention."

John Springs felt no eagerness to send his young son to France, so 1831 found Leroy back at Mount Zion Academy. There his mother wrote to him on March 1: "You being rather predisposed to those winter fevers, I cannot be content without hearing from you often. . . . Your brother Baxter and sister Sophia are back in school. . . . It is reported that gold is being coined at your Aunt's mine. I know not the truth for I have not seen any of them. They say, two thousand dollars a week."

The oldest Springs daughter, Mary Laura, went off at the age of sixteen in 1829 to a school for young ladies at Salem, North Carolina. Christmas vacations were then unknown, for she wrote home on January 6, 1830:

"We spent our Christmas pleasantly indeed, and on that day received many presents from our dear Inspector and Tutoresses; and likewise recited our dialogues to the inhabitants. There was a curtain drawn across the center of the chapel which formed a separate room for the musicians and on the center of this curtain was the name Jesus printed in large golden letters; the rest of the curtain was handsomely decorated with artificials and evergreens and paintings which represented the birth of our Saviour to which our dialogues alluded.

"We had a prayer meeting in our chapel on the last day of the year held by our dear Mr. Reichel who offered a very fervent prayer in behalf of the Tutoresses, girls, their friends and relations. We likewise attended one at the large church between 8 and 9 o'clock; another between eleven and twelve which, when it commenced striking 12 there burst forth a band of music composed of various instruments such as organs, violins, flutes and trumpets, the sound of which echoed through and through the church. The minister who was preaching was stopped by the sound of music that was heard. After it ceased, there was offered a prayer for the congregation. It was truly effecting indeed. I do not do it justice.

"Father, you wrote me about my last letter being so badly written.

Indeed I was very much confused, but hope you will excuse me. My promotion in the first class must not be forgotten."

Later that year, at seventeen, Mary Laura was sent to Philadelphia to complete her education. Her letters reflect intense delight. Philadelphia was a big city, gay and stimulating. The experience was an adventure from the start. Enroute, in the care of Uncle Eli Springs, she met friends at Salem, North Carolina. "When they heard I was for Philadelphia," she said, "they laughed saying that they supposed I was going to get the polish." Afer visiting Washington, she proceeded by steamboat up the Chesapeake, through the Delaware and Chesapeake Canal, and up the Delaware to Philadelphia. There, Uncle Eli placed her in a Mrs. Sarazin's School.

The school cost $400 a year and offered five courses: chemistry, ancient geography, French, painting, and music. Mary Laura lost no time. She reported: "Mrs. Sarazin and the ladies encouraged my commencing the French language which I have already attempted. It is the only study in the afternoon. The opportunity to learn it is very good owing to the number learning and speaking it in the school. There is also a French lady living in the house who assists in teaching. . . . I hope that within a year I shall have made some progress worthy of the labor and expense. . . ."

Yet Mary Laura, in the process of acquiring "polish," remained aware of the extremes around her. Philadelphia, she commented, "gives us an idea of the different classes of mankind as this city affords instances of the contrast in that respect; while we are enjoying the greatest luxuries that wealth can afford, others again [are] in the most forelorn and helpless condition."

John wanted Leroy to go to college but had promised to let him make his own decision on leaving the academy. Now he wrote like many a parent:

"You speak of getting through your studies. . . . I am determined to do my part. If you do not do yours it will be your loss, but I will not agree for you to quit school, if it takes seven years, until you *learn to spell,* a thing that any common boy learns by the time he is ten or twelve years of age. I still observe misspelled words in your letters. . . ."

John also expressed misgivings at the speed with which Leroy claimed to have learned bookkeeping: "I know that it is considered a simple, easy science, but also know that few men are capable of going into the counting room of a commission house, or an extensive wholesale dealer, and making correct entries." He added a common doubt, "It may be too that you have not a competent teacher."

At the close of the session, John wrote Leroy that his formal studies at the academy were ended, "You are now launching out into the world, and will have an opportunity of forming some acquaintances with mankind, the study of which you should attend. You will have a chance to see and learn some of the virtues, as well as the vices of the world. Strive as much as possible to practice the former and shun the latter. Let your expressions and conduct be governed by truth, candor, and honesty; it is a course that will wear much the best. They will stand by you and be your support when others fail; and oh! My Son, remember the fond hopes and expectations of a father, who seems to act on this theatre of life, not so much for himself as for his children, in order that he may render his offspring useful and ornamental members of society. . . ."

Although John apparently clung to his intention of sending Leroy to college, the young man went farther much sooner than his father expected. Leroy and a friend his age obtained parental permission to visit Charleston in October, 1831. John sent them down in style in his two-horse carriage, writing a pass or permit for the slave coachman Nathan to return alone unquestioned. Both boys had ample spending money. Gaily they decided to take the steamship from Charleston to New York. On arrival, they paid a week's hotel board in advance and proceeded to crowd in all the sightseeing, amusements, and shows possible.

Finally down to their last cash, they bought theater tickets. But an older man stepped up just then. Leroy courteously stepped aside from the box office. When he moved back to pick up his tickets, they were gone.

Penniless and friendless, the two youngsters roamed from door to door through the business section of New York hunting jobs. They were thoroughly discouraged when Leroy suddenly saw a sign over a commission house with the name "Spring." He introduced himself to the kindly, elderly head of the firm, who was also interested in the similarity in their names. Through this, Leroy got a temporary job and his friend found one nearby. His new employer wrote John Springs, whom he knew slightly. This "resulted in an amicable settlement by which Leroy remained in New York instead of going to college."

No doubt, John and Mary must have been shocked to find Leroy, barely twenty, suddenly settling in distant New York. John immediately wrote, sending the name of a firm which Leroy could consult if in need of advice. He added some characteristic counsel of his own:

". . . but they cannot give you character; that you must form for yourself. I know your habits heretofore have been active and correct. If you engage with a fixed determination to apply yourself industriously and exert yourself to promote the interest of your employer, you may in a short time form a character for yourself that will be your best recommendation. Always endeavor to observe the strictest integrity to your engagements and account for every dollar you spend. On no occasion absent yourself without the knowledge and permission of your employer. I wish you now to be placed in the most advantageous circumstances for your interests and improvement, and to make salary no object. I particularly advise that you endeavor to make yourself acquainted with bookkeeping and the French language. I have it in view, if we both live, to set you up in business for yourself. You may, and no doubt will, find many more temptations to draw you off from business and fall in with bad company, than you have ever before known, but remember, my son, that your best guard and defense against vice and immorality will be close application and attention to your business."

Leroy found himself so carried away by his fascinating surroundings that he waited many weeks before writing. When he did, his father replied bluntly: "You make a lengthy apology for not writing, but to me not altogether satisfactory."

On the recommendation of his uncle Eli Springs, Leroy got a job as a salesman with the New York firm of Lee, Powell & Company, soliciting accounts. The boy, overwhelmed by this responsibility, appealed to his father as though John Springs could produce miracles or at least ready customers. In reply, John referred to his own store, J. & E. Springs, Charlotte.

"You are already beginning to solicit the influence of my character and acquaintance to patronize you in your business," he wrote Leroy. "It shall be most cordially extended. . . . [but] you know that I live myself rather an obscure country life. I am pretty extensively known from Charlotte through South Carolina and part of North Carolina and the firm of J. & E. Springs, for a village establishment, is extensively known and stands fair, but I have not any particular acquaintance with merchants. . . . But whatever I can do in promoting your interests and those of your employers' shall be freely rendered.

"I am vain enough to believe that it is only necessary for it to be known to a great many merchants of North and South Carolina that I have a son in New York for them at least to call and see you, and then the balance will depend on your courtesy, smartness and correct conduct towards them. Your being from the South I have no doubt is itself sufficient to create a small partial feeling in your favor, independent of acquaintances and family influence."

Meanwhile, John was busy at Springfield, and Austin, having completed his schooling at the University of Virginia, was home to help him. Between the two of them, they supervised the hauling of forty-six bales of cotton to the Nation Ford. There they had the cotton loaded on a flat boat which floated down the river to Camden in five days. The cotton was sold for ten cents a pound. On the return trip, John and his son brought two pairs of mill stones to be used in a grist mill which William E. White and John were erecting at the Ford.

Austin had recently received a magnificent gift. John had turned over to him about 1,238 acres near Nation Ford, on the west side of the Catawba, that he had named "Springsteen." The land was rich and fertile. It consisted of three tracts, the Baxter plantation and Henderson and Ticer places. The transaction was a business-like one. John retained title to the lands until "some future time at my discretion." He painstakingly listed by name a gift of nineteen Negro slaves, ten of them adults, total value $6,600. Then he added to the list everything including "cash given you since you started to College in 1827— $2,500," and livestock and grain. The total came to $21,173. The list ran:

The Baxter Plantation and whole of the Henderson place including the Mill and Land attached to it, containing about 1,075 Acres		$ 9,000
The Ticer Place—163 Acres		$ 1,000
Negroes: Africa and Jinney 50 & 45 years old	2	500
Cato and Granby 24 & 22	2	1,000
Ann and her Child Jane 26 & 3	2	500

	Patience 20 and her Boy Allen 2 months	2	500
	Cela 16 and Mary 14 years old	2	700
	Legion 12 Linney 10 & Eliza 8 yrs. old	3	800
	Bob 30, Harry 24, Grandison 22, Smith 19	4	2,000
	Lambert and Harriot 11 and 9 years old	2	600
		19	
Horses:	Big sorrel Horse Buck 10 years old		$ 90
	Sorrel Horse Nubbin 7 years old		100
	Chunky Sorrel Purch 13 years old		60
	Sorrel Horse Pinder 8 years old		60
	Young Sorrell Charley 4 years old		90
	Grey Colt 2 years old		100
Cattle:	1 Yoke Oxen and Cart		80
	3 Cows and 1 calf		30
	3 Steers and 1 Heifer		35
Hogs:	28 Head at The Plantation		60
	13 Hogs at the Mill		25
	1 Wagon, Chains, Bridles & Harness in Full		120
	Ploughs, Hoes, ————— Gears & sundry Tools		30
	2700 lbs. Pork put up at the Plantation		140
	1200 Bushels Corn at 75 Cents		900
			$18,520
	1 Good Saddle		15
	Cash gave you since you started to College in 1827		2,500
			21,035
	J. & E. Springs bill for 1830 against you		38
			$21,073

By the following summer, however, John thought he spied cause for complaint against Austin:

"He is now on his plantation with nothing to do that I know of, at least I don't think he attends to anything much. There is plenty for him to be employed at if he were industriously inclined, but he is perfectly a man of pleasure and I don't believe ever will bother his head much about the things of this troublesome world."

Still, the young man seemed to know what he wanted out of life and was content to take his time about getting it. John concluded that the best way to fan Austin's enthusiasm was to encourage him to improve his plantation. So he imported an expert to plant experimentally grafted trees at both Springsteen and Springfield, praised Austin's interest in pest control and his writing on the subject for periodicals of the day, and helped to stock the Springsteen stables with pedigreed horses. Here John heartily approved Austin's approach. In training, Austin never put harness on a riding horse nor a saddle on a driving horse. Two of his fiery saddle horses, Dill and Mouse, became so noted that "the memory of them has been handed down in a family history almost as human members."

In June John sent his youngest son, Baxter, over to the Providence section of Mecklenburg County to be enrolled in a school there. "He seems to be popular," John explained, "and appears to be fortunate in ingratiating himself into the good graces of the people where he has been."

During July John wrote many letters to Leroy in New York. He wrote in a calming vein, because there were problems again:

"Leroy, I presume you are under considerable excitement and a hub bub in New York respecting the Cholera. I would not have you by any means to be alarmed. (As Thomas Jefferson said) don't give yourself uneasiness about evils that never happen. I would not advise any person to run headlong into danger but I would disapprobate fleeing unnecessarily from it. Live temperate and prudent. Keep good hours. Don't go out too much in the damp night air. Be moderate in your diet. And I would advise you (not merely on account of the cholera, but for the good of your health and habits in general) to refrain from drinking almost everything but water. I would recommend strongly not to taste ardent spirits. If I used anything more than simple water it should be Soda water. This, at the present time, is my own course and am sure I profit by it. When Lee Powell and Company get alarmed and leave the city, then it will be time for you to think of cutting dirt, but don't think about quitting without consulting me or as long as two or three remain in the House. If you will examine the account from Europe you will find that when the Cholera has raged the worst that perhaps not one in a hundred of the population has taken the complaint and perhaps a third of that number have died, and we are not secure in any situation in life. If you were to flee you might get shipwrecked. You might be blown up by the bursting of a boiler in a steam boat. You might get your neck broken by the capsizing of a stage or the limb of a tree might fall on you and knock out your brains. Again, I repeat, don't be alarmed unnecessarily."

Older brother Austin undertook to cheer Leroy with a letter on July 6, 1832. He discussed courting, crops, deer hunting on Sunday (highly illegal), and social doings. A bold character in the latter was a friend, David Lowery, who outdid the rest of the beaus in the stylish tightness of his trousers. Austin reported:

"Lowery entered the room dressed for the party in an extreme tight pair of inexpressibles. He said that the girls applied their kerchiefs to their faces and made for their rooms as he supposed that they thought he entered the room in his drawers. He tells another very good anecdote upon himself. When on a visit to North Carolina—having called at some house—he could hear the children whispering 'that man had mighty tight pantaloons on.' At length the Gentleman of the house enquired of him why he had his pantaloons so tight. He replied to him that the tariff was so very oppressive that he could not afford them any larger."

By late summer, the cholera in New York was so grave that John warned, "Quit the city and retire to some country seat. I would by no means wish you to return home at this warm and unhealthy season, but you must in some measure exercise your own judgement. In New York you are visited by Pestilence and here we shall have Famine. We are still dry and the crop of vegetation literally burned up. . . ."

Leroy took his father's advice and went to board with a gentleman in the country. That gentleman was soon "seized with a violent attack of cholera." As younger brother Baxter expressed it, "That plague is surely coming nearer and nearer us."

Leroy escaped the disease, but New York palled on him. He yearned for home and wrote his father accordingly. John on November 11, 1832, expressed surprise "to learn your apparent determination to return home. "I am much inclined to believe that, unless the state of your health and constitution absolutely require, it would be considerable loss to you returning home. It would break off your mind and attention from your pursuits and business, which of itself is considerable. It would cost from $100 to $150 which is some object in these Tariff and Nullification times."

Talk of a split in the nation persisted. Although a new Federal tariff in 1832 did away with some of the objections to the 1828 one, Southern agriculturists still felt that it favored Northern industry at their expense. In October, 1832, the Governor summoned the Legislature into special session on the issue. John hurried to Columbia. There he participated in action calling for a State convention. There were rumors that if South Carolina balked at paying the tariff on imports, a United States Navy squadron might blockade the coast. John wrote his son Leroy:

"The Northern and Western people have been deluded by thinking the Southern States would accept the late bill of 1832 as a compromise and that it was all bluster and talk in South Carolina but she will perhaps convince them that she is in earnest, and the frigates you mentioned may begin to take their stores and fit out for the blockades. We have made a beginning and God knows where we will end, but with the Southern States it is completely a question of freedom or slavery,* and when that is the issue there is no counting of cost, and it is not a time to look back or dally by the wayside. I will not continue the subject as it is out of your line of business, and you will have an opportunity of being more fully informed of our Political movements by reading some of the Southern papers and others.

"If you write on receipt of this, address me at the seat of Nullification in Columbia. If the Cholera should not Nullify the Nullifiers, I expect to be there. Adieu."

Cholera did not "nullify the nullifiers," and in convention assembled at Columbia November 24, 1832, they declared the new tariff unconstitutional, null and void. The ordinance also provided that if the United States Supreme Court upheld the tariff, South Carolina would secede from the Union.

President Jackson, the former Springs neighbor from the Waxhaws, called on Congress to give him authority to use the Army and Navy to collect tariff duties at Charleston. The issue shook the nation. Many people outside of South Carolina agreed that the tariff was too high, but felt that secession was going too far. Under a timely compromise, South Carolina withdrew her Act of Nullification and the possibility of war in the 1830s was averted.

*The reference was to enslavement of the South by the North, not Negro slavery.

CHAPTER SIX

IN 1833 JOHN SPRINGS suffered a severe loss in the death of his brother and business partner. Faithful "Uncle Eli" died on March 13 after a three-day illness. The duration is indicated by Dr. M. Dougherty's bill of $2.00 a day for the three days, paid by John as executor on July 31. Another of the good doctor's bills reveals further tragedy, "visit to Mrs. Springs in labour and delivered, $7.00," on June 21. Eli's only son, Eli, Jr., was born posthumously then and died within the year.

John was now burdened with the affairs of his widowed sister-in-law and her three small daughters, Mary Laura, Elizabeth B., and Catherine V., a burden he willingly and ably assumed.

During the Christmas season of 1833 sorrow came again to the Springs family. John's father, Richard, the gallant Captain of the Revolution, who, though eighty years old, still dressed in fine, imported clothes and rode his handsome grey mare, died on December 22. The following day, the long funeral procession proceeded to Unity Church. The weather was miserable. John placed an extra blanket over Mary's knees, because she had taken cold and was susceptible to severe coughs. After the burial John and his family went directly to Springfield. By that time a cold mist was beginning to freeze. Mary went to bed, shivering with a chill. Outside the sleet bounced off the window sills like beads of glass.

The next day Mary insisted on rising and making the usual Christmas arrangements for the large household. Although ill, she presided at the holiday feast. In her black mourning dress, her pale face seemed all the whiter. John grew more worried as Mary's cold grew worse. The following week she was unable to leave her bed. Outside the trees shimmered in their icy splendor. The peacocks refused to leave the tall oak trees. They roosted quietly, with their frozen tails hanging like iridescent robes.

John sent the overseer to Charlotte with a note for Leroy, who had recently arrived from New York, instructing him to come home and bring Aunt Sophia and Dr. Ross.* By Wednesday, January 2, Mary's lungs were so congested that her breathing could be heard outside her room and in the library where the children sat around the open fire, talking nervously in whispers. John never left Mary, day or night. He dozed occasionally but always he was there to reach out for her hand and speak a comforting word should she stir or open her eyes. Nathan tiptoed in during the night to put more logs on the fire or replace the burned down candles. John sat and waited, his heart consumed with fear. Only the flickering shadows dancing on the walls shared his anguish.

When dawn broke, John sent a Negro boy over the river to Spring-steen to tell Austin to come at once. Dr. Ross said it was only a matter of hours. John knew now his Mary was slipping away from him. He sat helpless and pathetic. Agony shone on his face. His Mary, to whom he had said: "Oh, my Dear, what would the world be to me, were I deprived of you, the only object that appears to render life desirable." And Mary had called him "Dearest Love."

At one o'clock that afternoon Mary's short, heavy breathing suddenly stopped. John held her in his arms, sobbing ever so softly, almost as if he were soothing her pains away and remembering "the happy days and hours we spent together, and the distance we are now separated."

Now John was faced with being both mother and father to his children. To them he was devoted, indulgent, and gentle. In his realistic way he tried to do what was best for them. He studied each one individualy. Austin, he reasoned, was well settled on his plantation. True, this oldest son, who personified the gentleman of leisure and genial country squire, was not destined to come up to his father's hard-driving standards, but John took consolation in the fact that Austin was now completely independent of him.

Young Mary Laura was at Springfield. Her schooling was finished and she had assumed her mother's duties. John could talk to her,

*Mary Springs' sister, Sophia, married Dr. Joseph Ross.

soothe her in her sadder moments and encourage her in her social activities. She would be all right, he reasoned.

Leroy, now, he thought, what would be best for him? Responsibility and work. That was what Leroy needed. He had promised the boy that he would set him up in business. He would keep his promise. He would turn over his Charlotte store to him. And this he did, three weeks after Mary's death. Typical of John, he itemized everything carefully, and presented it to his son:

"A list and valuation of Property given off to Leroy Springs by his Father January 21st, 1834."

Brick House Corner Lot and improvements in Charlotte. Title to be made at some future time	$11,000
Stock gave you in the firm of Springs & Dinkins	6,000
My profits in said firm from 23 March 1833 till 21st Jan. 1834 at which time I put you in possession	1,500
Cash furnished you at different times when you started to school at Winnsborough till your return from New York. See schedule on my Book	1,450
1 Bed, bed stead, 1 pr. blankets, 2 pr. sheets, quilts and counterpane	70
1 English cow and calf	30
Cash to pay for corner Lot no. 12 Part of Masons Lot in Charlotte	500
1 Set silver table and 1 set teaspoons	30
	$20,580

Next, John considered Baxter. The boy, fifteen when his mother had died, was preparing himself for college. Professor Robert J. McDowell had established an excellent school at Rocky River, a few miles north of Charlotte. That, John decided, was the place for his youngest son.

And now, Sophia. She was thirteen, small for her age, vivacious, pretty, and extremely affectionate. She was like a little princess and Springfield was her court. Having known nothing but this beautiful, happy life of affection and care, her world had suddenly broken apart with her mother's death. The selection of a school for her was John's hardest task. He knew he could not send her as far away as Charleston or even Salem. So he settled on Charlotte. There, on February 25, he enrolled her at the Southern Female Institute, headed by Mr. and Mrs. A. J. Leavenworth. Although he visited her often she cried for days with homesickness and was often ill. John would ride up to Charlotte and sit with her for hours.

"You and I," wrote Sophia to Baxter, "seem to be the chief objects of Pa's care, as the rest are grown, and I think that he comes as near filling the place both of a father and a mother as any person could. I can say that you and Pa occupy many of my lonely hours." Gradually, however, she cheered up and became her usual exuberant self. She wrote:

"There was a caravan of animals and circus men here the first day of this month. I went up to Leroy's that night and we went to the circus. Mr. Leavenworth suspected me a little but did not say anything. The next day he went with all the young ladies to see the animals and I went with the rest. We happened to get there just as the circus commenced and the manager told us that if we would stay until it was over that he would open the animals again so that unexpectedly we saw them perform."

And later:

"We had the pleasure of walking to the pond the other evening to see the young men skating and we had also the pleasure of sliding across the pond and I do not think that I ever enjoyed myself better. The Young ladies class in chemistry have lectures three times a week after night and two nights this week Mr. Leavenworth exhibited the exhilarating gas. Mr. John Wilson was the first one that took it and he was very happy indeed, danced all over the floor. Then Dr. Louis. He was very angry and knocked down two or three. Mr. Foster, he just went about clapping his hands. I get very homesick at times but I soon get over it. I think that I have learned more this session than any other. We write composition on slates every other Friday and the other Fridays we bring in written composition. I am now studying U. S. History and expect to take natural philosophy. I saw a letter of yours [Baxter's] that Pa had and he praised your good spelling very much. I cannot think that you think much about me or you would let me hear from you. Oh, you don't know how I want to see you. I would give you a battle of fun."

By 1836, Sophia was in full rebellion against her schoolmaster. She wrote Baxter on November 9: "I am more discontented this session than I ever was before or than I expected to be. Mr. Leavenworth is more strict than ever. I have not been up the street but once since I came here. I really believe that some of us will get married. . . ."

Three months later, she reported: "It is very dull here."

Leroy was not only the first of the five children of John to strike out for himself in the world, he was the first to marry.

Pretty Amanda Moore of Yorkville, South Carolina, set October, 1835, as the date of her wedding to Leroy. The ceremony would take place at the home of her parents, the John Starr Moores.

Leroy broke the news to his brother Baxter, who had progressed by that time to the University of Virginia: "This will inform you that I am to be married on the fifteenth of this month and should be glad if you could make it convenient to come on the thirteenth. You will have to go down to the old man's and go in the carriage with Mary. There will be a dinner at the old man's on the sixteenth from whence we expect to return to Yorkville again."*

Friends and relatives came from near and far to the wedding ceremony. The following day the carriages lined up to take the families and guests to Springfield where John had planned his elaborate entertainment for the bride and groom. Outwardly he was jubilant, but more than once he felt a great lump in his throat. If only his dear Mary could have lived to see this happy day!

Never could there have been a more beautiful background for a dinner than that of Springfield. Never could there have been a more gracious or handsome host than John, for this "old man," as the boys called him, was not forty-nine years old, with thick, brown wavy hair which was slightly greyed at the temples, cheeks that were ruddy and tanned, and a figure as erect as a soldier's.

The following April 20, John had the pleasure of giving away his oldest daughter, Mary Laura, as a bride to Adam Brevard Davidson, grandson of a lifelong family friend, the gallant Major John Davidson, signer of the Mecklenburg Declaration of Independence.

The wedding took place by candlelight at Springfield, with Sophia and "Cousin Eugenia" as candle holders, and Mary Ann Irvin and Mary McCombs as bridesmaids. Nearly one hundred guests attended,

*According to the early letters which described weddings, it was the custom, if the wedding was an elaborate one, for the bride and groom to remain at home for several days, or even a week, participating in entertainments.

a large gathering in that period of sparse population. John had expected not more than seventy.

Brevard took his bride to Rural Hill, the ancestral home of the Davidsons, in the Hopewell section. It was an imposing two-story house of dark pressed brick, with massive Corinthian columns supporting the roof, which extended over wide piazzas front and rear. On the main floor, the partitions between the spacious parlors could be raised from the floor and fastened to the ceiling with immense hooks, thereby throwing the rooms together for balls and important occasions.

True to his generous nature John showered Mary with gifts. And, also true to his nature, he made a complete inventory of the valuations of those gifts. Among them were twenty slaves valued at $7,450 and a 959-acre plantation.

Inventory of the property given to Mary Davidson and charged to her on my Book and valuation given to her in December 1836:

From	) To your expenses at School in Salem &		
1828	) Philadelphia, Etc. Etc.	$ 1742	
to 1831	) 1 Side Saddle & Bridle	20	
1836			
Aug.	1 Cutting box & knives $9, Pr. Wedges 2,		
	Mattocks $4, Grindstone $5	18	
	1 fine Mahogany bedstead $40, Bureau &		
	closing flap $45, Set Tables $90	175	
	2 Beds, 3 Pr sheets, 2 Pr Blankets, quilt coverlid,		
	Curtains, 3 counterpaines	100	
	Table cloths, Towels, Etc. Etc.	10	
	2 Pr Candlesticks snuffers & Tray	4	
	Silver soup spoon, set Table & Teaspoons,		
	salt spoons & sugar Tongs	41	
	1 Set knives & forks complete	15	
	Bill of Crockery ware bought by Leroy	34	
	1 Doz. Chairs lost in the steam boat	15	2174
Dec. 9	3 Cows, two yearlings 60, 1 Sow & 4 Shoats		
	from Duffy	75	
	3 Heifers & 2 steers from Home 60, Stack fodder		
	from Duffy 12	72	
	3 Bus salt, 5 Meal & Corn	8	
	250 Lb. Bacon at 15	38	

	New Waggon gear & Harness for five Horses	250	
1	Pr Horses, 4 yr old 250, Spotted filly 4 y. old 125, Sorrell filly 3 y old 110	485	928
	Dixon Plantation in Lincoln containing 959 Acres		5000

Negroes:

1	Bill, black Smith, 51 years	1000	
3	Ann, 42 years old, 300, Fanny 21, 450, Wilbert 14, 500.	1250	
3	Rhody 12, 350. Hannah 10, 300. Nancy 7, 250.	900	
2	Humphrey 5, 250. Cela 3, 200.	450	
4	Tom 30, 600. Julia & child 500. Austin 7, 300.	1400	
2	George 5, 250. Lemuel 2, 200.	450	
2	Burrow 54, 400. Sirci 14, 400.	800	
3	Peggy 50, 200. Henry 18, 500. Alick 15, 500.	1200	7450
20			

Dec. 14	To 193 Bus. Corn 145. Cash to furnish Plantation 300	445	

$15,552

It had been with some hesitation that John had agreed in 1835 that Baxter, like his older brother, Austin, should attend the University of Virginia. Soon, however, he had his doubts that his decision had been a wise one.

"I anticipated you would find some wild young men at the University and that it would cost you a good deal of money," he wrote his son . . . "I have sent you there not for the purpose of spending money, any more than is absolutely necessary. . . . The best way to keep from extravagance and spending money uselessly is to employ yourself closely at your studies. Another good way is to keep a constant account of your expenditures, for your own satisfaction but more particularly mine. If a student spends more than $400 a session, the rules and regulations of that institution as published to the world and which the faculty have promised should be observed are all *fallacy* and *humbug*. Why is the money required to be placed in the hands of an officer if it is not for the purpose of controlling the expenditure of the students?

"Your moral, upright, correct and economical deportment will now be put to a severe test in your collegiate course, and it requires you to summon up all the resolution you possess, and a great degree of perseverance, and a fixed determination to pursue the paths of virtue and moral rectitude, to preserve you from falling into habits of extravagance and its companions, vice and immorality. You will now in all probability in the course of the next four or five years form habits, be them good or bad, that will most likely abide with you through life."

Like most students who are busy enjoying themselves, Baxter seldom bothered to write to his father. John's next letter took a stern and tart tone:

"I received a few weeks since from Wm. G. Pendleton, your Proctor, a letter stating that you were in arrearage and that it became his duty to report you. I felt insulted, not at him but at you. I answered him (which he will no doubt show you) that I had no certain information that I had a son at the University since the 10th of January, but if I had one still there and he needed funds, if he would give himself the trouble to let me know it, I would endeavor to furnish him.

"Mr. Pendleton will, no doubt, think I am a strange kind of man. I had, I confess, strange feelings on reading his letter, to think that you would suffer me to be dunned by an officer of the Institution without letting me hear one word from you or communicating your wants. It is pursuing the same course Austin did when there. I scarcely ever heard from him, only when he wanted money. . . ."

Then John, having delivered his sermon, relented as fathers will.

"I am enclosing you a Hundred Dollar Bill of the State Bank of North Carolina. . . . I presume it will be good at Charlottesville. . . . Acknowledge its receipt and if you need more I will then forward. . . . Affectionately, your Father, John Springs."

To enliven further the already lively life at the University, Baxter and his friends formed a little orchestra. Hastily he wrote Leroy. Would he buy him a flute on his next trip to New York? Leroy obliged. He advised Baxter on April 3, 1836:

"I have purchased you a fine German 4-keyed flute, silver. It will cost you $22. I have also purchased a case for it to preserve it from abuse."

The campus harmony that was melody to Baxter must have sounded more discordant to his father. In June, 1836, John ordered Baxter home from the University of Virginia. He sent the boy a $50 U. S. bill with instructions to "return by Fredericksburg, Richmond and Raleigh, and spend a day at each place, and from the latter by way of Hillsborough, Greensborough and Salisbury."

Once home, Baxter was hustled to Yorkville State Academy for a brush-up course in mathematics under Professor John A. Alston. After two months there, he entered the South Carolina College (now University of South Carolina) at Columbia. There he found he had to start anew in the freshman class. His father, displeased, commented:

"It would seem your time has been measurably lost at the University of Virginia. . . . Without application and industry, you might remain in college till you are 40 years of age to little purpose. But I am flattered with a hope (natural to every father) that you will do well, that you might render yourself an ornament to your little patriotic State, useful to yourself, and an honor to your family and friends."

At that, to all indications, Baxter finally buckled down to work. But he enjoyed getting mail from his friends at the University of Virginia reporting on the gay pace there:

"Old Conway gave a first-rate dinner today. There was wine aplenty. Two fellows were so green as to be afraid to drink of the wine, for fear they would be sent off. Such greenness does deserve exemplary punishment!"

"Vangle has been suspended for a fortnight for having an eggnog frolic in his room during Christmas."

"There is a rebellion now in progress at the University. The faculty forbid the military company to use muskets. They persisted. The faculty then disbanded the company and ordered them to deliver up their muskets. Forthwith they refused and stacked their arms on the lawn, then danced around them, fired a salute, then went to the top of the Rotunda, fired another volley and rang the bell. They got drunk and cut a great many shines. There seems to be some chance of a reconciliation and a return of the students."

"Seventy of the students were in Richmond making all sorts of a row about town in theaters, etc. I reckon they'll repent finally."

Baxter smiled at the way his old schoolmates were whooping it up, but conscientiously resolved to stick to his books and please his father. Nevertheless, he felt unhappy and let his father know it.

"You say," John replied by mail, "that you reflect much on the subject of fixing some definite course through life, until at times it throws you almost into melancholy and renders you unsociable. I think that is wrong. You should first make yourself a first-rate literary scholar. You have three or four years to determine what course you will pursue. Why should you feel discouraged?

"Can you point out any distinguished man of the present or former day who has opportunities or advantages superior to those I propose furnishing you? Have there not many risen to distinction with much more limited opportunities? Look at the addresses of all our leading men and see what great stress they lay on an educated community for the well-being of our form of Government. Look at the great Jefferson in his old age, with what zeal and fervor he got up his favorite object, the University, and on his anticipation of the great good it was to do by diffusing and disseminating literary knowledge."

John's lengthy letter to Baxter continued in a serious tone:

"We are not permitted to look into futurity—Some great Revolution and convulsions in our Government and the Governments of the world may be ahead, some of which may take place in your day, if not mine. To preserve our government in its purity requires much talent, much watchfulness, and a bold and fearless independence to pry into its operations and expose and detect the corruptions that are to be feared are daily creeping into it under the hypocracy of the public philanthropy, patriotism and great devotion to the public good. And it will require well informed minds, deep perceptions and penetrating judgments to separate the wheat from the chaff."

CHAPTER SEVEN

THE PANIC OF 1837 shook the American economy, banks included. Martin Van Buren's inauguration ended the period of expansion and speculation under Andrew Jackson. Some six hundred banks failed, prices slumped, and unemployment soared.

John Springs, as director of the Bank of Hamburg, had grave problems. That bank had always commanded great respect throughout the country and it was one of the banks whose notes were always honored. If John had anything to do with it, the Bank of Hamburg would continue to have the confidence of the people, and accordingly he journeyed there in March to see what steps should be taken to insure the safety of the bank. At the meeting of the Directors it was decided to sell $200,000 worth of stock to increase the bank's capital. John, the second largest holder, now had 555 shares of stock.

What started this panic and why was the money situation serious? It had all started far back at the close of the war of 1812, when money became scarce. The westerners imported goods from the East and, in turn, shipped their products east, but the balance of trade was in favor of the East, which left the westerners in debt. The latter needed a greater supply of money. For instance, one letter John Springs received from Tennessee in 1833 had this to say about the situation there: "This land can not now be sold for $2.00 per acre for cash in hand because money is scarce and there is a large quantity of land on the market and the custom is to give a credit on land. I presume the land could be sold for as high as $3.00 per acre if the resident could take some horses or other property for payment or give time."

In order to relieve such situations as this, and because the individual states under the Constitution of the United States could not issue or make any money legal tender except gold or silver, the state banks under charter came to the rescue by issuing bank notes which circulated as money. By 1820 the number of these state banks reached 300 and grew to 788 by 1837. There was much friction and jealousy between these state banks and the Bank of the United States, which had been chartered in 1816, because the latter was managed under such regulations that it was always able to pay its notes in silver and gold. Some state banks were stronger than others and the value of their notes fluctuated according to the soundness of the bank and the distance the notes were from the bank. For this reason many business men preferred notes of the United States Bank. But Andrew Jackson withdrew all Federal funds from the Bank of the United States and placed the funds in various state banks. When these smaller banks received the large deposits they were able to extend their loans and enlarge their issues of currency. This made for easy money and speculation. Jackson realized this evil and attempted to correct it. Senator Thomas Hart Benton proposed a measure which would have forced all buyers of public lands to pay in gold or in silver. Congress refused to adopt this policy. Jackson, taking matters into his own hands, issued on July 11, 1836, what was known as the "Specie Circular." This was virtually an adoption of Benton's policy and it was put into effect. The state banks had little coin in their vaults to back up their notes. The public panicked and anyone who had loaned money tried to call it in. The borrowers had not made the quick money they expected in the wildcat speculations and were unable to meet their payments. Banks, factories, and business houses all over the country failed. And John's stock in the Bank of the United States, which he had had for years and on which he had collected excellent dividends, started dropping, dropping, until ultimately he would lose most of his investment. He stubbornly refused to sell or to lose his confidence in the Bank, saying, "I prefer the glory of a total loss."

Leroy felt the pinch of the panic in his mercantile business. His father noted: "Some 12 or 14 persons have blown out in Charlotte and I believe they all owe Leroy. One-half of the people there won't work or use any industry to make a living but depend on getting a support *on credit*. As soon as they are pressed upon to pay they blow up and go elsewhere to set up again on credit."

Within two years, however, Leroy was recouping in his own way.

From the landing of the first Springsteens, the family had always invested in land. A friend wrote from Mississippi in 1839 that "times are unusually hard here. Everybody broke. Everyone being sued, both rich and poor. Land at Sheriff's sales selling for 75 cents to $3 per acre." So it was not surprising that John Springs noted in his correspondence: "Leroy has been laying out money for lands in Mississippi."

One April afternoon in 1837 John approached his home with peculiar and mixed emotions. A feeling of melancholia hung over him. His mare trotted briskly up the avenue approaching the house. He could see Wheeler already at the head of the drive, waiting to take his horse. The beauty of the scene before him would ordinarily have pleased and soothed him but today it only saddened him. He remembered what it had meant to have Mary waiting to greet him. Now, it was only Wheeler who said "Evenin', Suh."

He dismounted, threw the reins to the darkie and entered the house. No one, he thought, to whom he could talk. No one to encourage him. He had tried so hard to be a bulwark to the children. But he needed someone, too. Nothing could fill the emptiness that was inside him. Not his children, not his friends, not his business. The truth was, he was lonely. And it was spring.

He strolled about the house. It was quiet. There was a delicious odor of pastries and spiced ham permeating the air. Nancy, the cook, would have a fine supper for him, but he would eat alone.

Rushing out of the house, he went for a walk in the woods. He had a lot of thinking to do. He cut across the side lawn and was soon in the woods. The banks of the brook were green with wild cress. The pungent odor of wild plum filled his nostrils. The young new leaves of the honeysuckle ran riot up the many cedar trees. The bare limbs of the scalybark trees looked strange with their bulbous leaf buds ready to burst open, while the stately elms looked fairy-like with purplish-brown tufts of young flowers drooping from their limbs. In the distance the lowing of the cows reminded John of his loneliness.

He circled back toward the house and as he entered the boxwood garden a great crested flycatcher flew overhead and lighted in the magnolia tree, giving a shrill whistle. John sat down on the bench and waited to see if the female would answer. Even the birds felt the urge for mates, he thought. Here was beauty and tranquillity. Springfield was as radiant as a young girl, as dignified as its "Massa John," but it was nonetheless a lonely place.

John made his decision right then and there. He would marry again. He would ask the widow, Margaret Smith, to become his wife. He had known her as Margaret Allison for many years. He had known her late husband. He admired her. They were congenial. She would make him a good wife. His mind was made up. And yet John was a practical man. He weighed every aspect of such a marriage. He would not wish to jeopardize his children's inheritance in the event of his death. Likewise, if Margaret Smith should become his wife and he managed her estate, it would not be fair for his children to participate in her estate at his death. He returned to the house, sat down at his desk and drafted an article which he carefully labeled "Marriage Agreement."

Margaret Smith did accept his proposal of marriage. She did sign the agreement on April 15. And she did marry John on May 25 of that year of 1837.

Six weeks later Margaret was dead of fever.

John did not file any letters or papers from May to October. Their absence speaks louder than any written words. His unhappiness and frustration seem to cry out from it. Not until November did he resume his correspondence. Then he wrote Baxter a pensive letter: "What shadows we are and what shadows we pursue. We must all needs die and are water spilt on the ground, that can not be gathered up again; and ought to admonish all of the necessity of our being up and doing; and urge us all to be living in such a way that we need not fear to die; and inspire us with desires to render ourselves useful what little time we are here."

From this date on, John Springs plunged into business, politics, and travelling. He continued to be indulgent to his children and they continued to be his prime interest, but many of his letters had at the bottom, "I write in haste." Besides banking, he entered the manufacturing field; he organized companies to build and operate railroads; he helped create insurance companies; and he became one of the first trustees of Davidson College (1838) and contributed regularly to it. His influence was far reaching. His advice was sought on every hand and followed. His wealth was shared by many unfortunate ones but never advertised. His life was full.

An economic and industrial revolution had been going on in the United States, a land unrivalled in opportunities for expansion and growth. But more than an economic upsurge was responsible for the success of John Springs. There was his ingenuity, his enterprise, his thrift, his keen ability to sense a situation, his understanding of people, government, and economy. There was also the fact that people trusted him and therefore they listened to him. This gave him a certain power, influence, and command of attention. Yes, he was well on his way to success in 1838. His investments showed a profit, even after the panic of 1837, evidence of the soundness of his judgment in such matters.

He bought stock in the Commercial Bank of Columbia, South Carolina, and the Merchants Bank of Cheraw, South Carolina. The $10,000 that he invested in the State Bank of North Carolina had doubled its value in two years. He noted at the bottom of his ledger in 1838, "Owing to the present great pressure . . . in business and the great downfall in property it is difficult to ascertain what my stocks are worth, but I am confident it will be very moderate to average it at 10 percent advance which will be $142,175."

John was almost rampant on the subject of President Van Buren's policies. A special session of Congress had been called by Van Buren the previous year and he had recommended a measure which would provide for the borrowing of $10,000,000 through Treasury notes. He had also recommended an independent Treasury or a Sub-Treasury in order that the government could take care of its own funds without depositing them in state banks or one centralized bank. When Congress passed these measures John Springs did not hesitate to voice his opposition. He did a characteristically American thing: He switched newspapers in disgust.

To Baxter he wrote, "Go to Mr. Weir, the Editor of the *Times and Gazette,* and tell him to discontinue my paper. He has been haulting between two opinions and finally has come out on what he believes to be the strong side of the currency question. . . . I don't believe in the Sub-Treasury and Specie currency. . . . I view it as most unsafe. A great many of the Sub-Treasury officers would use the funds for corrupt purposes and for their own private emolument."

John further objected that the plan "would be making one currency for the Government and another for the People, and would be commencing hostilities against the whole Banking System. . . . It is another Administration experiment on the currency and the best interest of the community. The Government has already experimented the currency almost to death to the great injury of the good of the Country!"

And John continued forcefully: "Does any business man of intelligence and experience believe the present state of affairs ever would have existed to their present extent if General Jackson had left the deposits where they were in the United States Bank and Congress under judicious regulation had rechartered their institution?* . . . So said a majority of Congress and the People, but General Jackson said no—he would try an experiment. And Van Buren has pledged himself to carry out the Glorious Principles of his Predecessor. . . .

"The people I expect have been taken by surprise. They have been struck dumb. They remain mute, but they may sometime regain their speech, rouse up from their stupor and speak out. You are authorized to tell Mr. Johnson, editor of the *Telescope,* you have heard of one man from York who is not a Sub-Treasury Van Buren man."

Early one morning John sat down at his desk in the library and penned a letter to Baxter, who was then finishing his junior year at the College of South Carolina and "aspiring for one among the highest honors" of his class and Society. There was no hurry to get the letter off because, as he said, "it will not leave now for four days." And as for any mail coming up from Columbia, "I could get letters much quicker from New York," complained John. Anyway, this particular morning he was not in a hurry, so his pen was the medium of expressing his thoughts to Baxter: "The time will soon come when it will be necessary for you to make some practical application of the theories you have acquired; a period which will be all important. Indeed your future usefulness to yourself, to the community and to the country is greatly dependent on the application, industry, ambition and energy with which you now apply yourself in improving the means and opportunity you now enjoy. Your time is now a golden time. And one day mispent or lost can never be recalled or can hardly ever be regained."

Then, in a humorous vein, John added: "Miss Sarah Pettus is married to a Baptist Preacher, Mr. Bracker. This makes three Baptist Preachers in the course of three months have taken wives in this neighborhood and they go in for the handsomest and richest. I think the young men ought to assemble themselves together and remonstrate

*The charter of the Bank of the United States expired in 1836 and the bank was chartered under the State of Pennsylvania.

against any more young Baptist Preachers being permitted to come to Flint Hill church."

John Springs' philosophy was a wonderful tonic. By 1839, Baxter was in his senior year at South Carolina despite an illness. Wade Hampton, later to win fame as a Confederate cavalry general and post-war Governor of South Carolina, wrote to John from his plantation at Millwood, near Columbia, "I regret to hear that your son has been indisposed. I have not seen him, but will endeavor to do so very shortly and will try to prevail on him to come and see me occasionally."

As Baxter recovered, John felt cheered. "My mind," he wrote the boy, "is much relieved of its anxiety and solicitude by hearing of the improved state of your health, but do not let this prevent you from continuing a course in your diet and exercises. When you walk, do it briskly and with energy. The latter is a word I lay much stress on. It is an ingredient of the mind and body, without a good degree of which I think a man might live and die a cipher, a perfect automaton."

Sophia, now turning seventeen and blossoming into peach-like beauty, returned home from school in Charlotte and spent part of the summer of 1838 with her father. John, fondly studying his youngest child, concluded she was ready for a more sophisticated education than the Charlotte of that day offered. So, to Sophia's delight, she was enrolled in Madame Talavande's French School for Young Ladies at Charleston.

John gave his daughter a lavish wardrobe to meet every occasion in Charleston. The dressmakers bustled over the finest silks and linens from Charlotte. Sophia spent much time shopping and being fitted. Before she finally packed her trunks, she spread the wardrobe across her bed and surveyed her pretty new clothes. They must have looked impressive.

There were four dresses and a cape that Mary Porter, the dress-maker, had made for her in July and August. Next were three dresses of silk, muslin, and calico sewed by Mrs. Doucin in the latest style. Miss Johnson had fashioned two "morning gowns" and six exquisite "pocket handkerchiefs." From the skilled hands of Miss Martha Mon-roe came a beautiful "dress with tippet to match." Petticoats and under garments trimmed with many yards of "lace edging," ribbons and innumerable minute tucks lavishly applied lay ready galore. So were her hair combs of "shell," her hose of cotton and of silk, and her gloves.

The Springs carriage was literally crammed with trunks and clothes boxes early in November when coachman Wheeler snapped the reins over the beautiful pair of greys and John and Sophia waved goodbye to the Negroes lining the driveway to see "young missus" off to school in Charleston.

On arrival, John explained to Madame Talavande that he wished his daughter to be a "parlor boarder." This meant giving her the freedom, under proper chaperonage, of course, to accept social invitations and attend places of amusement.

John then whisked his charming daughter back into his carriage for a final round of shopping that father enjoyed as much as daughter. It was Sophia's first chance to buy in a town where ships daily unloaded beautiful merchandise from abroad. She purchased an imported bonnet ornamented with ribbons and flowers, cost $17; sixteen yards of imported silk to be made into a dress by R. Aveille; English silk hose at $2.50 a pair from Harwood & Company, 112 King Street, and fourteen yards of plaid, "spider net" lace, silk handkerchiefs, a comb and brush, cakes of soap, and papers of pins. John, pleased with his daughter's good taste, cheerfully indulged her.

Madame Talavande charged $500 a term, $100 more than John Springs had paid for his oldest daughter Mary Laura's finishing school in Philadelphia. The sum covered board, tuition, music, books, stationery, and laundry. John soon learned, however, that the good life in Charleston involved other expenses. By the end of the term, he had handed out an additional $200 for such carefully-recorded items as "Theater," "lectures," "Omnibus," and "passage to and from Sullivan's Island, Carriage."

Life in Charleston, then a center of plantation aristocracy, was very sociable and very elegant. To be even a junior part of it gave Sophia polish, poise, and confidence. Many exciting events took place. A lecture by "the world-famous traveler, Mr. Buckingham," drew an audience of 1,056 including Sophia and schoolmates. Well-known actors such as the Ravel family performed for enthusiastic audiences. At the opera, "Madame Otto and Messrs. Bishop and Brouf sang entrancingly." In February there was a week-long holiday for the annual races. And of course, Sophia added, "the battery is always delightful!" There society drove in its carriages or promenaded. Enchanted, she wrote brother Baxter:

"I am very much pleased with the school and teachers. Mrs. Talavande is extremely kind. She is very familiar with the girls out of school but when she enters the classroom everything moves. I do not think she is much taller than I am. I have taken lessons in French and English, on the Guitar and Piano. I wrote to Pa the Friday after he left me and received no answer. I am glad you have received a letter. I was afraid something prevented his writing."

Among the teachers, Sophia's favorite was "Nenaine," who taught her the beautiful penmanship so characteristic of the day. Sophia wrote, "Pa stated that he was more pleased with the evident improvement in my writing and that he would not begrudge all it cost him if I could write such as my Nenaine." Write she did, for in another letter she said, "Nenaine says I will ruin Pa with the cost of postage." And later: "Nenaine is extremely kind to me and indulges me a great deal. She is trying to get a house on the Island [Sullivan's Island, a resort] so I expect we will all have fine fun there soon."

By May, when Sophia reported happily that "the time appears to glide away quite fast" toward her return home, her father had a fresh surprise in store for her. John Springs and all his family thoroughly enjoyed traveling. For the summer of 1839 he planned nothing less than a pleasure trip to Philadelphia, New York, and Quebec to show Sophia and Baxter the sights. To John, travel was another form of education.

If the three traveling Springses paused to write home, none of their letters appears to have survived. But it is easy to imagine Sophia's girlish enthusiasm in embarking at Charleston for Philadelphia, Baxter's walking the deck chatting with influential planters and politicians and, most of all, pretty ladies, and John's quiet pride in his two handsome children.

The one way of following the three is by their bills. John typically saved them all. As those from Philadelphia predate the New York ones, they evidently stopped there first, probably visiting Leonidas Springs of that city, John's nephew.* John bought for himself Italian silk cravats and black satin stocks. Then from "David S. Freeland, 22 Market Street, Wholesale and Retail Hat Warehouse," he purchased 30 black wool hats for his slaves.

In New York Sophia went on a shopping spree. Between July 15th and 17th, the bills show, she bought kid gloves; rib and plain silk hose; a Chinese lacquered fan from Tiffany & Young, 259 Broadway; French

---

*Leonidas Springs was the son of John Springs' sister, Margaret, who married her first cousin, William Springs.

shoes and corsets; fine wool for a full-skirted riding habit; and many yards of French satin, muslin, and "Chenny silk" for gowns.

For his plantation mansion, and gifts for his daughter Mary, John bought from Nunns E. Clark, 137 Broadway, a "crotch mahogany round corner Piano Forte" at $375, a "crotchwood square Piano Forte" at $270, and two piano stools for $40. He also purchased $242 worth of table and bed linens, blankets, and other drygoods items. Other purchases consisted of a rocking chair, many yards of carpeting and matting, a pair of gold mirrors, and a 102-piece set of white and gold china. At Fellows, Wadsworth & Company, Jewelers, 17 Maiden Lane, John spent $608 for table silver. And here he did something he had looked forward to doing for a long time. He bought Baxter a $150 gold watch.

Father and son then visited Howard Keeter & Scofield, 88 Broadway, at Wall Street, and were fashionably outfitted with such articles as "wool black cloth dress coats with silk buttons and edges corded" and "French Moleskin vests."

The long trip through New England to Quebec was made in August, with many pleasurable stops. Not until October did they return to Springfield.

The trip was marred for John somewhere along the line by an accident in which he broke his arm. Sophia wrote after their return, "His arm gives him more pain now than it did soon after he had it set. I am afraid he will always suffer from it at every change of weather and when he uses it too much."

Baxter, now a graduate of the College of South Carolina, remained at Springfield that fall and winter. He was working on "a Journal." He also assumed many duties of running the plantation, thereby relieving his father.

John and Sophia journeyed to Charleston in November for what was to be her last year at Madame Talavande's. By January Sophia reported: "I have spent the time very pleasantly, and I hope profitably also. . . . Weeks and months pass away without my scarcely being conscious of it. I have some very pleasant acquaintances here. I think *hospitality* is justly applied to Charlestonians."

CHAPTER EIGHT

ONE WOULD EXPECT JOHN SPRINGS to be concerned with many people in 1840, but the least likely of these would be Indians. Yes, Catawba Indians!

Springfield was situated in a section which, for generations, had been called The Catawba Nation, laid out in 1763 for the use of the Catawba Indians. The history of this land, going far back into early days, was well known to John Springs, because his land was leased from the Indians by virtue of a law passed by the South Carolina legislature in 1808, giving the Catawbas power "to grant and make leases for life or lives, as well as for a term of years." For a long period of time, especially in the 1830s, the State of South Carolina had made unsuccessful attempts to buy the Catawbas' land. In December of 1839, by order of the legislature, five Commissioners were appointed by Governor Patrick Noble to meet the head men and Chiefs of the Catawbas and to enter into negotiations with them for the cession to the State of their interest in the Indians' lands. John Springs was one of the Commissioners.

And so on the morning of March 14, John, accompanied by Austin, rode to the Nation Ford and there met with the following Indians, who had ceremoniously given themselves military ranks: General James Kegg, Colonel David Harris, Major John Joe, Captain William George, Lieutenant Phillip Kegg, Colonel Sam Scott, and Lieutenant Allen Harris.

On April 3 of that year, a report, signed by the four Commissioners, was sent to Governor Noble. Part of the report, written in John's hand, follows:

". . . that similar commissions have been made from year to year from 1830 up to the present time, without being able to affect anything, a majority of the Indians being indisposed to cede their claim, or remove, and it is believed a treaty could not have been effected on any reasonable terms. But now your commissioners met them at their own particular request. Some of their leading ones have for the last two or three years been passing and repassing to Haywood County, North Carolina, and seem to have been forming a friendship and connection with a remnant of the Cherokees that remain in that section.

"The Catawbas have leased out every foot of land they held in their Boundary, the propriety and expediency of which we need not now enquire. Some remonstrated against it, while others (with the Indians) contended they had a right so to do, and for the last few years they have been wandering through the country, forming kind of camps without any homes, houses or fixed residence, and destitute of any species of property, save dogs and a few worthless horses. They now seem desirous of having a tract of land on which they can again settle and build little houses, according to the number of families, and procure some cattle, hogs and poultry, which they were once in the habit of owning.

"Your commissioners would with due defference state in behalf of the Catawba Indians, that probably they are entitled to some favour from the State or at least to its sympathy and kindness. Their Chief (General Kegg) remarked, that when they were a strong nation and the State weak, they came to her support, and now when the State was strong and the Catawbas weak, she ought to assist them.

"One of your commissioners states from his own knowledge and recollection, that during the Revolution, they left the State, he thinks, for about eighteen months, or at least removed their women and children to a place of greater safety. By which move they lost their stock and poultry. While in the mean time a number of their Warriors were in active service in the American cause. Several of them were in the battles of Guilford, Hanging Rock, and Eutaw, were in several scrimmages with the Tories, and were particularly useful as guides, scouts and runners, and never were known to be in a British or Tory camp. They have now lived in the midst of a dense white population for more than a half century, and your commissioners all concur in testimony that they never have known or heard a dishonest charge made against a Catawba or their meddling with anything that did not belong to them, and have always been harmless, peaceable and friendly. But (as is perhaps characteristic of Indians generally) they are indolent and improvident, and seem to have little idea of laying up for their future wants. Your commissioners believe that if they would have agreed to have paid them (the Indians) in hand, for each one to have used as he chose, they might have effected a treaty for one third or even one fourth the amount.

"From a once populous tribe they have dwindled down to 12 men, 36 women and 40 young ones, in all 88. Nine of whom are connected with a family of Parmonkey Indians and it is believed will not remove. They have been urging a speedy Treaty as some of them are going off immediately to Haywood County and they wished to know before they go that they might make arrangements for a permanent move. . . .

"Your commissioners are of the opinion that there are between five and six hundred white families living on lands under lease from the Catawba Indians and from six to eight hundred voters. And the lands have been divided and subdivided into various small tracts, of which transactions no regular record has ever been kept. This is a matter of wonder that the lessees have not got into more difficulties and litigation.

"Your commissioners beg leave to report a Treaty herewith annexed and recommend that the Legislature of the State would ratify the same, believing its terms are as moderate as the State ought to desire, and as liberal towards the Indians as they would be likely to use judiciously. . . .

"Your commissioners have the following short Traditionary account of the Catawbas. In 1763 it seems King Hagler was their Chief, who was killed by a small party of Shawnees. He was succeeded for a short time by King Prow, and after the American Revolution, they became so Republican that they would not have a King. They then chose General Newvevir as their Chief. He was succeeded by General Scott, him by General Ayres and he by General Harris. The four latter of whom were personally known to the commissioners. And James Kegg now claims the Generalship. He says as being their senior, about 55 years of age, and being a full blooded Indian and the only descendent of the Newvevir family, and in a talk or kind of speach to us said—The State ought to give him the money to buy the land. He wanted title in his own name and was willing the State should tax them and make them subject to the Laws and then they would be entitled to the privileges and immenities of Citizens. But the other Indians are not willing to entrust him with it nor would your commissioners recommend that he should have anything to do with more than his part.

"General Kegg says he wants to marry his women to the Cherokees; and then by the laws and customs of Indians, they would all become Catawbas and in that way strengthen his Tribe."

" (signed) John Springs
David Hutchison
E. Avery
Allen Morrow"

An interesting notation which John had made was the fact that residing with the five or six hundred white families on the Indian Land were 2,085 Negro slaves.

This then was the story of the land which was being farmed by John and his neighbors. The acreage included what is now Rock Hill and Fort Mill, South Carolina. In March of 1841 John received a title to his plantation from the State of South Carolina.

CHAPTER NINE

BAXTER SPRINGS LEFT his father's plantation in 1841 for a tour of the South. He might even go as far as Texas, he thought, and see the Republic which President Tyler wanted to annex to the United States. Going first through Georgia, Baxter stopped in Milledgeville to visit his father's first cousin, Thomas Baxter. While there he decided to ride to Sparta and visit Thomas' brother, Eli. That was the extent of Baxter's tour. Once at the home of his Cousin Eli, Texas was forgotten. Never had he enjoyed a visit more. After several weeks, though, he reluctantly turned his horse toward South Carolina. Having made plans before leaving home to study law under Judge Thomas J. Withers in Camden, he knew the Judge would be expecting him.

Baxter was no more than settled at the Davis Brick Hotel in Camden than he received a letter from his father: "I am gratified you seem pleased with Camden and your studies. I know you will find the people hospitable, kind, civil and polite; a community where an improvement of manners may be acquired. . . . I have no doubt if you conduct yourself with moral propriety you may be able to associate with the most respectable families."

Baxter became a popular bachelor in Camden society. His diary, with daily entries, attests to that fact. There were such notations as: "This morning I arose much later than usual, as will be the case without fail if one eats a late supper, drinks wine, smokes and dissipates the night previous." Or this: "This evening the field was crowded with young men, old men and boys playing cricket. As I returned to the hotel I saw the Miss McWillies all seated on the steps at the door, for the purpose, it would seem, of ogling." Or this: "This morning attended church. Sat with the Shannons by special invitation, also went home with them. The table was well spread, the wine good. There is much hospitality, liberal feeling and kind-heartedness in old Camden."

"The dancing room" was mentioned often in Baxter's diary. There he met the belles of the town and once recorded: "I added to my stock of human nature in observing and speculating upon the different mannerisms of a certain young lady. We danced until one o'clock."

Another day Baxter was enthusiastic about a new invention. "At ten o'clock this morning," he recorded, "I sat for a miniature which was taken by the Chittons of New York. It was done by the method of Dagueratype, which is certainly the most correct manner of delineating to the shape and features of the face now extant. As correct as a mirror. It is, so far as I could observe, a species of mirror with a silver plate (very nicely polished) inserted behind which received the impression and then acted on chemically—brought the color even to the minute folds of a vest or the checks of a cravat."

The party that claimed the greatest space in Baxter's diary was at the Kennedy's home. He described the day: "Tom and Billie Shannon and Haile were the only young men going. The young ladies went on earlier in the morning. It was six miles and we had a glorious ride of it. The gold mine, (the $80,000 Miss Winn), Miss McWillie, Miss Dessausure and Miss Lenoir of Sumter were the young ladies. We spent a most glorious day. Kennedy and his Lady are the fairest samples of the tone and general hospitality that is ever to be met with in the country. We amused ourselves in a variety of ways: I first took a game of drafts with the gold mine, in which I proved successful, and she again in a game of Back Gammon. Others were playing whist on the Piazza. Our dinner was sumptious, well served and bountifully spread. The liquors were old and genuine. My share of carving was bestowed upon a piece of fine Corn Beef. Drank first to the ladies, then to Mrs. Kennedy and to Miss Winn by my side. After dinner we amused ourselves with walking, gaming, etc. Though a little disappointed in Miss Lenoir from the representation given of her extreme beauty, I never-the-less found her quite pretty and interesting. After tea we all danced until half past eleven, then started for Camden. We rode the six miles in about thirty minutes. The carriage having about five minutes start of us, we rode nearly half speed for two miles before we caught up. Dashing up beside McWillie's carriage I rode the rest of the way in the delightful entertainment of both myself and the young ladies by funny songs and other frivolities and maneuvres. And was paid the compliment by one of the young ladies of being all life to the company. We arrived at Camden safe and joined in a dance at the Dancing Room at 12 o'clock precisely, which I call fashionable with a vengeance. There we danced four Cotillions and dispersed. Seeing the young ladies to the carriage and bidding them goodnight, I mounted my horse and galloped to the hotel. And thus gloriously has one day been spent, at least as far as regards pleasure."

As might be expected, the notation in Baxter's diary for the following morning was: "This morning I rose at seven with a slight headache."

And also as might be expected, John Springs wrote to his son: "From your letters it would seem you are much favored with animated parties, the civilities of the town and fashionable amusements. You say if I have any *loose* money you would like to have the use of it. I have heretofore been fortunate enough to be able to procure money enough for my necessities and that of my children, but if I had ten times as much I would have none to spare for indefinite or useless purposes. And you have not stated that you needed any for a definite purpose or particular necessities."

However, John could not bear for his children to want something and not have it, so in his next letter he wrote: "I now forward a check for two hundred dollars. I never have yet, out of the thousands of dollars I have furnished you and my other childen while away from home, had one statement to show how they have been expended. I know this is not right, and I have been remiss in my duty that I have not enforced it by order for I have always requested each one to do so. . . . I heard a man say that you were sitting for Mittag to paint your portrait, but I did not believe it. Nevertheless, it may be true. If so, I hope you will not call that a necessary expense. And besides a great piece of vanity and folly! What have you ever done to render your likeness a matter of interest to future ages? A man ought to marry, clear a field, plant a tree, write a book, or perform some meritorious deeds to perpetuate his name before he thinks of leaving his likeness as a bequest to posterity."

To placate his father, Baxter wrote a long letter on the excellent farming methods used by the low-country planters thereabouts. But this only annoyed John and he lost no time in answering: "You think since you went to Camden you have learned much by observation in the art of planting; that the people below have a slight in dispatching work which we are ignorant of (perhaps so) . We cultivate, and that well, ten acres of corn, six of cotton and about six of small grain, to the hand, thirty five to each horse. At any rate I wont give up that any of the low country Negroes who are fed on a peck of corn per week can do more work than mine. I would like to see some of them in the same field that could hoe or pick out more cotton than Bright and several of my hands. I know some push harder but I am satisfied with fourteen hours good labor out of twenty four. The low country has great advantages over the up country in some respects, contiguity to market, navigation, and their lands lying level. But we enjoy some and make more beautiful grain crops and of course a greater abundance of everything else. They buy their horses and mules, their flour, pork and often other necessities. Whereas we make them all in abundance or at least all who manage well can do so. I have raised my own horses and oxen and have never yet bought the first barrel of flour or pound of pork since I kept house."

While all this correspondence was going on, Austin Springs was faced with a political question. This oldest son of John's was well endowed with social graces and good looks. He made friends easily and through his contacts he was drawn into politics. He wrote to Baxter:

"I was at York Court and was waited on to know if I would agree to be a candidate for the Legislature. I replied I did not wish to be, although frequently solicited. . . . If a person is ignorant of himself and wishes to become acquainted, let him come out as a candidate for public office. He will then hear all the faults he ever had and many added to the list he never possessed. This I know from experience, for there were continually some slanderous reports in circulation against our Father whilst a candidate. . . . For a public character it requires a person of phlegmatic temperament who is callous to anything like feeling whose feelings can not be touched if he has any. This will not be the case in the sanguine temperament so characteristic of our family."

This would not be the end for Austin in politics, however. He would eventually be drawn into it.

A long newsy letter came to Baxter from his cousin, Julia Baxter, wife of Judge Eli Baxter in Georgia. When he looked at the envelope a picture flashed through his mind of all the happenings of his visit to Sparta the previous year.

The Baxters lived on a plantation called Cornucopia. Eli and Julia had four daughters and one son, Eli, Junior. The older son, Andrew, had died a few years previously.

Baxter remembered vividly the day of his arrival at Cornucopia. He had ridden out from Sparta alone. When he had turned into the road leading to the house he had found himself on a long avenue, under the shelter of dozens of gigantic oaks, with their immense limbs branching off in every direction and giving off a coolness which was particularly refreshing to him. He had allowed his horse to walk slowly in order that he might survey the scene before him. The white "mansion house" had stood at the end of the drive. A lawn was in front of the house and it was separated from the driveway by a low, white fence. The gate was standing open, showing a brick walk leading to the steps of the piazza. The house was framed, painted white with the exception of the blinds which were dark green, and it stood two stories in height with large brick chimneys at either end.

As he had ridden nearer the house he had noticed the adjacent gardens with beautifully shaped boxwoods and hundreds of roses, which he had later said were the prettiest ones he had ever seen.

He had decided at once, as he gazed around with a feeling of intense pleasure, that this plantation had been well named. Truly, it had looked as though it were overflowing with flowers, fruits, and plenty.

The barking of the dogs had announced his arrival long before he had circled up to the gate, and some one, seeing him, had rushed back into the house. By the time he had ridden up to the entrance there had been four beautiful young ladies waiting to greet him. Then their mother, Julia Baxter, had rushed down the steps and embraced him.

"This," she said to her girls, "is your cousin Baxter Springs from Carolina. Baxter, these are my daughters, Elizabeth, Jane, Julia Blandina, and Mary Frances."

Yes, thought Baxter, he would never forget that visit. He was charmed and thrilled with Cornucopia. It was the most hospitable place he had ever known, the most abundant in enthusiasm, laughter and joy. And the daughter, Julia Blandina, or Blandie as she was called, was a very attractive young lady!

All these recollections were rushing through Baxter's mind as he opened the envelope to read: ". . . Your short but very agreeable visit at Cornucopia last summer is remembered with much pleasure and interest. I am happy to hear you are engaged in the study of law. I know your father wished it, and young men of education and talents should certainly have a profession in the event of their being compelled to depend on their own exertions for a living. And if they are not, it is certainly more commendable to make a support than live on one our fore fathers have made for us. . . . I think Mr. Baxter is quite in the notion of going to see you all, particularly since the reception of your letter. . . . Can't you steal a week from your studies to come and spend a few days with us? . . . Blandie has been in school in Eatonton since last winter. She will spend the month of June at home. Elizabeth says tell Cousin Sophia she's so anxious to make her a visit she will almost be tempted to take the stage some dark night in disguised costume! (I would like to take a peep at her just then with a dark lantern.) "

Baxter was anxious to have his Georgia cousins up for a visit, but his father wanted to make his own plans for the summer and informed Baxter: "I would be glad to receive a visit from any of the Baxter family, but if they do not come in the month of July they might find us missing in August." Upon receipt of this letter, Baxter hurriedly sent a note to Cornucopia and Julia answered:

"I ought in good manners to have answered your very interesting letter sooner but I have been all the while in a bustle and hurry. . . . We went to Eatonton to attend Blandie's examination. It went off as such things usually do with *great applause* and closed by the young ladies of the school giving a *tremendous* and *splendid* party. The preparations for the supper were very *sumptuous*—Pyramids of cake almost as large as mountains—Ice lemonade and creams in profusion. . . . On our return from Eatonton some parties and dinings were given to my daughters—and as a matter of course we gave some ourselves. Cornucopia has been one continued scene of gaiety for the last few weeks. We now have some friends from abroad visiting us. . . . But to the point. We had a consultation this morning about our visit to Carolina. Now perhaps Sophia wants to go north this summer. If so, do be candid and let us know it. We have lost one of our carriage horses and Mr. Baxter can not get a match as yet— though we have a very good horse that works well with the old carriage horse—one is white, the other dark bay. Mr. Baxter says he can go with us after the first few days in August. . . . Jane and Blandie have gone to ride on horse-back. They were finely equipped with riding habits, hats and feathers, etc. . . . I must close as there is company in the drawing room, and forward this letter, so long delayed already."

John Springs grew tired of waiting to hear from the Baxters and penned a letter to the Judge saying he was taking Sophia to White Sulphur Springs, Virginia, on the day after the Springs-Moore family gathering, which was August 11. Therefore, the Eli Baxters did not come to Springfield that year.

The family gathering was a great success. No one enjoyed it more than John. He enthusiasticly wrote Baxter about it:

"We had a full meeting at James Moore's made up of Springs and Moore families. I have never seen a company enjoy themselves more. The girls danced, the boys stamped, the old ladies gabled, the men talked, the dogs barked, the geese hollowed, the hens cackled and the roosters crowed. . . . I expect to leave in the stage tomorrow evening with Sophia and Elizabeth Springs in company and if I can contain myself may remain at White Sulphur and the watering places in that vacinity till the 10th of October."

John and the girls, on their route through Virginia, stopped for a few days at Red Sulphur Springs where John reported: "Within a circle of forty miles from here there are Salt, Blue, Gray, White Sulphur, Hot and Sweet Springs. . . . We find no acquaintance here but will at the White. . . ."

White Sulphur Springs was an elegant resort and, without any doubt, a gathering place of the aristocrats. But let John tell it:

"This is where the world, comparatively speaking, is in some degree to be seen in miniature. It is Saratoga over again, though on a much smaller scale. The number at any rate not exceeding two hundred. It takes a great many people to make a world, but there are to be seen dignified Fathers, jockeying Mothers, dashy Sons, flashy Daughters, brisk Widowers, gay Widows, tidy old Bachelors, spruce old Maids, strutting Dandies, and dashing Belles. The smooth faced Lad, the mustached one, the whiskered tribe of various grades and sizes from the small, decent, moderate to that of an old Hi Gent—are all here to be seen promenading the long piazzas and gravel walks in groups and parties of various sizes. Some individuals seeming to look upon themselves with so much consequence as though the things of the world could not move in regular progression without them. Whereas, if they were struck from existance, as they will shortly be, they would no more be missed (comparatively) than a house fly. *No Poor Folks here*. Not even Mediocrity. *All rich.*

"There is a corps of horse jockies that flount and cut many capers on horse back. Riding dandies. Walking beaus. Belles on horseback. Fine ladies on foot. And there are the hunting gentry. The pack for their convenience consists of some sixty hounds, kept in kennels. They take out some twenty at a time to insure a good cry which is echoed from mountain to mountain, as the buck bounds from hill to hill or crosses the little limestone rills and creeks running clear as crystal in which you may see a pin to the depth of seven or eight feet. Then if this cry of twenty hounds should chance to force the timid deer into a field or open space then they let loose a corps of grey hounds (that are held in strings by some footman for the purpose) that will run under the buck as he bounds or lopes and take him running two hundred yards or less.

"For the amusement of the sporting there are to be seen all the various kinds and sizes of the canine race, among them the pointers and setters for the benefit of those who think they are good at a shot on the wing. And these sportsmen recount marvelous fetes that would baffle a hunter of the Rocky Mountains to best. So wags the world— that I am ready to say with the Psalmist: '*O Lord* how wonderfully and fearfully are we made. The Heavens declare thy glory, the firmament showeth forth thy hand works.' "

Returning to Springfield in October, John and Sophia found the weather unusually warm. "I was ready to conclude we were home too soon," said John. But soon the days turned cooler and John was "all in a hustle to start the wagons to Cheraw" with his cattle for the stock exhibition. His bull "took the premium of the silver cup," but he noted, "Times in Cheraw were more dull than I have ever seen them. I must look for some other market for my bull calves in future."

The following month John began to sense a change in the economy. He could foresee a depression coming. He warned Baxter: "New cotton from this section has been sold in Columbia for five cents. I think I can discover hard times about to break over the country. We have been peculiarly blessed with a succession of good crops and an abundant supply of provisions, but let there come a bad season and then we may cry hard times in earnest. Distress will then likely pervade the country. Not half the people can ever pay their debts from the products of their labor at present rates and a great portion can not do it after giving up their whole effects. I fear I may suffer considerably from my liabilities from some of my friends."

John was right in his forecast. Hard times came. Markets were depressed. His bank stocks dropped and business in general slacked off. He was serious when he expressed himself to Baxter:

"I am of the opinion that the life blood has been steamed out of the government, State and Federal, and the people. Such a state of affaires in the course of my experience I have never before witnessed. The people and the Government are without money, credit and friends. It is a time of distrust, jealously and fears. The country is literally ruined and I can only attribute it to misrule, mismanagement, wild speculation, theories, extravagance and imprudence, owing to our imperfect and corrupt nature. We certainly have been Providentially blessed beyond any other people. The country abounds in plenty. Yet there is a general cry of distress. No doubt He in His wisdom has ordered this for wise purposes and ought to teach us that 'this is not our abiding city,' that we must all go hence. Of which I was sensibly reminded yesterday while riding to church in company with Bell and Sophia, when my filly, cold and in a way of play, very suddenly sprung and pitched me off my balance. I received a most dangerous fall on a hard road, but somehow saved myself from injury by easing myself down by the stirrup, though my shoulder and head first struck the ground, but I was not the least hurt. I view it almost as a miracle and so do those who saw me."

John's preoccupation with business kept him close to Springfield. Sophia grew restless. "I tell you," she exclaimed, "this child *does* want to go to Charleston this winter a little of the worst, but Papa only laughs and says 'no doubt'!"

In December John took his daughter to Charlotte for the holiday season and he returned to Springfield. In January, after Sophia had reported her Christmas the merriest she had ever had, John traveled to Charlotte to see her. He explained his trip to Baxter: "I was in Charlotte on the sixth. Blundered in upon quite a large private party at Leroy's. The parties kept up for ten or twelve days during the time they had a Miss Mutz from Lincoln, who is of fine size, handsome, sings and plays well, dances admirably, and rich as poison. The boys designated her the great Western. Mrs. Osborne gave a party for her. Mr. Julius Alexander gave a party, and a hop was given at Col. Gaither's, and others in anticipation. There have been two or three balls. Sophia has been honored with invitations to them all. So they go. The people of Charlotte are like the Negroe's tailor, *poor* and *pert*."

CHAPTER TEN

THE PROSPERITY OF JOHN SPRINGS extended to many enterprises but was firmly rooted in the land. Wherever he invested and whatever he did, he was first and foremost a planter. His crops, his livestock, and his farming operations always remained dear to his heart.

Even on summer vacations he thought of livestock and farming. As he and Sophia would go through the country by stage he would observe: "Some good cattle, horses and sheep in the Valley of Virginia, though I think no cattle that surpasses my own. Have seen no bull to equal mine." In Tennessee he would report on the crops and once volunteered: "Their cattle and hogs are small and miserably trifling. The farms, little towns and villages of Tennessee manifest a great want of energy, industry and neatness."

For years John had bought cows from dealers in New Jersey and from his good friend, Colonel Wade Hampton, of Columbia. Hampton had written him once:

"Your calf was got by a Roan Bull imported from England by myself, out of a red cow who was also thorough bred and bred by me. This cow was descended from a pair of English cattle, imported into this country by my Father about the year 1802. This pair was equal to anything that I have ever seen. The Bull Hector became so heavy it was necessary to castrate him. He was fed two years and then slaughtered, weighed 2425 lbs. meat."

John had been delighted with this addition to his herd:

"The calf Col. Hampton sent me, price $100, is the finest I have ever seen. Austin says his overseer says it is from the finest cow Hampton owns and that he has selected it and taken pains with it purposely for me. I have already broken him to lead and have him in good training."

John never exhibited his stock in Charlotte. "I will not show," he said once, "because they rather object to my coming in, saying I have the start of the rest of them. I will stand by and let Leroy and Brevard Davidson exhibit." Then he had added humorously: "The Mecklenburgers are taking a popular course. They are going to exhibit *Daughters*. The female youth and beauty of the land are to be present at a splendid Ball, given the same evening as the Fair."

Time and time again, John's methodical approach to farming paid off. He kept his ledgers in plantation style, not on the basis of so much raised *per acre* but so much *per field hand* or slave. In one bumper year, he figured his cotton crop amounted to "four bales picked to the hand." He also figured he raised that year 200 bushels of corn and six of wheat per hand, plus 500 pounds of pork and 100 of stall-fed beef. He almost chortled:

"My last killing of hogs at home was twenty two, with the lightest weighing 206 pounds and the heaviest 400 pounds. Ask the Piney Wood or Swamp Planters if they can beat that! It may be asked what does all that amount to. I will answer that my Negroes look slick and greasy; horses, hogs and cows look saucy and corn fed, down to the chickens. And my cotton brings twelve to fifteen dollars a bale! What signifies money if a man can make all he needs. . . ."

Cotton was always on John's mind. During his yearly visits to Charleston, he never failed to advise his sons about the cotton market. From the day he began planting Springfield until the day he died he seldom wrote a letter without quoting the price of cotton or describing its growth, its picking or its shipping. His letters might have been enthusiastic over the fact that Charleston was in a "bustle with people attending the races" and "Sinkler's Jeff Davis won the three mile purse" or that he had "witnessed wonderful doings of a jugler at the theatre," but he was more particular to close his letters with a sentence about cotton. "The Hibernia steam packet from London is in. Cotton was firm." Or, "My agent sold fifty bales at 7½. A bad sale."

The spring of 1843 was a miserable one as far as weather was concerned. John and Sophia, returning from Charleston, found the roads in a muddy mess. "We arrived home through rain, snow, sleet and freezes. Our carriage met us a mile this side of Lancaster. Could not get to us for the creek. We nearly swam at the one below Lancaster."

The domestic matters at Springfield were about as well as could be expected under the circumstances. "The most backward spring I have ever seen," complained John. "Everything now has the appearance of the dead of winter. No appearance of the Dogwood blossom, which from tradition we have been taught to believe was the true indication of the season for planting maize or Indian corn."

Spring finally arrived and the month of May was everything that could have been expected. Mary and all the little Davidsons came for a visit. "A fine, hearty, mischievous little band," John called the children. Sophia went to Charlotte for a round of parties and a celebration on May 20. Concerning the latter, John facetiously recorded: "Major Edney is to review two regiments of Infantry and one of Cavalry. He will show out large as life. He will no doubt give them a military address and make a fierce show off in politics, urging with great emphasis his claims to the support of the Whigs in that Congressional District."

Although John spoke humorously of the Major boosting the Whig party, he himself would soon be doing the same thing. With great anger and sarcasm he condemned the evil practices which were creeping into government. The spoils system of rewarding the faithful party workers was one target of his anger. He compared these "office hunters" who were "foaming and boiling over with patriotism" to those who followed Christ for the loaves and fishes which they received.

"Alas! frail human nature is the same now," he declared. "I greatly fear that Government patronage, both State and Federal, is producing that sort of patriotism that is engendering intrigue, fraud and corruption that will one day undermine our Republic, which is now the admiration of the wondering world. Great and awful will be the crash. We once had patriots with whom the loaves and fishes were no part of their object, whose aim was Honor, Glory and Liberty, who labored, toiled and endured all sorts of deprivation, exposure and hardship without fee or reward save that of redeeming their country from bondage. They shed their life's blood freely for their country's good and to save from Monarchial slavery we their descendents. But I greatly fear since that time patriotism has been terribly adulterated."

Unexpected developments arose in John's situation and the national political scene. On April 1, 1844, he wrote to Baxter:

"Fifteen Indian Land people met and insisted on running my name as a candidate for the Legislature from this part of the District. . . . I told my friends my politics, and that I would not sacrifice my principles for any place of honor or profit. . . . They insisted on using my name. I heard a day or two afterwards some were saying my politics would not do and that I would get a licking, but they only wanted to withdraw their support. I don't consider them personal friends. I did not expect my friends would want to run me after avowing my opinion, but they still insisted. I believe I would not have consented except, had I not, they were going to run Austin and they were of the opinion I would run better. I knew it did not suit Austin as he and Springs Moore are commencing their merchandising business in York and it is a miserable policy for a business man to engage in politics."

John yielded to importunings and became a candidate, but he was handicapped by his views on national politics, in which he refused to bend. He bitterly opposed Van Buren, because of his fiscal policies while President. Early in 1844, Van Buren, having been unseated in the previous election by William Henry Harrison and "Tyler too," attempted a come-back. He set out to capture the Democratic nomination at the national convention in Baltimore. John meanwhile came out strongly for Henry Clay, the great Westerner and Whig, as the man likeliest to whip Van Buren. But Southerners at the convention sidetracked Van Buren and nominated James Knox Polk. This literally struck home at John, for Polk was a North Carolinian, born only three miles from Springfield. Naturally, the local vote swung to Polk. John, however, stood steadfastly by Clay and made no bones about it.

No one was more dumfounded by John's candidacy than Austin, who confided to Baxter:

"The old man is again in the field for the Legislature, a thing I never dreamed of until Tuesday night. As I was going with Dr. Moore to supper he told me that the old man had been spoken to run and he was to let his friends know at Court. When I went to York on Monday of Court some of my friends observed they were using my name as a candidate and urged me to declare myself as such. I replied that it was time enough to do that; that I did not know that I was their choice and would not wish my name to be used if any other was preferred. I observed I was going into business in York and that I did not think under the circumstances it would suit me. They replied that the kind of business I proposed doing would not interfere and they hoped I would allow my name to be used. I gave my consent Tuesday that my name could be used. That night I heard the old man spoken of.

A few of the Indian Landers got together in a room and I requested if the old man would agree to run I preferred my name should be withdrawn. You will perceive that we were very awkwardly situated. I am very well satisfied that I am out of the scrape. And I fear the old man's politics will operate against him. I saw Parson White yesterday and he said that Starr Moore and other personal friends would not vote for him on party grounds. The old man will not be silent on his politics. I think he is right in not concealing his politics but it will injure him in his election as it will prevent some of his personal friends from voting for him if he runs on party grounds."

Austin's prediction and other prophesies of "a licking" proved all too true. John made a bold and forthright campaign for the South Carolina Legislature. He told voters of the York District that he had hoped for a Presidential contest between John C. Calhoun and Henry Clay, "the two greatest Statesmen of the age," but that the nation had been "deprived of beholding that glorious conflict by a few Party Conspirators and political jugglers"—a cry of backroom politics echoed in Presidential election years many times since. John explained where he stood:

"When I consented to be a Candidate, it was at that time fully expected Van Buren would be the nominee, and then told my friends I would not vote for him under any circumstances, and Mr. Calhoun aside, I preferred Mr. Clay to any other candidate that could be started. It has turned out, however, that Van Buren is not the nominee, and I congratulate the State, that she is absolved from an alliance with a man who holds two sets of principles, one for the North and another for the South."

Continuing his campaign, he spoke on local as well as national issues. "The people ought to arouse from their lethargy and attend to their own business," he exhorted, "do their own reading and thinking and act accordingly. They are falling fast into a state of apathy, becoming careless and indifferent to their best interests, and trusting too much to others to do what could be better done by their own energy and action."

But John could not turn the national tide, and with it he went down in defeat. He stood fourth among eight candidates from York District. "I will not complain," he said. "I have no ambitions to gratify. . . . Neither do I desire to sail with the popular breeze into the Legislature under false and deceptive colors."

Apparently, John was less upset over losing the election than he was over the prospect of losing Sophia, who was being courted by three serious suitors, any one of whom might win her hand. There was Mr. R., Mr. Pope, and Mr. Myers.

John requested the aid of Baxter, who was now a full-fledged lawyer, having passed his Bar examination in December of 1843. "Can you tell me something of Mr. Pope? . . . I would like to have your opinion of Mr. R."

Baxter's reply is not known but it must have been unintelligible to John who wrote: "You are beginning to write like a lawyer. (I mean your handwriting.) They generally write more unintelligibly than any set of men, one attainment I neither admire or approve. The general purpose of writing is to be understood by those with whom we communicate."

William R. Myers seemed to be leading in the race for Sophia's hand. He was a very attractive young Charlotte lawyer, formerly from Wadesboro, North Carolina. John termed him "too sporty." The thought of living at Springfield without Sophia was indeed gloomy to him. He made arrangements to take Sophia to Deaver's Springs, in the mountains of North Carolina. At least a change of scenery might change Sophia's mind about William. So off they went, leaving Baxter in charge of Springfield.

Austin joined his father and Sophia at Deaver's in late summer, and amused them with the account of his vacation. His first stop had been at Glenn Springs for a cavalry review. While there he had bought a military outfit from one R. A. Cates, who apparently was dropping out of the service. Austin had paid $99.25 for the outfit and he displayed it with pride. It consisted of: "a fine guilt scabbard sword, a black leather belt with gilt mountings and chains, one pair of gilt epauletts, a drooping plume, a red sash, one pair of military gloves, a fine cocked hat, a military coat, and one gilt sword nob and palmetto." It is not surprising that Austin confessed, "I became quite the lion with the ladies."

"The place to cut a dash and splurge is Athens," continued Austin. "It is celebrated for its great display of beauty and fine vehicles. My visit was made more pleasant by meeting with Mr. Eli Baxter and his two daughters. I could scarcely get off from going home with them."

Then Austin described his visit to Madison Springs: "I was so fortunate to meet with a couple of Charleston ladies at this place whose acquaintance I had made at Deaver's Springs. Through them I made the acquaintance of all the ladies. We had dancing every night, but there was only one other gentleman besides myself who could dance. . . . We spent the mornings in rolling nine pins. The ladies put in an hour or two and then the gentlemen until lunch."

Austin found the atmosphere pleasant at Deaver's Springs too. He wrote to Baxter: "General Thompson and daughter of Greenville are here. To use a Kentucky expression, she is a bully woman. She is one of the most accomplished, pleasant ladies I have ever met and she would be a beauty if she had a little more of the bacon and collards about her. She is rather delicate."

All too soon September was over and it was time for the Springses to return home. John almost dreaded to see Springfield, because the drought had played havoc with the crops. It had been the driest summer ever known in South Carolina since the State was settled by white people. And the drought had stretched far south, even into Alabama. Not that John needed corn—his cribs were filled, four in all, but he hated to see his neighbors suffer. Fortunately, he had stored the surplus from the bumper crop of the preceding year.

But corn and drought were soon forgotten as far as John was concerned. Sophia announced her engagement to William Myers!

Typical of John, he buried his feelings deep within him and took Sophia to Charleston to buy an elaborate trousseau. From that city she wrote: "Most of my time has been spent in King Street looking at pretty goods and spending money." That was December. The wedding was set for the following December. Engagements were long in those days.

While Sophia fluttered about preparing for the wedding and being courted by the twenty-nine year old Mr. Myers, John occupied himself with a new project. This time it was not banking or planting; it was manufacturing.

Mr. Hiram Hutchison, President of the Bank of Hamburg, had conceived the idea of building a cotton mill. He wrote to John:

"Four of us, H. Hutchison, Otis Mills, William Gregg and Jack Smith, have obtained a charter for a Cotton Manufacturing Company. Capital, $300,000. We expect to take $100,000 of the stock and *select* our co-partners for the other $200,000—not more than twenty stockholders in all. Do you wish a cut? If so, say the amount and authorize me to enter your name."

John bought 300 shares for $10,000. Hutchison outlined plans to purchase 9,000 acres on Horse Creek between Hamburg and Aiken, within a mile of the railroad and with "two valuable falls and plenty of water at all times." The waterfall would have a drop of 37 feet, providing power enough for 10,000 spindles and 400 looms.

"It will be a year before a Superintendent is needed and we do not expect to find a suitable person for less salary than $2,000," wrote Hutchison. Thus the Graniteville Manufacturing Company, one of the South's first cotton mills, came into being.

For one last fling of traveling with Sophia, John took her to Saratoga in the summer of 1846. He had begun to like his future son-in-law and was more reconciled to the marriage. Besides, he was glad to get away and be gay with his daughter. Springfield had been rather depressing because wagons were constantly turning into the drive, bringing people wanting corn. The country was going hungry because of the drought the summer before. To each man John had the same answer. He would give him enough corn, at $1.00 per bushel, for his immediate needs and some to take on with him, but as long as the man had a horse and wagon and money to get him to the mountains where corn could be obtained, John could sell him no more. To those who had no horse, wagon, or money, he furnished corn.

Baxter bore the brunt of this situation while his father was away. He wrote: "A woman came here this afternoon from nine miles beyond the river, representing her condition and that of her children as destitute and lamentable in the extreme. Of course she was not to be resisted. I am a poor fellow, daily bedeviled, having nothing to relieve the monotony of my solitude, save the bewailings of the widow and the cries of half starved children on the one hand, and the *soft harpings* of moping, lazy, 'no-corn-making' sons of b—— on the other."

In response to Baxter's query, "Do you still intend to feed Mrs. Hazel? . . . Have you promised corn to Mrs. Sembler?" John replied from Saratoga: "I am under no promise to furnish any individual with corn, but, of course, expect to divide out what I have to spare among the poor people for they will suffer without help." Then John added bits of interesting news.

On his way north he and Sophia had remained in Washington to witness the closing days of the Congressional session, when President Polk's plans for a lower tariff and an independent Treasury were passed. John explained: "After a session of eight or nine months the two houses of Congress broke up in much confusion or rather a row. Some bills were lost for want of time, one was a two million appropriation asked by the President to negotiate peace with Mexico who already owed this Government some eight or ten millions. It is said to be evidently with a view of purchasing California, including the bay and port of San Francisco."

Then John related an interesting experience: "I have seen President and Mrs. Polk. The former distinctly recollected my name and manifested much pleasure at seeing me. He said he would have been pleased if he had been at leisure enough to have talked about his native place. I had the first interview with him one morning of not more than three or four minutes, there being eight or ten hangers-on waiting for an audience with him. I relieved him by telling him at once that I did not appear for the purpose of annoying him, that I had no favor to ask for myself or friends. He replied: 'You are a happy man, a happy man!' "

John, relaxing in the cool breezes of Saratoga, gave his impressions of that resort: "I am better pleased with the visitors here than formerly. I find a graver, plainer set of people, not so much show off, dandyism, black legs and rowdys."

From New York City, en route home, John made an observation which, being a business man, interested him: "The empire state and New England people seem both to have money and leisure time to spend it. I have taken a glance at many manufactures as they are everywhere dispersed about the land."

Arriving at Springfield in October, John was happy to be home. He always missed the plantation when he was away from it, because it was like a balm to his soul. Others felt that same way about it. Even John Bell, the former overseer who went to Perry, Alabama, to work for General King, wrote back to Springfield that same month:

"Many is the time I have been present with you in imagination and passing from one field to another examining the cattle, horses, barns and all other things pertaining to the Plantation. I must tell you the truth. I would rather live with you for one hundred dollars per year than to live here for my present wages. If I was back in that little house I left you could not run me off with all the dogs you own."

CHAPTER ELEVEN

SOPHIA'S WEDDING TOOK PLACE on schedule, by candlelight. An "elegant" affair, friends called it. John was keyed with excitement. But when the bride and groom departed for Charleston, and the last house guest had left, he was in the depths of depression.

Once more he was alone at Springfield, except for Baxter who was out of the house most of the time attending to his duties on the plantation. The elderly squire remained in his library most of the time. January always dispirited him. It reminded him of Mary and her last days with him. He read Sophia's letter, posted from Charleston: "Amid all my pleasures I have had several good cries when thinking of home and its dear inmates. I have experienced so much kindness and affection from the best of brothers and the most indulgent Father that I feel like expressing my remembrance of all these things and although my conduct may not at all times have been as it should have been, it must not be attributed to a want of affection."

Then John took up William Myers' letter, and admitted to himself that he was beginning to have great respect for this new son-in-law of his. "Sophia and I," wrote William, "have anxiously looked for a letter from you but have been disappointed. . . . We have not, I am sorry to say, written as frequently as we should have done. This, I trust you are satisfied, doesn't by any means arise from the fact that you have been forgotten. Very far from it."

John tried to read his books, but this grew tiresome. He made lists of what should be done, such as, "Have turnips shortly set round the garden for seed; put part of the hands to putting manure in pens; don't forget to take down all the hams and shoulders the last of the month and have them covered in ashes; send two logs to the mill, one sawed in two inch plank for the cotton screw, the other into inch plank; plow the corn land with two horses, the cotton land with one." But he grew fretful doing this. He tried to write, to catch up on his back correspondence. He wrote to his cousin Andrew Baxter in Athens, Georgia, and received a prompt reply which said, among other things, "I can appreciate your feeling that your place is rather desolate without Sophia."

John examined his inventory of the gifts he had given Baxter in former years and the money he had spent on him. Then he made an important decision. It was not an easy one to make, but he knew he would do it someday so it was better to get on with it.

He decided to give Springfield Plantation to Baxter.

His son, he knew, would cherish and care for it as he had done. He remembered what he had told Baxter on the boy's graduation from college: "You are embarking on the journey of life and like other travelers a day lost keeps you as it were a day back in your progress."

John reasoned that his son had every right to feel that he was not being held back. Baxter had chosen Springfield as his career, and John was happy in that choice. He recalled the question he had put to Baxter when he had passed his Bar examination: "And now what are you going to do? Are you going to practice or are you going to return to the Plantation and enter practically the study of improving the fertility of a small portion of the earth, and rendering yourself useful in the community by experimenting and practicing in the pursuits of Agriculture?"

John knew in his heart that he had been afraid Baxter would not come home and work the land. He wanted his son to make his own choice, but he also remembered that he had hopefully written: "Had you not as well visit home at least for a while?"

Now the choice had been made. Baxter had turned to the soil. He had come home.

"He shall have Springfield *now*," John decided.

The squire laid the blue sheet of paper in front of him. Across the top was written "Cash and Properties given off to Andrew Baxter Springs." The first item was dated November 23, 1835, "Tuition and Board at Rocky River Academy." Then further down was listed, "University of Virginia." Then "flute." John had to smile when he remembered Baxter trying to play his flute. And so the list went on and on.

"College to Columbia"; "gold watch"; "tour of the North"; "Cash for Camden"; "Cash for Mississippi." The sum total of all these various expenses amounted to $4,755.26.

John turned over the sheet and entered the date, "January 9, 1847." Then he listed his new gifts to his son:

"The plantation I live on and all the improvements, 1126 acres.

"The Ross Place including the Bennet tract S.W. side Steel Creek, 390 acres.

"The Darnall Place where T. Kimbrell lives, 142 acres."

Underneath this were listed the following negro slaves:

Name	Age	Description	Charge
Sampson,	age 69,	old and blind	Charge naught
Nathan,	age 51,	value	$ 800
Abram,	age 48,	and unsound	200
Phill,	age 35,	stout and waggoner	525
Arthur,	age 34,	not very stout	475
Eli,	age 33,	ox driver	500
Solomon,	age 29,	stout and willing	550
Albert,	age 28,	stout, active and stubborn	550
Plato		stout and biddable	550
James,	age 24,	very stout and very willing	550
Washington,	18,	fine boy	550
George,	age 6,	— — — —	225
Jack,	age 4,	— — — —	175
Elam	age 1,	— — — —	125
Cela's William,	6,	— — — —	225
Handy	age 4,		175
Cynthia's Caleb			125
Jane,	age 40,	unsound, sore leg from an old burn	200
Cela,	age 31	a good negro	400
Cynthia,	age 26	valuable woman	400
Sarah,	age 16		400
Laura,	age 13		350
Mary,	age 13		350
			$ 8,400

John then extended his list of gifts to include the following horses: "Whip," "Prince," the Jackson horse, the Kendrick horse, the Owens horse, the bay mare and the Whip filly. Added to this were two yoke oxen, four cows, six heifers, two little steers and the Wade bull, forty head of hogs, all the plantation tools, two wagons, an oxcart, corn, oats, fodder, clover, and five English saddles and bridles.

When his list was completed John folded it and placed it in his "day book." Once this decision was made he felt relieved. His course seemed plain to him now. He would not sit around and mope. He would travel; he would be up and doing things.

When Sophia and William returned from their wedding trip, they went straight to Springfield for a visit. John presented Sophia with gifts in the form of land, Negroes, silver and furniture, all valued by him at $20,000. Among these was a lot on East Avenue in Charlotte, on which they would later build their home.

Then John went off to Charleston and left Baxter as master of Springfield.

By the time he arrived in Camden he was ill. He later wrote Baxter about this trip: "I travelled eight miles in the dark and through the Waxhaw wind, and I have taken cold from which I fear I will suffer. ... I drew off a schedule of your money and property which I intended to hand you. It lies in the day book. Put it by and take care of it."

Regardless of his cold, John took the morning stage out of Camden the following day, arriving in Columbia at daylight the next morning. "We had a full stage last night," he explained, "and the curtains had to be closed down. Otherwise we would have suffered from the state of the air."

Upon his arrival in Charleston, John was "rather better," and immediately attended a meeting of the South Carolina Railroad. An idea was in the back of his head. A new project. A railroad running from Columbia to Charlotte! "The people here seem to be interested in the subject and I believe if we would do our part up the country, the State or railroad company here would be 2/5ths in the Road—Though it would cost much money," wrote John to William Myers.

No invention ever had a greater influence on American history than the locomotive, and nothing sparked John Springs' imagination more than the growth of the railroads. He had realized their importance from the very beginning when the first American locomotive had run along a six-mile track at Charleston. Then, about 1834, when that line had been extended for 137 miles inland to Hamburg, South Carolina, just across the Savannah River from Augusta, Georgia, he had sensed what this, the longest railroad in the world, would mean to the little town of Hamburg. He had concluded that a fine future awaited that village, which was already a raw cotton center, and within two years he had joined with Hiram Hutchison and John Blackwood in forming the Bank of Hamburg.

Now, John, cognizant of the importance of a railroad to Charlotte, began working towards this end.

In answer to John's letter from Charleston, William Myers replied on February 23, 1847: "I have shown your letter to Mr. Osborne and others, and all concur with you in the opinion you have given as to the importance of immediate action in securing subscriptions to this enterprise. There is to be a meeting in the Court House tonight."

As matters progressed, there arose a difference of opinion as to the route the line should take. Two rail connections were possible, at Camden or at Columbia. John favored the Camden route over Columbia. With typical directness, he presented a powerful argument for the railroad in *The Charlotte Journal:*

"The South Carolina and Charlotte railroad I believe to be a project of paramount importance to this and the surrounding country. . . . It would give a new stimulus to industry, economy and enterprise and create a market for innumerable articles now wasted and lost.

"I know of no other town or village that is surrounded to the same extent by so rich and fertile country as the town of Charlotte, producing all the great staples of cotton, tobacco, flour, corn, and grain in great abundance and variety, in a circumference of from 60 to 80 miles around, abounding with some as rich uplands as perhaps the sun shines on. At the risk of the charge of egotism I will say that, having travelled more or less through the old thirteen States and three or four of the new, I have come to the conclusion that, originally and naturally, the country between the Yadkin in North Carolina and the Broad River in South Carolina, an average distance of about 100 miles, and about the same distance up and down, forming an area of 100 square miles, is the most fertile, productive region that I have yet seen, and capable of the highest agricultural and manufacturing improvement, abounding with almost unlimited water power; and this opinion has been accorded by many others who have travelled through the country.

"I need not be told the project is impracticable and therefore inexpedient. I have recently seen too much of Rail Roads penetrating mountains, encountering rocks, hills, water-courses, and all kinds of obstructions and difficulties to yield to that opinion. I need not be told that it will cost too much money, and if made would not pay. I believe the road can be made and would pay well. No one can appreciate the business it would likely do. I need not be told the country is not able to construct it—this, I am disposed to dispute. I believe we are entirely competent to effect it, if we only determine that we will, and this, I believe, to be all that is necessary to succeed. But there must be a unanimity of feeling and action; everyone, from the least to the greatest, must put his hands to, as they will participate more or less in its beneficial results. Few are so poor that they can take but one share, and if he is willing and able to work, he can go to the road and get his $10 to $15 a month and work out his stock. Every man who can raise his $5 (and if he has it not I would urge him to borrow) ought, when the books are opened, to come forward and take his own or more shares according to his ability. The big things of this World are made of little ones, and if this work is effected, I believe it will be by small subscriptions, there being perhaps but few large capitalists who can spare large amounts.

"I have no hesitation in saying real estate would immediately be enhanced to double its present value. I do not desire to hear men object and say they are in debt and have nothing to spare,—this will be an effective way to get out of debt and to remain so. I do not wish to hear young men say, 'we will leave the thing to others of more age and experience'—the vigor of youth is the favorable period for energetic action. I do not wish middle aged men to say, 'we are now under heavy expenses, raising and educating large families'—this will the better enable you to discharge those duties. Neither do I desire to hear old men complain they are too old and can not live to enjoy its benefits. We are all laboring for those who will succeed us, and this would likely be doing the greatest good for our posterity; but it will be necessary for all, old and young, rich and poor, to make an energetic, vigorous, effort to effect so great, meritorious and worthy purpose, and success will then, undoubtedly, crown our efforts.

"I need not say Charleston, the Rail Road Company and the State of South Carolina are all looking to this project with a becoming degree of interest and solicitude, and I can not believe the old North State and the chivalrous State of South Carolina are going to be outdone in enterprise and liberality by their neighboring Sister States. I see stated that Virginia has chartered a road from Richmond to Danville. . . . if that road is made and the one to Charlotte fails, it would draw off much of the trade of the rich valley of the Yadkin to Richmond.

"Under all the circumstances, are we to remain quiet and at ease, are we to continue to fold our arms and look passively on whilst in the midst of as fine country as any people can boast of, we are becoming literally surrounded by Rail Road enterprise? They are constructing North, South, East and West, above, below and on each side of us. I feel forcibly the importance of the subject, and am now ready to buckle on my armour and appear in conjunction with all who may feel a proper interest in the enterprise, and am willing to be found wherever it may be expedient to place me, either in the front, middle or rear of the contest; and propose that the word *Failure* should be stricken from the vocabulary—we must not entertain such an idea, but adopt the maxim of old Rough and Ready,* 'we never surrender.'

"These are some of the opinions I entertain, and will be ready, to a liberal extent, to back my judgement with my means."

Never resting in his efforts, John wrote to friends North and South, far and wide, in behalf of the project. Not all applauded. His friend Green Kendrick, of Waterbury, Connecticut, warned "I fear the project will not meet with as favorable a response from capital generally as from yourself."

Yet John persisted, undaunted. On April 27, 1847, supporters of the railroad project from South Carolina and western North Carolina convened in the Presbyterian Church in Charlotte. As the first order of business, it was moved and carried "that John Springs, Esq., of South Carolina, be unanimously chosen President of the Convention." Typically, John called for the meeting to be opened with prayer by the church's pastor, the Rev. Cyrus Johnston.

The convention elected the Hon. D. M. Barringer of North Carolina and John Bryce, Esq., of South Carolina, as vice-presidents, James H. Witherspoon and W. J. Clawson of South Carolina, and C. J. Fox and J. W. Hampton of North Carolina as secretaries. A roll call showed an attendance of more than one hundred from the South Carolina districts of Kershaw, Fairfield, Richland, York, Lancaster, and Chester, plus the city of Charleston, and from the North Carolina districts

*General Zachary Taylor, hero of the Mexican War, was known as "Old Rough and Ready".

of Gaston, Lincoln, Burke, Davie, Caldwell, Rowan, Union, Iredell, Cabarrus, and Mecklenburg.

A committee met and brought in a lengthy report, the gist of which recommended "the speedy completion of a railroad communication between the town of Charlotte and some point on the South Carolina Rail Road."

But what point? Camden or Columbia? The proposed Columbia route lay nearer to John's plantation. But he favored the Camden connection, because, he said, it could be built over easier terrain for half the money. "I am solely governed by expediency," he wrote. "If a Columbia road was ever built it would come nearest me. I have 16/20 of the same banking interests in Columbia as I have in Camden."

Before adjourning April 28, the convention resolved that rail connections between the projected Charlotte and South Carolina railway and Danville, and Abington, Virginia, and Jonesboro, Tennessee were "of great and increasing importance." It set up county or district committees of ten to solicit for the sale of stock, and provided for further conventions.

Soon the summer heat descended on Springfield. The sun rose and shone on the fields with such intensity that the slaves were drenched in sweat by eight o'clock in the morning. From the stables came the laughter of Negroes, currying and brushing the horses. The peacocks were screaming at each other, and the blue jays quarreled with the cat birds. It was all music to John's ears. He sat on the piazza and drank in the beauty of the place.

Tomorrow he would leave Springfield for a few weeks. He was taking Sophia to the mountains. She was expecting a baby and he was fearful that she might take a summer fever if she remained in Charlotte. She had accepted his invitation and William had agreed it would be healthier for her to be away during August and September.

John went across the piazza and down the steps, moving with great vigor. His shoulders were straight and square. His white linen suit was immaculate. He was, as he expressed it, in "the enjoyment of his usual health." He strode around to the stables where Wheeler saddled his horse for him. Putting one shining boot in the stirrup, he swung into his saddle with the ease of a young man. He was off to survey Springfield and say goodbye for a little while. Baxter had hired a new overseer, Wylie Glover, and John wanted to see how things were going. Even the previous overseer, John Bell, had been concerned about the new man and had written Glover a note from Alabama: "I understand you have stepped into my shoes as overseer. I tell you, Sir, if you intend to follow me you must be Solomon in the head, Sampson in the arms, and walk like you had hot rods under your feet all the time. Lay aside your old rifle gun and fishing rod and go it like a tiger. Keep your eye shined on everything on the Plantation. Keep your business planned at least one week ahead. Be sure you make your calculations so that no change of weather will flustrate you in the least if it rains so you can't plow or hoe. Perhaps there is something wanting in the barn yard or a piece of fence to reset or new ground to work out, which always works best when it is a little wet. I hope you will excuse me for making free to advise you, but, Sir, you are at home if you will play your cards right and I know it."

In an instant John was out across the fields. The darkies all looked up because the old squire of Springfield was coming. As his mare picked up her way down the rows between the cotton, John could see that the crop was flourishing. Springfield is doing well, he thought. He knew he would leave it in good hands.

While John and Sophia enjoyed the mountain coolness of Asheville, North Carolina, a struggle raged in Charlotte over whether to locate the railroad along the Camden or Columbia route. William Myers reported by letter to John on a double convention held in Charlotte that September. South Carolina stockholders met at the church, North Carolinians at the courthouse. The South Carolinians' spirit ran high, William said, while "gloom and despondency might be seen in the face of every North Carolinian." The reason was apparent. The South Carolinians had been far more successful in selling stock than their neighbors. Further, the subscription for the Camden route that John favored came only to about $275,000, whereas the Columbia subscription amounted to about $670,000. That settled the issue in favor of Columbia. William Myers reported:

"North Carolina is not degraded. Though her pledge has not been fully redeemed, at all events her honor has been saved. The $600,000 (necessary to get a charter) was raised the first day and the charter secured. . . . Mr. Palmer has been elected President of the road. Your friends were more numerous than his and I am satisfied if you had rendered the smallest amount of service to the Columbia route you would have been elected by acclaim. As the matter stood, it was thought that it would be an act of too great injustice to Mr. Palmer."

John and Sophia arrived in Charlotte the first of October. William joined them and the three went to Springfield to await the arrival of Sophia's baby. The child was born on November first, a fine boy. No one was the least surprised when he was named John Springs Myers.

CHAPTER TWELVE

THERE WAS NO QUESTION about it, John Springs liked to travel. He liked to get out and see things, keep up with what was going on, meet people, hear their opinions of conditions. Travel relaxed him. He had said once: "If there is any such thing as being rid of the cares and troubles of this world, it would seem that when an individual is placed at such a distance from home and his business that he can hear or know nothing of it, with the means of procuring all the comforts he may desire in the midst of pleasant association, he is perhaps approaching as near to quiet and happiness as is to be expected in this world of care and trouble."

John said goodbye to the land of cotton and journeyed north in the summer of 1848. Philadelphia was his first stop. There he enjoyed the company of his nephew, Leonidas Springs. But he had been there only a few days when he received a letter from Baxter, who needed supplies for a company which he, Austin, William Myers, and William E. White had formed for the purpose of constructing railroad beds for the new Columbia to Charlotte line. Would his father, Baxter inquired, consult some practical railroad operator for advice as to the purchase of carts, implements, etc.? "Give me information," he continued, "as soon as possible. I would respectfully suggest when you come to contracting that you haul out five or ten dollars, and give it to some Yankee to contract for you. Otherwise, knowing by the keenness of his vision that you are a southerner, *pregnant with money, generous in feeling, chivalrous in spirit* the son of a —— will cheat you to a dead certainty."

John evidently planned to purchase the excavating and grading equipment in New York, but he never got around to doing it until a month later. He had other things on his mind. Stopping for only one day at the Astor House in New York, he hurried on to Newport, Rhode Island. He was courting. Yes, courting an attractive widow, Elizabeth Hill of Waterbury, Connecticut. She was a neighbor of his good friends, the Green Kendricks. An inkling of what went on in Newport is given in a letter written by the Reverend A. J. Leavenworth, who was then the head of a school for young ladies in Petersburg, Virginia.

"I was truly delighted," wrote Mr. Leavenworth, "with the account you gave of your stay in Newport. What a mockery of life is such a scene! What vanity. What ostentation. What display. What empty pomp. What conflicts of pride and poverty, of envy, jealousy and passion that daily exhibit themselves upon the Stage. Lord what is man!

"Your account of your lancing with the widow was amusing. I had thought it not improbable that you would bring things to an issue; and perhaps if I had been there to offer a friendly hand such might have been the case. I should gladly serve you; but whether such a course would have been best, your judgement is worth a hundred others. The common sense, practical views which you express on the subject are deeply sound and full of moment. Still, I pitied you. How could I do otherwise than pity you—when you and the widow turned your backs upon each other. ' 'Tis sometimes sad to part.' But both of you are young yet and perhaps you will gather fresh energy for an encounter next summer."

When John went back to New York, he was on a spending spree. He bought such items as a French bed, ornamented with pilasters, gilt chairs, marble top tables, carpeting, table linens, china, and books. Then, finally, he ordered the equipment for Baxter's construction company. All in all, it was a satisfactory trip, with the exception of his disappointment in his courtship. But John did not give up easily. There would be another summer. He would return. And with this thought in mind he turned his eyes homeward.

The year 1849 was important. It was the year of the gold rush in California, which indirectly brought about a new period of activity throughout the country; it was the only year General Zachary Taylor presided over these United States because he died in 1850, leaving his Vice President, Millard Fillmore, to take over the Presidency; it was the year of the cholera epidemic which stretched from North to South and West to the Mississippi. But these were not the most important facts as far as the Springs family was concerned. No, there were other things vastly more important.

John Springs was married. Austin was married. Baxter became engaged. Mary had a new baby. And poor Leroy lost his wife, his "little Amanda."

Yes, 1849 was an important year.

In February, Baxter received a letter from his cousin, Julia Baxter (Mrs. Eli Baxter), written from Cornucopia:

"Blandina went on to Washington City in December with her cousins, Mr. and Mrs. Kaufman, from Texas. We have written her to stop in North Carolina on her return to Georgia and make Sophia a visit. . . . She had made the acquaintance of several of the Carolina members and may possibly come under the protection of some of them if they come direct to Charlotte. It has occurred to me that perhaps you, your Father or Brothers would be going on to attend the inauguration of General Taylor, as a good many are going from this place and Blandina could return with you to Charlotte."

When Baxter read his cousin's letter, he was pleased and excited that Blandie was really coming to Carolina. He longed to be in Washington too. He thought of the gaiety, the crowds, and the thrill of being there at this time. He tried to picture in his mind what Blandie would be doing. But what she actually was doing was told to her mother in her letters:

"I am perfectly delighted with Washington. For the last two weeks, I have been out every night to splendid parties. . . . I have plenty of beaux to go with me everywhere. Engagements for three days ahead. I went last night to hear Madame Bishop sing. Was perfectly enchanted. I never heard such a voice. . . . My principle beau has left for New York. Col. Duncan will be absent a few days. Tonight I shall first go to the theatre to see Macbeth and then to a very large party at Mrs. Patten's. Cousin is mad because she is not invited. I told her she would not get out with me to return the call so she could not expect to be invited. I understand the world and his wife is to be there. I shall wear my blue tarleton with a white sash that looks more like a mantle than a sash, with a white head dress. My beau tonight is General Edney of North Carolina. I don't like him very much. My beau last evening was Mr. Gales. I am going with him and Mr. Duncan to

Mount Vernon this week sometime. . . . I went to the Capitol today with Col. Gaines but it was snowing the first part of the day. . . ."

Blandie, always full of enthusiasm, wrote another day to her mother: "I sent a letter to Jane yesterday. She wished to know about the fashions. I told her the dresses were tight waisted and many had steel or silver buttons. That is a very fashionable trim. Everything is trimmed in velvet. Crimson Moire trimmed with dark red velvet. . . . I was returning calls all day. Made twenty five calls and found few at home. Returned at four and found nineteen cards left for me, Mr. and Mrs. Johnson* among them. Stephens† is considered the smartest Whig from Georgia and they say Cobb‡ rules all the Democrats in the House. . . . Our hotel is considered the gayest in the city; Willars the most aristocratic. Coleman's used to be the most fashionable. At the different hotels they have commenced having receptions in the evenings. On Friday night all the ladies from Coleman's came over here; brought all the beaux they could start. I was the fidler and we had a very pleasant evening. On last night we all from this house went to Coleman's but they set us back completely. They had four harps and two violins playing most divinely and the room was crowded, all dancing. I think it was the most pleasant evening I ever spent. I had *six* beaux by me all the time."

A few days later, Blandie was still reporting the gay times of Washington: "Saturday night I went to a splendid party at Dickersons. Four rooms were opened, had a handed supper. I went with General Edney. He is most anxious to be Minister to Spain. He said he loved Cousin Sophia Springs for seven years. . . . I went to the fourth assembly ball last night. It was beautiful. Madame Bodicks was dressed in a gold dress and looked splendid. I was introduced to the French Minister, a very pleasant young man, also the Spanish Minister. I went to the ball with Mr. Gale and wore my white tarleton. Cousin David gave me a beautiful set of curls to wear on the back of my hair which looked *killing.* . . .

"There will be two inauguration balls. They have built a splendid room for one. I don't think I will go to that one because there is only one door to the room and it is to be lighted with camphene, which

---

*Evidently this was Herschel V. Johnson, who was United States Senator from Georgia and later Governor of Georgia from 1853 to 1857.
†Alexander Stephens, Congressman from Georgia, later Vice President of the Confederacy.
‡Howell Cobb.

is very dangerous. . . . The city is very crowded. I hear there never were such preparations as are being made for the inauguration. . . . President and Mrs. Polk have asked me to join their party on the sixth of March. They go through Georgia. I guess it will be very pleasant, but I can't tell until I hear from Cousin Sophia."

Blandie received a letter from Sophia and immediately made arrangements to go to Charlotte. She had an exciting but sometimes uncomfortable trip south. She wrote to her mother after she arrived at Sophia's:

"From Raleigh to Charlotte the stage was so crowded I felt like fainting several times, and it was only the lively company which kept me up. I spent a very pleasant day in Raleigh. We went to the splendid state house, considered the finest in the United States. We had an elegant dinner and left at two o'clock on the stage, arriving at Chapel Hill at nine o'clock that night. We stopped at an old maid's. She keeps the principal hotel. The University of North Carolina students call her 'Aunt Nancy.' We had traveled with a young Mr. Tyler who was going there to college and when we stopped at the hotel about twenty five students ran out to the stage as if they expected a host of acquaintances. When they spied Tyler they said 'how do you do' as if he had been President. I was very much pleased there. Thirteen or fourteen of them came in and were introduced. They were very pleasant and I would have liked to have spent a day there. They enquired after several Georgia boys—said all the wild boys were from Georgia. They said if I would remain, twenty of them would go home with me, said I must come back in June.

"We left at eleven o'clock, they all hoping the stage would break down before we got out of town. We arrived in Greensboro at two o'clock at night. Mason, who was in the Cabinet, was in our group, also two members of Congress. Greensboro is considered one of the prettiest towns in North Carolina but I could not see much of it. I found a piano, banjo and a guitar. Though it was in the night, I raised the piano and played several tunes and set them to dancing.

"We arrived in Charlotte just at dark. I remained with Cousin Leroy Springs and his wife all night and the next morning at eight o'clock. Cousin Sophia came down. I was asleep but she came in my room—was glad to see me and wanted me to go immediately home with her. I was so fatigued I told her I would remain with Cousin

Leroy until the next day. She said Mr. Myers had looked for the stage every night, and that Cousin Baxter had been up to meet me but had returned home. I like Cousin Leroy very much. He's quite good looking and all sorts of a business man. Mr. Myers is a very handsome man too and just as clever—very pleasant manners. He and Cousin Sophia live in a beautiful place, the prettiest situation in town. She has everything very comfortable around her and a darling little boy named Jack Springs. She treats me just like homefolks and is as sweet and clever as can be.

"I wrote you a long letter about the inauguration but did not send it, as that time I thought I would go home direct from Washington. I received three beautiful bouquets the evening of the inauguration ball (ten dollars apiece). I wish you could have seen them. They were so beautiful."

Spring came early to Springfield that year. The plantation seemed to be showing off its pretty dress to Cousin Blandie. The dogwood gave the woods an appearance of snow on the trees. The peach and apple blossoms were a mass of delicate coloring. The crocuses and daffodils showed their pretty heads in the boxwood garden and the Judas trees were fairylike with their delicate, lavender blossoms. In the fields the moist, freshly plowed earth was being laid off in rows, ready for the cotton seed. The house stood white and impressive in its quiet beauty.

The sound of hooves, the barking of dogs, and the crying of peacocks announced the arrival of the William Myerses and Blandie. Baxter stepped out on the piazza, and as he gazed at Blandie's pretty face under a most attractive little bonnet of white horsehair, he was immediately jealous of all the men who were in love with her. He was excited over the idea of showing her Springfield, a pleasant excitement that he had never experienced with the other young ladies of his acquaintance. He was suddenly glad he had worn his new suit from Boston and he was suddenly glad, too, that at long last he could introduce this young lady to his father, because, try as hard as he could, he had never gotten her out of his mind since his visit to Cornucopia.

Baxter's father was waiting at the steps when the carriage came to a halt. John stepped forward, kissed Sophia, welcomed Blandie to Springfield, and shook hands with his son-in-law.

As Blandie looked at Baxter who was descending the steps, she was conscious of his grey broadcloth suit, his black cravat, his shiny black boots, but above all she was conscious of his handsomeness, his dignity, his smile, and his voice. He was speaking to her. "Well, Blandie, at last you have come to Springfield."

She would always remember how her heart pounded with excitement and pleasure.

She liked Springfield from the first moment she saw it; and she liked its master, so much so, that she remained several weeks. Sophia was careful to give the two ample time to be together. She liked Blandie. What a good match for Baxter, she thought.

There were rounds of parties, balls, picnics, barbecues, and long rides through the countryside. They went up to Charlotte part of the time. Wherever Blandie went, Baxter followed. He was enchanted. He was in love. By the first week of May when Blandie left, she and Baxter were engaged, but they had decided to keep it a secret for a while. He made her promise that she would write from Edgefield, South Carolina, the second stop on her journey home. A cousin, William Harris, was her escort. "After we left you," she wrote, "we traveled for several hours very quietly. Cousin William endeavored to keep up the conservation but for the life of me I could not talk. I knew I ought to try and make myself agreeable, yet I was so gloomy and sad I felt like communing with my own thoughts. . . . I often look at the little key you gave me and intend to keep it by me all the time. . . . I sometimes think, Cousin Dearest, I will let you write to me as you would to any other cousin, and anything you may not want to write in the letter, write it on a half sheet of paper and put it in the letter. I can always open it by myself. Cousin, I can't let three months pass and not hear a word from you. . . . I guess you will think you have quite a *foolish* cousin!"

John Springs, highly pleased with Blandie, decided he would write her a letter. He wanted her to like Baxter, and, like Sophia, thought it would be a good match. "I know not how many letters you have to read," he wrote, "or what part of them you may deem merit answers, from the many acquaintances and the favorable impressions you made during your trip to the North. Nevertheless, none of all those considerations shall prevent me from performing a pleasant duty of letting you hear from myself, and something relative to the many acquaintances you formed during your sojourn among the Catawbas and in Charlotte. . . .

"And now what shall I say about the young people? The gentlemen of your acquaintance are dashing and cutting about, pretty much as you left them. Mr. W. D. may be seen in the course of most any day dashing through the street with his buggy and pair of fine bays, accompanied by his large, imported dog, wagging his bushy tail and looking up wondrously in his master's face. While others might be seen at the nine pin alley and perchance a few might be found at *our house*. And when the sun shines, little groups may be seen under a shade tree discussing matters of state and other dignified subjects; while some may be seen sauntering along the street flourishing a cane and puffing a cigar. . . . I can't undertake to say how the ladies are employed in doors, but they, too, have important matters of their own to attend to, the rumors of the country, how certain ladies were dressed at church last Sunday, *match making* and all the little tales of the town have to be analyzed and adjusted. . . .

"Like the New York Editor who received a great number of challenges to mortal personal combat (for certain of his publications), which he filed away and numbered with a promise they should be attended to when regularly reached, so I wish you to do with this scroll, and when its turn is reached I shall expect to hear from you. . . . And now the last parting word, farewell, a word that makes us linger yet!"

Blandie answered this letter promptly, expressing her appreciation to "Cousin Jack" for his arranging for her to travel as far as Edgefield under the protection of William Harris. "I don't know when I've seen strangers I was more pleased with," she wrote. "They have elegant manners and live in great style."

Baxter followed Blandie's suggestion and tucked little love notes into the envelopes of his newsy, impersonal letters. Blandie thrilled to every word and wrote: "Oh, how I wish I could see you, if only for one hour. I feel I could talk always!" On June 10 he gave her the news of the neighborhood and teased her about her beaux and her stay in Edgefield: "It seems Cousin Blandie was not in so great a hurry after all to reach her sweet home, having *only* stayed two weeks at Edgefield. Ah! but you are a cute little somebody. I thought there was something in your eye not satisfied with the conquest of all the North Carolina beaux; you tarry by the wayside to ensnare the unwarry. Charlotte, your headquarters and place of many sensations, they say is now 'killing' dull. The young men that are its life have all fled with Cousin Blandie. . . . Mr. Myers and Sophia were down last week and spent several days with me. They said they had come down to take a fish and feast on strawberries. Little Jack (Sugar Plum) was along with them, big as life and lively as a cricket, and made no small show in the strawberry line. 'A dish of ripe strawberries all smothered in cream' is about all I have lived upon for the last six weeks. All the berries needed was a little ice; there being no hard freeze the past winter, I had none put up."

To this letter Blandie replied, hoping to make Baxter jealous: "I guess, Cousin, there is a day coming when you will wish you had never seen me, but I will try to make you a *good little wife*. I think I hear you say, 'Blandie had better say a *bad* little wife.'

"I know it must be forced work to write those letters but you must keep it up a *little* longer as no one suspects here. . . . They thought I was engaged to Duncan. Oh! Cousin, you can't think of the variety of reports they have in circulation about my stepping off the carpet. Three young men were here last evening. Said they heard I was to be married in two months and that my wedding dress had come. Four young men had bet five hundred dollars I would be married to a young lawyer in this state. But how I shall fool them! The home folks don't know what to think of me. I praise every body so they can't find out who the favored one is. . . . I often think of that famous and long to be remembered ride to Aunt Peggy's that Sunday evening. Indeed all the evening we talked of only the commonest of subjects. I can't account for it."

The last week in June, John Springs sat in the drawing room of the Springs town house on the Square in Charlotte in a state of complete depression. Even the arrival of a new grandchild at Mary and Brevard Davidson's could not lift his spirits. Amanda was dying. A deep gloom had spread over the house. The children no longer frolicked through the halls. They sensed the seriousness of their mother's illness. Only the baby of one year cried occasionally. The servants tiptoed through the house. The doctor remained with Amanda constantly.

All the happiness was going out of his son's life, and John was helpless to do anything about it. The candles, flickering in the crystal chandelier, reminded him of Amanda's life flickering on the brink of death. The house was still. Indeed, never again would the house on "Springs Corner" escape from the stillness of that night.

The following morning, death cast a shadow so deep over the house that light and sunshine could never bathe it away or erase it from

Leroy's mind and heart. He afterwards expressed himself in a letter to Blandie, answering her letter of condolence:

"I am indeed a most disconsolate and heartbroken husband, and feel that all I most cared for in this life has departed and left me forever. All my future hopes crushed and expectations blasted, and each succeeding day can only bring to mind the sad reality of my loss, with the rememberances of those happy days and years that have passed and gone forever, and a once happy home now made desolate by the absence of her whom I have delighted to cherish and most fondly loved, and with whom I can truly say I have enjoyed all the happiness possible pertaining to the married state.

"It was to me a gratifying mark of respect, as it has never been done before, to find on the day of her funeral all business suspended, and all the stores and shops shut up; and to see so much respect and interest shown, not only by our relatives and friends but by all the citizens of every class. A deep shade of gloom seemed to be cast over the community and a solemn stillness was made to pervade the whole town. At the toll of the deep and solemn sound of the church bell, all flocked to the house of mourning, where every eye wept, and it will long be remembered by all present on that mournful occasion. It was said to be the largest funeral ever witnessed in Charlotte.

"You will, I doubt not, be anxious to know what I intend doing with my little children. My kind father, to whom I can not feel too grateful and who could not have wept more genuinely over his own than he has done on this occasion, has generously offered to take Margaret and Julia Amanda and educate them at his own expense. Although I thought Julia too young to send away from home, yet I have thought best to do so and have yielded to his wishes in the matter. He has just returned from entering them in school in Salem and is here at this time. Aunt Tirza [Mrs. Eli Springs] and her girls have taken our little Laura. Buenna Vista, the baby, sister Sophia has taken. So my two youngest will be situated so I can see them every day. That I may be able to raise them to reflect back the virtues of their mother is my most anxious wish and great desire."

Not even a cholera epidemic raging in New York City checked John's ardor for Elizabeth Hill. The first week in August found him on his way north. He addressed a letter to Baxter from the Astor House in New York on August 15:

"I reached this city on Saturday the 11th and went out to Stratford, sixty two miles, the same evening, where I was expected. I was met with a kind reception from Mrs. Hill and treated with special attention from all her friends. I will return to Stratford Wednesday, the 22nd, which day is fixed upon to consummate our engagement, after which we will make an excursion to the East. I had expected we would have been right off, but Mrs. Hill is desirous of having her relatives present and my making their acquaintance, so that we will remain over night and leave the next morning. She has one sister in this city (Mrs. Clinch), one in New Haven, two sisters and one brother in Stratford. Their wealth, intelligence, and, I may say, splendid style in which they live, and the elevated stand they occupy in society greatly exceeds any anticipations I had formed, and my fear is that she may be disappointed in her expectations of me and mine, though I have endeavored to prepare her mind for the worst. I will have nothing to show her, among my friends, that will compare favorably with that of hers, but I imagine she is more restricted in means than any other member of her family. I hope you will not detract from our *enjoyment* by giving us a cold or unkind reception on our return."

When the letter arrived at Springfield, Baxter was absent. He had lost no time in getting to Cornucopia. His father's letter was forwarded to him by Austin, with the statement: "I found a letter at your place from Father which I enclose to you without comment."

Two weeks passed, and John, honeymooning in Newport, wrote to Baxter again:

"My marriage to Mrs. Joseph A. Hill came off on Thursday, the 23rd, which rather contrary to my expectations, proved to be a large affair. The ceremony took place in church at the tolling of the bell and where assembled a greater number of witnesses than I had ever before seen at any one marriage; I being a South Carolinian, and about to take off from their midst a favorite member of a large family and highly intelligent and respectable train of connections. . . . We reached this place last evening by train and steamboat. . . . I find Mr. Clay, two sons and a daughter here, and their great fancy dress ball is to come off on Friday. There is much company here. . . . Show this letter to Austin and do write me immediately. Oh! Baxter, I remain your affectionate Father."

Baxter was disturbed by this turn of events. He was in Georgia, hoping to plan his wedding to Blandie and eventually bring her to

Springfield and suddenly he was faced with the fact that his father was bringing a wife home to Springfield, too. Baxter did not like the situation and he did not know how to meet it. At the same time, John craved his son's approval of his marriage and was hurt when the following letter arrived from Baxter:

"You state you were to be married on the 22nd of August and hoped I would not give you a cold reception on your arrival. I shall under no circumstances desire to do so. I entertain at no time the slightest objection to the object of your affections. I have no doubt that your good sense and judgment in everything else will likewise be exemplified by your wisdom and discretion in this. The only sad thought I've had was that at this time of life you should marry at all and this has been the feeling of the others of your children. Besides, I felt that it placed me in a peculiar position myself, if I thought proper to marry. It virtually excludes me from entertaining any views of the kind."

John was upset. This letter was a blow to him. He answered it promptly: "In your long looked for letter there are not those expressions or manifestations of kindness to which I think I am entitled, but they contain some evidences of your fears that I might interfere with your arrangements or deter you from marrying, in which you are much mistaken. Almost the last thing I said to you was not to hesitate a moment in carrying out your own wishes; that I would not interfere with you; that I had given up the plantation to you and was willing to give up the house whenever you wanted it. . . . We have set the 15th of October to be home, where I wish my children to be present to receive us. . . . I think it is only necessary for you to know and see the lady I have married to be pleased, and respect her. You will soon discover her to possess superior attainments, intelligence and good sense, with a proper dignity and deportment."

Meanwhile, Austin exploded his own marital bombshell in a letter to his father. After expressing the hope that his Father's marriage would greatly contribute to his happiness, Austin continued:

"The marrying mania appears to attack your family suddenly, you taking the lead. However, there is one member of the family who does not marry *often*, but the fit is decidedly on him now and if nothing should turn up to prevent it, he will . . . bid farewell to Bachelordom. I hope it will meet your approbation. You are acquainted with her and I have no doubt but you will be pleased with my selection.

"You recollect becoming acquainted with the Misses Bobo's at

Alexander's. We afterwards met them at Warm Springs. They lived at that time in Unionville. Dr. Bobo, their father, has since inherited the Musgrove Mills and removed to them on the Enoree—a place distinguished in the history of our State and so eloquently described in 'Horse Shoe Robinson'—Mary Musgrove the heroine. Colonel Williams defeated Colonel Innis and the Tories at this place (Laurens District). Miss Janey Bobo is a descendent of the Musgrove family. She and I have appointed the last day of October for the consummation of our marriage. I hope you will give us your approving smiles and your presence. Her parents proposed if we would wait until an addition was added to their house they would give us a large wedding. I objected for several reasons not necessary to mention. Her parents told me they were not willing for her to leave them immediately—for which reason I urged our immediate marriage, as I was not prepared to remove her at this time so she could spend the most of her time with them.

"I hope you will return in time to give us your approving countenances. Remember me kindly to your Lady. May the Disposer of events bless our unions, is the sincere prayer of your affectionate son."

Under those circumstances, John and his bride arrived at Springfield, a mature but handsome couple. John was a vigorous 62, his bride possibly in her 50's. They did not linger at Springfield. On November 9, Baxter wrote to Blandie:

"Pa has moved bag and baggage this week to Charlotte. He has been from time to time much away from me, but have felt it no separation like the present. This is what I mostly regret in his having again married. I feel quite isolated and little, I assure you, as the sole occupant of these premises. Never before have I felt so sensibly the weighty cares and responsibility now hanging over me. I now truly feel the want of one who would share my joys and sorrows and strew the pathway with flowers. Who, dearest, is better fitted than yourself?"

Part Three

CORNUCOPIA

Cornucopia, Hancock County, Georgia, built in 1823.

CHAPTER THIRTEEN

LIFE HAD NEVER BEEN quite as exciting to Blandie. Julia Baxter noticed the difference in her daughter. Was it love, she thought, that made Blandie sing all day? Was it love that made her daughter watch breathlessly for the mail each morning? Yes, love brought about a great change in a girl. Julia remembered so well, remembered the days when she herself was being courted by Eli Baxter. Had it really been thirty years ago? It seemed like yesterday.

As Julia Richardson, she had been the pampered and indulged daughter of Daniel Richardson and his beautiful Virginia born wife, Frances Long. She had grown up accustomed to wealth, position, and all the finer things of life. But with it all, Julia had never been spoiled. Her family had been a happy one. Visitors coming to their home had been enthusiastically welcomed and entertained. It had come natural to Julia to like people. She had grown into a charming, gracious lady, with great vitality and enthusiasm for life. She had been considered pretty and had been described many times as a "southern belle and heiress." There had been something very special about her and Eli Baxter had realized this the first time he had met her.

Eli and Julia had been married in 1819 when he was twenty-one years of age and she was twenty-three. Already he had been admitted to the Bar by a special act of the Georgia legislature, because he was only twenty when he passed his Bar examinations. He was practicing Law in Sparta, Georgia.

For four years Eli and Julia lived in the town of Sparta, but all the while they dreamed of a plantation which they would name Cornucopia. They would call it that because they wanted it to abound in cheer and hospitality, as well as the good things of the earth. Finally, the house was built four miles out from town and Eli moved his little family there.

Situated in a grove of tremendous oak trees, the house was sparkling white in its new coat of paint. It sparkled inside too, because Julia was a genius at efficient housekeeping. She loved and soothed her babies and gently directed her slaves; and above all she catered to every want and comfort her husband could desire. She adored him. And it was to her that he was indebted for much of his success. Her financial background made it possible for him to take his nose out of his law books at the age of twenty-three and run for the state legislature, beating the oldest and most experienced politician in the country.

Eli Baxter was a quiet, shy man. He forebore to take the prominence in the debates of the General Assembly to which his mind and fine speaking ability entitled him. He was easily embarrassed. Julia realized all these qualities and by her own exuberance and enthusiasm she was able to push him into successful situations which he would never have attempted or attained without her encouragement. Above all, Eli was a family man. His wife and children came first in all his considerations.

Eli continued being returned to the legislature but never became an outstanding debater until the session of 1833 when the question of South Carolina nullification was introduced. Unable to restrain expressing his strenuous opposition to that question, he entered the debate and delivered a series of speeches which at once raised him to the first rank of parliamentary speakers in the State.

The following year he was earnestly solicited by his party, who were in the majority, to become a candidate for Congress, but he steadily and repeatedly refused. He felt his obligation to provide a larger income for his family. In 1835 he was re-elected to the Legislature and was the first to introduce a bill for the establishment of a Supreme Court. At that time, and for ten years afterwards, this measure was unpopular.

The prominence which Eli Baxter had attained as a political speaker and his great popularity with people suggested him to his party in the year 1839 as a candidate for Governor of the State, but his unconcealed difference of opinion with some of the leading men on a question of national policy, and his known unwillingness to receive any office which would conflict with his duties at home, prevented his nomination. It was said that no man in the State, of his character and talents, ever evinced less desire for and love of office.

As a lawyer, he had an unusual career. He had never been a close student of the science of law. When he first began to practice he became well acquainted with the fundamentals of common law, displaying great ability and success, often to the discomfiture of routine lawyers of small caliber. He was often careless in the preparation of his cases and, being a very absentminded person, he often misplaced his brief, that is, if he had made one. He was thus thrown on the resources of his own mind and ingenuity, displaying such eloquence that he was the admiration of the court, the bar, and the country. His opponents at the bar were never sure how to meet him. There was always his timidity and reluctance to speak, his embarrassment in the beginning of a case. He would often yield the place of leading counsel to other lawyers because he shrank from addressing a jury. But when he was compelled by his associates and clients to take the lead in a cause, the very irregularity of the energy of his mind, its impatience of restraint by ordinary rules, its contemptuous refusal to be bound by regular procedures, and the vehemence of his eloquence made him one of the most formidable competitors in a company of eminent lawyers.

The great qualities of Eli Baxter's mind and heart were best displayed with his wife and children. He showered them not only with love and consideration, but with every comfort, beauty, and luxury that could be had. His greatest satisfaction was spending his time at Cornucopia with them and the host of visitors who came to partake of his generous hospitality. Truly, he was a happy man in a happy home. Only one sorrow, and that was a great one, had come into his life. His oldest son Andrew had died after a short but promising business career in Augusta and Sparta.

In 1849, Eli was elected Judge of the Superior Court on the first ballot taken in the General Assembly.

Six babies were reared at Cornucopia—Andrew, Elizabeth, Jane, Julia Blandina, Mary Frances, and Eli, Jr. (Blandie was born on October 24, 1827.) These children grew up frolicking over the plantation, riding ponies and horses, fishing, hunting, and entertaining their neighbors in a most sumptuous and exciting way. As the girls grew older, the piazza at Cornucopia became a mecca for the younger set.

Elizabeth was witty and a tomboy; Jane was sweet with a quiet voice, but always laughing; Blandie was bubbling over with enthusiasm and ideas. She would plan a barbecue. Or should it be a dance? Would she let Charles be her beau for the evening or should it be Bob? Or would it be her handsome cousin, LaFayette Lamar from Augusta, who was coming to visit? No, she would save him for her cousin Sally, who was spending several weeks at Cornucopia. And so it went, on and on, an endless round of gaiety. No wonder cousin Sally wrote, "I have been so happy I had hoped to remain a month longer, but I am compelled to leave this happy, thrice happy place!"

The party given for cousin Sally was a spectacular affair. "It was something *extra*," wrote Sally. "You never saw the beat of the cake. Why, there was enough for a wedding. And the finest show was orange trees in full bearing. Mighty pretty *fixins'*."

There was no denying the fact, thought Julia, there were many young gentlemen in love with Blandie. But somehow, where Baxter Springs was concerned, it seemed to be different. This was no simple flirtation. However, Julia sensed that her daughter would prefer to keep this fact a secret for a while so she said nothing. Finally, in August when Baxter came for a visit he asked for Blandie's hand.

The question now was *when* the wedding would take place. Blandie explained by letter to her fiance: "Since you left I have had another talk with the old folks. They tell me they want me to do just as I please about everything and I have concluded to have a large wedding so I can have all the kin folks to come." Then Blandie added another thought: "I would have given anything in the world to have seen you meet your Papa and MaMa and heard what the old man said to you. How do you like your MaMa?"

Blandie set the wedding date for the first week in December, and Baxter, filled with excitement, began making his plans accordingly. But he hardly had time to digest the good news before another letter arrived. "Well, Cousin dear," Blandie wrote, "Ma has changed my plans and blown them sky high. She says when I wrote last she had not heard from the Charleston schools, and now she is obliged to take Fannie there the last of November, so our affair can not come off in December."

To this Baxter replied: "Oh, Cousin, you surely do not appreciate my feelings or sympathize with my condition, or you would not be putting me off with 'a hope long deferred.' I need not say, Cousin

First courthouse of Mecklenburg County where Declaration of Independence was signed, May 20, 1775.

Second courthouse of Mecklenburg County stood at northeast corner of West Trade and Church Streets in Charlotte.

Third courthouse in Charlotte stood at southeast corner of Third and South Tryon Streets. Monument in front was dedicated to signers of Mecklenburg Declaration by the Hon. Adlai Stevenson.

Independence Square in Charlotte, N. C., 1875. The left foreground shows the "Springs' Corner."

An early
Pullman car.

The Central Hotel on the southeast corner of Trade and Tryon Streets, Charlotte, N. C., in 1890.

A railroad train in 1859.

Charlotte Female Institute.

Carolina Military Institute, Charlotte, N. C., established 1873.

St. Nicholas Hotel, Broadway, New York City, in 1857.

The Charleston Hotel, Charleston, South Carolina, in 1882.

The Mills House in Charleston, South Carolina, in 1861.

Harrison Phoebus
(PROPRIETOR HYGEIA HOTEL OLD POINT COMFORT, VA)
Lessee.

Greenbrier "White Sulphur" Springs,
ON THE CHESAPEAKE & OHIO R'Y. W. Va.

1883

The children of Blandie and Baxter Springs. Top, left to right: Eli, John, Richard Austin. Center: Baxter, Jr., Bleecker, Alva. Bottom: Brevard, Johnnie (on nurse's lap) and Eli, and Leroy.

Eli Baxter Springs at the time he was Mayor of Charlotte with offices in City Hall (left) which stood at North Tryon and Fifth Street.

Richard Austin Springs

Brevard Davidson Springs

Leroy Springs

Top left: Caroline Clarkson (right) photographed on her wedding day with her maid of honor, Isabell Irwin, Dec. 17, 1884. Top right: Brevard Davidson Springs and Caroline Clarkson in 1884. Right: The residence of Blandie and Baxter Springs in Charlotte at the northwest corner of South Tryon and Stonewall Streets.

Children of Caroline and Brevard Davidson Springs. Top left: Marguerite. Top right: Blandina. Bottom left: Esther. Bottom right: Eli Baxter Springs, II, as a cadet at Virginia Military Institute.

A New York newspaper cartoonist's humorous conception of Eli Springs I.

Left: Lt. Eli Baxter Springs, II, France, 1918.

Right: Mrs. Eli Baxter Springs, II, Rye, N. Y., 1934.

Below: Mrs. Eli Baxter Springs, II, with her daughter Katherine and son Eli, III, Rye, N. Y., 1936.

Right: P.F.C. Eli Baxter Springs, III, U.S. Marine Corps, 1951.

Left: Katherine Springs, daughter of Mr. and Mrs. Eli Springs, II, 1951.

Top left: Eli Baxter Springs I, II, and III, New York, 1931. Center left: Eli Baxter Springs, II, III, and IV, Charlotte, N. C., 1964. Center right: Eli Springs, II, welcoming President Dwight D. Eisenhower to Charlotte, May 20, 1954. Bottom: Eli Springs III, ready to take off from Charlotte in 1960, flying a plane of his own design and make.

dearest, I have often, often thought of you. This is a cold, blustery, gloomy night and I a poor, devoted, deserted being with not a soul to whom I can express a thought or communicate an idea. But I will not complain."

Springfield was being put in spotless order. Baxter wanted everything to be fresh and beautiful for his bride. Supplies of delicacies were ordered from Charleston, and Baxter himself was preparing to be a very well dressed man. He wrote to his friend and agent in Charleston, Joseph H. White, and requested the latest in the way of stylish suits. White replied:

"I feel highly honored in attending to your commands. I have exerted myself in selecting your 'suites' and do sincerely hope you may be pleased. The goods are of the latest style. Thinking you might have forgotten to order gloves, I've taken the liberty of sending you a pair. I know Athens to be a fashionable place and have given you an everlasting pair of green pants for the second day. The vest intended to be worn the second day can't be surpassed on this side of 'Jordan's stormy banks.' Now, old cock, you must fling those Georgia boys clear out of the house. Lord! If I only had time to go, clear the track, you sinners all! Bac, I wish you more luck than a Jack--- could pull down a mountain. You sneaking devil, you! Allow me to congratulate you. May your future life (as has ever been the past) be one of peace and plenty."

February 12, 1850, was the date set for the wedding. That day Cornucopia was alive with excitement. Carriages and horses lined the driveway. Smiling Negroes were on hand to take the horses away to the stables. Gentlemen helped their ladies up the steps to the wide piazza. Judge Baxter stood in the doorway greeting his guests. He was dignified in his black suit. His gold shirt studs sparkled against the background of white linen. His curly hair, which never looked quite combed, gave him a boyish look in spite of his fifty years.

Inside the house everything from the crystal chandeliers to the guests was sparkling. Young girls in their prettiest silks, laughing and giggling, were going up and down the stairs, all anxious to have a word with and see the beautiful bride in her chambers. The gentlemen, immaculate in their blacks and greys, moved about the rooms, smiling and bowing to the ladies, but invariably finding themselves in little groups of men only. In the drawing room chairs lined the walls, and here sat the older ladies, chatting in an endless babble. The room was elaborately decorated. The spacious hallway, which led from the front to the back of the house, was filled with guests who were being served wine.

Finally, the wedding hour approached. A hushed silence spread over the house. The sound of music came from the drawing room, and Blandie, looking more ravishing than ever in her Brussels lace gown, descended the stairs. Walking in front of her were her two sisters, Lizzie and Fannie, lovely in pink tarleton dresses. Blandie, on the arm of her father, entered the drawing room. Baxter was waiting, impeccably dressed. He was so completely entranced with Blandie's loveliness that he hardly remembered the words of the minister, while the mysteries of love made Blandie's heart palpitate with great wildness.

When Blandie and Baxter arrived at Springfield, it was late in the afternoon of March 1. Wheeler pulled the horses down to a slow trot after they entered the cedar lined driveway. The dogs, Paul, Silas, Laird and Henry, on seeing their master, began to run furiously around the carriage, barking and wagging their tails. Waiting in front of the house was Nathan, his white teeth shining in a broad grin. As Wheeler checked the horses at the steps, Nathan stepped forward with the greeting, "We'come home, Marsa and Missy." On the porch stood two Negro women, clean and neat, with their aprons freshly starched and their black heads wrapped in white cloth. They were Nancy and Sarah, who would wait on and serve their new mistress.

Baxter stepped down from the carriage, looking every inch the Southern gentleman in his brown frock coat and velvet vest. He extended his hand to his bride whose eyes were sparkling beneath an exquisite "Neapolitan" bonnet which had two huge roses perched in the front, decorated with sprays of green wheat. They entered the house and Baxter led Blandie to the parlor on the right. There, much to her delight, was a new rosewood seven octave, Gothic alcove pianoforte. This was Baxter's second wedding gift to her. The first had been a handsome gold watch which he had given her the morning after their wedding.

Three days later, a letter arrived from William Myers in Charlotte: "I write to advise you of our good luck. We have a fine daughter* born this morning at six o'clock. Sophia is doing as well as could be expected. The child is perfect in every respect, weight 9½ pounds. Say

*Sophia Convert Myers who married Colonel Hamilton C. Jones in 1873.

to Blandie we hope to welcome her to our home as soon as it meets with her convenience. You must bring her up shortly for it is not right that you should have her all to yourself, for you must recollect there are some old beaux of hers in these parts that may claim the right, at least, of seeing her once more, though she be Mrs. Springs."

About this same time, John Springs sent a letter to Baxter from Charleston. It concerned Henry Clay, that venerable gentleman whom John had met at Newport and who was one of his political idols: "A rumor was afloat here yesterday morning that produced much excitement; that Congress had broken up in a *row*. It was even stated that Henry Clay had his throat cut; that Foote was killed, etc., but it turns out all to be without any good foundation. Still much solicitude exists as to the proceedings and doings by Congress."

Baxter went to the library immediately and answered his father's letter. He too had heard reports and rumors of what was going on in Washington. The situation seemed to be growing steadily worse, and the subject of slavery and its spread to the new territories was the basis of the trouble.

Actually, when Congress had convened a few months back in December 1849, the Union was threatened because there were fifteen slave holding states and fifteen free states when the question arose of admitting California as a free state. This would break the balance of power and give the North a majority in the Senate. There was also the question of New Mexico and Utah and whether they should be slave-holding or free states. Delegates from some of the southern states met in Nashville with the intention of expressing a solid opposition to any plan which would close California and New Mexico to slavery.

In the spring of 1850 the moderate leaders in Congress united to bring about a settlement to the problem. Their spokesman was Henry Clay. He argued to have California admitted as a free state and let New Mexico and Utah be territories open to slavery. Let slave trade be abolished in the District of Columbia and force the North to co-operate in the return of runaway slaves. This was Clay's famous compromise. But John C. Calhoun opposed this plan.

On March 4, the same day that John Springs had written his letter to Baxter, Calhoun made his last appearance before Congress, speaking against the compromise. The old politician was so emaciated and weak that he had to be carried into the Senate chamber. He was too ill to deliver his speech and a colleague read it for him.

Calhoun placed the blame on the North for creating the crisis, saying they were attempting to interfere with the institutions of the South when their own institutions were not endangered. He advocated the permission of slavery in new territory because that territory was the property of free Americans and the people should be able to move into those territories with their personal property, even though that property be slaves. He said the fugitive slave law should be enforced. He even went so far as to propose an amendment to the Constitution which would permit two Presidents, one for each section, and each having a veto power against the other.

On March 7 Webster gave his famous answer to Calhoun's speech. He said the North and South were both responsible for slavery in the country and that Congress had no right to interfere with slavery in the states where it already existed. He also stated that he believed the fugitive slave law should be enforced. He appealed to the men of the North and the South to lay aside their differences in order to save the Union. His speech eventually did much to bring about the passage of Clay's Compromise, but the speech so infuriated the anti-slavery people of New England that they burned him in effigy and accused him of treason to his State.

This, then, was why John Springs felt anxious about the proceedings in Congress. He soon relaxed from his worries, though, when he and Elizabeth came to Springfield for a visit the end of April. It was good to be home, John realized. Even though he had turned the place over to his son, it was home and always would be. He enjoyed riding over the plantation, talking to Baxter.

"I would not think of planting cotton until next week," he said. "And then if it will do without, I don't know that I would turn the ridges. Cotton doesn't plant well nor come up so good till it gets a rain after it's plowed."

Blandie spent much of her time that spring answering her mail. One letter, which had arrived after her wedding, had been forwarded to her. It was from one of her cousins, William H. Ogbourne, who lived at "Cherry Hill" outside of Montgomery, Alabama. Part of the letter explained: "On the 27th of February, Sue and I are to give a large party. I am now having a ball room built in the rear of the house, which is built expressly for the occasion, with a spring floor, on the 'Remington Aerial Bridge' principle. Can't you come out to Cherry Hill for the party?" Blandie giggled over the idea of a springing floor.

Maybe some day she could go to Montgomery and see this new contraption!

She rose from her desk, threw herself across the bed, and opened a letter from her sister Fannie, who was in school at Charleston. She had read it before, but on a lazy afternoon it was pleasant to think of her family while the soft breeze blew from under the oaks into her room and across her bed. She read:

"I received a letter from Ma telling me about your new piano. Mr. Oats told me it was one of the finest he had ever had in his store.

"I have a new grenadine dress. The material cost $1.25 a yard which was a great deal to pay for a summer dress but it is very fine. Ma also got for me a fine white dotted swiss and pink muslin. The dresses were sent from New York and had low necks with three flounces.

"I suppose Cousin Baxter is wrapped in grief and melancholy at the death of Calhoun. His is one of the few names born not to die. Mrs. Dupre has put us all in mourning and seems perfectly surprised at our wishing to go out, dance, sing, talk or do anything but lament the death of the great statesman.

"Miss Sparks cut me out altogether with Mr. Dunwoody. He is coming next week to see her. They are to ride horseback and as they are both very near sighted, I am to go ahead to show the way for fear they should break their mutually precious necks."

Blandie smiled at the humor displayed in her sister's letter. Fannie's a lot like Ma, she thought. This brought her to thinking of her mother and she rose to find her mother's last letters and enjoy parts of them again: "Never a day passes and seldom an hour without our speaking of you and wishing that we could enjoy the sunshine of your bright face. . . . Your Pa often speaks of you, says 'Blandie married beyond my expectations for a real clever fellow. I feared she would marry a dandy.' . . . He will be at leisure until September. Talks of going up country in June. I think he only wants to see you and Baxter. . . . So you are thinking of going North in August? We hoped you would come to Cornucopia. We will have a great abundance of fruit. The turkies are very fat and the lambs too. . . . My 'cloth of gold' rose is in full bloom. Dr. Whitten said my yard was decidedly the prettiest in the country. . . . I have ordered Italian silk for a new dress. It will be made into a low neck evening dress with a full skirt. My new hat I bought in Charleston has flowers and ribbons on it and cost $3.00. . . ."

It would be nice if Ma and Pa could come to Springfield and see this lovely place, thought Blandie. Her Pa had been so anxious that she should be a good wife, a practical wife. She had shown Baxter her father's last letter and it had brought forth smiles and a humorous remark. The letter had read:

"Blandie, let me urge upon you always to have a view to your husband's money and never draw too heavily upon him. Take a timely interest in all his plans and progress, and you will truly give encouragement to his industry and promote especially his interests and happiness. Now is the time to be industrious and economical. Become independent now. With independence all the enjoyments of life are under your control. A taste for employment is one of the greatest blessings of life. It gives health and contentment and, consequently, happiness. Employment will soon come to be interesting. . . . Something of its products should always be saved. . . . I am not the advocate of saving everything and spending nothing. That is the miser's philosophy, but make all you can, save it and spend it in moderation, and enjoy it, taking care never to spend the whole."

Blandie felt a great love for her father. She had pride in his being such an outstandingly good Judge, but she felt most tender toward him because of his kindness, his comforting presence.

May and June were delightful months at Springfield. Blandie planted roses which were sent from Cornucopia. She busied herself about the house. She and Elizabeth, who had become very much a part of the family, went for drives in the late afternoon, while Baxter and his father talked about planting, politics, and business. Often Jane and Austin would ride over from Springsteen or Sophia and William would drive down from Charlotte.

Each day was pleasant. Each day was thrilling to Blandie because she was happy, happy to be in love with Baxter and happy because they were going to have a baby. At night in the privacy of their room, they would talk about their plans. Blandie wanted to have her baby at Cornucopia, and Baxter knew she would like to spend the summer there too. The baby was due in November, so he suggested that they leave for Georgia the end of July and make a pleasant easy trip. John and Elizabeth would be leaving at that same time for Newport and Connecticut.

Baxter kept a detailed expense account of the trip. At every stop Blandie bought watermelon. She craved it all the way from Lancaster to Camden, to Branchville and finally Augusta! From there a smoking little train took them to Atlanta for a ten-dollar fare, but there was still the item of watermelon on the bill!

At Marietta, Georgia, the travelers paused for a week's visit with Blandie's sister, Jane, and her husband, Dr. Alva Connell, and then continued to Cotoosa Springs, a large summer resort which they reached by train and hack. On the way, yes, there was watermelon! The next stop was Chattanooga, where they had a horse ride up the mountain with dinner at the top. Following this was Rowland Springs, and finally they arrived in Sparta where the Baxter carriage was waiting to take them to Cornucopia. The entire trip had been like a second honeymoon, with just the two of them together, dreaming and planning.

When the carriage turned into the avenue leading to Cornucopia, it was nearly twilight. At first the trees blocked the view of the house, but when finally it stood before them, with the pale pink sky overhead, it looked like a beautiful picture that might not be real. Baxter remembered Blandie's words, "I know you were monstrous pleased with Cornucopia." He was, he had to admit, more than pleased with it and he secretly wondered how Blandie had been able to tear herself away from it.

Stepping down from the carriage into Baxter's arms, Blandie cried out with joy and ran into the house. "Ma! Pa! We're home," she shouted. And in a few moments she was being kissed by her parents and welcomed by a group of laughing, wide-eyed, shiny Negro servants. All were talking at once. All were laughing. That was the way it was at Cornucopia. It was a "thrice happy place!"

CHAPTER FOURTEEN

AUGUST WAS A LAZY MONTH at Cornucopia, a restful, satisfying month. The mornings were cool and Baxter enjoyed getting out early, riding over the countryside before the dew was off the ground. He liked to examine the ways of the Georgia planters and compare them with his own methods of farming. Often he would ride over to the Cain or Ponce plantations and chat with those gentlemen about crops and politics. When he would get back to Cornucopia Blandie would have had her breakfast in bed, and often he would enjoy a second breakfast of figs and cream while he talked to her. It pleased him to watch her eyes sparkle as she listened to him and as she talked. There was one thing certain, Blandie, like her mother, was never at a loss for enthusiastic conversation.

The late mornings were spent on the piazza, talking, reading, and waiting for Tom, the coachman, to come from Sparta or Mount Zion with the mail. The newspapers and letters which he brought were filled with the serious subjects of slavery, secession, California, New Mexico, Texas, and the state of confusion and bitterness in Congress, particularly since the death of President Taylor on July 9.

A letter from John Springs, written from Washington and dated July 22, 1850, explained conditions there:

"I have attended the Senate every day where I have had an opportunity of seeing and hearing some of the great men of the nation. President Fillmore (President through and by the grace of God) has seized the helm of state and sent in his Cabinet nominations yesterday. . . . Our representatives from South Carolina, including the Senators, seem to despair of any satisfactory adjustment being made; that the thing is now reduced to two desperate alternatives, submission or disunion. The majority seem determined to ride rough shod over the minority, in perfect disregard of the Constitution and in violation of all law and justice. It seems to me the great fault is in the South, for I am told the North was alarmed at the Nashville convention, and if the slave states had all united and spoken out they could have made their own terms, but the partial manner in which it was attended rather had a tendency to weaken the South and show our want of unanimity among ourselves. Disunion seems a common theme spoken of by Southern members. . . . There is no hope of anything decisive being done on Congress adjourning soon. The North is determined to urge or force their measures on the South before they break up."

John spent eight days watching the Senate debate Clay's compromise, hoping to be present when the vote was taken on this great "Omnibus Bill," but he was disappointed. "Its fate is doubtful," declared John. "I heard Mr. Clay's great effort which was certainly well worth listening to. It was mortifying to see that almost all the discussion was among the southern members. The Northerners sitting quietly, perhaps giggling in their sleeves at the Southerners squabbling. I believe there is more wholesale rascallity in the two houses of Congress to their number than in any body or place in the United States."

The August evening breeze blew warm across the lawn of Cornucopia. A faint perfume of roses drifted in from the garden. The house was thrown open and the sound of music came from the inside. Blandie was playing the piano. Baxter, with his flute, and Lizzie, on the harp, were accompanying her. Fannie was dancing the polka with Eli, Jr., and Cousin James Skinner was clapping in time with the music, occasionally demanding his turn with Fannie.

In the slave quarters another kind of music was filling the air—a low, mournful spiritual, sung only as darkies one generation away from the wild lands of Africa could sing.

Julia and Eli sat on the piazza. The Judge held a small glass of brandy in his hand and as he talked he took an occasional sip. He spoke of Cornucopia, its prospects for the future, and he talked of Texas. It seemed that more and more often his thoughts were on that far away state. But Julia, taking these thoughts merely as dreams, went on planning her own little projects for Cornucopia. She would build her arbor beyond the rose garden and soon they would begin on the majestic columns which would be added to the façade of the house.

Late that night, Blandie lay awake and listened to the sounds of Cornucopia. The crickets and frogs created a symphony of monotonous discord, with now and then the lonesome sound of a whippoorwill adding his peculiar note. But there was something missing. At first she could not sense what it was. Then she remembered, remembered her first nights at Springfield when she had been awakened by the blood curdling screams of the peacocks which had frightened her. But later she had begun to be thrilled by their wild cries and now she realized she missed this occasional strange, savage noise. She immediately regretted that she would not be returning to Springfield with Baxter. The nights would be long without him at her side. Already she was beginning to dread the day of his departure.

That day came in September. Blandie could not hold back the tears. After he had gone she wrote: "I felt so lonely, Bac darling, when I went into our room and you were not there, I had a good cry and concluded never to go upstairs again." Later she would write sorrowfully, "You may think it very silly, but I am so easily frightened now that you are not with me. Ma sleeps in the room with me and tells me how foolish it is. I think now if I always had you, my own dearest, by my side I never would get frightened again."

When Baxter returned to Springfield from Cornucopia, he found the plantation in good condition. Glover had "tramped out the wheat" and "hulled up the rye"; he had "cleaned up all the stubble land" ready for plowing and had completed most of the new fencing. The flower beds around the house had been worked and weeded, and the ditches in the field cleaned out. Taking all things into consideration, Baxter felt that the plantation had not suffered from his absence. However, there was one thing that bothered him. He found, as his father had before him, that Springfield could be a very lonely place. He could break the monotony by going to Charlotte, but Leroy was in the North and Sophia had taken her children to the mountains, so he chose to remain at home and watch eagerly for letters from Blandie. And he was not disappointed. The letters were long, affectionate, and newsy. One of them threw Baxter into immediate action. Blandie had written: "Our figs are giving out but we have peaches, and you have apples. I wish I had some."

Baxter strode out of the house and called to one of the Negroes to bring baskets and follow him to the orchard. If Blandie wanted

CORNUCOPIA 127

apples, she should have apples! With the greatest of care he selected the most perfect specimens, being careful to leave a few green leaves and stems on some of them. "They look pretty that way," he said. Soon the apples were on their way to Cornucopia and soon Baxter had a letter from his wife:

"On Wednesday morning Mac returned from the railroad bringing the barrel and box of apples. Now, old man, you wanted to take us by surprise by not saying one word about it in your letters. I tell you it was not long before Fannie and I got into them, and such delicious apples I never tasted. I thought all the time I was taking them out, you had with your dear hands helped to put them up, but I tell you what, old man, when it commenced getting toward the middle of the barrel your little wife had to give it up. She could stretch no further. . . . When I opened your last letter Pa said, 'I want you to make haste and read all the love and marrying to yourself and then tell all the news about his crops out loud.' I told him it was *all love* and *marrying* and nothing about the crops. He laughed very heartily."

Interspersed in Blandie's love letters were many paragraphs on politics. This was now a subject of great interest to the women as well as the men. For instance in October she wrote:

"This is court week in Sparta and I understand there is greater excitement there than has been for many years. . . . Ma and the girls have been every day this week and have gone again today. The men who are for the Union spoke yesterday and today those in favor of dis-Union will speak. Monday Mr. Stephens* spoke. He is for the Union. Pa is strong for the Union. Great excitement prevails over the State. The ladies can't go in the streets of Columbus because there is so much excitement. I expect the convention in Milledgeville will draw a great mass of people. I don't know which side is right. I did not like Stephens speech for he said a great deal against Carolina. Pa's friends are besetting him to speak today but he thinks it is best not to do so. He will go down to the convention and speak there. He is a candidate to go for the Union. I am rather inclined to go with the dis-Union men, but, old man, whatever you are for I know is right and I am there."

Evidently Baxter was making speeches too, because Blandie wrote another time: "I read about what you said about old Georgia. Ma and

*Alexander H. Stephens, Congressman from Georgia, and later the Vice President of the Confederacy.

all exclaimed how they would have liked to have heard your speech, but they are not half as anxious as your little wife, or in other words, your 'little un.' " Then, because she could never get Springfield off her mind, she added: "Bac dearest, I wish you would open my piano, bless its dear heart, and touch all the keys a little. It might help it. Or get Janie to come over and play it."

Because Baxter knew that Blandie was interested in all political views, he sent her his father's letter. John Springs had written from Niagara Falls:

"I have not knowingly met an avowed Abolitionist in the course of my travels, but here was struck by the appearance of a very conspicious sign *'Free Soil House,'* and have no doubt but the great mass of people in all the free states are Free soilers.* I think also the opinion prevails that no one state or more has a right peaceably to secede or withdraw from the compact, and if any attempt of that kind is made by the South the course would be to treat them as rebels, and to put them down by force of the sword, over run them by power and numbers and whip them into subjection. . . . *Suppose we get into conflict!* It would be one of the most unnatural, bloody struggles almost ever heard of. It would be brother against brother, the father arrayed against the son and the son against the father."

John wrote again, this time from the Astor House in New York on October 2: "A runaway rascal, James Hamlet, has been arrested here by the Marshall and his posse and has been delivered to his owner in Baltimore. So far so good! I believe by a large majority of the people the law is a popular one but is producing great excitement among the colored gentry. I see it stated that about three hundred of them had left, armed to the teeth, for Canada, all runaways, denouncing the country and the people that won't protect them. Meetings are being held in all the principal towns and cities. One took place here last night, made up of blacks and a few abolitionists. The strongest resolutions were entered into, calling on all the patriotic lovers of liberty to join and aid in resistance to the fugitive slave bill and asking for contributions from every one who is able to give a cent to aid in resisting the law. I read a part of their proceedings this morning in the New York Herald. The Editor remarks that the law shall be faithfully executed, but my own private opinion is that it won't afford

---

*Those who wished to prevent the spread of slavery were called "Free-soilers." Martin Van Buren was nominated for the Presidency in 1849 by the Free-soil party.

much relief or security. Think it would have been better, as some member proposed, to have paid the owners for their property out of the U. S. Treasury. Collections are also being made to pay passage and expenses of part of the runaways to Canada so as to get them out of reach and that is rather gratifying to the citizens here. They don't want them. I do wish there were a way to get our free blacks to the free states. I would be willing to contribute liberally to that object."

The latter part of October, Baxter felt it was time for him to be on his way to Georgia. Blandie was getting nervous. She said, "Lizzie has been counting for me by the moons." But Baxter was more nervous than his wife for fear he would not be there in time for the birth of his child. October 30 found him at Cornucopia, anxious and waiting for the event. A state of tense excitement gripped the entire family. John Springs wrote, "We will be solicitous to hear from you."

On November 5 the baby was born, a large healthy boy. Blandie bore him with more than the usual pain and stress. It was a "tedious labour," as Dr. H. S. Burt expressed it. The baby was named John Springs.

Baxter remained with his wife for two weeks after the child was born. Then he returned to Springfield. His wife's letters were enthusiastic in her description of the baby. "He's a complete night owl," she wrote, "but he looks so sweet and innocent and beautiful I can't get mad with the little darling. It is astounding, old man, how large his eyes have grown in a week. . . . I continue to improve very fast. My whole study and aim is something to eat! Ma had me a large pone of light bread and a large cake made just to keep in my room. You would laugh, Bac dearest, to see me and our darling little one eat so much. I tell you, old man, we'll make way with everything when we get home, so you had better be looking around."

Christmas found Blandie in her own home. Baxter marveled at his wife's energy. She moved about the house, superintending the slaves in their cooking, cleaning, and sewing. She entertained guests and showed off her new son to all the Carolina folks. Her spontaneous charm seemed to make her home more gracious and hospitable than ever. Quiet old Springfield was coming to life again.

Blandie often thought that living with Baxter was like living with all the security and tenderness of her father combined with all the excitement of a knight in shining armor, as the story books would say. Her flirtatious romance had ripened into a tender, passionate love.

She was astonished that her husband could frolic with her as a child, or consult with her as a business partner, or forget all except being her lover. Then there was the baby to love and care for. Even John Springs made the remark, "They are so much occupied with the baby that they can think of nothing else."

Shortly after Blandie left Cornucopia, Julia Baxter had a very interesting trip. She was most ecstatic when she wrote of hearing the very popular Jenny Lind sing:

"Fanny and I set off for Charleston on the cars to hear Jenny Lind sing. As soon as the car reached Augusta I went off in full speed to get Lizzie to go with us. She was soon ready and the omnibus called for us. We had time to go to the United States Hotel for coffee before leaving. At Hamburg we found scores of people bound for Charleston. Upon arriving we went straight to the Charleston Hotel. After dressing we went into the parlor. I assure you I had to keep both eyes wide open to see everything. The first thing that attracted my attention was Mr. and Mrs. Barnum* being introduced to some persons near me. I fixed my eyes on the great 'humbugger.' He wore two splendid diamond rings. Mrs. Barnum was dressed in black, wearing a good deal of jewelry—and Miss Barnum made quite a figure in the circle. Tickets for the concert were five dollars for the first evening and six dollars for Saturday night. The orchestra far excelled anything I could have imagined—it was enchanting. 'Come Over The Moonlit Sea' was magnificent. In a few moments Jenny Lind came skipping out from behind the scenery, looking more like a fairy, first courtseying very gracefully, and then she commenced singing. Such applauding I have never heard! She was dressed in a blue silk, with a real lace bertha and her dress was trimmed with blue fringe. She wore one diamond bracelet and one cameo breast pin, with bright red roses in her hair. Her 'Home Sweet Home' surpassed everything. I felt completely overwhelmed and melted to tears. Billeta sang several duets with Jenny. It is said he is her favorite of all her orchestra. Jenny and all her company were staying at the Charleston Hotel. I saw her passing to her room. Barnum would not allow her to appear in public."

Julia Baxter was not the only person to have Charleston on her mind. Mrs. John Springs' eyes were turned in that direction, but for a different reason. Charlotte was experiencing a smallpox epidemic.

---

*P. T. Barnum, the great showman, paid Jenny Lind $1,000 a night for 150 performances. The famous Swedish singer remained in America for two years.

"Your Mother," wrote John to Baxter, "has become uneasy under the circumstances and won't leave her room. We expect to leave shortly for Charleston and will send Wheeler, the carriage and horses to the plantation. Leroy's Negro, Napoleon, has smallpox."

By January 15 John and Elizabeth were safely and comfortably settled in "one of the finest rooms of the Charleston Hotel, number 120 at the head of the private stairs."

Sophia had packed bag and baggage and gone with her children to Springfield to escape the epidemic. On March 15 Leroy sent a note down to Baxter: "The smallpox has entirely disappeared and Charlotte is now beginning to assume its usual appearance of business and life." The next day Sophia put her little family in the carriage, had the baggage loaded in a wagon, and departed for Charlotte. When she rode into town she found a great commotion. The old Female Academy was on fire. The flames were pouring out from every part of it, and all hope of saving it was gone. "It gave me rather sad feelings," said Sophia, "to see the old house where I spent so many days and knew every nook and corner so well entirely destroyed."

The summer months of 1851 brought forth many letters on politics, exchanged between Baxter, his father, and his father-in-law. The Judge, being a strong Union man, was gratified by the fact that Baxter was opposed to separate state action. "I have as an American citizen," said the Judge, "felt a good deal of alarm about the course which Carolina would pursue and I still have apprehensions, but I have confidence in the intelligence of the great mass of the people, and I now tell you that the plain, staying home, unpretending class of men, who do not want office, will put down your office seekers and holders, the babbling politicians who have nothing at stake in society, some of whom would like to see the elements of society thrown into anarchy, society distracted by factions, law giving no protection to life, liberty or property, knowing that they may gain by these conflicts and storms of passion.

"If Carolina should secede the consequences will be disastrous and destructive to all the great interest which the American people have hereto held so dear. If she drops silently, safely and peaceably from her sphere the consequences are the same. She will never regain her position and the American Union is dissolved forever. I know the advocates of this policy anticipate great things from a Southern Confederacy. . . . With a Confederacy of a few states what an abject miserable creature we should be. We should be the object of insults upon the land and powerless to resent it; our will impoverished by our culture; the white man driven away by the slaves, we shall be the weakest Republic that has had a place upon the catalogue of states. I know that a certain portion of slaves make a state stronger but when the slave population will treble the white then it is a source of great weakness.

"I have no sort of respect for a little Republic. The history of the world does not furnish one example where a little Republic has enjoyed for any length of time peace, independence and happiness. Have a large Republic. Here I differ with your leading men. In their zeal for a Southern Confederacy they have thrown themselves upon the doctrine of Kings, that a Republic is unsuitable for an extensive tract of country. For myself, the extent of this Republic has been its salvation. Its future prosperity depends upon its continuing expansion. I hope to see it embrace all North America."

When Austin Springs announced that he was in favor of separate state action, John Springs, vacationing in New York, was so agitated that, in his next letter, he forgot to describe the elegant dinner party he and Elizabeth had attended at the home of the famous merchant prince, A. T. Stewart; he forgot to tell of their sojourn on Long Island; in fact he forgot to describe anything except great concern over his son's decision. He wrote vehemently to Austin:

"I regret to learn that you have joined the immediate secession party. I will not pretend to dictate your course to you but recommend that you very gravely consider the matter before you lend whatever influence you have to so important, momentous, dangerous and hazardous move. . . . My mind is, I think, made up on the subject. I don't think the Government will hang together long. I am ready to join in a Southern secession, but not alone, single handed. I am of the opinion that secession and revolution are synonimous terms.

"It is, perhaps, practicable to effect either peaceably, but do not think it probable that it would begin and end so, but likely would lead to a civil conflict of the most horrible kind. The General Government would have to acknowledge the seceding party a free and independent sovereignty with liberty to make all her own commercial regulations and enter into treaty stipulations to that effect. Think you she would stand by and see foreign importations into Charleston duty free or at a less rate than she charges?

"I am aware that some of our political leaders, in their bursts of patriotism, say that dollars and cents are not to be taken into account, and that they are ready to sacrifice commerce and all the great interests, together with all their own effects and even their blood on the altar, to vindicate what they consider our wrongs and violations of our Constitutional rights, but from long experience I have always deemed it prudent and right on undertaking any matter or new enterprise to sit down and cooly calculate the gain or loss likely to result.

"After hearing a long discussion on the subject between a young Mr. Hayne of Charleston (son of R. Y.) and a New Yorker at Lebanon Springs, in a casual conversation with the latter I remarked that the Northern people were not aware of the Southern secession feeling that prevailed, or they would not agitate and irritate; that there was a prevalent opinion that we must separate shortly. I said to him, 'Let Congress meet, repeal the fugitive slave bill and abolish slavery in the District (neither of which we had much interest save the principle. From the former we expected no benefit) of Columbia and they would find that feeling would develop itself, and as an individual I am ready for it and would rather be pleased that they should do so and bring this agitation to an issue. I do not believe the North will cease their aggression until the issue is made. With the North it is a matter of political principle; at the South we have $1,500,000,000 at stake. The North is determined there shall be no further extension of slavery and in the South we are determined we will not submit to restriction and the issues might as well be made up at once.' He looked at me with perfect astonishment and remarked that he was much surprised at such an expression of feeling from a staid looking gentleman of my age. He then replied, 'We will take care of that. We are determined not to do anything to increase the agitation or give the South any new plea for discontent. We are fully sensible of the value of the South to the North and could not part with you.'

"I think this gentleman spoke the feeling of the intelligent mass of the community. It is not fair to take all our inferances from a few fanatical Abolitionists. I believe now if a Southern Convention would assemble and it were possible for them to unite and lay down some principles and make certain requisitions for our future security, I believe they might be met and granted by the Congress of the United States, rather than see the South secede."

The month of August, as far as Baxter was concerned, was hot, humid, and harrowing. As a newly commissioned Captain in the State

Militia, he was supposed to attend Reviews and encampment during the month. He hardly knew if he would make it or not. His worries at Springfield had doubled. Following a terrible drought, the plantation had suffered, first, a damaging hail storm, which had ripped leaves from everything growing. Second, a tumultous freshet had washed across the land in such floods that ditches had disappeared, bridges had washed out, and bottom land where corn was planted was swamped.

Now on top of it all, and of much more concern, baby Jack's sickness, attributed to teething, had grown extremely serious. In fact, it was so alarming that Baxter had sent word to his father, who was then in the social whirl of Newport, that he feared for the baby's life. John had sympathetically answered:

"With emotions of sorrow and feelings of sympathy I now proceed to reply to your letter in which you seem to anticipate the bereavement of your first born, and I sorely regret I can not be present; not that I could render you any essential service but that I might sympathize with you in distress and exercise a father's influence in consoling and comforting you. I would say trust in *God* in whose hands are all our destinies.

"You are now able to appreciate the great anxiety and suspense of parents, the constant watchings of the changes of every symptom, the alternate fears and hopes to which the human mind is subject. . . . I will remind you of the great uncertainty of all transitory and earthly things. . . ."

John, of course, had no way of knowing, but the day he wrote his letter was the day little Jack was buried. The shadow of death had engulfed Springfield many times before but not since Mary Springs' death in 1834 had the plantation been so unconsolably grieved. Strong black Negro men wept as they worked in the fields, the tears mingling with the beads of sweat which ran from their brows. Their little "Marsa Jack" who was someday to be the master of Springfield lay in the parlor, white and cold like a doll. Isaac Spencer, the carpenter, had just finished the small coffin and Blandie had laid her baby to rest for the last time.

There was no need for anyone to attempt to describe Baxter's or Blandie's misery. It was tragedy, complete and pathetic.

And far away in Newport, John Springs wept.

In his gentle manner, he tried to console his children with a letter:

"I received the letter dated September 9th telling me that the dear little fellow had died the evening before and was buried that afternoon. When I last saw him he looked as promising and as much like living as any other child, though I had some fears of his passing well through the warm season on account of his being so full and fleshy. I am aware both from experience and long observation that it is a sore bereavement under any circumstances to lose a beloved child, and it is more especially so in losing a first born and only one, the *pledge of mutual love.* And now what shall I say in the way of comfort, consolation and advice? I will undertake to say but little. You are both young and the world is before you, and I trust you have resources within yourselves. You can look to the future with hopes that are denied those in more advanced life. You no doubt will sustain and be far more dependent on each other. Do not sit down quietly and brood over your misfortune or give way to melancholy."

It was several days after the baby's death before Blandie could bring herself to write a note to her mother. It was a short one, for her heart was torn in writing it. On Monday morning, September 15, the letter was delivered to Cornucopia. Julia sat down to answer, but as she said, "I could not command my feelings sufficiently to do so." Finally, the letter was written. "I feel calmer tonight," she wrote, "and trust you have passed the first bitter pangs of grief and are experiencing a ray of calm and quiet resignation. . . . My dear children, this is your first sore, bitter trial in life. I trust there is much happiness in store for you both."

It was Baxter who made the decision to go to Georgia. It was time, he thought, for Blandie to be at Cornucopia. She needed the warmth and love and gaiety of her old home. She acquiesced because it really did not make any difference to her what she did. The fact that another baby was on the way did not seem to comfort her.

But they waited until John and Elizabeth could reach Springfield, because John had requested: "I hope you will not go to Georgia before our return. We expect to come right to your home." And because he could not get little Jack off his mind, he added: "Last night in a vision I saw your dear little boy playing in his mother's arms, in all the health and sprightliness in which I left him. But, alas! On waking I found it all *a mournful delusion.* A dream!"

CHAPTER FIFTEEN

FEBRUARY 2, 1852, WAS A COLD, blustery day, but inside the house at Cornucopia all was sunshine and joy. Blandie had just given birth to a son, and he had been promptly named for his grandfather, Eli Baxter. The Judge was bursting with pride and termed the baby "that cute little rascal."

From Charleston, John Springs, happy over the baby's arrival, was filled with memories when he wrote to Baxter: "Your Mother joins me in congratulations to Blandie and yourself on the happy result of her perilous situation, and hope you may receive consolation in this birth of the second son for the loss of your first, the dear and promising little Jack."

Eight days later, Baxter departed for Springfield. He had been absent from home for nearly four months. He had a lot of catching up to do. One matter required his immediate attention. A group of citizens from York District was urging him to run for the legislature. After giving the matter serious consideration, he consented.

The coming campaign promised to be a spirited one on the national and local level. The chief talk was going to be the Compromise of 1850. There was much debating about the candidate the Democrats would put in the field. No one dreamed at the time that a "dark horse," Franklin Pierce, would be nominated on the 49th ballot and would oppose the Whig candidate, General Winfield Scott.

Baxter plunged into campaigning. He rode to all parts of the District, giving his views on separate secession and the general political picture. His wife admonished him: "Do, dear Bac, take care of yourself and don't ride too much in the hot sun."

Blandie, recuperating at Cornucopia, was fretful to be home. "What beautiful weather!" she wrote. "I feel as if I would go crazy if I can't turn my steps homeward soon. I know you wish me to wait until the train runs to Ebernezer, but if the tracks are not soon completed I must come on anyway." Then she added patheticly: "I wish you would please have Jack's dear little wagon fixed with the rockers for a cradle. I feel very attached to that little wagon as if I never wished (if I gave way to my feelings) it used by anyone else."

Blandie arrived with the baby during the first week of April. The train she was riding puffed into Ebernezer, South Carolina, on tracks that were slowly but surely approaching Charlotte. When she stepped from the train and saw her husband standing there, neatly dressed in his new dark green suit which had recently arrived from his Boston tailor, she tingled to her very toes.

Baxter's campaigning efforts proved effective. York District had one of the greatest turnouts at the polls it had ever had. He led the ticket of those running for the legislature. No one was more pleased than the Judge when he wrote:

"The result of your election was certainly flattering and I hope you will render to the people, who have given you such high evidence of their good opinion and confidence, such service as will increase their confidence and attachment. I am also pleased at the result of the Presidential elections and if General Pierce does not put in his Cabinet that fellow Douglas and that Republican Soule I shall anticipate a good administration of the Government. There was never a time since the first administration of the Government when the country required more sound and conservative men at the head than now. The morals of public men have become loose, if not corrupt."

The Reverend M. Anderson wrote to Baxter: "I believe I can with truth say that South Carolina has never honored any son as she has honored you in placing you by a most handsome vote at the head of her representatives ticket, although you lived in an extreme corner of the District, have never mingled very much with the people generally and had not condescended to the low tricks of the demagogue nor the humiliating system of electioneering usually practiced by candidates for popular favor."

Mr. W. B. Withers of Beatties Ford, North Carolina, had this to say: "I see that you have been directing your attention to politics in addition to your farms. I wish you every success—and mind you, your

State is very excitable and nervous at times—though truly noble—so keep your head cool and calm in all cases of sudden boil. Though the above advice is hardly applicable to you for caution is one of your characteristics handed down from your ancestors."

October 21 of that year of 1852 was the day the first passenger train rolled into Charlotte. John Springs exclaimed, "Huzzaw! We *have* a railroad! I expect in future we will go from Springfield to Charlotte by train. Is it not a great change in the condition of the country?"

All the Springses were present on that eventful day, because they anticipated "frolics and fine doings." They were not disappointed. It was a gala occasion. An estimated crowd of 20,000 jammed the streets of Charlotte, and for a town of little over a thousand in population this was quite a crowd. A band was sent up from Columbia to play for the festivities. A barbecue was served on the lawn of the Female Academy and after dark there was a display of fireworks which preceded a dance.

Immediately after this momentous affair, Baxter and Blandie returned to Springfield and the former made preparations to assume his duties in Columbia. The Governor had called the legislature into session for the first of November. A new Governor was soon to be inaugurated.

This time it was Blandie who was lonely at Springfield and she addressed a letter to her husband at the American Hotel in Columbia and in it was: "I miss you, my dearest Bac, very much, but I try to keep my mind so engaged as not to think of it. Some of the Negroes have been sick. I was in Nancy's house last night until one o'clock. Her baby was very ill with croup, but is better today."

Blandie joined her husband in Columbia in time for the inaugural ball. Fannie came up from Cornucopia for the event, traveling "under the protection of Mr. Alexander Stephens." Bubbling with excitement, Blandie described the ball:

"The Ball I would not have missed for anything. There was a party there, just from Europe, who were vastly entertaining to me. They dressed, acted and talked Parisienne in every word. It consisted of three young ladies, a matron, the mother of one of them, and a widow, sister of the matron. I heard that the widow's dress cost one thousand dollars! I scrutinized her well. Her dress was a pink silk, with three deep flounces of lace, each flounce of lace put over different colored silk flounces, the first pink, next white, next blue. It looked odd and singular enough. Her head was a complete net work of flowers. She was Mrs. Smith and is engaged to the present Governor, Mr. Winston. The most striking of the young ladies was Miss Gardner. She was dressed with exquisite taste. I can not describe her dress. It was odd and new to me. She wore a massive gold necklace and bracelet. She attracted *universal* attention, but her dress was evidently *not admired,* though to me it was beautiful. An old gentleman said to me during the evening that he had been a year in Paris and saw no *naked* bosoms or saddle racks. A saddle was the only thing he could compare her dress to. Miss Winston, another of the ladies, wore a facsimile to Fannie's tull dress, embroidered with straw. It looked very sweetly, but her hair was put straight back as if she were going to bed. Not an ornament or flower about her whole person. That was *too plain* and would not have done for any other than the Governor's daughter. The other lady was more of a *bell* than any of the others. The old dowager was no less striking. Her toilet was very elaborate indeed. She wore a maroon velvet but I haven't time to expatiate on her."

Springfield was covered in sleet and snow when Blandie returned and she felt a great letdown after the social whirl of Columbia. "Oh, my dearest Bac," she wrote plaintively, "I only need your dear self to make all as bright as sunshine, but, my own dearest, I cheer up with the hope that not many days shall pass before I shall be made happy by your presence." Soon it was Christmas and Baxter arrived bringing gifts for all. He had come to the conclusion, he said, that no one in Columbia could surpass his Blandie's "stylish mien and classic air!"

Christmas at Cornucopia was happier than was expected because the Judge arrived from Texas in time to celebrate with his family. Julia Baxter told of his homecoming: "I was out in the yard planting violets and hyacinths when Becca said 'yonder comes Master walkin' down the lane with his red blanket 'bout him!' We all set off to meet him. He had come from Double Wells in a wagon. He is delighted with his trip and is determined to settle his plantation next winter. He is 'brim full' of Texas."

There was no doubt now that the Judge was serious about moving to Texas. Julia realized it, and yet she would not face the fact that she might have to leave Cornucopia. She seemed to be putting it out of her mind. Her next letter to Blandie, dated January 20, said: "The new columns to the front of the house are completed. They look quite city like. I am having a new gate put at the first steps, and Mr. Sharpe is making new windows of large panes of glass for the drawing room and sitting room."

Julia probably knew that she would eventually go to Texas with her husband because her greatest desire was to please him. He always came first in her life. But it was hard to think of leaving the plantation. The little things about it that she adored, her flowers, her boxwoods, her neighbors, her relatives, were very important to her. She would not accept the fact that it was useless to plan her projects, to go on making Cornucopia more beautiful. It was much more pleasant to think of the new, elegant drawing room curtains or the newly built green house across the lawn.

But Texas and Cornucopia were both temporarily forgotten when Blandie wrote that she was to have another baby in August. Would her mother please come up to Springfield? Off Julia went, leaving the Judge to face a momentous decision.

It seemed that Mr. Baxter's term as Judge of the Superior Court was to expire the following year and his friends were wanting to put his name up for Governor. Lizzie was all excited over the idea. "I'll join Ma at Springfield and then return to canvass the state for Pa for Governor," she wrote. Unfortunately, the Judge would not allow his name to be placed in nomination. This had happened before.

When Julia Baxter returned to Cornucopia in March, she thought the place looked so elegant, and the garden had never looked prettier. She decided to give a party. Her description sparkled: "The Spartans came out about half past eleven. I had cake and wine. . . . At one o'clock your Pa came from Wilks Court. At two o'clock Mr. Ponce and Dinas came in one conveyance and Mrs. Ponce with Miss Hernandez, from Cuba, in another. At three we dined. I had quite a variety of everything, beautiful celery, which very few raise in this country, with chicken salad. We had Madeira and domestic wine with the dessert and two bottles of champagne with the fruits. Your Pa has lately got a basket of champagne. I had the cordial stand set on the table with the dessert. Fannie prepared a dish of orange and grated coconut. After dinner Miss Hernandez played a few pieces on the piano. Then came Fannie and Mr. Johnston with their delightful music, he on the flute. Everyone seemed perfectly charmed. Your Pa asked for an old Virginia reel—all laughed. . . . The Wisteria and flowering cherry are in full bloom, and my rock mound has hearts ease on the edge and verbena all over. Everyone admired these very much. . . . Miss Hernandez has the most splendid jewelry and dresses. She wore no bonnet. Said she wished the Americans would adopt the Spanish fashion of wearing no bonnet—only a scarf."

Miss Hernandez created quite a stir in the neighborhood. Even the Judge was captivated by her charm, saying, "She is really clever and entirely without affectation." Elaborate plans were being made for her amusement. Lizzie kept Blandie posted on the details:

"Miss Hernandez is a perfect jewel of the first water. She is the most stylish looking person I have ever seen and makes herself as pleasant and interesting to our country beaux as if they were the 'elegons' of New Orleans. All the young gentlemen of the country have called. Next week is Court week. The week after, Miss Hernandez spends here with us at Cornucopia. Ma says she will get all the young people together and give her a frolic. All of Miss Hernandez's summer muslin dresses are perfectly round waisted with sashes tied in front, fall very low off the shoulders and look as though they had no lining. I will examine them and get the idea! She has a diamond bracelet as large as the palm of my hand. Said 'twas sent her from Spain by some of the 'Aristogue.'"

In May, Julia, packing to go to Augusta for the State Convention, reported that they would stay at the newest hotel, "The Augusta," in spite of the fact that the Judge said there was more "tom foolery" as to service there than at any hotel he had ever seen. Then Julia added in this letter to Blandie: "Your Father's biography* will come out next month. He sent one hundred and ten dollars for the engraving of the likeness. A great swindle, your Pa says."

In the last week of May, the youngest member of the Baxter family, Eli, Jr., having graduated from the Marietta Military Institute, was ready to go north and enter West Point. The morning he left, his mother wept and said, "I regretted we had ever thought of sending him to West Point." But Eli, Jr. certainly did not regret it. Accompanied by Major Brumly from the Institute, he took in the sights of Washington, Philadelphia, and New York en route to the Academy. From the fabulous new St. Nicholas Hotel in New York he, with a humorous eye to his mother's love of decorations, reported: "The dining rooms

*The biography of Judge Eli Harris Baxter was published in *Eminent Americans*, by John Livingston.

are finer furnished than any rooms I ever saw in my life. It will take Ma all the *remainder* of her life to *overtake* the St. Nicholas *dining room,* let alone the *parlor.*"

But what impressed young Eli more than anything else about the hotel was the Bridal Chamber. "It surpasses anything I ever expect to see as long as I live," he wrote. "The man that furnished the room furnished Victoria's room and he says that this is far more fashionable and finer than hers. The cloth that is on the chairs is worth a hundred dollars a yard. The covering for the bed cost a thousand. The whole room cost twenty thousand dollars. It has been used only one time so far. A man had been to California and made five hundred thousand dollars. He came back and married a factory girl. They slept in this room the first night. It cost $150 for the night!"

Julia and the Judge went north that summer of 1853 and vacationed at Saratoga. It was agreed that they would return home by way of Springfield in time to be present at the arrival of Blandie's baby in August.

Meanwhile, Blandie was spending a very quiet summer. The weather was hot but the piazza at Springfield was a pleasant place to relax. She liked to listen to the humming of the darkies as they worked the cotton, up one row and down another. She liked to watch her little son as he toddled about the yard with Betty, his nurse, running after him. In the twilight hours, when all was quiet, she would seat herself at her piano and allow her emotions to express themselves in exquisite music, while Baxter listened with profound admiration.

By August Springfield was in the midst of torrential rains. Everything was flooded. The grass was overtaking the cotton fields. "I am having a time of it," complained Baxter to his father who was in Connecticut, "McAlpin Creek was over the handrails of the bridge. I fear my cotton crop will be poor."

But that was not all that Baxter was fearing. He had a problem that was not unusual to slave holders. He asked his father for advice:

"I gave you intimation when you were with me that certain persons were tampering with my Negroes. I have been ferreting out some of it and the investigation develops conclusively that fact, that I have been feeding for some time past a large and lazy, worthless, white family or gang near me. I have suspected it for some time but have no proof except what some of my Negroes tell me, which you are aware is not sufficient for legal procedure. My design now is to institute at a proper period such means and stratagem as will enable the law to reach them or break them up. Before doing so, however, knowing the malignant spirit and desperate character of their main 'chief and counsellor' had I not better have insured my entire premises. You will remember Bales has always believed his house was burned through spite. I have no other fears in taking any course except some private injury of this character. Could you not affect insurance favorably for me at the North and what are your views regarding it?"

John Springs answered from Stratford, Connecticut:

"It is certainly very aggravating to have a worthless population getting their living off you in a stealthy manner. William Myers thinks he has the same thing going on at his plantation but I think Brevard Davidson likely suffers more than either of you on his Dixon plantation. I advised him to make an example of one of his Negroes, Henry (Arthur's brother), by sending him to Mississippi. I don't believe flogging will stop it. It is difficult to get such testimony as will insure conviction. I have done so three or four times but it is a most unpleasant, exciting, unthankful, unpopular and unprofitable business. Some would be gratified and give you credit for ferreting out villainy, while others would charge you with seeking undue advantages and taking advantages of the necessitious and grinding the poor. Still I think it would be well to procure the testimony and at least hold in terrorum over them and compel them to quit the drive, but if you once commence a prosecution it is not easy to drop it after it reaches the solicitor's hands, and if you take any of them I doubt if anyone so degraded could give security, so would have to go to jail. In that case would advise to take their own single bond of recognisance and before court they would likely cut out and leave that state. I did so in one instance and in that way got clear of the nuisance.

"I never insured any property, and as to my own part would not do so, but if you are determined to do so would prefer the Officers in my own state. I imagine they pay losses promptly. I have no faith in Wall Street people. Would rather rely on William B. Heriot, William Loyd, or William M. Martin of Charleston. But whatever you do, you should act boldly, openly and independently, avoiding what might be unjust or mean, and trust to consequences. A man is not apt to suffer from performing his duty to himself, his family and the community, and those who are so low, degraded and mean do not often have the courage to perform a bold or daring act. As to the loss (although I am aware it is very aggravating) if you take care of your meat and money, your Negroes can not carry off any great amount, especially if they do not use your horses, which you might ascertain by visiting your stables a few times before daylight, in which case you would be justified in punishing severely on detection. I have sometimes thought the most efficient punishment would be to send to Mississippi. Exercise vigilance and patience and you may ferret out the rogues of both colours after a while."

Unfortunately for Baxter, a third problem arose. And this one was far more serious than bridges and floods and stolen food. It came on the heels of the wet weather, which usually brought illnesses. This year it took the form of dysentery. People all over the South were dying. On August 22 Austin reported to his father that all were sick at his place. His overseer was gravely ill. "I do not know," he wrote, "how long I will have enough Negroes to attend the sick here and in the neighborhood."

It was in the midst of this epidemic that Blandie's baby boy was born on Saturday evening, August 21. And she was thankful that her mother and father had arrived from the North in time, because Baxter was in a terrible predicament. Little Eli was taken ill the day after the baby arrived. "It was unfortunate," Baxter said, "on his Mother's account for she could but feel much solicitude about him. And I have besides a very sick family of Negroes. Mary, one of them, I think is doubtful of recovery. She is difficult to restrain or control. Both the Nathans are down. Little Nathan bad. Also Solomon. Tempy, one of Blandie's women, has a high fever. If Northern Abolitionists could only know my fatigue, loss of sleep, anxiety of mind, etc, as well as that of others similarly situated, they might justly conclude that *we* were, bonafide, the slaves."

The Judge did not tarry long at Springfield. He left Julia to entertain Blandie with the stories of their northern trip, which she did hilariously, declaring she was "through with the water" after their rough voyage from New York to Charleston.

John Springs, from Connecticut, wrote his congratulations to Blandie and Baxter and continued: "You asked for suggestions of a name for the baby. I will not suggest a name for the boy. I will say, however, *Leroy* is a name I am rather fond of and you have the names of a number of distinguished characters to choose from. *Andrew* is the old family name as well as *Richard*."

By the time October had rolled around, Baxter felt more relaxed. Blandie and the children were well, and the Negroes had recovered sufficiently to be back at work. Therefore, he hoped he might be able to exhibit some of his prize stock at the Georgia State Fair in Augusta. He asked his father, who was then in New York City viewing the much publicised Crystal Palace, if he would like to go. "Judge and Mrs. Baxter still hope you and Mother will meet them there," he wrote. "I should like to be present, but my business is behind and I do not know yet if I shall be there."

John and Elizabeth went by boat to Charleston and there took the train to Augusta. When they arrived, they found the Baxters, together with Lizzie, Jane, and Dr. Connell. Thousands of visitors were in town. Not a room was vacant anywhere. The streets were crowded with farmers, aristocrats, children, Negroes, horses, carriages, and wagons. A festive spirit had spread through the town.

John Springs arose early the following morning, which was Tuesday, October 18. He dressed with meticulous care, selecting light doeskin trousers, a ribbed silk vest, topped by a black frock coat. After saying good morning to Elizabeth, he descended the stairs of the Planters Hotel, looking hale, hearty and handsome. Following a substantial breakfast, he set out for Hamburg, shunning the omnibus which could have carried him there. He preferred to walk. As he had said many times, "I deem good exercise necessary."

His first stop was at the Bank of Hamburg where he was warmly welcomed by Cyrus Hutchison and John Blackwood.* Several hours were spent in discussing business and going over the profits of the bank.

As noon approached, the gentlemen left the bank and walked one mile to a barbecue, where a great crowd had gathered to celebrate the opening of the Fair. Here John was the center of attention among the men who were eager to have some news from the North on the slavery question.

What did John think, they asked him, about the impending crisis? What did he think would be the effects in the North of the exaggerated accounts of the evils of the slavery system as recorded in the much talked about *Uncle Tom's Cabin* which that woman from Cincinnati had written? What did she, a Yankee, know about the South anyway? How did John think the South was going to regain its bal-

*John Blackwood married Laura Springs, daughter of Tirzah and Eli Springs.

ance of power with the free states? Did he believe there would be war with Spain over Cuba? And what about all this talk of the organization of the two territories of Kansas and Nebraska? Would the Missouri Compromise be repealed?

No doubt about it, John Springs had a good audience that day, and no doubt about it, he gave his views eloquently and frankly.

Late in the afternoon he was driven back to the hotel by friends. He had not realized he was tired until he was suddenly exhausted. When the carriage stopped in front of the hotel he found Elizabeth seated on the upper piazza with the Baxter ladies, all dressed in their prettiest silk dresses. He bowed to them and entered the hotel. Slowly he climbed the stairs. Strange, he had not noticed that morning how steep and long they were. But he would soon be in his room where a servant would be waiting to bring hot water for his bath. Maybe he would have his tea in his room and not go down again. He would send his apologies to Elizabeth and his cousins. A depleting exhaustion came over him, so profound that his legs weakened under him. And he was hot, terribly hot.

That night John became ill. He sent for Dr. Connell who pronounced his trouble "billious fever." Elizabeth and the Doctor thought he would be all right, but before day light John sent his servant to awaken Elizabeth. When she entered his room she had a great feeling of alarm. As she afterwards wrote, she "apprehended the worst." She found him "labouring under distressing sick stomach, with considerable fever." At once, she sent for Dr. Connell who prescribed six grains of calomel in broken doses. On Wednesday he was as well as could be expected. Elizabeth sat with him until eleven o'clock that night. At midnight she sent for the Doctor. By the time Dr. Connell arrived John was delirious with little or no use of his legs. Elizabeth frantically asked the Doctor to call in another physician, which he did, but that Doctor made no sure suggestion, only recommended morphine. John would not swallow anything. By morning it was very evident that he was no better. Elizabeth asked for a third physician. When he arrived all three Doctors consulted. A large dose of quinine was recommended, with a blister between the shoulders. It was then one o'clock. John seemed not quite so useless and not so delirious. But still he said nothing. He moaned.

Elizabeth slipped quietly out of the room and telegraphed Columbia to send word to Baxter at Springfield by way of an open note to come at once. Word came back that the wires were out of order.* She sat down and hastily wrote to Baxter: "I think him very seriously ill but hope for the best. Send word to Sophia, Leroy and Austin that your Father is down gravely ill. Do come on without delay. He is very anxious for you to come. He has every attention. We are at the Planters Hotel, the best in the city. . . . Your Father brought on his sickness, I think, by fatigue."

John moaned softly as if he were dreaming. He was dreaming. His life, like a river, stretched behind and before him. The abundance of it all, his passion for truth and knowledge, his ambitions and love for his children, his dedication to his home and his country, his love for his dearest Mary, the tenderness he felt for Elizabeth, all this seemed to ebb and flow as his consciousness came and went. He knew, jut as his heart knew, that now the time had come and yet he had no words to express himself. He tried, but the words would not come. He could not hear his voice. He was grateful to them all. Somehow he must let them know this. Especially he wanted Baxter to know. And Elizabeth too. Did he hear her voice? Yes, through the shadows there came her voice. "Johnny," she said.

That was good. He would rest now. He closed his eyes.

John was dead.

John Springs, Esquire, master of Springfield, was dead.

At five o'clock on the afternoon of October 21, the telegrapher at Columbia took down a message coming over the Washington and New Orleans Telegraph line. It read:

"For the President or Agent of Charlotte R. R. Mr. John Springs of York District died this morning. His remains will be forwarded to Columbia by tomorrow Saturday's train. Can an extra train be furnished on Sunday morning to convey him to Charlotte. (signed) Eli Baxter."

The following morning, Baxter Springs received a dispatch which read:

Columbia, Oct. 22, 1853

My dear Sir,

The enclosed dispatch will convey melancholy tidings for you. It

---

*The first telegraph line was completed in 1844 between Washington and Baltimore in time to carry the news that Polk was nominated.

came last night. I will have a train ready to start up with the funeral party in the morning. Sympathizing with you in your bereavement, I remain

Yours truly

W. M. Stockton

On Saturday evening the body of John Springs arrived in Columbia, the town which had seen him rise and speak calmy but constructively before the South Carolina Legislature; the town which had watched him exhibit some of the finest specimens of stock the upper country had ever seen; the town which had watched him promote and increase the banking interests of not only that city but the entire State.

It was right that John Springs' body should be carried over the Charlotte-Columbia railroad, a project he had worked on so industriously and supported so wholeheartedly, being one of its largest individual subscribers. And it was right that his body should pass slowly by the fields and forests of Springfield, and finally come to rest in the cemetery back of the Presbyterian Church* in Charlotte where he was an elder for so many years. All this was fitting, as were the lengthy newspaper columns throughout the South that paid tribute to him. But the greatest tribute was written by his son on the back of the last letter John had written to Baxter from New York. One simple sentence. "This letter stands in the sad relation of being the last from an affectionate Father to his son."

It was natural that Baxter and Blandie named their new baby *John Springs*.

---

*John Springs' body was later moved to Elmwood Cemetery in Charlotte.

CHAPTER SIXTEEN

CORNUCOPIA IN NOVEMBER OF 1853 was a beehive of activity. Julia and the Judge were preparing to leave for Texas. It was agreed that they would both go out, establish a residence, get the plantation started and return to Georgia in the spring. Julia expressed it this way: "We can use our Texas home to go to for variety." Never did she admit or dwell on the possibility that she might someday live there permanently.

The Judge's nephew Andrew Baxter was going, too, taking his wife and children with him. The two families planned to travel together.

Fannie Baxter wrote to Blandie on November 10: "We are in such a vein of hard work. Ma is really over run with work, not that she has more to do than usual but a shorter space to do it in. The Negroes start to Texas the last of this month. Four Negro women are hard at work to get them equipped in time. I fear you will have a fatiguing trip getting here with your little ones."

Baxter brought Blandie and the children to Cornucopia for a two-weeks visit. Blandie found it difficult to reconcile herself to her parents going so far from home. "The very thought of Texas is anything but pleasure to me," she said. John Springs' sudden death had made her realize the unexpectedness with which tragedy can strike. It was like Jane Connell had said, "Verily we may exclaim 'What shadows we are and what shadows we pursue.' "

Eli Baxter was having his problems. Every Negro who was going to Texas wanted his or her mate to go, and sometimes this meant buying those Negroes from adjoining plantations. One man, forty-five years old, had to be bought at a cost of nine hundred dollars.

Blandie had a delightful visit. "I scarcely have time to do anything," she said. "Guests are coming all the time. Last evening we had company until twelve o'clock. . . . Ma pets little Eli so much I fear we will have no control over him." On the last day of November, Blandie and the children departed. They rode in the carriage as far as Double Wells, the nearest railroad stop. As usual, Baxter had preceded them, rushing home to attend to business, so they made the train trip to Springfield alone.

The night before the Baxters departed, Julia wrote to Blandie: "All's ready. The trunks are packed and I feel really bound for Texas. All in the house are asleep except myself. I must say goodbye to you and Baxter, also my darling boys. I miss little Eli very much when I go out to the store room. He was always after me. I received your note from Double Wells. How rejoiced I shall be to get letters from you in Texas."

True to her word, Julia kept her family well informed of every detail of the trip to Texas. "On our arrival at Atlanta," she wrote, "it was raining torrents and we all ran a hundred yards to the La Grange cars in inch deep water. I sat near the stove but my feet were wet until our arrival in Montgomery after dark. Montgomery is a beautiful place. The town is very gay. The ladies are dressed magnificently, with embroidered coverings. We are in delightful quarters, waiting for the Alabama Steam Boat which leaves tomorrow evening. Mr. Allen and the wagons reached here Friday, all well and gay. Henry and all went to the boat yard. Henry said, 'Master, don't let them put me in the boat with all them bales of cotton. They'll never find me alive.' All the Negroes send 'howdy.' . . . We hear the cholera is in New Orleans and my heart sinks within me when I think we are going in the midst of it. . . . Cousin William Ogbourne came in to inquire for us. He sent his carriage in and we went out in the afternoon. He lives in beautiful style."

On December 14 the Baxters were on board the Steam Boat *Mobile*. "We sailed from Montgomery Monday evening," Julia explained, "in the greatest excitement and bustle I ever witnessed. The boat caught fire last night, but it was extinguished before the women and children knew it, or we would have had a scene. Fifteen families are on board, all bound for Texas, besides hundreds of immigrants and a thousand bales of cotton. The Captain seems to think we need not fear cholera in New Orleans. A Physician on board this boat was taken sick yesterday. He said it was cholera and left the boat at a little town on the river.

It created alarm and excitement, particularly among the Negroes and immigrants.

"The steam boat is very large, fine accomodations. Fruit and fish of all kinds is forbidden on account of the cholera. We expect to arrive in New Orleans Friday morning and leave there Saturday afternoon. . . . All the Negroes keep well and hearty. Ivan is employed to wait on the table. Jim was also engaged, but Henry slipped in the dining room to wait on table too and the Captain dismissed them both forthwith. Jim's little boy strayed off to some other Negroes just before leaving Montgomery and could not be found for an hour or more. Jim ran about like a mad man in a rage."

New Orleans might have been visited by cholera and Julia might have meant it when she said her heart sank when she thought of going in its midst, but she saw New Orleans nevertheless. She hired the chambermaid at the hotel for a guide and, taking her niece Mattie Baxter with her, she procured a carriage and rode all over the city. Meanwhile, Judge Baxter was buying provisions to be loaded on the *Mary Bess*, the boat which would take them up the Mississippi and Red rivers to Alexandria, Louisiana.

Julia and Mattie soon found themselves on the main street of the city. "Just at the corner," Julia wrote, "was a milliner's shop. I gazed in admiration and thought I had never seen anything so splendid, even in New York. We passed on from shop to shop until we reached a china store. I could scarcely get away. . . . At sunset we returned to the boat and found a worse crowd than on the Alabama. Human beings were like bees over the boat. There were twenty families. Of all the medley of children, maids, etc.—I never could have imagined such a motley crew. The children got to fighting——"

Then in a plaintive tone, Julia added: "I never feel faint hearted about going to Texas only when I think of my children and grandchildren. When my thoughts reach West Point I feel a 'nothingness' come over me which is only relieved by tears."

The Steam Boat *Mary Bess* was nearing Alexandria on December 18 when Julia continued her letter: "We have very comfortable berths and a dandy of a Captain. He said I should have brought my daughters as young ladies are scarce in Texas. The table excels any steam boat at the North, quite as good as the steamers between Charleston and New York. Pa praises the good eating all the time. Says I have fattened twenty pounds.

"I have been perfectly charmed and delighted with the beautiful improvements on the banks of the Mississippi River. We are never out of sight of sugar plantations—one continuous village, the most beautiful yards of shrubbery, groves of orange trees loaded with fruit, just on the bank of the river. We saw a magnificent college and large convent for the education of young ladies. Some of the private residences are most beautiful. Colonades all around. It is decidedly the finest improved country I have ever traveled through. My trip on the Mississippi and Red rivers is worth six months seclusion in Texas. So far I have been highly gratified, *not withstanding* I have had to wait on sick Negroes.

"Feb is sick but out of danger. Maria has had a very severe attack of croup, the worst I ever saw. Your Pa and I have been doctoring her every day. She would have died without our attention. In fact your Pa has had to quarrel and almost fight to get the Negroes made more comfortable on these boats. They are crammed and jammed down in the bottom of the boat with all sorts of dirty people. Feb says to tell Sarah and Mac she 'helt' out mighty well on land but the water scares her. Jerry cried like a child today about Maria. All the other Negroes are well and very much delighted. They come out on the lower deck in the day time and sing and dance. Edmond is one of the merriest and Peyton is always in a broad grin. Henry is ready to say something funny every time I see him. They often say, 'Miss, tell them all howdy at home when you write.' "

The following day the *Mary Bess,* after a week on the rivers, docked at Alexandria. It was pandemonium. There were at least fifty dogs on board, all barking and scrambling to get on shore. The passengers were in a hurry. The Negroes and mules were coming off the boat. Cotton was being shifted on the dock, ready to be loaded.

That afternoon the Baxters pitched tents, made a camp and spent the night. They boiled a ham, broiled sausages, ate heartily and "all was life and animation, singing and rejoicing in the divers camps." That is, all were happy except Mattie Baxter. She was pouting. The prospects of riding in a wagon were dreary indeed to her. She wanted Andrew to buy her a carriage. But when Julia said she was going in a wagon, Andrew said Mattie could do the same. Finally, unable to withstand his wife's anger, he weakened and bought her a sort of Jenny wagon at forty dollars. Mattie called it a hearse. However, this broke down the second day, and Mattie moved back to the wagon.

The Judge was able to buy a side saddle for Julia so that she rode horse back part of the way, and of course, wherever it was possible, they all rode the stagecoach.

Mattie seemed to look on the dark side of the whole business. "She was astonished," said Julia, "at my cheerfulness and at my talking to the ladies on the boat, because they were plain people."

Julia's description of their trip from Alexandria to Cherokee City, Texas, was in great detail. She wrote:

"The first day we left Alexandria, we traveled twenty two miles through a very beautiful country, large fields of sugar cane. The Negroes commenced eating. Your Pa soon stopped them for fear it would make them sick. We passed a number of beautiful flower yards, mostly shrubbery. One attracted me so I sprang out of the wagon and went in the yard. There was a cypress as tall as a Lombardy poplar. The lady and her son came out, told me the name of the cypress. It had been brought from Cuba many years since. I got some cuttings and made the young man promise to send me some seed in a letter. That afternoon it commenced sleeting, blowing and then raining. We slept and ate supper at a Mr. Henderson's, a large brick hotel, very good (no flour bread). He told us frightful tales of the cholera. Said the sugar plantations were the main cause, and the Negroes over eating. Our Negroes slept in a large school house that night.

"After the first day's travel, we passed almost a wilderness country to Sabin River, which we crossed Christmas day. We expected to have crossed it the evening previous but we encountered the worst roads in the world, and it rained some every day. Yet your Pa never took the slightest cold. One night it rained several hours. The tents kept us dry and, strange as it may seem, we slept well. We had a feather bed unpacked on which we slept every night. I never had such an appetite in my life. We broiled as many birds every night as we could eat. Partridges were in abundance. We purchased butter and lived on the fat of the land. The Negroes kept up their laughing and singing all day. Henry often blew his horn.

"On our arrival in Sabin Town your Pa and I dressed and went to Mr. Austin's store (Sunday). He is your Father's agent and insisted upon us going to his house to pass the night. We did so. I had heard Dr. Connell speak of Mrs. Austin. Well, I found her a perfect lady. We entered a very pretty flower yard, large Cape Jasimines, orange trees and grape arbor. In the house all looked like comfort and, I may say, elegance. The parlor was well furnished and had a grand piano. Mr. Austin's Mother was extremely pleasant; loaned me a cap when I took off my bonnet. But when we were asked in to supper I opened my eyes wide. Silver forks, rich silver doily rings and everything to correspond. There were jellies, etc., a pair of wild duck dressed most deliciously and a dish of fresh broiled venison. You may guess we ate a hearty supper. Had a pleasant, comfortable bed, etc. The next morning Mrs. Austin had a delightful breakfast. She gave me a venison dried ham and some sausages to take with us. As we travelled along, every person knew 'old Colonel Daniel Richardson.'*

"I must tell you of Henry meeting his father, 'Georgia Phill.' Phill gave Henry six silver dollars—offered him a gold piece but fool Henry would not take that 'brass money.' Several of the old Georgia Negroes came out to talk to ours.

"We took the stage to Sabine and stopped at Mr. Sexton's. Spent the day of the 27th there. Mrs. Sexton had a dinner party that day. Large fat turkey and everything. She is a real piece of affectation, rather pretty, favors Blandie. We stopped for part of a day at San Augustine. We passed a night with Mr. Polk, your Pa's kin, five miles this side of San Augustine.

"We arrived here yesterday afternoon. Found a beautiful level country, but rather a poor prospect as regards good houses or pretty yards. The house we are in is a comfortable, double hewed log cabin. There is a shelf on which I put the books and divers little things. We have one chair, which we borrowed. We found a sort of camp meeting bedstead on which we placed our feather bed and I assure you we slept as if on 'downey pillows,' after camping out ten days.

"Today we are all astir. Caesar is busy making little benches, shelves, etc. The wagon has gone to the saw mill—your Pa with it. Some of the Negro men are at a neighbors to kill some hogs. The other wagon is preparing to go to Alto for salt which is five dollars a sack. They will also get nails, etc. Of all the many families in our company on the trip, we are the only ones who have kept in good health. This is entirely owing to your Father's direction and management. . . . He begs me to keep cheerful and not to think of home."

Julia did try to make the best of her situation in Texas, but a month had not passed before she wrote: "It is said 'variety is the spice of life.' This variety, I think, has lost its spice. . . . The Negroes say I am glad

*Julia Richardson Baxter's brother.

to look at the stage as it passes. They will call one to another and say, 'Tell Miss the stage is coming.' The stage has two pairs of fine matches. I often think of Lizzie. You know her passion for fine horses. Our stage driver is from North Carolina. Says he knows all the Springs family by character, that they are 'mighty clever and well off.' Who of us could convey more meaning and sense in fewer words?"

The Texas plantation was named, of all things, *Cornucopia.* "The name is totally inapplicable at present," wrote the Judge, "but it is a compliment to my old home where I raised all my children and where I spent so many pleasant hours."

To create a home out of a log cabin was a new experience for Julia. But she tried anyway. She made mattresses. She planted roses in the yard, around which the Negroes had built a fence. She had the Judge buy a milk cow with calf so they could have butter. She bought chickens so there would be fresh eggs. The Negroes went hunting for birds, deer, rabbits, and 'possum.

When the month of May had rolled around, a new house was almost completed. It would be ready for the Baxters when they came again. It was time to return to Georgia. But it was the end of June before Julia and the Judge passed through Marietta on their way home. "I did not think they looked well," said Jane Connell sadly.

During the summer of 1854, Baxter Springs was running again for the South Carolina Legislature. As far as politics were concerned, the country was becoming more distracted each day. Men were slowly exhausting every means of accomplishing any amicable adjustment of their difficulties. Would the South, with its Negroes and plantations, win out or would the North with its industries rule the nation?

Stephen A. Douglas, senator from Illinois, had introduced a bill in the United States Senate which provided for the organization of the two teritories of Kansas and Nebraska. His bill advocated the end of prohibition of slavery in those territories and left that question to be decided by the settlers themselves. With the passage of this bill, the Missouri Compromise was in reality repealed and the North felt it must fight to keep slavery from spreading over the West. One result of the passage of this Kansas-Nebraska act was that the Whigs and Free-Soil Democrats joined hands with anti-slavery forces and formed the Republican party. There was a rush to settle Kansas by both slave holders and those hostile to slavery. A period of violence between the two factions followed. All the while the tempers of South Carolinians rose higher and higher, and there was more and more talk of secession.

Baxter, still opposed to withdrawing from the Union, had certain factions working against him, trying to defeat him in the election. And defeat him they did. But there would be other campaigns and other years. He would win another time.

Blandie was almost glad Baxter had lost the election. She was having another baby in February and it was a comfort to have her husband near her as much as possible. Due to her condition she had postponed a proposed trip to Cornucopia to see her parents. Instead, she had sent them a small deguerrotype of the children, showing Johnnie sitting on nurse "Aunt Betty's" lap while little Eli stood beside her. The picture created quite a commotion the day it arrived. "Nothing of the kind has ever produced such excitement in this house," wrote Julia. "Your cousin James was the first to get sight of them. He shouted so loud everybody (Negroes and all) ran to see what in the world it was. So we all exclaimed aloud and made a great fuss. Eli's likeness I think very good—and old Betty's can't be beat. Johnnie has grown very much. Now I am more anxious to have them than ever. You and Baxter must just 'pack up' and come along."

To have a serious discussion with her Father was one reason Blandie had wanted to visit Cornucopia. She worried about her Mother. There was still talk of selling the plantation. Was this the reason the enthusiasm had vanished recently from her Mother's letters? Why did the place have to be sold? She put the question directly to her Father in a letter. He answered:

"In reference to the sale of Cornucopia, I think your views and comments are like the other children. I, too, am attached to it, in fact I love the old place as one of my children, but we have to separate before a long time and therefore it would be wiser to make it when it would be more advantageous. Its cultivation can not be profitable. The fields have become exhausted. I have no new lands to clear to relieve the old. This year I will make plenty of corn, but I will not make more cotton than will pay the overseer. . . . We have but little of the company of our children. Lizzie and Fannie are away from home a great deal of the time, and when we have none of our children with us the place seems lonely and desolate."

In October Julia expressed herself to her daughter: "Blandie, the thought of going to Texas without seeing you almost crazes me. If you can't come here, I must go to your house." And so Julia journeyed to Springfield with something of desperation in her heart. She dreaded her second trip to Texas. However, Julia Richardson Baxter was a very remarkable woman. She would not persuade her husband to give up Texas, since that was what he really wanted, so she accepted it and made the best of it. That was why the Judge was able to report from the Steam Boat *William Jones,* on the Alabama River, November 18: "Julia had a great deal of reluctance in leaving on a *Friday,* but so far everything has turned out well. She is in fine spirits. The crowd is gay, which just suits her."

But Julia was right about Friday being an unlucky day. She explained why to Blandie:

"Your Father *would* set off on Friday and all the bad luck has come on him. On board the Steam Boat was a man with delirium tremens. Your Pa attempted to feel his pulse— (just like your Pa) —the crazy man mistook him for a person with whom he had had a quarrel. So he took a chair and knocked your Pa on the head, cut a small gash. The blood flowed as if an artery had been cut. Eli was near and seized the man, telling him it was his father. The man knew your Father in Georgia as he was from Atlanta, but in his crazy feelings did not recognize him. He fell on his knees and wept, begged pardon a thousand times. As soon as I heard of it of course I was much excited, so altogether we had quite a scene. A physician examined and dressed your Father's wound. Said it would be well in a day or two. I kept it tied up a day and night."

The Baxters remained in Texas for five months and this was the extent of their bad luck for that season. When they were ready to return to Georgia, Julia confided to Blandie: "We expect to ride to Alto and make some farewell calls. I would not care much if they were 'farewell' for a long, long time."

With his active political career at a temporary standstill, Baxter Springs concentrated on other matters, and one of those was the settling of his father's estate. He and William Myers were co-executors according to the will. On October 24 (1854), William sent a note from Charlotte down to Springfield: "Please bring up with you next week the little black trunk of your Father's. All the legatees will be

here at that time. We must try to divide the stocks and bonds at least."
Settling the estate would take time. There was half a million dollars
to be divided.

Several banks, Hamburg and Chester among them, had asked Baxter
to become a Director. John Blackwood was only one of the bankers
who said: "We look to you to take your Father's place in our
meetings."

Life now was becoming more complicated for Baxter as far as business matters were concerned. He was being called away from home
more and more often. Besides the bank meetings, there were meetings
to discuss railroads, mills, insurance companies, agricultural affairs
and State Militia. Blandie understood that all these demanded much
of his time. "My home has many charms," she wrote to him, "though
the greatest charm of my heart is absent. I think of you often, my dear
husband, and long for your return. Yet I know I can't always have you
by me. For us to prosper you must attend to business and perhaps be
called away often from home."

February 9 (1855) was the day Blandie's baby arrived. A tiny, black-
haired girl! Lizzie and Fannie had come up from Cornucopia to help
usher the little one into the world. And Sophia had come down from
Charlotte the day after. So the reception committee was large and
enthusiastic. And because the baby was named Julia, there was great
enthusiasm in Texas too! "I feel quite complimented that the little
girl is called for me," wrote the proud grandmother. "I shall expect
to see a perfect beauty! You say her complexion is sallow. The more
saffron like and yellow the skin the first month, the more fair and
beautiful will be the complexion afterwards."

When the Baxter sisters left Springfield they took little Eli with
them to Cornucopia. In April, Fannie reported that the child was
running around the plantation with all the Negroes spoiling him and
"taking care not to let him tumble down the stairs. Harriet and Becca
have walked after him all day. Rose will be his regular nurse."

"We had a rich scene," she said, "with Eli last Tuesday when Dr.
Connell's brother came out. Eli took a tremendous fancy to him,
would climb in his lap and jabbered at him incessantly. Mr. Connell
asked him if his Father drank, to which the little fellow replied, 'Yes,
Farder drinks water, Johnny drinks brandy and I drink toddy.'

"When I asked Eli what his Mother would say to him when she
came, he answered, 'She will say *good morning!!*' He is a little tiger.

I think you will not find him very much subdued, on the contrary, very effectually *spoilt*. We go on the principle of improving his health, not his manners or temper!"

Great plans were being made for a family reunion to honor the homecoming of the Judge and Julia, but the Baxters were having difficulty getting home because of low water on the Red River. Julia was once again showing her good sense of humor when she explained the reason for their delay:

"We are here on the Red River, twenty miles below Alexandria at a place called 'Sraggy Point' *stuck* fast in the sand, where we have been for the last twenty four hours. The river is *extremely* low—and 'tis said misery loves company. There are three other boats in sight of us, all in the same fix. The passengers are visiting from the different boats. This, the *Rapides*, is a very large, fine boat, magnificently furnished and every luxury the earth affords on the table. A number of pleasant ladies on board, also some agreeable gentlemen. My husband is dressed out in white pants, buff vest, shiney boots and is playing the agreeable in the ladies saloon—something a little unusual for him. If my face were not Georgia bound and I anxious to see my dear children and little ones, I would be as happy as the case would permit of. Mrs. Sexton and Eli amuse themselves a great deal at the backgammon box. James Skinner keeps just enough brandy in his head to make him extremely polite. Mr. Sexton and I put on a little dignity for the respectibility of the party.

"From our plantation in Texas to Alexandria we had a very pleasant journey, being in our own carriage and traveling leisurely. The first day we dined at Capt. Wolf's, which is a most charming family. . . . The next day we spent in Nacogdoches at Col. Raguets. . . . Court was being held there and all the 'big bugs' were there with an eye to politics. By arrangement, General Rusk and General Houston were to make speeches the day we chanced to pass, and we were highly gratified at hearing them both. General Rusk spoke in very good taste, though it did not strike me as being remarkable in any way. But 'old Sam' (as he is called in Texas) far excelled my expectations, not from oratory or deep intellect, but his overflow of mannerisms, sarcasm, wit and new fangled words. For instance, he called Abolitionism 'negro-ology.' General Green, he styled 'General Tom Jefferson Dog Green.' He commented largely on Texas Rail Roads. Said he did not know that he would ever ride on a railroad in Texas but would be thankful if they did not *ride him* on a rail. There is great excitement now about his being a candidate for the Presidency. A party of young men in San Augustine drew up some resolutions against the old General. He styled them 'two year old yearlings, scarcely old enough to be marked, and not worthy of being branded.' His speech all together was very amusing and his dress rather singular for an Orator—blue gingham summer coat, blue checked vest, and on the little finger of one hand he wore an immense diamond ring sent him by the Pope of Rome for his protection to the Catholic religion in Texas. On the other hand he wore three very large rings with sets the size of a ten cent piece. Whenever he was a little sentimental, placing his hand on his breast, the rings made quite a display. I was introduced to the General and had some conversation with him. He desired to be particularly remembered to my daughter, Blandie."

Cornucopia was literally running over with adults and children when Julia Baxter, Eli Baxter, Jr., and the Judge arrived the latter part of June, bringing with them the Frank Sextons from Texas. Baxter Springs, typical of this increasingly busy man, had deposited his family and hurried away to attend to business. Dr. Connell accompanied Jane and their children, Alva, Jr., Baxter, and Mary Julia, to Cornucopia. Lizzie and Fannie had everything in readiness. There were dinner parties, with the neighbors and Spartans coming out in full force. The neighboring Ponces gave elaborate entertainments, and so did the Greens and Richardsons. And of course there were always the proverbial political conclaves, because the local Know-Nothing party* members were just waiting and itching for the Judge's return so he could help them campaign in the up-coming election. In fact, they insisted that he run for the state legislature.

"They are anxious for Pa to say he is a Know-Nothing," wrote Blandie to Baxter. "Many people in Sparta want to know his views. I think Pa takes a very sensible view of it. He says he won't or doesn't belong to the order but thus far he agrees with them in their efforts to prevent immigrants from coming to this country for the 160 acres

---

*The Know-Nothing party actually began as early as 1830 at a time when Irish immigration was increasing steadily. The foreign immigrants, particularly the Irish, critisized our American institutions. Many secret organizations, thinking this criticism un-American, formed the basis of the Know-Nothing party, which derived its name from the fact that none of its members ever knew anything when questioned. They supported candidates of other parties but never gave public endorsements. They fought public aid to Catholic schools and opposed the great power the Irish had captured in politics. In 1854 they changed their name to the *American party* and ceased to be secretive.

of land Congress has voted them. He says he doesn't want to prevent them from coming, only not to give them any inducement. The Know-Nothings are two to one in this county and a reliable member of the party told me that if Pa had been in the State he would have been nominated for Governor."

Blandie, being a most feminine creature, adoring admiration, added teasingly to her letter: "Everyone is remarking that I look as well as I did before I was married. So you see, old man, you were right as you always are." Then she wrote: "Johnnie and Eli came in today with their faces flushed. Pa looked at them and said they were such fine looking boys he wished your Father could have lived to have seen them now."

Before the summer was over, the Judge was in the midst of a very hot political campaign, as was Dr. Connell, each running on opposite sides of the ticket. "Pa was waited on," explained Fannie to Blandie after the Springses had departed from Cornucopia, "by a committee of Know-Nothings from Sparta, begging him to go in tomorrow and make them a speech. There will be a great meeting there. Furthermore, they wish Pa to allow them to nominate him for Congress. Brother Eli is almost crazy for Pa to accept the nomination. I don't know how it would suit Pa to go to Washington now, because of his business, but I feel if I were a statesman like Pa and had judgement and influence like he had I would make it a matter of conscience to respond to the call of the people on so momentous an occasion."

Great excitement prevailed the day of the speech-making. "Men, women and children applauded, hooped and yelled," explained Julia Baxter. "I really felt nervous. However, there were no fights. Fannie laughed with all her might and main at the people applauding. Everybody is raving crazy! Your Pa's speeches have pleased the people so much he is sent for everywhere to speak for the party. I will try to get the newspaper pieces from the Chronicle and Sentinel and send you. They were so overwhelmingly complimentary."

The judge won his seat in the legislature. Dr. Connell lost his by twelve votes.

But all thought of elections and speeches soon passed from the minds of the Baxters and the Springses, because little ten-months-old Julia Springs, always a delicate baby, became gravely ill. Dr. J. M. Strong attended her daily. Finally, the child rallied sufficiently for Baxter to meet pressing business engagements in Columbia.

"Bac dear," wrote Blandie, "dear little Julia is still better. Dr. Strong said to tell you if he had known you had business in Columbia he would have told you you could go with all safety, so I hope, Bac dear, you will make yourself easy and come when it suits you."

Baby Julia might have seemed better but her condition suddenly worsened. On November 17 she died.

CHAPTER SEVENTEEN

CHRISTMAS IN THE YEAR OF 1855 was not the gay celebration that it usually was at Springfield. No one had any spirit for entertainment. Baby Julia's death had cast a great cloud of depression over the household. Baxter had his usual gifts of clothes and money for the Negroes. He ordered oranges, raisins, and almonds from Columbia. A home-made rocking horse for Eli and Johnnie was made by the slaves and was a delight to the boys.* This was about the extent of Christmas. It was a rather sad affair.

Like his father had done before him, Baxter Springs found his solace in work. He expanded his agricultural program by planting a new orchard and by producing more small grain—rye, barley, and wheat—for the market. He added more full-blooded cattle and was shipping his calves all over the state. He wrote articles for the newspapers concerning his views on agricultural improvements. He was involved in politics. He became more and more interested in railroading, for everywhere enthusiasm was unbounded for this great new method of getting places and for making money. He began to question the wisdom of planting so much cotton when the railroad, running through the lands of Springfield, could haul small grain and cattle to market.

Work, coupled with the joy of being with his wife and sons, was healing Baxter's sore spirits caused by the death of his baby daughter. Not so with Blandie. She was completely crushed. A calmness settled over her but it was the calmness of resignation and despair. There was a somberness about her life now. The old gaiety and flamboyancy was gone.

They sat together for tea in the late afternoons, Blandie and Baxter,

*This rocking horse is now being used by the fourth generation of Springses.

and they sorted their memories just as Blandie often sorted her little Julia's clothes. They reminisced and then calmly they planned for the future. There must be plans because Blandie was going to have another baby. Would she remain at home or should she go to Cornucopia? She decided she would remain at Springfield.

It was at this time that Baxter began a new project, one which would keep his wife occupied and entertained. The house at Springfield had stood for fifty years without major repairs. It was beginning to show its age. The majestic columns which adorned the front of the house were deteriorating. Baxter engaged Mr. Jacob Graves, a Columbia architect, to come up, survey the situation and draw up a plan.

Mr. Graves suggested doing away with the tall columns, lowering the porch roof and supporting it with a series of smaller, Ionic columns. A wrought iron balustrade would surround the porch. A nursery, with a bathroom, and a new pantry would be added. Baxter and Blandie agreed to the new plans and soon a band of carpenters descended upon the house. All was noise and confusion, decisions to be made, colors to be selected, and plans made for new furniture, draperies, and carpets.

And thus it was that Blandie, unconsciously, eventually found solace in work, just as Baxter had done.

Early in 1856, Baxter announced his candidacy for the South Carolina legislature in a letter to the *Yorkville Citizen*. The editor of the *Yorkville Enquirer*, the other county seat paper, also endorsed him. One of the most explosive issues of the time was "Bleeding Kansas," over which both anti-slavery and slavery men armed and finally fought. The *Enquirer* editor, John S. Miller, told Baxter: "Write me a letter on the necessity of the South aiding Kansas and I'll publish it. I am heartily tired of these dreamy abstractions and idle speculations as to the probably beneficial results of this or that line of policy. The Kansas battle is worthy of our steel. We can there meet Yankee Abolitionists as Southerners should meet them, with sword in hand. In fact I can not but regard the people of Kansas and the 'border ruffians' as solving the great problem of our existance, as slave states."

The issue centered on whether Kansas should be a slave or free State. It threatened to split the heart of the nation, and finally led to Civil War.* Southerners maintained that the United States Constitu-

---

*President Woodrow Wilson, in his *Proper Perspective of American History*, written while a Princeton University professor, commented: "Kansas shows us that the problem was not South Carolina."

tion with its provision protecting personal property gave them the right to settle in Kansas with their slaves. Northern Abolitionists collected funds in churches to buy guns to arm the anti-slavery element. Fanatical John Brown butchered pro-slavery settlers at Osawattomie in the first real bloodshed. The South then sent funds to arm its people. Baxter and A. Whyte of Rock Hill solicited contributions in their area. "I have deep interest," said Baxter, "in the struggle for Kansas to maintain her rights and her triumph over abolitionism, fanaticism, villainy and outlawry and fully appreciate the issue as alike important to themselves and the South generally."

Congress had to take up the question, had to take sides. To do so meant many bitter debates in which tempers flared. Could Congress prohibit slavery in a territory belonging to the Union? Was the Missouri Compromise constitutional? These questions would be settled finally by the Supreme Court in its Dred Scott decision. The South, in winning the decision, felt that she had a legal right to her position. Only an amendment to the Constitution could change this. But the North refused to accept the decision of the Supreme Court.

Amid the excitement of collecting funds for Kansas and the noise of the carpenters' hammering, Blandie gave birth to her baby on June 10 (1856). Mrs. John Springs, writing to Blandie from Wilmington, North Carolina, gave a picture of what happened: "I send a hearty greeting to the little stranger who, it seems, was in such a haste to make his appearance in this world of strife he could not wait for Mother, Doctor or aught beside. Perhaps it may be ominous of his future life, a real go ahead character, destined for the future chivalry of South Carolina. I was a little disappointed it was not a daughter, as it would have filled the aching void in your heart but let us be thankful, dear Blandie, for what God designs. I sincerely hope by this time you and the little one are getting along finely, though surrounded as you must be with noise and confusion . . . I suppose your mansion goes on rapidly. You will be so grand in your new abode."

Much to the delight of his Uncle, the baby was named Richard Austin Springs.

Blandie remained quietly at Springfield until fall. Then she took the three boys to Cornucopia while the interior of the house was being painted. But this particular aspect of the decorating progressed entirely too slowly to suit her. She postponed returning to Springfield until December 17, the appointed day for her parents to depart for

Texas. She sent many instructions to Baxter: "Walnut doors are far the prettiest and most fashionable. The knobs should be silver. Pa says to tell you to have a gold knob to your front door to be talked about. I was very amused at him and told him you had an elegant knob. . . . I think the cornices in the parlors should be bright yellow and then streaked. The grapes should be bronzed."

During the first week of December Blandie wrote four letters, complaining of the painters' procrastination. "I hate to be separated from you so long," she deplored. Then she became ill. Baxter rushed to Cornucopia. When his wife was well enough to sit up, he hurried back to Springfield, determined to prod the painters along at a more rapid rate. Two days after his departure Blandie wrote: "I feel like chatting with you this morning. I am improving and think I will get well fast. Ma was taken with chills and fever after you left, brought on I think by exposing herself. After the first chill she *would* get up and run about the house and had the second chill. So last night, the time for her third chill, Pa was doing everything to keep it off, but she is so fidgety Pa can't do much with her. He is nursing her and me too. I wish, dear Bac, you could look in about bed time and see us all getting to bed. I could almost kill myself laughing at Pa trying to keep Ma in bed. To keep off the chill he is having hot corn and bricks put to her. She says she will be steamed to death!"

On New Year's day, Blandie was showing her irritation when she wrote: "I think the painters have treated you shamefully. I have been from home two months and now the painting is not done. It is well I am not a man or they would have to leave my premises quick. I have decided to leave here next Thursday, the 8th of January."

April in New York! It was something Blandie and Baxter had planned and looked forward to for a long time. They left Springfield the end of March amid a great confusion of hugs and kisses bestowed by plump little arms and wet little faces. The children had a new housekeeper, Miss Betsy, to care for them, and it appears that Fannie and Lizzie were at Springfield too.

By the time the steamship from Charleston arrived in New York, Blandie was beginning to look and act like her old self again. The unhealthy pallor of her face had changed to a healthy pink glow. The sparkle had come back into her eyes. Her laughter had a merry ring to it for the first time since before her baby's death. She chattered with great enthusiasm as the carriage took them to the very elegant St. Nicholas Hotel on Broadway. For three weeks they remained there amid splendor and excitement.

Blandie was swept into this gay city life with such a burst of ecstasy that she blossomed as a flower suddenly discovering the sunshine. Baxter took her to the fashionable eating houses, to the theaters and opera. Dinner in New York was an adventure, with new wines to sip, new foods to relish. They danced too, and the eyes of others followed this attractive couple as they twirled around the floor. The glitter had come back into the lives of these two people who had been so sad, so serious.

Blandie exclaimed over gorgeous gowns to buy and exquisite furniture to be selected for Springfield. One can almost hear her say with great exuberance, "Isn't it simply *killing?*"

Every morning as she awoke in her soft, luxurious bed, Blandie wondered what new delight she would discover that day. And Baxter's greatest delight was seeing her sparkle with happiness and thrill to his love for her. He was indulgent. He was tender. He kept flowers and fruit in her room.* He bought her many gifts, among them a rich pearl and gold pin and an eleven-piece English porcelain dresser set with a pair of vases to match.

For the parlors of Springfield they selected two large gold framed mirrors to go over the matching mantels, handsome carpeting for the floors, and lace curtains with silk damask draperies to go over them.

Baxter watched with adoring eyes as she purchased a white hat, a black lace hat, and an exquisite pink cape. He heartily approved of her new evening gown of brocade, trimmed in fringe and tassels, her new traveling dress, her silk gown with cape to match, her duster, all from an exclusive dress shop on Broadway, and last but not least her new fur muff from A. T. Stewart's.

The three weeks passed far too quickly. Their trunks were packed, sent to the depot, and the Springses were off on the cars for Philadelphia. There they stayed at the Girard House on Chestnut Street between Eighth and Ninth streets.

It did not take Blandie long to find what she wanted for Springfield. At Charles H. White's, 250 Chestnut Street, she found the latest styles of furniture. There were European sofas, tête-à-têtes and étagers. And there were so many beautiful dining tables she hardly knew which one

*Listed on the hotel bill.

to select. Finally, she chose a mahogany extension table which could seat sixteen people.

Leaving Mr. White's shop, she and Baxter walked down Chestnut Street to Bailey and Company, jewelers and manufacturers of silver. Here they bought gifts for the family, including a hundred dollar silver pitcher for Jane and Dr. Connell, and nearly four hundred dollars worth of silver for themselves. To this was added a painted pin and bracelet for Blandie, to match the earrings Mrs. John Springs had given her several years back.

Next, they visited the ornamental iron works of Wood and Perot on Ridge Avenue, below Spring Garden Street, where they selected two iron settees, elaborate with grapevine designs.

Only one sad note shows up in the records. Amid all the happy shopping excursions, Blandie and Baxter did not fail to remember. There was an item of two small grave stones, made of Italian marble, one for little Jack and one for baby Julia.

Springfield in May was a very busy place. A landscape gardener arrived from Columbia to lay out the new gardens. The boxwood cuttings from Cornucopia were ready to be set out. Then one night during a severe electrical storm, a great cry went up. One barn had been struck by lightning. The fire spread quickly. Other barns caught. Every person on the plantation, black and white, worked all night beating out the flames and hauling water. Fortunately, the fire did not spread to the main house or slave quarters. Thus it was that, unintentionally, even the utilitarian part of Springfield was rebuilt.

On May 23 John Blackwood, always a true friend, sent a note up from Hamburg: "I am very sorry to learn from the papers that you have met so serious a loss as the destruction of your barns, etc., by lightning. As you will likely wish to rebuild and have lately paid in what money you have to spare, I have thought it might be agreeable to you to have the use of some means to replace your buildings. If so we, the Bank of Hamburg, would cheerfully let you have whatever amount you would like, and I now enclose a stock note which you can fix to suit your convenience as to time and amount."

Money was generally tight throughout the country that year, but apparently Baxter had no financial worries, even though he had spent a considerable sum on his home and new investments. His bank and railroad stocks were paying excellent dividends. In June he sold his cotton for 14½ cents, considered a good price.

But financially, things were different with his brother, Leroy. For a time, Leroy's newest project, a steam powered flour mill (the first in Mecklenburg County), had prospered to the point of supplying flour to the whole country around. That year wheat advanced in price. Leroy invested in large quantities of it, only to find it molded by dampness and unfit for use. This was his first great loss. Others were yet to come. He had overextended himself. Money was scarce. His creditors took advantage of the situation. He, who had been considered one of the most successful financiers in the State, was now being pushed to the wall. At times, Leroy was outraged that this financial ruin was closing in upon him, and yet at other times he was too broken to care. Actually, ever since his wife's death he had lacked the incentive to accumulate money. "What is wealth," he had once said, "when I am deprived of all that was nearest and dearest to me?"

Baxter and Austin felt pity and compassion for their brother. They came to his aid immediately, but they could not bail him out of the depths of his debts. "Take care," Judge Baxter warned his son-in-law, "how you contract liabilities for him lest you might be put in a situation where you could not assist him."

Everything Leroy owned had to be liquidated, including his town house on the Square in Charlotte. Members of the family bought the home and furniture. The mill, the vast real estate holdings—all—were swallowed up.

"I feel truly sorry for Leroy," lamented Judge Baxter. "He's honest, too confiding and generous in expanding his business too much. He has been ruined by dishonest agents."

By late November, the economic situation had reached a panic condition. Baxter received word that one of the banks in which he was a Director had experienced a run on it, due to cotton buyers not being able to give the bank the security it required. From the Hamburg Bank came this message: "Our main efforts have been directed to keeping the 'old ship' above the waves and make a safe harbour. Our object is not so much to *make* money as to keep what is already made." From Philadelphia Leonidas Springs reported to his cousin Baxter: "Times are awfully hard here."

Bank after bank held to its reserves and reduced its loans. Business houses failed all over the country. The panic of 1857 went down in history as a disastrous affair.

But panics, business failures, and depressions never hold back babies when they are ready to be born. Such was the case at Springfield on December 18. Baxter and the Judge had gone up to Charlotte on the very early morning train, leaving Blandie with her mother. Suddenly all was confusion. Julia Baxter explained it in a note which she sent up to Charlotte on the next train: "Baxter, soon after you left this morning, Blandie was taken sick. I sent for Dr. Williamson and called for assistance. Before five o'clock another fine boy made his appearance, not waiting for the arrival of the Doctor. We shall be happy to see you and the Judge this evening."

The little boy was ceremoniously named for his father. Then the Baxters departed for Cornucopia, not waiting for Christmas. Their eyes were on Texas.

The year 1858 was ushered in with peace and contentment. Blandie and Baxter had now been married eight years. Little Eli was in school. Johnny would soon be there, too. Richard Austin was now a child of one and a half years, looking for all the world like his grandfather, John Springs. In the nursery, baby Andrew Baxter slept angelically. This year was destined to be a good one, not too eventful, but a profitable, happy year. What happened? It was like this.

The panic had opened up opportunities for anyone having cash to invest. Baxter began buying more railroad stocks, such as the Mississippi Central, the Memphis and Little Rock, the Atlanta and La-Grange, the Atlanta and West Point, and the Georgia. Besides this, he was able to buy adjoining acreage to his plantation. He now owned 2,242 acres. His slaves numbered fifty-six, but he bought no more because the price of a good man had skyrocketed. He agreed with his father-in-law when he said, "I can't afford to buy Negroes at such prices and if they don't get below their present cost I shall never buy."

The Judge made another comment and it was of interest to the entire family. He explained that his son, Eli, Jr., who had been studying law instead of completing his education at West Point, was ready to hang out his shingle and practice, "that is if he gets any practice." Eli, Jr., proved to be an excellent lawyer and a brilliant statesman. The following year he would be elected to the Texas Legislature, being that body's youngest member and representing the most intelligent, as well as wealthiest, county in the State.

In March of that year of 1858, Leroy came to Springfield to recover from an illness, but how could he actually recover when his spirits were so low? Eventually though he would get himself together and take his three youngest daughters to Petersburg to live with Margaret, his oldest daughter, who had married a promising lawyer by the name of John Lyons.

By midsummer it looked as though President James Buchanan's term would be taken up with the subject of slavery. One event after the other brought more friction and tension between the North and the South. The country was discussing the Lincoln-Douglas debates. Abraham Lincoln, running against Stephen A. Douglas for the Senate, had suddenly loomed upon the political horizon when he said: "A house divided against itself can not stand. I believe this government can not endure permanently half slave and half free. I do not expect the Union to be dissolved; I do not expect the house to fall; but I do expect it will cease to be divided. It will become all one thing or all the other." The clouds were beginning to gather, clouds which would eventually form a tremendous, thunderous storm.

In September, Blandie left her children at sleepy, quiet Springfield and journeyed south to visit her sister Jane Connell in Marietta. Baxter accompanied her that far and then continued on a business trip. But the elaborate round of social engagements at "Major Brumley's, Governor McDonald's, Mrs. Stewartson's, Mrs. Harrisson's, etc., etc.," did not keep Blandie from missing her husband. "I am invited out every day," she wrote, "and am happy, yet I can't but let a sigh escape when I think you are away from me. I don't think I can remain contented two weeks longer without turning my steps home to be with my own dear husband, for, even if he doesn't think so, I can't be happy unless he is with me."

Blandie would have another baby in February.

And so it was with the Springs family in 1858.

The year that followed was similar to the preceding one. Trips to Charleston, Columbia, and Georgia. The same Directors meetings for Baxter, except now there were more, because there were more investments and responsibilities. At home the plantation was being enriched with a remarkable new fertilizer, super phosphate, which Baxter was buying in Baltimore. A rust free wheat was being planted and harvested which created much attention among the farmers. Letters were coming in from all over the state asking for information and seed.

The new baby, who arrived on February 25, was named Alva Connell, which delighted Jane, who had come up from Marietta to attend her sister in her confinement.

Something else was born that year. It came to light in New York City in a minstrel show. It was a song which caught the fancy of all who heard it. It would one day catch the spirit of the South. It was called "Dixie."

And something very shocking happened that year 1859. It was John Brown's raid on the Federal Arsenal at Harper's Ferry, Virginia. The fear of a slave insurrection had long been prevalent in the South and to have Northerners openly side with Brown and his attempt to arm Negroes caused Southern tempers to flare in open criticism and anger. Even those who opposed slavery denounced the North.

When Baxter and Blandie went to Cornucopia the following month, which was November, they talked for hours with the Judge on this subject. Baxter explained that one of his Negroes had run away, taking a horse with him. And Brevard Davidson had had trouble too. His Negro girl, Gincy, had run away after setting the cook house on fire. Fortunately, the fire had not spread to the handsome and elegant residence. Jane Connell remarked that she thought the happiest people were those free from the worry of slaves. The Judge concurred but nevertheless said to Baxter, "If you can buy a girl big enough to wait table and bring in breakfast, I will pay $600. Or if you can get a woman with first child for $1,000, please buy."

The Negro situation was dynamite and yet slavery was an institution which was part and parcel of the life of a Southern planter. Generation after generation it had been an accepted fact, an accepted way of life. And as far as the Baxters and Springses were concerned it would continue to be right up to the proclamation of emancipation.

South Carolina had a white population of nearly three hundred thousand but she had nearly four hundred thousand Negroes. Georgia had a little over a half-million whites but also nearly a half-million Negroes. In the event of war, would the Negroes be loyal? Would there eventually be a bloody uprising in the South with blacks fighting whites? An attempt to plot just such a thing was reported to Baxter in detail early in 1860 by his friend, the Reverend Archibald Whyte of Rock Hill, South Carolina:

"It seems that on Friday last, a negro . . . was about to receive chastisement for some misdemeanor. He proposed, if spared the whipping, to disclose a matter of great interest to the community.

"It seems that a family of the name of Pugh, consisting of a father and two sons, with some women, have long been suspected of trafficking with negroes and who, for a similar offense, had been expelled from Chester. The negro boy (Dave) said that - - - Pugh, one of the sons, was engaged in training the negroes of the country to the art of loading and shooting guns. Pugh had told them that he had joined the 'Minute Men,' but if forced to go to Charleston he would feign sickness, return and help the negroes kill the men who were at home, also the old women and the children—divide the property and the negroes should have their choice of the young for wives. This statement, at first, would seem incredible and one which would not be entertained by white men. Yet it is one, as we know from what has transpired elsewhere, which is adopted to the capacity of negroes. Besides, it is corroborated by the negroes who have been under Pugh's training.

"Instead of proceeding immediately to arrest the Pughs, it was deferred till the next night. A large company proceeded, towards day, to the premises of the Pughs. Two of the company blacked themselves and proceeded to the house, sending Dave in and they remaining without. Upon Dave's going in, he was asked for his name and also who was with him. He named two neighboring negroes, and asked Pugh if he had 'any of that good thing.' Pugh said he had and told Dave to go towards an outhouse where it was kept. Pugh then stepped back, brought out a gun and said to Dave, 'You damned rascal, I mean to punish you for betraying me.' The negro started to run and received a shot in the thigh. A number of shots then passed between the two white men and the Pughs in which the first named Pugh received a wound in the foot. The rest of the company coming up secured the old man and his two sons, the women taking part in the fight. The men were taken to York, but Stilwell refused to put them in jail (probably for want of a regular committment) . They were left under guard until Monday.

"On Monday an examination was held and some twelve citizens called to sit upon the case. Some eight or nine were for hanging them forthwith, but finally yielded to the opinions of three or four old men, some of them Elders of the church, who probably thought the evidence incompetent and the punishment too severe. It was finally agreed to shave one half of the head, give each fifty stripes, dispose of their property, give them the proceeds, and send them out of the country. It remains to be seen whether the clemency is misplaced. They owned a piece of land said to be worth $300, three negroes and some bags of cotton. It is said they will be sent from Chester, where they are now in jail, on Monday. The most active of the three is represented as a hardened wretch who was not in the least cowed either by the whipping or shaving and it is not unreasonable to suppose that they will find their way back on some suitable occasion.

"A nephew of the old man Pugh, of the same name, has been in the neighborhood selling liquor. He was ordered to leave the neighborhood but instead of that he had the curiosity to remain and witness the trial of his uncle and cousins. Upon his approaching the crowd, the young men stepped out in line, intending simultaneously to shoot him. There again Frank Love interposed by getting between the parties. After consultation Pugh was taken out, shaved, blacked and received twenty-five lashes, and sent off on the cars on Tuesday with a paste board placard on his back labelled 'To the Sheriff of Mecklenburg County of N. C.' . . ."

Notwithstanding the fear in the hearts of the Southerners that the slaves might rise up against them, there was a greater fear that the South was losing her rights under the Constitution of the United States.

Baxter Springs reflected long on the condition of the country as the year 1860 began. He constantly remembered his father's words: "I shall be willing to see you suffer death standing up for Constitutional principles, for the purity and welfare of the country."

Part Four

THE THUNDER AND THE FURY

The original Springfield as it was remodeled in 1856.

CHAPTER EIGHTEEN

"The day of compromise, concession and submission has passed." These were the words of Eli Baxter, Jr., spoken from the floor of the House of Representatives of Texas, but they could easily have been those of the average Southerner. People who had never believed in secession as an answer to the South's problems were now willing to pull out of the Union. For instance, Eli said, "The Harper's Ferry excitement has made the 'Lone Star State' truly a Southern rights State and I trust to God she may ever remain so."

The political pot was boiling. There were now eighteen free states and fifteen slave-holding states. The pot would soon boil over into what John Springs had once prophesied would be "a civil conflict of the most horrible kind."

Abraham Lincoln made his famous Cooper Union speech in New York on February 27, 1860: "If slavery is right, all words, acts, laws and constitutions against it are themselves wrong and should be silenced and swept away. If it is wrong they can not justly insist upon its enlargement. All they ask we could readily grant if we thought slavery right; all we ask they could as readily grant if they thought it wrong. Their thinking it right and our thinking it wrong is the precise fact upon which depends the whole controversy. Thinking it right as they do, they are not to blame for desiring its full recognition as being right; but thinking it wrong as we do, can we yield to them? Can we cast our votes with their view and against our own? . . . If our sense of duty forbids this, then let us stand by our duty, fearlessly and effectively."

That same month, Baxter Springs' good friend, Frank Sexton, sitting at his plantation in San Augustine, Texas, was feeling depressed because "the prospects for the perpetuity of the Federal Government upon the plan contemplated by our Fathers who organized it seems just now peculiarly gloomy." He questioned Baxter: "What do you think the South ought to do? I know that you have always been among the most moderate of the school of South Carolina's Statesmen. But are you now able to see anything for the South to do but assert her own independence on the event of the election of a Black Republican President?" Baxter found this a very difficult question to answer.

The Presidential election was the important issue of 1860. The same question was asked over and over. Whom will the Democrats nominate for the Presidency? Baxter received many letters concerning the National Democratic Convention to be held in Charleston April 23. It was important to him and his York District friends that the right delegates be sent from their section. A letter from William R. Robertson suggested: "Let us knock our heads together and see if we can't get Franklin Gaillard, the editor of the South Carolinian, elected. I believe between you and myself we can accomplish the matter."

There's little doubt that Baxter went to Charleston to witness the Convention, because it was one of the most important events ever to take place in the South. On the outcome of this meeting rested the fate of the Union. Charleston was not a good place for the Convention to be held. It was a hotbed of fire-eating secessionists. This would make it even more difficult for the Democrats of the North to get together with those of the South.

The six hundred delegates comprised a serious body of men. At the beginning of the Convention it was clear there would be a split on Stephen A. Douglas, the choice of the North and West. The South, remembering Douglas and his popular sovereignty policy would have none of him.

For one week the Convention debated and argued over a platform. None could be found acceptable to all. Finally, a vote was taken on two platforms, one a majority report and the other a minority report. The former was a Douglas platform which caused the South to line up against the North in the voting. The majority report or platform was adopted. Promptly the delegates from Alabama withdrew from the Convention and were followed by South Carolina, Georgia, Florida, Louisiana, Mississippi, Texas, and Arkansas. This made it impossible for the remaining delegates to elect a candidate as that election required 202 votes which no man received.

On May 3 the Convention broke up, failing to accomplish its purpose, and scheduling another meeting for June 18 in Baltimore. The Southern Democrats immediately called a meeting in Charleston and adopted a platform. Later they met in convention and nominated John C. Breckinridge of Kentucky as a candidate for the Presidency. The Convention which met in Baltimore nominated Douglas. Another group, calling themselves the Constitutional Union Party, nominated John Bell of Tennessee. Thus the Democratic party was split and this division would, later that year, give the election to Abraham Lincoln, the Republican's choice.

While all this excitement was going on over the country, Blandie remained quietly at Springfield, awaiting the arrival of another baby. On May 27 Dr. E. D. Williamson was hastily summoned. There was no time to lose. Her two previous babies had been born before the doctor could get to her. Faster and faster the doctor prodded his horse and because of his haste he was at Springfield in time to deliver the fine healthy boy whom Blandie and Baxter named for their brother-in-law, Brevard Davidson. They had hoped for a girl. As Mrs. John Springs said, "Another son! Well, better in boys than girls, say I. Surely a 'troop cometh' and enough to settle a territory of your *own* name. Tell Blandie not to be discouraged. She has time enough yet for as many girls. I think if she had denied herself some of those luxuries like strawberries and cream (the very mention makes my mouth water) her little Lordship might have been less bulky."

Election day soon rolled around. November 6, 1860. The day the die was cast for nearly half a million men who would die in the war to come. Abraham Lincoln would be the President of the United States and he pledged himself to keep it united.

The Southern secessionists organized for action. Four days after the election, Baxter Springs received an urgent letter from his friend Robert Gadsden McCaw, York District representative in the legislature in Columbia. The legislature had approved calling a State convention to discuss South Carolina's secession. McCaw informed Baxter: "All parties are united. . . . My object in giving you this information is that you may prepare the minds of our people for the change. For the State will secede whether York is willing or not and I do not want the Submission men of our district to have a place in the convention as it will be a reflection on our district after the act of Secession is passed. The news from Georgia and Alabama is cheering, which gives great encouragement to the members of the cooperation party in 1852. In fact they all advise prompt and speedy action. Col. Preston and Gov. Manning say our salvation depends upon the action of this State. . . . Shape your course that none but safe and conservative men shall be sent to the convention from York."

York District called their meeting for November 22 and the following notices were distributed throughout the district:

"Carolinians: The wrongs and insults of years are at last presented in a tangible form for redress. The South is rising to take into her own hands a nation's rights; to act as freemen—to act the part of those who know their rights, and knowing, dare maintain them.

"Shall we who breathe the spirit-stirring air of proud King's Mountain,* prove deaf to the voices of Georgia, Alabama, Florida and Mississippi? Is this a time to counsel delay? Shall we fail in the crisis of our destiny? While a glorious Southern Confederacy is offered us, shall we still sleep in the fatal embrace of Northern fanaticism?

"Our State, our glorious Palmetto State, is rising in its might from mountain to seaboard. . . . the deep-toned voice of liberty is heard, demanding action. Action! Action! . . . And as men who will represent York District, we present the following names, contented to trust the destiny of our beloved State in their hands, as being men whose every aim will be 'their country's, their God's and truth's': Samuel Rainey, Sr.; A. Baxter Springs; Wm. B. Wilson; Dr. R. T. Allison; Dr. A. I. Barron.†

These five men were elected delegates. York District responded heartily. Soon Baxter's friend, the Reverend Whyte, was writing him about raising "Minute Men" and recruiting cavalry. South Carolina was arming, although Lincoln at this point had not said whether he would resort to coercion by soldiers if the Southern States attempted secession. He still contended that slaves were the personal property of their masters and as such those masters were entitled to protection under the Constitution. He had not given up hope of preserving the peace and the Union.

The State Convention was called for December 17. Baxter began making plans to attend. Blandie began making plans to visit Cornu-

*The Revolutionary victory over the British at nearby King's Mountain.
†Samuel Rainey, member of S. C. Legislature for eight years, was a planter of Guthriesville, owning sixty-nine slaves. William B. Wilson, lawyer, was a former member of the S. C. Legislature; Dr. Robert Turner Allison lived at Meek's Hill and practiced medicine for forty-five years, a former member of the S. C. Legislature; Dr. Archibald Ingram Barron lived at Yorkville and practiced medicine for fifty years.

copia before the departure of her parents to Texas. There was much confusion, much packing on her part, and a general flurry about the household.

Finally Blandie and the boys were off. The baggage was piled in the wagon which followed behind the carriage. Blandie was almost hidden under a sea of little boys, lunch boxes, and blankets. At last Baxter had his family settled on the train which took them to Columbia. There he left them to make the rest of the journey by themselves. In a few days he received a letter from Blandie: "We got along very well after you left me. The conductor was very attentive and the boys got up quickly without any trouble. They seemed very much disappointed that they could not tell you goodbye and asked why I did not wake them up. . . . We got to Double Wells at three o'clock. I dislike very much the way they do on the Georgia cars. They never call out what station it is and if you are not alert they pass on in a few moments and you are never thought of. I got a servant to come and let me know when we reached Double Wells, but the conductor came and wanted me to get off in a minute. I told him he had not let me know and I could not get my children ready in a moment. . . . York had a good fire and a pot of coffee waiting for me which Ma had sent to Double Wells. We started in half an hour and came by moonlight. The roads were very wet and heavy. . . .

"This State, as Carolina, is in great excitement. Pa is very despondent about the government. He says war seems inevitable and the country will be ruined, slaves gone. It will be worse than the French Revolution—equality and fraternity will be the motto! . . . Mr. Toombs* promised Mr. Stephens* to use his influence with Carolina to wait and see what the South would do. But Pa fears it is too late. Former Governor Morehead of Kentucky was in Sparta the other day and said all the States were waiting on Georgia. Someone told him Georgia would go out. 'Well,' he remarked, 'you can come and get our slaves for nothing.' Stephens told Pa that Orr, Hammond, Gist† and many of the Carolinians were conservative, and that they were for a Union of the South. Everybody seems despondent."

The Georgia Legislature had called for an election of delegates to

*This is Robert Toombs who became Secretary of State for Jefferson Davis, and Alexander H. Stephens, who felt that Lincoln's election did not necessitate secession. He had been a fellow Congressman with Lincoln.

†James L. Orr, James H. Hammond, and Gov. William H. Gist were prominent South Carolina leaders. The latter, like John Springs, had advised concerted Southern action rather than South Carolina seceeding alone.

attend a convention on January 16. A member of the legislature, one David W. Lewis, was on the committee of the State of the Republic. He afterwards recorded in the Milledgeville, Georgia, newspaper: "The question before our Committee was, What shall we recommend to the Legislature for the action of Georgia? Going from the meeting to my lodging I met Alexander Stephens in the street. He asked me if the Committee had agreed on any measure. I told him that the Committee had instructed me to invite him and other distinguished citizens to meet in council and agree upon a report. . . . His only reply was, 'Be certain to invite Judge Baxter to the meeting.' Such an estimate of the Judge's wisdom and character from such a source renders comment futile. Georgia never had such a host of worthies in her Capital at once. Nearly every man upon whom she had conferred high honor from 1840 to 1860 was there. . . . Judge Baxter was opposed to secession, preferring to wait for a gross violation of the Constitution before taking the perilous step. But when secession was lawfully decided by the voice of the people, he was for maintaining that decision at all hazards."

Blandie and her children arrived in Columbia on Friday, December 14, where Baxter was waiting for them. He accompanied them to Springfield and immediately returned to Columbia to prepare for the opening of the convention on Monday morning. He was tense with apprehension, but comforted to some extent by the speech President Buchanan had made several weeks previously, in which he had said:

"Let us take warning in time and remove the cause of danger. It can not be denied that for five and twenty years the agitation at the North against slavery has been incessant. In 1835, pictorial handbills and inflammatory appeals were circulated extensively throughout the South, of a character to excite the passions of the slaves, and, in the language of General Jackson, 'to stimulate them to insurrection and produce all the horrors of a servile war.' This agitation has ever since been continued by the public press . . . and by abolition sermons and lectures. . . . How easy would it be for the American people to settle the slavery question forever and to restore peace and harmony to this distracted country! They and they alone can do it. All that is necessary to accomplish the object, and all for which the slave states have ever contended, is to be let alone and permitted to manage their domestic institutions in their own way. As sovereign states, they, and they alone are responsible before God and the world for slavery existing among them. For this the people of the North are not more responsible, and have no more right to interfere than with similar institutions in Russia or Brazil!"

There were many Northerners who agreed with President Buchanan and deplored the possibility of a break between the two sections. Even Baxter's tailor, John Earle, Jr., of Boston, expressed such sentiments in a letter acknowledging Baxter's payment of a bill for a new frock coat, pantaloons, surtout and silk vest: "We are all feeling sadly at the stormy prospect before us and yet we entertain strong hope for the Union. We fear your citizens at large are too much influenced by the one sided reports and by the *false* statements respecting the general feeling of the North towards the South to act judiciously upon the question before them. Even here in old Massachusetts, the very hot bed of anti-slavery fanaticism and where every wild 'ism' has a foothold, the people at large would respect the rights of the South and the number who would sanction the language of the Garrisons* and Phillips† and such as they, are few and their influence extremely limited. . . . While the subject is up for discussion the South should insist upon such a guarantee of their rights as to forever shut the mouth of the abolitionist croakers and thereby prevent so sad a catastrophy as the dissolution of this proud confederacy of independent states—God grant that the day may be far distant when these shall be other than united in interest and destiny."

Baxter rose early on the morning of December 17. The gravity of what lay ahead weighed on his mind too much to allow him to sleep. He made his way to the dining room, which was packed even at this hour, because all of Columbia was crowded. There was much going on in the town. The legislature was in session; a new Governor was to be inaugurated; and the Secession Convention was opening. When Baxter finished his breakfast he joined his York fellow-delegates and together they walked to the Baptist Church on Plain Street where the convention was to be held. Although the morning had only begun, gentlemen were assembling in the pews and aisles of the church.

---

*William Lloyd Garrison, editor of the abolitionist newspaper, the *Liberator,* wanted the South to secede because he said "it is in the power of the North to deluge her soil with blood and inflict upon her the most terrible sufferings but not to conquer her spirit or change her determination."

†Wendell Phillips was a violent abolitionist. When South Carolina seceded he said, "Who dreamed that success would come so soon? South Carolina, bankrupt, alone with a hundred thousand more slaves than whites, four blacks to three whites, within her borders, flings her gauntlet at the feet of 25,000,000 of people in defense of an idea to maintain what she thinks is right."

This was no ordinary group of men. Here were planters, statesmen, scholars, lawyers, doctors, men of the highest caliber, some of whom had been Congressmen, Senators, Governors, Legislators. They were grave, serious gentlemen, all here to perform a serious duty.

Moving among these men, Baxter shook hands and spoke to many of his friends. He passed from group to group. Former Governor John Lawrence Manning, a planter with well over six hundred slaves, stood talking to another plantation owner, T. L. Gourdin. Here were two of the wealthiest men in South Carolina. Baxter joined them for a while, then left to talk to a group of staunch state's righters, former Governor John Peter Richardson, J. I. Middleton, who was himself a son of a former Governor, and F. H. Wardlaw of Edgefield. Soon former Congressman James Orr joined them, accompanied by C. G. Memminger, who would in the not too distant future be the Secretary of the Treasury of the Confederacy. Then there was young Thomas Y. Simons, Jr., a lawyer from Charleston talking to Barnwell Rhett, a very enthusiastic secessionist of that same city. Soon former Governor John Hugh Means strolled over to enter the conversation. And thus it went on all morning until the one hundred and seventy delegates had assembled. Probably never was there a more distinguished or more solemn group to meet in the State of South Carolina.

The session began at noon with the election of General David F. Jamison* as temporary president. Jamison, standing under a blue flag suspended over the rostrum, proclaimed "our fixed determination to throw off a Government to which we have been accustomed and to provide new safeguards for our future security." He listed the South's grievances, asking:

"Did the Constitution protect us from the jealousy and aggressions of the North, commenced forty years ago, which resulted in the Missouri Compromise? Did the Constitution protect us from the cupidity of the Northern people, who for thirty five years, have imposed the burden of supporting the General Government chiefly on the industry of the South? Did it save us from Abolition petitions, designed to annoy and insult us, in the very halls of our Federal Congress? Did it enable us to obtain a single foot of the soil acquired in the war with Mexico, where the South furnished three fourths of the money, two-thirds of the men, and four-fifths of the graves? Did it oppose any

*General David Flanel Jamison, lawyer, planter, member of House of Representatives from 1836-48, author, Secretary of War under Jefferson Davis, was from Barnwell District.

obstacle to the erection of California into a free-soil State, without any previous territorial existence, without any defined boundaries, or any census of her population? Did it throw any protection around the Southern settlers of Kansas, when the soil of that territory was invaded by the emissaries of Emigrant Aid Societies, in a crusade preached from Northern pulpits, when churchmen and women contributed Sharp's rifles and Colt's revolvers to swell the butchery of Southern men? And has not that Constitution been trodden under foot by almost every Northern State in their ordinances nullifying all laws made for the recovery of fugitive slaves, by which untold millions of property have been lost to the South?"

Jamison vehemently concluded, "Written Constitutions are worthless, unless they are written, at the same time, in the hearts, and founded on the interests of a people."

When his address was over, he was wildly cheered and applauded.

The delegates, including Baxter, proceeded to the main business: Approval of a resolution, "That it is the opinion of this convention that the State of South Carolina should forthwith secede from the Federal Union, known as the United States of America." It passed with a roar.

A smallpox epidemic in Columbia caused the convention to adjourn and meet next day in Charleston. Baxter, exhausted but unaware of it because of the tense excitement, packed his bag and boarded the train. In Charleston, he went to the Mills House at Meeting and Queen Streets, bathed, dressed, ate a substantial dinner, and attended a four o'clock meeting at Institute Hall. The next day the convention was moved to the St. Andrew's Hall because it was less noisy.

On Thursday came the climax. The committee to draft the ordinance of secession presented its work. Chairman John A. Inglis read it to the final words, "that the union now subsisting between South Carolina and other States under the name of the United States of America is hereby dissolved." The applause was tremendous. But there were tears as well as cheers. The ordinance passed unanimously.

It was agreed that the signing would take place at seven o'clock that evening at Institute Hall in the presence of the Governor and both branches of the legislature. The convention then recessed until six-thirty in the evening.

At the appointed hour the one hundred and seventy delegates, together with those invited to witness this great signing, moved in a body from St. Andrews Hall to Institute Hall. As they passed through the streets great crowds cheered and waved their handkerchiefs. When the procession filed into the hall the galleries were already filled with ladies. On the rostrum were two palmetto trees flanking the President's chair.

The convention was called to order and opened with a prayer. The Attorney General, I. W. Hayne, reported that the ordinance had been engrossed with the great seal of the State affixed to it. The delegates then came forward, in the alphabetical order of their districts, and signed their names amid great applause. Next to the last name on the document, written in a clear manner, was "A. Baxter Springs."

It took two hours for the signing. Then the President rose and in a dramatically clear voice said, "The Ordinance of Secession has been signed and ratified, and I proclaim the State of South Carolina an Independent Commonwealth." With one accord, cheers went up in a storm of enthusiasm. The demonstration was tumultuous. The palmetto trees were stripped by souvenir hunters.

Outside in the streets the news spread like fire. Guns boomed, bands played, and church bells rang. Horses were shying in the streets while people ran in every direction. Hardly had the convention adjourned before the Charleston *Mercury* had an extra on the street with huge headlines, "The Union is Dissolved." In the meantime the telegraph wires had crackled the message to Washington where aging, worried President Buchanan was receiving the word while attending a wedding.

Baxter sat up that night and wrote to Blandie. Christmas was only five days away, but he knew now that he would not get home for several hectic weeks. Suddenly he felt lonely, tired, exhausted.

CHAPTER NINETEEN

On Christmas eve, Blandie was lonely for her husband. She sat beside the open fire after her little ones had been tucked snuggly in bed and there, in the chill of the late winter evening, she wrote: "I miss you, my dear husband, in every way that one can miss another who is dearer to them than anything on earth. I want you to put your arms around me."

But then, for fear Baxter would worry about her because she was lonely, she added: "But remember we are getting along finely and really I think the servants wish and try to do better than if you were here, and I only want to see your dear self when it is convenient for you to leave for I know you are in a great good cause.

"I see from the papers that great demonstrations have been made in every town on account of the bright news from Charleston. This morning's paper says that the President contends for the revenue and all the public buildings. I think it is outrageous. I would fight to the last before I would give them up. What is glorious—Georgia will secede the 17th of January, so all is right there at last.

"I received your kind welcome letter Saturday. Oh! it does me so much good, by dearest Bac, to get your letters. I try not to expect one every day, but still I look in the bag with eager eyes hoping to find one."

Blandie managed to get through Christmas day, making merry for the sake of the children and the Negroes. The following day she wrote to her husband: "I hoped in spite of everything that you would get home for Christmas and spend at least a few days with us, but your last letter made me give up all hope. . . . The children were in great glee yesterday. We put little dumb watches in their socks with raisins, candy and chestnuts. They all seem delighted. Little Bac soon broke his open to see what was inside. . . . Yesterday I gave the Negroes their clothes and told them what you said about the money. Also gave them as much molasses as you usually give them and some flour. They all seemed pleased."

Launching a "sovereign State" on its own was a complicated matter. The convention continued in session at Charleston even on Christmas day. It demanded that the United States yield its forts and arsenal in and around Charleston. The following evening, the United States garrison on Fort Moultrie, under the command of Major Robert Anderson, slipped quietly into boats and rowed over to unmanned Fort Sumter. Governor F. W. Pickens of South Carolina notified the convention:

"I considered the evacuation of Fort Moultrie, under all the circumstances, a direct violation of the distinct understanding between the authorities of the Government at Washington and those who were authorized to act on the part of the State, and bringing on a state of war."

From Rock Hill, the Reverend Mr. Whyte wrote his views to Baxter, referring to Major Anderson as "the commandant": "I am slow to believe that instructions to abandon Moultrie and occupy Sumter emanated from Washington, and suppose that the commandant was governed by some false rumor and acted under panic. I was led to believe from your letter that neither the Convention nor any portion of the grave and thinking portion of the population would favor precipitate action. I take it for granted that the commandant would have persons on the alert to gather up, and communicate to him, any information which it might be important for him to possess. These persons might have heard thoughtless youth talking of taking the Forts, and as a matter of course communicated the rumor to the commandant. He has assumed a high responsibility."

Blandie was overwhelmed at the turn of events and the prospect of war. She poured out her anguish to Baxter: "My heart is filled with sadness, my own dear husband, at the intelligence in your last letter. As Carolinians we are certainly in the right and I trust in the mercy, wisdom and justice of our merciful Father to guide and direct us. Oh, my dear Bac, the greatest thing that we have to apprehend, I fear, is that we are and have not prepared ourselves sufficiently for this war.

The enemy has the advantage in her equipments. I think the South now should be united to a man. I have very little hope that North Carolina will act promptly. William Myers said they would submit to Lincoln's administration unless he committed an overt act.

"We found yesterday we did not have salt enough for the hogs that were killed or lard cans, and Eli and Austin needed shoes, I needed stamps and pens, and Wash said his feet were on the ground, so I took $20 of *my* money, which was gold, and started to Charlotte. When I got to the station I found Austin about to get off. He said he would go with me, that he had come over to assist me in anything he could do. He took on a memorandum of what I wanted and got it all done."

Baxter managed to spend most of January at Springfield with Blandie and the children. Each morning his newspaper brought important news. South Carolina had now been joined in her secession by Mississippi (January 9), Florida (January 10), Alabama (January 11), Georgia (January 19), and Louisiana (January 26), and on February 1 Texas joined the Confederacy. The latter state was late because of complications. Eli Baxter, Jr. explained to Blandie what happened.

Governor Sam Houston was a Union man and fought the calling of a Convention. He refused to convene the legislature but the people made such an uproar that the legislature met and legalized the election of delegates to a Convention and gave that Convention the power to exercise the will of the people. Eli, having been elected a delegate to that high-spirited assembly, voiced his opinions to the Convention. He declared himself a Southern Rights man who thought it time to stop suffering any further encroachments by the North upon the cherished rights of the State of Texas. He was ready for secession. The Convention was ready for secession. And so Texas went out of the Union.

Immediately, Governor Houston declared Texas an independent republic which did not need to join the Confederacy of Southern States. Regardless of their Governor's wishes, delegates went to Montgomery and voted Texas into the Confederacy. Sam Houston, still stubborn and refusing to swear allegiance to the cause, was deposed from the government March 18.

By this time, Baxter was making preparations to go to Charleston for the second session of the Convention which had been called for March 26, and he had already engaged his rooms at the Mills House.

He and Blandie had talked it over and agreed that he would go down first and, when his business was completed, she would join him for a vacation.

The South still hoped for a peaceful independence. Jefferson Davis had expressed this hope in his inaugural address: "If a just perception of mutual interest shall permit us peaceably to pursue our separate political career, my most earnest desire will have been fullfilled." Two weeks earlier, Lincoln had closed his inaugural speech with, "We are not enemies but friends. We must not be enemies. Though passion may have strained, it must not break our bonds of affection."

This, then, was the state of the country when Baxter checked into the Mills House in Charleston. He found many of his fellow delegates already there. Selecting a few of his more intimate friends, he invited them to his rooms. Servants brought brandy and champagne to pass among the guests. Baxter, always with business on his mind, cornered William Gregg, the guiding spirit of the Graniteville Mill, and asked, "How are things progressing at the mill?"

The past year had been very prosperous for Graniteville, Gregg explained, and it was expected that new orders would greatly increase. The mill now had a cash capital of $138,624 but he thought that amount inadequate for the extended business. With the present embarrassed state of the money market he felt it better to forego paying the usual four percent dividend and use that money instead to purchase cotton and pay labor. Baxter and Gregg both concurred in the opinion that the cash means of the company should be increased and that a stock issue would be justified. It would be a safe buy for any investor.

"What about the Bank of Hamburg?" questioned Baxter. "Will it pay $2 again on the next semi-annual dividend?"

"Yes, I believe so," replied Gregg. Then followed a discussion of other stocks and their dividends, paid semi-annually. South Carolina Railroad had paid $4.25; Bank of Charleston, $3.50; Camden Bank, $2; Merchants Bank of Cheraw, $5; Bank of Chester and the Exchange Bank of Columbia, $1.25 each, and the Charleston Insurance and Trust Company, $5.

Baxter was satisfied with his investments, but he was constantly on the alert for ways of making money. New enterprises and inventions intrigued him. If the critical condition of the times had not intervened, he had planned to invest in a new venture with three Charlestonians, establishing a line of Steam Propellers between Charleston and Liverpool.

The State Convention reconvened on a Tuesday "to consider the Constitution of the Confederate States of America, which has been adopted and submitted to us by the Congress at Montgomery, with such other questions as the exigencies of our situation may require."

After meeting through Friday, the Convention recessed over the week end so the delegates could accept an invitation of General P. G. T. Beauregard to visit the fortifications erected for the defense of Charleston harbor. Baxter spent the week end pleasantly, dining with friends, visiting the exclusive Charleston Club and the Art Gallery on Meeting Street, and shopping for supplies for Springfield.

During the following ten days the Convention ratified the Confederate Constitution, which was patterned after the United States Constitution in many respects, by a vote of 138 to 21. It then approved Jefferson Davis as President of the Confederacy and Alexander Stephens as Vice President, transfered forts and other former United States properties taken by South Carolina to the Confederate Government, and committed a volunteer force to the Confederate service.

Word spread meanwhile that a powerful Union fleet was headed South to reinforce Fort Sumter. This meant war. Baxter immediately thought of Blandie who was probably at that very moment leaving home to join him. He hurried to the office of the American Telegraph Company and wired her not to come.

Blandie, not knowing anything about the sudden turn of events, had already boarded the train, accompanied by several trunks of her most elegant clothes. When the train stopped at Winnsboro, the conductor was handed a telegram for Blandie. She, who had been so radiant at the thought of being with Baxter in Charleston, now hurriedly gathered up her bonnet and wrap, said goodbye to the passengers sitting around her, and left the train, a sad and confused person. The conductor kindly wired the following message to Baxter: "Winnsboro, April 8, 1861 . . . Mrs. Springs got your dispatch and stopped here. She will return on the up train today."

Baxter received another telegram that day, this one from John Lyon, his nephew, from Petersburg, who asked, "Has Sumter been attacked or any attempt to reinforce been made? Telegraph us." Baxter replied: "Not yet. Official information that it will be reinforced if possible. The attempt will be made and we shall defeat it.

Collision momentarily expected. No longer doubt war is intended and we are ready and willing. Chestnut and Wigfall, aides to Beauregard, just left for scene of action."

The Convention adjourned April 10. The following day, shortly after noon, a boat flying a white flag made its way to Fort Sumter from Charleston, carrying three officers, who, upon their arrival at the fort, conveyed General Beauregard's message to Major Anderson. The fort must be evacuated. After a consultation with his officers, Major Anderson declared that surrendering the fort was against his sense of honor and obligation to his government and he could not comply.

The next day, April 12, Major Anderson was given another opportunity to surrender but refused, hoping to hold out until the ships arrived from the North. The Confederate messengers receiving this answer realized the situation futile and handed the following message to Major Anderson:

"Sir; By authority of Brigadier General Beauregard, commanding the Provisional Forces of the Confederate States, we have the honor to notify you that he will open the fire of his batteries on Fort Sumter in one hour from this time. We have the honor to be very respectfully, Your obedient servants, James Chestnut, Aide-de-camp; Stephen D. Lee, Captain C. S. Army, Aide-de-camp."

At 4:30 that morning of April 12, a ten-inch mortar shell burst above Fort Sumter.

War had begun.

Within five days, Lincoln declared a blockade of the coast. Baxter could not forget what his father had said in 1851. Although John Springs had been dead nearly eight years, the words came back:

"If South Carolina becomes a separate nation, will she have the means to maintain it, of either men or money? The latter your politicians will tell you, is not to be taken into account; that dollars and cents are mere trash compared with freedom and independence. But I say she can't move without the dollars. How is she to fortify herself? Does she expect men to defend her and to fight her battles without being fed, clothed and paid? Suppose the Federal government should block our ports and cut off our communication with others in the way of exports and imports?"

True, his father was speaking of South Carolina alone. Now she was not alone; there were seven states joined together in a Confederacy, but, Baxter reasoned, there would be need for money and men to keep that Confederacy free, to fight the war which was now beginning. That was his first duty.

With the fall of Fort Sumter, President Lincoln called for seventy-five thousand troops. President Davis issued a call to arms. Two days after Lincoln's call, Virginia seceded. The thunder and fury of war was now ready to roll across the land, gathering momentum each day.

No one was more disturbed than Mrs. John Springs, living far away in a home she had bought in Stratford, Connecticut. She expressed her feelings to Baxter on April 15: "The papers bring us the intelligence of the surrender of Fort Sumter, and while I rejoice on the success of the brave South Carolinians, I am mourning over the condition of our once glorious country. . . . What is to become of us God alone knows. Terror and dismay have taken hold of me, and I take no rest, day or night. I can not let the mail leave without writing you my feelings for my heart is so sad. I need the sympathy of *those near to me* and God alone knows how I miss the protecting love of your beloved Father. Oh, Baxter, when and where is this trouble to cease and what is to become of us? It is needless to say where my sympathies turn in this time of trouble. My heart goes out in all the fullness and affection for the interest of the South and then I turn with mournful feelings to my *native* land to see its sad position. This morning I felt as tho' I would pack up and go off to you all . . . but then I am tied here by necessity. Perhaps it is best under the present excitement as I am in my own home and living as economically as possible, not knowing what may be in store for me. I am so miserable about our country's affairs and fearful the mails may be stopped and then I could not hear from you all."

Baxter worked tirelessly organizing his company of volunteers in York District. William Myers, as Captain, was recruiting a company in Charlotte, because North Carolina had seceded on May 21. Out in Marshall, Texas, Eli Baxter, Jr., now a Lieutenant, was busily organizing a company which he planned to take to Virginia as soon as possible. In Marietta, Georgia, Dr. Alva Connell was doing the same thing.

Arkansas had added her name to the Confederacy on May 6 and Tennessee seceded June 8.

Most of the Southern troops were leaving for Virginia. With the capital of the Confederacy moved to Richmond, nearly thirty thousand Union soldiers had been ordered into Virginia for the purpose of taking that city, thus hoping to end the war quickly with one bold stroke. Austin Springs left in June with his Regiment for Richmond.

A letter from James L. Orr written on June 16 from Anderson, South Carolina, to Baxter explained: "I have heard that you have a company raised for the war. . . . I am now engaged in raising a Regiment. . . . I require three more companies. If agreeable to you and the men of your command to join my Regiment, I should be most happy to receive you if you can report within a week from this time."

Baxter's recruits left, but he himself was detained by a letter from C. G. Memminger, Secretary of the Treasury of the Confederacy, appointing him York District Commissioner to enroll every planter to subscribe "the portion of his crop which he is disposed to lend for the support of the Government."

While Baxter made his rounds raising supplies and rallying recruits, letters came from his friends in Virginia. On June 20, his neighbor Joseph Nivens wrote: "I am at a place called Old Town Point, where two creeks empty into the James River. . . . A battery is being erected at this place. . . . According to 'Fuss and Feathers' '* war policy, Richmond will be taken by July 4th but they have made but little headway in Virginia. . . . We have gotten our rifles so now we are riflemen instead of musket men. I tell you we are getting pretty well prepared to butcher Yankees. . . . If they can't fight any better than they did between Newport News and Yorktown they had better quit. . . . I'll tell you when I heard the way the Yankees had treated the women at Hampton I felt like I could wade up to my neck in Yankee blood."

The first major engagement of the war was fought on Sunday, July 21, at Manassas along a creek called Bull Run. The battle terminated with the Yankees retreating in great panic towards Washington. The South was jubilant over this victory, but many asked the question: Why did Beauregard and Johnston not pursue the Yankees into Washington? W. J. Campbell wrote to Baxter concerning this battle: "It was a bloody fight. Killed more than could be buried. I could count fifteen or twenty dead just in thirty or forty yards around. And the most and finest horses were dead. . . . I tell you it takes lots to keep this thing going. Many of our boys are sick. The day after the fight it rained all day and night. We had not even a blanket or shelter. . . .

---

*Seventy-five-year-old General Winfield Scott, head of the United States Army, was called *Fuss and Feathers*.

The boys are looking for you. If you can, let my wife know when you're coming and fetch that flag along with you."

In August, Baxter was in Richmond with recruits for the Sixth South Carolina Volunteer Regiment. He was not very contented about leaving Blandie at Springfield because she was six months pregnant. However, her mother had promised to get there as quickly as possible and he could only hope for the best. Soon after his arrival in the capital he found his brother-in-law, Eli Baxter, Jr., looking extremely handsome in his uniform and apparently quite the idol of his men.

The Texas troops, camped at the Fair Grounds, had been properly recognized by President Davis in a ceremonial speech during which he presented the "Lone Star" flag to Colonel Lewis Wigfall* who accepted it on behalf of the Texas soldiers. Afterwards, Wigfall had marched his troops in a lengthy drill, which Lieutenant Eli Baxter, Jr., thought was an unnecessary hardship on the men considering the temperature was in the upper nineties. He and Wigfall did not get along well.

Baxter Springs quartered his troops at the Fair Grounds where hundreds of tents were pitched in encampment. Here green recruits were being drilled by cadets of the Virginia Military Institute under orders from their mathematics instructor, General Thomas Jonathan Jackson, who had been given the name of "Stonewall" at the battle of Manassas.

Making his way to the War Office, Baxter presented a letter of introduction, written by James Chesnut, Jr. and addressed to Colonel Bledsoe, Assistant Secretary of War. Here he received instructions and prepared to leave for Manassas.

Meanwhile, a letter arrived from Blandie who was doubly concerned now that her only brother and her husband were headed for battle. She did not share the joy which most Southerners felt after the victorious battle at Manassas when she wrote: "Poor Ma is perfectly broken hearted and crushed about Eli. I trust and pray he may be spared. He is Pa's and Ma's all. Tell him for me to try and take care of himself. And now, my dearest Husband, do for my sake and your

*Louis T. Wigfall, hot-headed duelist, native of Edgefield, South Carolina, was U. S. Senator from Texas until his withdrawal March 23, 1861; was a prime performer in the fall of Sumter; achieved the rank of General; represented Texas in the Confederate Congress.

little childrens' take care of yourself. Had you not better get yourself two net shirts and put them on, not heavy ones but such as will suit the fall weather. I am sorry you did not take a blanket. I heard this morning there was a great deal of sickness in the Manassas camp. So many drink from the water it keeps it muddy. . . . I will send this letter to Richmond. God bless you, my dear Bac, and guard you from every danger."

Eli moved with his troops to a camp near Bull Run. His letter of August 22, 1861, addressed to Baxter, was postmarked "Tudor Hall, Virginia": "We reached this point in safety. . . . Wigfall has been disipating since our arrival here but is now quite cool. We are very polite towards each other. I shall remember your injunctions given in Richmond. . . . I understand Dr. Connell has left for the seat of War and will be ordered to this Department."

On September 6, Blandie addressed a letter to Baxter at Fairfax Court House, Virginia: "I was rejoiced to receive three letters from you this week. I wrote you that Ma came on last Thursday, the 29th of August. She is so restless and unhappy about Eli that she scarcely knows what she is doing.

"Our Society is very busy making soldiers' clothes. We will send off next week for every soldier this side of the river two woolen shirts and drawers and socks. As soon as we receive the measurements for the military suits we will make them and send them on. I heard each Regiment would have a hospital. If so, I would like to know so we could make up a box.

"The little boys all ask if Father is well and when he is coming home. If I could only know you are well and not in danger I would be satisfied, no matter how long you have to be away. . . . Give my kindest regards to Cousin Fed Moore and John White. God bless you, my own dearest Husband. You are never out of my thoughts."

While Blandie and the other ladies of York District sewed and worried at home, the Confederates extended their skirmish lines past Falls Church, Virginia, almost to Washington.

Baxter's cousin, Fed Moore from Yorkville, was in that vicinity and wrote him the latest news: "Baxter, we have been absent from camp for a week on pickets the other side of Falls Church, a very dangerous post. Our pickets were fired at all the time until Col. Windor, with two pieces of artillery, made a charge on the enemy and completely routed them, they outnumbering us three to one. Our lines extended within the District of Columbia. We are under marching orders at this time. Be not surprised to hear of a general engagement before many days as troops are moving forward in large numbers today. . . . Enclosed is a letter which was directed to you at this camp. Thomas Kimbral has died since you left. Youngblood and Parks will both die in less than twenty four hours with typhoid fever. . . . Lieut. Love requests me to acknowledge the receipt of the money you sent. He will apply it to the use of the camp sick. We, as well as the camp, thank you."

This was the last letter Baxter received from Fed Moore, who was killed in action a few weeks later. Captain John White later told the story: "Pood Fed Moore was a victim, a brave, noble and generous man. The Yankees (it not being in our power to carry off his body) robbed his person of everything, even the buttons of his clothing."

Sometime in October Baxter arrived at Springfield. He was ill. Blandie was startled when she saw him. He was pale and drawn, showing his years for the first time, and his hair had begun to grey at the temples. He was badly in need of a rest, but, his duties as Commissioner for subscriptions for the Government needed his immediate attention. One of his fellow delegates to the State Convention, W. B. Wilson, wrote: "I regret to hear that you have been so unwell. I would like very much to see you. . . . Mr. Memminger states that the Government intends to provide a mode for the planters to obtain advance on their produce to enable them to meet the government taxes, and that Treasury notes will be issued for the purpose. Something must be done. There is now not cash enough in the District to pay its taxes. I hope nothing will prevent your coming to our meeting."

Blandie's baby arrived November 12. Dr. E. D. Williamson's bill reads: "Visit to Mrs. Springs in haste. Attention half day. Obstetrical services." And thus was born Leroy Springs, a baby destined to grow into the precocious, bombastic, aggressive, assertive, and attractive owner of the largest cotton mill in the world under one roof.

Now there were seven sons at Springfield. Baxter's kinsman John Blackwood offered his congratulations: "You perhaps might like a little more variety in regard to sex, yet the country may need all the soldiers it can command. I congratulate you and Cousin Blandie."

Then, referring to Federal seizure that week of Hilton Head, South Carolina, between Charleston and Savannah, Blackwood added: "It grieves me to know that the vandals have got a footing in South Carolina, not so much on account of the harm they have done, but for the glorification that they will make over it in Yankeedom."

Aside from the "glorification," the Federal forces turned Hilton Head and nearby Port Royal into a base for blockaders and siege operations against Charleston and Savannah. Some of Baxter's friends of the 12th South Carolina Regiment were engaged in the unsuccessful defense, and he sent personal checks to aid the wounded of the companies of Capts. W. H. McCorkle, John S. Miller, and G. E. McSteele, all local men.

Having Federal troops on Carolina soil was very disturbing to all Southerners. One soldier, A. B. Bale with the 6th South Carolina Volunteers, regretted it sorely. "I am sorry," he wrote, "to hear of those Yankees landing and planting their flag pole on the soil of South Carolina. That grinds us mightily to hear of such news. I think if they attack us here [Centerville, Virginia] we will give them some pills that will do their disease good. . . . I heard today from a letter from Rock Hill that the Negroes have been guilty of some outrages on some white women. That won't do. You must stir up the home guards and tell them they must put a stop to it."

The Federal invasion of South Carolina created a crisis that caused the President of the State Convention to issue a proclamation that the convention would convene in Columbia at noon on December 26. Baxter listened attentively to the President's opening speech: "Before your adjournment, on the 10th of April last, you devolved on me the very responsible duty of calling you together, whenever, in my judgment, the public exigencies should require it. . . . When you adjourned you prolonged your existance for eight months. . . . I was unwilling to assume the responsibility of permitting you to be dissolved. I have therefore called you together for the purpose of taking into consideration the dangers incident to the position of the State, and to take care that the Commonwealth of South Carolina shall suffer no detriment. . . ."

The Convention was in session for twelve days. One of the most important ordinances passed was one designed to strengthen the Executive department of the government by the appointment of an Executive Council, composed of the Governor, the Lieutenant Governor and three members elected by the Convention. This Council was to take over control of the military, declare martial law if necessary, arrest disloyal persons, impress private property, and expend public funds. In the absence of the Governor, the Council had full power to act.

It was eleven o'clock on the night of Wednesday, January 8, when the Convention adjourned and Baxter went back to the Congaree Hotel. The next morning he planned to shop for a few articles for Blandie and the boys. Then he would take the "up" train for home. Blandie had sent him a list, with the added comment, "Don't look for these things if you are pushed for time." As far as his wife was concerned, he always tried to find time to satisfy her every wish, but, actually, he thought, as he gave an exhausted sigh, he was very pushed for time. He had neglected his plantation and this worried him. Austin, who was at home from Virginia, had noticed it and had written the week before: "Wheeler was over Christmas day and informed me that your hogs had not been killed. If I had not been so engaged, I would have gone over to your place and had them killed. Dear Baxter, I am ready and willing to do anything to promote your interest."

Baxter had written his overseer to kill hogs the minute the weather permitted. He thought there was still enough salt to pack the meat down. He mulled over these things as he rode the train home, and, taking out Blandie's letter, he read it again:

"I received the package of candy this evening. I and the little ones shall enjoy it. . . . Yesterday morning was the coldest of the year. Hood had the hogs killed. . . . They weighed 4,481 pounds. . . . I got a letter from Lizzie last evening. She said all the planters had sent to Charleston and bought cards* and were going to make their own cloth. Had you not better look around for some? But do as your judgment dictates. If cloth is very high I will make the Negro womens dresses of osneburg and set Tom and the women spinning when the weather is bad. When you buy my thread I would rather have Singer Sewing Machine thread, but if you can't get it, buy Coate's thread. If you have time go around to Lec Monts and see if he has the Emperor Napoleon rose. Do get it for me if he has."

Baxter, bumping along on the train, smiled at Blandie's way of giving him instructions. Certainly, he had gotten her the Emperor Napoleon rose. He had sent it straight on and it had pleased her. She had

---

*Cards were wire-toothed brushes for combing and cleansing wool, cotton or other fiber.

written, "I received the rose yesterday evening and your letter. When I opened the bundle I was so pleased."

Then because his sons were so dear to his heart, he read again what Blandie had said about them: "The fields are white with sleet. The boys started to school this morning. Baxter started and *would* go. Eli could not keep him back, so I had to send Winnie for him up the road. He came back screaming 'I never get to go.' I could not keep from laughing, though he needs a whipping."

When the small, puffing train came to a shrieking halt at Springfield, Baxter found the little boys waiting for him. There was much jumping up and down, much hugging, much joy over the gifts he had brought them. Then they all tumbled into the carriage and Mr. Hood drove them up to the house where Blandie was waiting.

Coming home to Springfield was for Baxter a balm for the soul, just as it had been for his father before him. The stateliness, the peacefulness of the place had a soothing, quieting effect on a man when he was troubled and tired. Here he could pause, reflect on his problems, find understanding with himself and others. He could look up at the sky, listen to the wind in the oaks, he could see the love in his wife's eyes, hear the excitement of new dreams in his sons' voices. To enter the front door and see the roaring fires, one to the left and one to the right, to smell the enticing odors of good food, to have Blandie throw her arms about him and cry, "Oh Bac!," to sit after tea and talk to her, to thrill to her vibrant and tender love, all this was what he hungered for every time he left Springfield.

By the end of January, wounded soldiers were trying to get home. But that was a difficult undertaking. "Conveyances," explained Captain John White from Centerville, Virginia, "are very scarce and it is almost impossible to walk on account of the roads—the mud averaging about knee deep. I am unwilling for any of my men to start home until I am convinced they will incur no risk. The severity of the weather and bad roads are very destructive to our horses. Many are dying from poverty. I can count 60 or 75 dead horses in a mile of our camp. . . . Branch looks weak and feeble but he may be able to start for home. . . . Hamilton, who was shot through the body, the ball passing through his liver, lies quiet, and I think his recovery extremely doubtful. Nature worked a piece of his shirt (carried in by the ball) from his liver through the aperture in his side—the piece of cloth was 2½ inches long. . . . There is a fixed determination in our people to conquer a peace or die as free men. Baxter, ever since the battle of Drainsville I have felt a desire to kill a Yankee officer with my own hand and I live in hopes of being able to do it yet."

William Myers was sent with his company to the eastern part of North Carolina where he reported on February 7: "It is now certainly known that Roanoke Island will be the first point to which the enemy will pay their respects. I am now, and have been for some time, of the opinion that we can not successfully resist any point on our coast which the enemy attacks in full force. We neither have skill nor endurance of sufficient calibre to compete with them wherever their gun boats float. All the fortifications we have are of recent construction and of but little capacity to meet and resist the heavy force that will be brought against them."

From Adam Run, South Carolina, A. M. Kee, one of Baxter's neighbors explained: "Mr. Springs, we are getting plenty of good bacon, beef, flour, crackers, rice and more oysters than you could shake a stick at. We have no right to complain. But I fear our horses will go down hill. I think your black horse has distemper. Your grey horse doesn't look as well as he did when we left home."

The Governor of South Carolina again called on Baxter, this time as a Commissioner "to open books for the subscription of cotton." The Government needed all resources for the war effort and to this end Baxter worked diligently during the month of May. Meanwhile, his good friend Frank Sexton, who was then a Congressman from the state of Texas, urged him "to exert your extensive influence to keep the people in good heart. I know you will see the importance of doing all you can toward that end for just now our sky seems dark and lowering. Most of our important seaports have fallen and nearly the whole of the Mississippi is in control of the enemy. Texas, Tennessee and the Valley of Virginia, the great sources of our supplies for the Commissariat, are cut off. We have but little powder. Our manufacturers of arms are one by one being lost. Worse than all, I feel assured that the hopes of the people are drooping. I write you this, knowing that you deeply feel the magnitude of the contest in which we are embarked and upon the result of which depends the happiness of all we hold dear and sacred. You will of course understand me properly when I say that I would not speak to the people as I do to you.

"A tremendous battle is imminent at Corinth. It can not long be postponed. Will you believe me when I tell you a member of Congress said to me today that if Beauregard was defeated it would be the last of our 'organized resistance.' I begged him not to allow such a thought to enter his mind. . . . I think of the concluding sentence of Beauregard's order—'Our cause is just. God is with us and will give us the victory'—and am comforted."

Then Frank Sexton added at the bottom of his letter: "The telegraph reports Huntsville retaken by General Kirby Smith and that a battle has begun at Corinth. As tomorrow is Sunday—our great day for battles—it is believed the Waterloo of the war will be fought there. May God vouchsafe his favor to us in this hour of our peril."

The following month, which was June of 1862, Baxter was back in Virginia with the South Carolina troops, and Blandie was admonishing him: "Do, dear Bac, take good care of yourself. You know I am ruined without you."

CHAPTER TWENTY

PRIOR TO BAXTER SPRINGS' arrival in Virginia, his good friend Captain John White had been a faithful correspondent and reporter of the battles around Richmond. He explained what happened when Union General George B. McClellan was fighting his way up the Virginia peninsula in his drive on Richmond and his forces faced the Confederates at Yorktown. On Saturday, May 3, the seige of that town began. The Yankees kept up their cannon fire. The next day, which was the time the Northern army expected to storm the historic town, no Southerners could be seen. Upon investigation, it was determined they were retreating towards Williamsburg. Captain White, writing from a camp one mile from the Chickahominy River and twenty-six miles from Richmond, told the story to Baxter on May 13:

"Not long since, we commenced the retreat from Yorktown. The Yankee prisoners report McClellan's arrangements to route us at that place was complete. They say he was much chagrined and disappointed at our moving from the mouth of the monster guns he had placed in position to annihilate us—that he fully intended attacking us in the morning after we left. It requires at least a day to put an army of 60 or 70,000 men in motion. The van of the enemy was almost in sight of our rear guard. The close pursuit of the enemy forced Johnston to give them battle at Williamsburg to effect an orderly retreat. That duty was assigned to Longstreet's Division. It was not supposed that the fight would be so extensive, but Regiment after Regiment was called in, until 10 or 12,000 (I suppose) were engaged on both sides. The fight was close and furious, our men driving them from the field, when night closed the fight. I think our loss amounted to at least 800

or 1,000. The loss of the enemy was greater. We have in our possession eight cannon and destroyed ten or twelve (which we could not
bring away for want of horses) taken from the enemy. The fact that
we were on a retreat, the roads being awfully cut up, and not being
well supplied with transportation, prevented us from bringing off
many arms, etc. left on the battlefield. Our Brig. Gen'l Anderson
(from Sumter) acted very gallantly and received much praise. He is a
brave and fearless man. His brother was killed. He acted as Maj. Gen'l,
leaving Jenkins in command of our Brigade. Our Brigade supported
the Artillery, being placed in the redoubts. . . .

"The day of the fight was one of much anxiety and suspense to me.
Capt. Coker's company and mine were placed in a redoubt holding in
check four Regiments and six guns. We were expecting them to attack
us every hour. The Capt. of the Battery rode up to reconnoitre, when
Irwin Matthews fired, killing him—his horse was killed afterwards by
someone. The great blunder of the day was committed on our wing in
the evening. Gen'l Harvey Hill was ordered to make a strong demonstration, thinking that the enemy in front of our redoubt intended
attacking us. Instead of making the demonstration, an order was given
to charge—the 5th N. C. Reg't in front, 24th Va. next and the 6th S. C.
(ours) — (That may not be the order of the Reg'ts as my company and
Coker's being detached were ordered forward by themselves and I
could not see) The Yankee skirmishers ran in confusion. The Artillery men cut the gearing of their horses and left their guns, but the
Yankees held a redoubt in front of us. About the time N. C. Reg'ts
were ready to enter the fort—the order was given to face about and
retreat. The N. C. Reg't lost 200 killed and wounded. I think Hill
came up afterwards and remarked so I know his orders had not been
properly executed and that one of his Regts. had been badly cut up.

"The prisoners told us afterwards that there were two Divisions of
the enemy (30,000) supporting the front we charged.

"You see Gen'l Stuart's charge of Cavalry much praised in the Richmond papers. He charged back faster than he charged forward. Either
Longstreet or Johnston (so I hear) remarked that he went forward
like a rocket and came back like a meteor.

"After we left Yorktown our men did not sleep any more than four
or five hours during four days and nights. They had very little to eat.
Yet they all evinced a disposition to conquer or die. We anticipate a

great fight soon. If McClellan succeeds in taking Richmond he will do so when he shall have had half his army killed."

McClellan now marched on towards Richmond, a city which was in chaos with its wounded and dying, its citizens evacuating, and troops pouring in for reinforcements. The weather was terrible. The roads and fields were a mass of mud. Lying between McClellan and the Confederate forces was the Chickahominy River, over which all bridges had been destroyed except the one at Mechanicsville. Soon new bridges were built and the Federals were crossing the river. Seven miles out of Richmond, the road to Williamsburg intersected a road called the Nine Mile road. At this intersection there had once been a clump of seven pines. Not far away was a farm by the name of Fair Oaks. It was here that General Johnston decided to turn and attack the Yankees. That was May 30, a Friday. The following morning the heavens opened with a terrible thunderstorm that sent torrential rains down on the already wet soldiers. The thunder crashed and roared. Even the heavens had taken up the battle. The Confederates were slow to move because of this. Generals Longstreet and Hill waited for the sound of a gun which was to signal them that General Huger was ready to march. They waited. And they waited. It was near noon when General Hill, not waiting any longer for the signal, advanced. Captain John White went into great detail when he wrote to Baxter Springs about this battle:

"I will write you something about what I saw on Saturday, the day of the battle. Also give you a little of what I heard. I was told by a man (John Chestnut), who heard the quarrel, that the attack was delayed on our part for three hours on account of Huger's Brigadier Generals quarreling about rank. If that can be established, they should be court martialed and cashiered. Our Brigade did not fight at the point allotted to it—according to previous arrangement (so I've learned since). We were to support General Smith, but Huger failed to bring up his Brigade and Longstreet ordered Anderson to take his place. We, our Regiment, relieved a Georgia Regiment on the battlefield at 3 P.M. When we came up the Georgians were distant from the enemy about 100 yards. The space between them was covered with pine trees felled about waist high. The Georgians were lying down and the enemy were in ambush on the opposite side. We walked over the Georgians, climbed over the pines and drove the enemy in confusion before us. It was a trying time and many of our Regiment fell, among them Capt. Phiney in my company. . . . This was the first of a series of charges; six or seven made by our Regiment that evening. After the first charge we soon encountered the enemy in a similar position, in ambush well protected by dense pines felled about waist high, We charged them again and the enemy left in confusion. The enemy, with fresh troops, occupy advantageous positions and await our advance. We would yell and charge, never failing to drive them before us and always reserving our fire until they would rise to run, then we killed many of the scoundrels.

"Later in the morning we charged a Battery strongly supported by the enemy in rifle pits, forced them to leave in confusion, capturing three guns. Later still, in the evening, we had advanced so far as to be forced to present three fronts to fight on—the right, front and left. At that time Gile's (5th) Regiment came to our assistance. We whipped them and night came on after we had advanced one mile further into the lines of the enemy than any other corps in the army (so says General Anderson) .

"Baxter, we fought under the impression that it was a general route of the enemy, that we were driving General McClellan's grand army into the Chickahominy, that we were avenging the wrongs and insults done our people. Imagine our disappointment when we ascertained that many of our Brigades had not the heart and courage to charge through. We found that the Yankees had not been driven in many places one inch from their original positions.

"Baxter, I see our papers publishing our killed at 150. The Yankees know that to be lies. They have seen more of our killed than that. If we are afraid to tell the truth, we have not the nerve to do the work before us. . . . We have a well disciplined army to fight. The Yankee officers acted gallantly in endeavoring to rally their men."

By the end of June, with McClellan's Union forces camped four miles from Richmond, General Robert E. Lee, who had succeeded General Johnston after the battle of Fair Oaks or Seven Pines, had begun an effective strategy. The Confederates attacked on June 26 and were met with force by McClellan. For seven days the fighting went on. Richmond was saved. John White had so aptly expressed it to Baxter when he had said, "The Yankees are our superiors but they have not the cause."

Blandie wrote to her husband, addressing the letter to: Col. A.

Baxter Springs, care of Surgeon J. S. Baxter, 3rd Georgia Hospital, Richmond, Virginia, and on the envelope was a note asking to have the letter forwarded or delivered as soon as possible. It was dated July 5 and read: "Everybody seems crazy with the news. I feel so rejoiced that our victory has been so complete. I got no papers this morning which was a disappointment to me. I can't keep a paper an hour. Someone is coming for them all the time. . . . We are all well. I was very sorry to hear poor Col. Lee was killed.* We had quite an excitement yesterday. Someone had telegraphed Mr. White that John could not be found. . . . Poor Col. McIntosh—I wish it would prove a mistake that his leg was shot off. . . . Write me, my dear Bac, everything you know. So many people here want to know all about the men. . . . A letter came today from Lizzie which she had sent to Vicksburg and it had been mailed from there to Jane and she sent it to me. Brother Eli has gone to Arkansas. It is impossible for Ma and Pa to get home. . . . Please try to come home if you get sick."

By the end of July the situation looked brighter for those around Richmond. But all was not going well during July and August in South Carolina. A call had gone out for the State Convention to reconvene on September 9.

And so Baxter went home, arriving at Springfield August 15. He wrote wearily: "I got home last night about 2 o'clock and today I leave on business which will occupy all my time."

While the State Convention, which was virtually an emergency ruling body, was in session, Baxter received a letter from Blandie: "Now, old fellow, don't sit up all night and fail to get your rest. You have such a care worn countenance and I feel so anxious and uneasy about you. You must keep in mind you are my dear old fellow and I can't live without you. Life is a blank without your dear self."

When the business of the Convention was completed, President Jamison spoke to the delegates Wednesday, September 17, and said: "Connected as you have been with some of the most memorable incidents in the history of South Carolina, it will always be a subject of patriotic pride to me to have been a member of the Convention of 1860."

Now Baxter was ready to leave Columbia, but first he sat down in his hotel room and penned a letter to Captain John White, keeping

*Colonel Charles C. Lee taught with D. H. Hill in the North Carolina Military Institute in Charlotte.

him posted on the affairs of the South Carolina government. Captain White was on his mind because the 6th South Carolina Regiment under Lee had, several weeks before, fought the Yankees for the second time at Manassas or Bull Run, and Lee was now in Maryland confronting McClellan at a little town called Sharpsburg. Captain White later declared: "It seemed to be the general impression among the soldiers, that we should not invade Maryland. Many feigned sickness and a large number straggled behind the wagons; reducing the army to 30,000 (so I'm informed General Lee remarked) with which number he opposed McClelland with 140,000 at Sharpsburg."

As Baxter was writing to White, news crackled over the telegraph wires that a fierce battle was imminent. When it was all over, and the Confederates were back in Virginia, Captain White, writing from Winchester October 3, gave Baxter the details:

"The battle of Sharpsburg may be termed a *drawn fight,* the enemy sustaining a much greater loss.* The cannonading continued from sun rise to sun set and was terrific. The retreat was well conducted. The little village of Sharpsburg was strongly Union in feeling, was situated just in rear of our line of battle and was nearly annihilated by the Yankee guns. McClellan would have found our army in bad condition to fight, had he pursued vigorously, but I suppose he was too much crippled to do so. He did *attempt* a pursuit and Jackson awaited until he had marched about five thousand across, having his troops massed, he charged them, taking 300 prisoners, killing and drowning the remainder. The Yankees leaped from a precipice fifty feet high into the Potomac. The stream was blue with their coats."

The South Carolina legislature imposed another duty upon Baxter. It made him a Commissioner of the Soldier's Relief Board, charged with caring for the families of men at the front. He was then past forty-three and already burdened with efforts to keep the war machine supplied. He responded: "If my services are regarded more important than in the field of action I am ready and will endeavor faithfully to discharge the duties thereof. I have never, that I know, shirked responsibility or duty and I would not now like so to act as to give the appearance of it. I wish to serve where I can be the most useful to the country."

*The Union had 2,010 killed, 9,416 wounded, 1,043 missing, one General killed and eight Generals wounded. The Confederates had 1,890 killed, 9,770 wounded, 2,304 missing, three Generals killed and eight Generals wounded. Among the latter were Baxter's friends, Robert Toombs and Maxcey Gregg.

Baxter had the responsibility of securing supplies for the army as well as the home front. He began immediately to scour the country for what was needed. One very scarce commodity was salt, a necessary thing for man and beast. Another article necessary to the soldiers was shoes for their horses. Pots for cooking were essential to the Army. These required iron, which was a very scarce item. Speculators were going around the country buying up everything they could find and then selling for enormous profit. But this did not alter the fact that armies get hungry and have to be fed. Equipment wears out and has to be replaced. So Baxter again rolled up his sleeves and went to work.

He wrote to B. C. Pressley of Charleston, requesting iron and salt. The answer came back: "I deeply regret that we can not furnish you with any salt at this time. We are under heavy orders in small amounts to needy families. There have been six weeks freshets in the river, making it impossible to work. . . . Unless something can be done for us we can not do more than we are doing to relieve the army for salt. . . . We can not buy sheet iron or old boiler iron at any price. We would even make pans out of stove pipe iron but we can not get that. The speculators and extortionists head us off in every direction."

So Baxter tried R. C. Pearson of Morganton, North Carolina., who replied on November 19 (1862) : "I have not a sack of salt to my name and am totally at a loss where to look for it . . . short of the salt works in Virginia. It is no unusual thing to see dozens of wagons daily from the upper district of your State going there. . ."

Finally Baxter obtained four sacks of salt in Columbia for $507.20; six bushels from James W. Brown, Charleston, for $74, and eight bushels from Claussen Mills for $203.50.

The Reverend Mr. Whyte expressed it this way to Baxter, "Times are critical, finances deranged, and there are those who think the Legislature can put a stop to speculation."

Prices were going higher and higher. And money was going down. The Confederate Government had issued paper money not payable on demand, but at the end of the war. Consequently, as prospects for a victorious peace became dimmer the paper money became cheaper. For instance Private A. M. Kee, camped three miles from Richmond, informed Baxter of conditions there: "We can't stay here long because we can't get anything for our horses to eat. It is snowing and very cold. We have to buy more than half our food at exhorbitant prices. We can buy a pig that will weigh 16½ pounds for $6.00 and $2 for a turkey.* I have been buying oats for my horse and paid 25c for what would be called a good bundle. I don't like to pay the prices but we are obliged to have something to eat."

The government asked planters to curtail their cotton crop and increase their output of foodstuffs. Planting corn took less labor than cotton and released Negroes for work on the coastal fortifications. Every slave holder was required to supply a certain number of Negroes for that purpose.

Wheat was not only scarce but high. The Yorkville newspaper, in the fall of 1862, printed: "A. B. Springs, Esquire, has been selling seed wheat to his poor neighbors at one dollar per bushel. The writer has not heard of any being refused. Publicity is given to this fact neither to flatter nor to advance another in public favor, but to provoke others to imitate an example so benevolent and so patriotic."

During the entire year of 1862 the Eli Baxter family had been in a state of turmoil. The Judge and Julia had left Cornucopia in January and journeyed to Texas, but before their departure, they had enjoyed a visit from their son who was home on leave from Virginia.

While Eli, Jr., the dashing young Lieutenant, was at Cornucopia his mother decided to play the role of matchmaker. It was time, she thought, for her son to have a wife.

"I told him," explained Julia Baxter, "he should call on Mary Grimes, as she had sent him such a pretty scarf. So he and Lizzie went one evening and found her with a homespun dress on. Lizzie said 'How patriotic you are!' Miss Grimes remarked she had given all her pocket money to the soldiers. She thought it the duty of every lady to lay aside all extra dressing and extravagance these war times and assist, in all their power, the great cause for which we were struggling. I undertand she sews and knits every Saturday for the soldiers and had her summer bonnet trimmed to wear this winter. Eli said he looked and listened with astonishment. A young lady worth a hundred Negroes so economical! He set her down for a prize for any man, so he lost his heart, *at least for the time*."

When May rolled around Julia Baxter, in Texas, was feeling very far from her loved ones. "Oh, this dark benighted corner," she complained. "I have not received any letters from anyone. We are still at the plantation as we could not get home, but expect to leave here in

*At that time, turkeys were selling for $30 apiece in Richmond, Virginia.

a day or two for Shreveport where we will remain with Fannie* until the overflow of the Mississippi passes off. We are truly blockaded by water. At first I felt very unhappy and distressed over it all, but now I have made up my mind to be resigned and do the best we can. Perhaps the Yankees will take Vicksburg. If so there is no chance for us to see Georgia unless we run the blockade.

"Eli has been with us the past week. He certainly has a good, amiable and happy disposition. He seems as cheerful and bright as can be. His regiment is all complete,† he Lieutenant Colonel. He takes Jim, our old carriage driver, to wait on him. Says he has more confidence in him than any other Negro living. Eli paid an exorbitant price for his horse, five hundred dollars. He says Jim must have a good horse also. I felt very cheerful whilst he was here. Now he has gone I am sad again. We have promised to visit his Regiment near the railroad between Marshall and Shreveport. He says he will have a tent for our especial accommodation. We will go from Shreveport then. He thinks they will be ordered to Little Rock, Arkansas. Then I shall seldom hear from him, but the same strong arm can protect him everywhere alike.

"We have had a very exciting time here for the last two weeks. Had three Regiments of Cavalry camped in a few miles of us. They just swept the country of provisions as they went along. General Carter said they would allow 20c per pound for bacon. They took near a thousand pounds. Your Pa sold over eight hundred bushels of corn at $1.00 per bushel. They paid him two Confederate bonds, $500 each. But—oh—the botheration and trouble. They *would* come in the house to eat, twenty and thirty at a time. One day I fed, from twelve o'clock until near sundown, a hundred soldiers. They went in every room, just took possession of the house. Lizzie had her fun out of them. She made one soldier churn, another shell peas. They ate six pounds of butter each day and drank lots of milk.

"The soldiers pass in each direction, east and west. They are everlasting. I never could have believed three thousand men on horseback could have made such an appearance. They were four days crossing the river Neeches on a flat. We all feel willing to do all we can for the

*Fannie Baxter married Dr. William Ogden Cutliff of Shreveport in 1859.
†Lieutenant Eli Baxter, Jr. was sent to Texas from Virginia to raise a Regiment of Cavalry. Colonel Randon of Texas had received similar orders. The two jointly raised a full regiment, of which Colonel Randon was elected Colonel and Eli Baxter, Jr., Lt. Colonel. This Regiment was subsequently a part of Walker's Division of Infantry. This information taken from a Houston, Texas, newspaper of 1867.

Confederacy, but I really think we have had rather more than our share, and just to think the vile Yankee creatures are right in my way getting back to Georgia. I wish I could destroy them all with one blow—but this is sinful. How vain are all human calculations! I thought this summer to have all my daughters together at the old homestead. I pray this unnatural war will not last always."

Julia and the Judge were able to reach Cornucopia by midsummer. After a short stay there they went to Springfield to visit Blandie. However, the Judge was restless and worried over his Texas plantation. December found them once more across the Mississippi, and from Texas the Judge wrote to Blandie: "I don't like the aspect for public affairs or for peace. I believe I could have gotten an army of 50,000 soldiers from Georgia to Texas. Cars crowded, depots, towns and villages full of straggling soldiers.

"I don't like the aspects of things in this State. The poor men in army posts are resenting the conscript law. The exemption of men who own twenty Negroes is producing much excitement. In an adjoining county they shot the enrolling officer, burnt his buggy, and it is said the Governor has called out troops to cause them to subside. If this feeling should prevail to any extent the Confederate States are gone. They declare the war is the rich man's war, and declare they will not fight their battles. I fear if it is not suppressed it will inaugurate a conflict between the rich and the poor which will bring on a fearful civil war. Nothing can save us but peace.

"I have great fears for Vicksburg. If we lose that place the eastern army will suffer for meat. Texas has the most number of beeves. I expect nearly a thousand head going to the army and multitudes of sheep. President Davis should put all the available force of the West in striking distance of Vicksburg in case the enemy should attack it."

On Monday, December 22 (1862), Julia Baxter was greatly worried when she wrote to Blandie: "Yesterday I received the enclosed letter from Eli. Oh, what feelings I endured. I have been all the time hearing of the awful battle to come off at Vicksburg—I wept and prayed— finally concluded I could do nothing of myself except beg the Lord to spare Eli's life. Oh, how many noble, good men have fallen in this war!"

Eli's letter, which Julia Baxter enclosed to Blandie, read: "We are tonight encamped four miles from Little Rock enroute to Vicksburg. McCulloch's Division has been ordered to that point by a forced march. Gen'l Holmes told me today he feared we would not arrive in time for the battle and if we did, our hands would be full. He said, 'Colonel, I assure you there is hard fighting ahead for your command.' Gen'l McCulloch thinks we will have to engage the enemy between Monroe and Vicksburg. Our Division numbers eighteen Regiments and twelve thousand strong. My Regiment has suffered immensely from sickness. I fear I will not reach Vicksburg with more than four hundred fifty men. Some other Regiments much smaller. Ed Baxter has been discharged and gone home. The Medical examining board pronounced that his left lung was partly gone.* Tom Baxter is still here and well. I do not want anything in the way of clothing. I have a beautiful Colonel's uniform that I paid one hundred dollars for. I have paid a great deal for clothing this winter, though I have plenty of money, my pay being not quite two hundred dollars a month. My Reg't has warm clothes enough to last two Reg'ts a year.

"I may send Jim home from Monroe. He is nearly crazy to go. He is a great hand to make money, has purchased a gold watch. Lets a poor soldier ride his horse for three hours for a dollar. Will walk and carry another knapsack for a half dollar. Bought a sack of flour and dried peaches, made tarts and sold them to the soldiers for fifty cents a piece. He is a faithful Negro. We both enjoy good health. I walk eight or ten miles every day and let some poor tired soldier ride my horse. If we can get over to Vicksburg and have a battle with the Yanks I believe it will prove both beneficial to the health and spirits of the command. I shall go into the fight dressed very plainly. It is my opinion the great battle of this revolution will be fought near Vicksburg. The Yanks are determined if possible to get possession of the Mississippi."

The years 1862 was coming to a close and the Springses, as well as the Baxters, were fearful of what might happen at Vicksburg, and yet their thoughts were on Virginia too. The battle of Fredericksburg had been fought on December 13 and 14 and the casualty list was lengthy. "What a dreadful battle," moaned Julia Baxter. "Poor Tom Cobb†— a blank will be made in Athens not easily filled. And General Maxcy

---

*Edwin Gilmer Baxter, son of Thomas Baxter and first cousin of Eli Baxter, Jr., died shortly after this date.

†General Thomas R. Cobb placed his troops behind a stone wall on a hill at the boundary of the Marye estate. Behind him were the supporting batteries. Six times the Union forces advanced to within a hundred yards, only to be cut down. At nightfall the Yankees left 5,444 dead or dying on the field. General Cobb was killed and General Kershaw took his place. This battle cost the Union army 12,653 men, killed, wounded, and missing.

Gregg was one of Carolina's noblest sons*—It was a dear bought victory. How many more such are to occur! God only knows."

It truly was a dear bought victory. General Burnside who had replaced General McClellan, was anxious to show his initiative. He moved down the Rappahanock to Fredericksburg with one hundred and thirteen thousand men. General Lee placed his defenses south and west of the town. The Union troops crossed the river and attacked. The battle that ensued was so terrible that the Union General Couch cried out, "Oh, great God! see how our men, our poor fellows are falling!" And General Burnside, taking the blame for his Union dead, paced the floor, wild with anguish.

"The great blunder," wrote Captain John White, "with Burnside was, he had selected a Thermopylie to pass through to Richmond. He could not have selected a more dangerous or difficult route."

On December 15 Burnside's army retreated in the darkness to the other side of the river, leaving field after field covered with the dying, screaming in agony and freezing from cold, while everywhere lay the dead, already at peace.

"I did not dream," explained John White to Baxter Springs, "of the Yankees abandoning their proposed route to Richmond without making a greater effort than the fight on Saturday. It was no insignificant fight, it is true, but Burnside must have had 200,000 men and a loss of 15 or 20,000 is not much in such an army. . . . Kershaw's Brigade acted a conspicuous part in the fight on the left and in connection with Cobb's Brigade held Marye's Hill against 40,000 Yankees. They slaughtered the Irish Brigade of Meagher. The list of casualties in Gregg's Brigade bespeak for it a hot place in the fight on the right.

"We have made our last call for recruits and I think Lee intends hereafter to select advantageous positions and sacrifice as few lives as possible. Another series of battles similar to those around Richmond would ruin us. Baxter, our entire effective force here will not exceed 75 or 80,000. Half of our army is on furlough and in the various hospitals. The Medical is the deficient department in the Army— there are thousands of soldiers who spend nearly all their time in the hospitals."

---

*General Maxcy Gregg was killed at Fredericksburg.

CHAPTER TWENTY-ONE

BUSINESS, TO BAXTER SPRINGS, had always been a challenge. It was his forte. But the business of war was grim. It sickened him at times; it angered him at times; but forever and always it depressed him. How could he find supplies for soldiers and their families when those supplies dwindled every day and often were nonexistent? How could he alleviate the suffering of York District families when the Soldiers Relief Board gave him a token budget and very little grain? Fortunately, the citizens of Yorkville held a public meeting and agreed to give him one per cent of their wheat crop and two per cent of their corn harvest for relief.

He appealed to his friend R. G. McCaw, a member of the South Carolina legislature, who replied: "I am more than willing to vote for any increase of appropriation which may produce food and raiment for the poorer classes. I agree with you that the appropriation must be increased in proportion to the number of new troops mustered into the service. I also concur with you, were cards supplied instead of cloth our women could clothe themselves at a cheaper rate. I will take an early opportunity to see what the Governor has done in the way of procuring cards. . . ."

What could Baxter say about the home front to encourage the men on the battlefield? He found it difficult to dispute Sergeant A. M. Kee when that weary soldier wrote from a camp in Amherst County, Virginia: "I don't believe fighting will ever make peace. I think the thing will go on until one party or the other is starved out." What Kee did not realize was the fact that the North had plenty of food. Her ports were not blockaded. She had the whole world from which to gather supplies if she needed them.

The blockade was choking every Southern state. The army was in dire need of supplies and when they were available they reached the troops over slow and inadequate trains. But how could the railroads function properly when mechanical parts were wearing out and the North was the main source of supply?

Baxter had every available Negro on his plantation cutting wood for the railroad engines to burn. The President of the Charlotte-Columbia Railroad wrote to him: "I hope you have a good number of hands cutting wood all the while. We are depending on you giving us 1200 cords. It is very important. Make any contracts you can with your neighbors for wood and ties."

Another form of transportation was becoming scarce. Baxter was constantly looking for horses to send to the front. He had nearly emptied his own stables at the beginning of the war. He hardly knew where his horses were, except two, he had learned, were near Culpepper, Virginia, with the 1st Regiment, South Carolina Cavalry, and the soldiers at Amherst, Virginia, had one horse and one mule.

Speculators were having a field day all over the country. Judge Baxter wrote: "They trade in wool, sugar, cotton, molasses, beef cattle, corn, cloth, tobacco and poor hogs. They buy up poor hogs, drive them to Red River where they can get corn at 75c to fatten them."

Money was depreciating every day. Baxter had put thousands and thousands of dollars in Confederate Bonds. The low interest rate did not keep up with the inflation. Frank Sexton, writing from the Confederate capital, was correct when he declared: "The subject of our finances is indeed the one which, like Aaron's sod, 'swallows up the rest.' It is to be feared that in the vast multitude of counsel we are having on this subject we are likely to have obscurity rather than wisdom."

The South was discouraged over the lack of necessities, but the North had a different problem, that of morale. Baxter could see the trend from the letters that drifted back to him from the battle line, particularly since the terrible slaughter of Union soldiers at the battle of Fredericksburg. President Lincoln, discouraged, had used his *Emancipation Proclamation* to give purpose to the fighting, but, to use again Captain White's words, "they had not the cause." Sergeant Kee realized it when he wrote: "Colonel Springs, we have been paid our wages up to the 1st of January (1863). That is more than the Yankees can say. They are deserting every day, coming over and giving themselves up to our pickets. They say they are all whipped and won't fight any more."

And the same day that Sergeant Kee wrote, another soldier, Leroy Johnston, explained: "A Yankee deserter came over to our side. He swam the river naked, and when he got over he was so near frozen he couldn't speak for two hours. They wrapped him in some blankets and put him by a fire and he came to. He says they are powerfully demoralized. There were, he says, five hundred Yankees lay down their guns and went home. They sent out their Cavalry after them but they all got across the Potomac but sixty."

"We picket in two hundred yards of the Yankees," wrote J. Nivens, "just a narrow river between us. We talk to each other and change papers with them. They talk like they are very tired of the fun. They say we don't bite off the right end of the cartridge, and that we ought to bite of the ball and ram the blank cartridge down the shoot. Then we would not hurt so bad. They tell us they want to quit but they don't see any chance to get off. Colonel, I think they are tired, as well as some of the rest of us. If they come over here though, we will give them the worst whipping they ever have gotten yet. Old Stonewall Jackson and Longstreet have the boys to make the Yankees get."

The women of the South were in the struggle just as bravely as their men. Hundreds of spinning wheels came out of attics. Wool dresses were cut up and made into warm shirts for the soldiers. Carpets were being used for blankets. The women of Baxter's District were clamoring for cards to comb cotton and wool. He had been trying to get them. Finally, some came through the blockade into Charleston and he purchased two hundred. The agent apologized for the increased cost: "The advance in price has been caused by the requirement of the Government that we shall pay all import duties in coin or sterling exchange which multiplied that on these just received twenty five times. This is as low as the company can dispose of them."

In March (1863), having reports that his friends in the 6th Regiment of South Carolina Volunteers were very short of food, Baxter enlisted Blandie's and the boys' help in fixing up a large box of provisions which was sent north by friends. Captain John White, at Camp Blackwater, Virginia, gratefully acknowledged its arrival: "The non commissioned officers and privates of my company have unanimously requested me to express to yourself and family the many thanks for your liberal contributions of provisions sent in charge of the Grahams. The box certainly came to hand at a very seasonable time inasmuch as our commissary had just commenced to execute an order to issue half rations to this Regiment. As for myself, I assure you I appreciated your kindness, and to Johnny and Eli tender my many thanks. Baxter, without any exaggeration our Army is being fed at present on a very economical scale. When three days rations are issued, our men eat them in one day and a half. Our men have been guilty of killing many hogs in this neighborhood. Notwithstanding all this, the soldiers have been very cheerful and complain very little. My Regiment will make a good fight. . . . Our scouts report that the Yankees have been strongly reinforced."

John White was right. The Yankees had been strongly reinforced. "Fighting Joe" Hooker, the Major General who had replaced Burnside after the battle of Fredericksburg, was planning a maneuver which he said would send Lee in full retreat or surrender. But things did not work out that way. It all happened at Chancellorsville on the morning of May 1. The battle was a bloody slaughter for both sides. It raged all day and commenced again at midnight. That was the night Stonewall Jackson was shot, through error, by his own men. Over the same land on which the soldiers had fought at the battle of Fredricksburg, they now fought, bled, and died by the thousands. But the Confederates fought on, crying to one another, "Remember Jackson." The battle went into the second day, then into the third. John Nivens had been right when he told Baxter, "If they come over here we will give them the worst whipping they ever have gotten yet." The fourth day the battle raged on. When night came it was about over. The Yankees had retreated to the river. On May 5 they crossed over and settled in their camps. Lee had won again. After this, Baxter would receive fewer letters from his friends and neighbors who were camped on the Rappahannock. They had received that well earned rest they had been writing about, but they had not wanted it to be by death.

And on the battlefield lay two of Baxter's fine horses, dead.

The death of Stonewall Jackson cast a shadow of gloom over the South. Everyone from the highest to the lowest mourned. Blandie, who was a friend of Mrs. Jackson,* wrote to Baxter while he was away on official business: "I have heard of the death of poor General Jack-

---

*Mrs. Jackson was Anna Morrison, daughter of Dr. Robert Hall Morrison, founder of Davidson College. Mrs. Jackson spent much of her life in Charlotte, N. C.

son. 'Tis sad and distressing to think of it and I can't think of anything else. Oh, what a loss to our country. I really am afraid some misfortune is ahead of us. I long to see you back but hope you will be successful in your mission."

Blandie was very busy these days. She was supervising the plantation whenever Baxter was absent, and she had taken on a new task, that of nursing her brother-in-law Leroy Springs who had come from Petersburg, ill. Baxter had thought the change would be beneficial to him and had insisted that he come to Springfield.

Amid all the tension of war and anxiety over loved ones, there was one happy event which made everyone in the Springs family rejoice. It concerned Austin and Janie. After having been married nearly fourteen years, they had their first baby on May 20. Blandie, who had gone over to Springsteen plantation, sent a hasty note: "Baxter, I write this morning to let Leroy and you hear the good news. Janie was taken in rather slow labor yesterday about eleven o'clock and was delivered about eleven last night. She came through safely and presented Austin with a fine, plump little girl, who looks like Sophia and Austin. The child is named Mary Elizabeth.* Austin is delighted over the baby but seems a little disappointed it wasn't a boy."

Blandie at this time was expecting another baby. Seeing and holding Janie's wee little girl brought forth all the desire in her heart to have another baby as lovely as her little lost Julia. And so she waited and hoped.

While she waited, the war grew worse. And their brother Leroy grew weaker.

General Lee took the offensive. He marched north and crossed the Potomac, headed for a place called Gettysburg. Those who were not familiar with the name before that July of 1863 would surely have it engraved in their minds and hearts forever after. Lee's army was flushed with success. The South was optimistic, but the optimism was short lived. Gettysburg, the turning point of the war, sent the Confederates back to Virginia painfully and sadly thinking of their defeat. Captain White expressed it well when he wrote to Baxter:

"The Confederacy at present has every appearance of being in a critical condition; but the same God and Generals, who have led us heretofore, will establish for us yet our independence. . . . Vicksburg

*Mary Elizabeth Springs, at the age of eighteen, married Lysander D. Childs of Columbia, S. C. on July 13, 1881.

has fallen. . . . Old Lee is in contracted circumstances. Things look dark."

August was an exceedingly hot month. The humidity was oppressive. Blandie sat with a palm leaf fan, cooling her face. Her condition made her feel lazy. But her conscience bothered her when she was idle. There was so much to be done. Even the children were busy. Johnny and Eli were making sun hats from dried straw. They had made them for all those on the plantation and had even promised some to their father's friend in Winnsboro, Mr. W. R. Robinson, who just the week before had teasingly written to Baxter: "Ask my little friends Eli and John what has become of the hats they were to have made for me and my sons, Ebner and Tom. Tell them we are all nearly run out of something to keep the sun from boiling our brains, and that we are depending on them as our deliverers."

On August 14 Leroy died. This was the first break in the family since John Springs' death. It was depressing and another reason to feel a shadow of doom spreading over them.

The heat of August carried over into September and with it came the news of the battle of Chickamauga. All eyes were on Georgia and Tennessee that fall, but Blandie had eyes only for her baby who was born November 5. A little girl! Joy abounded at Springfield. The boys were fascinated with the idea of a sister. She was named Fannie Cutliff.

Baxter was absent from Springfield most of November and all of December. Where he was is not known. His files showed only a few terse orders given by the Chief Quarter Master of Armstrong's Division near Knoxville. He might have gone there, accompanying Captain John White and his South Carolina Volunteers who raced there by train when Knoxville was under seige. He left with Blandie an instruction sheet telling how much money each slave was to receive for Christmas. As usual, old Wheeler received the highest amount, with Betty, the children's nurse, receiving almost as much. The other forty-three Negroes received anywhere from $7.50 to fifty cents each.

The old year of 1863 rang out and the new year was ringing in, but it was a death knell to the hungry South. For instance, Charlotte did not have beef to feed the delegates of the General Assembly convening there and sent a message to Baxter: "If you can let us have two beeves we would be glad to have them sent up tomorrow.

. . . I beg you to remember we are a community in trouble for provisions for which to feed our guests." Baxter complied with this request and immediately sent the two animals to Charlotte.

It was no unusual thing now for Baxter to see undernourished mothers fighting desperately to find food for their children. He received letters like the one which read: "I have only one mess of meal in my house and that is borrowed. I have been borrowing the bread my family has eaten for a week. I have been down sick and my children cry when I leave them to hunt food."

Baxter saw determined women, who had never planted before, bent from hoeing in the fields. He saw women with hands calloused from chopping wood, hands which had once been soft and lovely. He saw women trying to control Negro slaves who had become lazy and indolent with no master at home to make them work. He saw unprincipled men becoming rich through speculation. He did not like what he saw. It showed in every furrow of his brow and every grey hair on his head.

Word finally came through from Texas. The Judge wrote in April: "You may not have gotten my three previous letters. . . . Our health is good. . . . Eli's Regiment has been ordered to Arkansas. In passing on from the late battlefield the troops came by here. He spent three days with us. His health was very good and he was in high spirits. He had two wounds, one on the arm and one on the leg just above the ankle. The one on the leg was swollen up and very black. . . . Your Mother is very anxious to go home this year and if she puts her head upon it she will go it."

The Northern populace had clamored for "something spectacular." The fall of Atlanta on September 2, 1864, was just that. Now Lincoln was assured of his re-election and now the war in the South would take on a new look. It would be waged against the innocent, the women, the children, the aged, their homes, their all. Sherman and his army would see to that.

On the night of November 15 Sherman set fire to Atlanta and ordered his sixty thousand troops, his twenty-five hundred wagons (each drawn by six mules), his sixty-five guns (each pulled by eight horses), his six hundred ambulance wagons and his tremendous herd of cattle to begin the march that would lead to Savannah. They marched out of Atlanta on four parallel roads. Part of the army went to Gordon, while part went to Milledgeville, the State capital. They remained centered around these two towns for several days. Sherman gave orders to "forage liberally." How those orders were carried out was explained by Judge Eli Baxter's neighbor, Mr. Ponce. When Blandie read the letter she burst into tears:

"Sherman's invasion through middle Georgia, embracing about twenty miles in breadth, is marked by desolation and ruin. The violation of black women was common occurence, and sometimes the white fell victim to the polution!!

"The taking, using and actual *waste* of property is immense from some plantations. They took *every mule, every horse* and much cattle and hogs. Many fattened hogs were killed and left on the ground to spoil. Their own jaded stock they shot, taking better ones instead. People's clothing, watches, plate, silver and gold coin and Confederate money was forced by violence from the hiding places, and if found on the person, was taken. Mills, gin houses, cotton and barns, and some private dwellings were destroyed and in some instances corn and wheat were also consumed. Through their track is a scene of ruin and confusion. Its effects will be felt all over the State. Not many Negroes were taken and most of them are returning.

"The most substantial loss is the want of mules and horses to work the ensuing crop. Consequently, bread stuff and meat are rising. Corn $17. Rye $15. Wheat $30. Many will find it hard to live and pay their taxes—and some will have to live on charity and pay no taxes. We were within four miles of the great raid and shall feel all its effects with regard to provisions.

"Our friend, Dr. Alva Connell, lost $60,000 in cotton burnt. It was deposited seven miles from town.

"Sherman is now encamped on the borders of the Savannah River, some twenty miles north west of the city. Our army is now within ten miles of his rear but what the result will be is uncertain. . . . God grant our forces may succeed against the ruthless foe."

The thought that Dr. Connell, who was already broken in health from his strenuous days of caring for wounded soldiers, was now financially broken, with his cotton burned, made Blandie hurt deep down inside. Poor Jane. How she must be suffering; and with young Baxter Connell fighting in Virginia, too. Jane had fled Marietta with her younger children when Sherman was approaching

Atlanta. Then she had fled from Cornucopia when he was approaching Milledgeville.

Sherman took the city of Savannah in time to present it to Lincoln as a Christmas gift.

But Christmas held no joy for Blandie and Baxter, who were now physically exhausted from nursing little Fannie through an illness of diphtheria. Everything seemed to be going wrong. A feeling of anxiety gripped them. They knew now the sun was setting on the Confederacy. Lee was trying to defend Richmond with an army of ragged, hungry, and tired soldiers. In the valley of Virginia, the Union General Sheridan had left what was once the grain supply for the army a blackened path. Even that month Baxter had combed the neighborhood for horses to send to Wytheville, Virginia, for Colonel Tom Osborne who had telegraphed Baxter in desperation, and who had written on Christmas day: "I should have acknowledged the arrival of the horses but just at that time the Yankees in heavy force appeared on our front and since that time we have had the most severe campaign of the war for so short a time. They have desolated the country contiguous to our line of march to a most fearful degree. Hope you had a merry Christmas."

Charleston was under heavy seige, but the Confederate flag was still flying from Fort Sumter, which was now a mass of broken rubble. Baxter had sent three of his Negroes, Jack, Nelson, and Calop, to work on the defenses of the city. He had also hired substitutes because he so desperately needed every hand possible for plowing, planting, and cutting wood.

Thinking of those starving on the home front and in the field made it impossible to think of Christmas holidays. For surely the South had a second enemy now—starvation. It came, not as a charge of grimy faced infantrymen, sweeping everything before them, or as an onrush of lathered horses and yelling men with sabers drawn, but rather it came insidiously with a weakness that drained the blood of life and pained empty stomachs with hunger and dysentery. It left shadows of what once were men, left them exhausted and dead on the battlefields or along the roads just as surely as if bullets had penetrated their hearts.

Blandie thought of all these things, but more than anything else, and maybe that was because it was Christmas, she thought of her

Ma and Pa. They, who had given her many happy Christmases, were probably worrying just as she was. No word had come from them for months. She knew there were letters somewhere which had not reached her. One of her Pa's letters had reached Frank Sexton in Richmond, who had written to Baxter:

"I have a long letter from Judge Baxter. It occupies some thirteen pages and is really a dissertation on our political and military condition. Are you not astonished that the Judge should have written so long a letter? There are many interesting points in it. While he complains much of Mr. Davis and of some features of the legislation of Congress, yet he approves entirely of our legislation of last session in regard to the currency and taxation. This was a great relief to me as I had favored those measures and it was of course gratifying to me to receive the approbation of a gentleman of such age and experience. But the *most* gratifying feature of his letter is that he scouts all idea of reconstruction and says plainly and unequivocally that we must *fight* until our independence is established and recognized."

Yes, thought Blandie, it was a sad Christmas.

January of 1865 was cold and rainy, but what sent shivers up and down the spines of the Carolinians was the fact that Sherman was marching toward Columbia.

Austin Springs sent a hastily scribbled note to his brother on January 12: "Baxter, times are gloomy. I go to Rock Hill today to make arrangements to send some hands to defend Columbia, although some of my boys are discharged from Charleston in bad shape and may never get well. Yet, I feel it my duty to do everything I can to keep the enemy from us."

Two weeks later, R. G. McCaw's letter to Baxter arrived at Springfield: "I was requested by the Governor to make an appeal to the people of York, begging them to send without delay their Negroes to Columbia for the purpose of fortifying the city. . . . It is thought if the city is well fortified it will divert the march of Sherman should he reach Branchville, as he did not attack any of the fortified places in Georgia. . . . If we can prevent his march through the center of our State it might be worth any sacrifice of labor on our part—and my opinion is that Charlotte will have to be evacuated as we can not hold the city and defend our line of railroads."

In the meantime, the soldiers from York who were around Richmond and on the coast of South Carolina were becoming increasingly nervous about the home front. Sherman's march was accomplishing the purpose with which he had set out. It was undermining the morale of the people. Joseph Parks declared from his camp below Richmond: "Lord, I do hate to hear of South Carolina being invaded. I do pray to God that something will turn up to prevent the invasion, but yet I am out of heart hearing of the fall of Savannah and the Yanks marching on our sweet old State where we have spent so many happy days. My whole prayer is for peace but really I am afraid many of us will be cut off before that day arrives. I am more uneasy now than I ever was. . . . I do hope and trust my dear wife and little children may be able to get along some way. . . . I can look around and almost see your good plantation, the place which I would be so much overjoyed to see."

A faithful correspondent had been A. M. Kee, but his spirits were very low as he lay in his trench between Pocataligo and Coosawhatchie, South Carolina, and wrote to Baxter: "Mr. Springs, old Sherman did get through to the water and his success in going through Georgia and the taking of Savannah has had a telling effect. A great many men of the 47th, 32nd and 5th Georgia Regiments are here doing picket duty with us. I tell you they are whipped. They are deserting every chance they have. A whole company, except one Captain, one Lt., one Sergt. and one private deserted in one of the Georgia Regiments. . . . Mr. Springs, you seem to be in good spirits about the war. I wish I could say I was in the same good spirits but I can't. I think that if our troops don't do better in the future we are gone. I hate to have to express myself that way, but I tell you there is nothing to encourage me here. My honest opinion is that the Yanks will be all over South Carolina in six months and then if ever a people suffered it will be ours. We are having it hard here. It rains most every day and we have to lie in the muddy trenches half of our time and the other half in camp in the rear of the trenches in a pond, you might call it. We are a sight—the dirtiest, ragged, lousiest set of fellows you have ever seen and we have no way to help ourselves. I am nearly naked and we are without shelter. Whatever the weather we have to take it as it comes. If I have to lie on the ground exposed to the weather much longer and me having chills and fever I am afraid it will fix me out. I have but little hope I will survive this war. If it goes on much longer there won't be many men left in the Confederacy."

Captain White, faithful, fighting John, expressed his opinion from more comfortable quarters, and if anyone ever deserved them, he did: "Being comfortably housed in quarters with a candle and a table, I drop you a note. So thoroughly saturated is the earth with water that all active military work has been suspended along our lines. . . . Wish I could have been home to have enjoyed an eggnog Christmas. Your humble servant spent Christmas on the cars between Gordonsville and Richmond. We had been ordered to the former place to drive back Torbert's Raiders. . . . I learn that there is much despondency among the people throughout the country. The recruits and the recruit conscripts are somewhat demoralized, but the old soldiers are as cheerful as ever. They still say we must conquer or die. . . . I have heard that you are going to assist in giving Sherman a suitable reception and greeting on his visit to South Carolina."

Judging from several letters written by soldiers, word had gotten around that Baxter was leaving home for the army. Possibly, with the advance of Sherman's forces he was to be ordered into service or maybe he had requested field duty. Anyway, the soldiers who were away did not like the idea. One Robert Philips, camped near Richmond, declared: "Mr. Springs, I was very sorry to hear by letter this morning that you were returning to the service. We poor men in the army had a faint hope that our families at home would to some extent be provided for and their sufferings relieved by men that we left at home, but as you have to leave home and our families left entirely in their destitute and helpless condition without any male assistance all our hopes are entirely fled away. When we anticipate the coming suffering of our helpless families and look at the condition of our army and how we are fenced in by our enemies, all hope is gone from us forever."

Sherman entered Columbia February 17. The Mayor surrendered the city to save it, but flames enveloped it by nightfall. More than a third of the buildings soon lay in ashes.

Baxter made immediate preparations for Blandie and the children to evacuate Springfield. He knew that if Sherman's troops followed the railroad, as they usually did, Springfield would go up in flames. Blandie packed her silver in a large box. The boys carried it down by the spring and buried it. Livestock was driven into the woods and guarded. The chickens were cooped up and carted away. Meat from the smoke house was hidden. Buckets and barrels were filled with water and placed near the house. Springfield was ready for Sherman.

The day after Columbia fell, Frank Sexton advised Baxter: "Congress will adjourn around the first of March. Events succeed each other so rapidly and unexpectedly now that it is impossible to say what may occur between now and then. . . . I shall be along as soon as I can get to your house, provided always that Sherman does not establish his headquarters at Charlotte. . . . I can not possibly stop but one day and hope you and Cousin Blandie will have your letters ready. . . . I wish to take anything I can for you to Judge and Mrs. Baxter. . . . There is no concealing the fact that we are now at a most critical period of our history. Still I do not despair. I can not think that it is written in the book of fate that we are to be subjugated."

Blandie had her letters ready to go to her parents. She had no way of knowing of the terrible tragedy which had happened January 3 at the Texas Cornucopia plantation.

The day after Christmas, Judge Baxter left his plantation and went to the county seat of Rusk on business. He had caught a cold before leaving, but he never took his physical ailments seriously and felt the cold would soon wear off. When he returned from Rusk, Julia could see that he was ill and immediately summoned the doctor, who assured her the Judge would be all right. On New Year's day, the Judge asked Julia to call in his most faithful slaves. He had wanted a minister but he knew there was none near. When the Negroes arrived, he requested that they sing to him. One by one the Negroes joined in, each coming closer around the bed. Their deep mournful voices gave forth a stirring, melancholy spiritual which brought tears to Julia's eyes. All the while, the Judge wept and prayed.

That night, which was Sunday, about midnight, Julia realized her husband was shaking with a chill. She hastily threw more quilts over him and put warm bricks to his feet. In a short while his tremendous shaking stopped. He lay quiet. Then he slept while Julia watched over him. After several hours had elapsed, he began to shake again and awoke. "My dear wife," he said, "I am dying."

Julia, frantic with fear, called Lizzie and together they tried to warm him. All the while the Judge was calling for Eli, for Fannie, for Jane, and for Blandie. He weakly repeated their names over and over, as if saying their names would bring them to him. Gradually he sank into a coma, his last mutterings being, "Eli—Eli." All day Monday he lay in a deep sleep, and on Tuesday at three o'clock in the afternoon he died.

When word of the Judge's death finally reached Springfield, Blandie and Baxter were completely stunned. Their tired voices, as they spoke between themselves of this tragedy, were hardly articulate and only half audible. To have her Pa so far away from her when he was dying; to have her Mother at this tragic moment without her children and loved ones except Lizzie—and thank God for Lizzie—was more than she could bear. Knowing that her father realized, in his last days, that the war was lost, that Cornucopia had been pilfered by the enemy, his Georgia Negroes demoralized and scattered, his son—God knows where—with three bullet wounds in his body, his oldest grandson facing a storm of lead fire while fighting with Lee in a line which grew thinner and weaker with every battle—knowing all these things frustrated Blandie to such a point that she became useless for anything but weeping. The beautiful life of Cornucopia, the gaiety, charm, and graciousness of the place, the love and tenderness which had gone into its making and its upkeep, all were gone, lost forever to all but memory. She remembered Jane's words of several years back, "I am writing on Pa's old desk and I tell you it looks like him. I feel a watering about the eyes and a sadness about the heart."

One of the Judge's friends, David W. Lewis, in a lengthy article for the Milledgeville, Georgia, newspaper wrote of Judge Baxter: "He showed even to the last, the forecast, the wisdom, the purity which ever adorned his public life, not less than his private one. He is one of the very few men who carried into their public service and into their public *acts* and *words* the same rigid integrity with which he dealt with his fellow-man. He is one of the very few who acted and spoke to and for his country and her interests as if he were speaking and dealing, face to face, with individual man. He is one of the few who never was a member of a clique—and who would have felt degraded by political combinations and alliances for mutual advancement, and who has never been known to resort to even the slightest device of the demagogue. As a statesman, a lawyer and a judge, it may truly be said 'the ends he aimed at were his God's, his country's and truth's.' "

Then Mr. Lewis gave vent to his feelings about Cornucopia: "Who could know old Cornucopia as the once happy abode of a cultivated, prosperous, unsevered family, as the scene of his early struggles in the business of life, and a little later as its ornaments and improvements kept pace with his successful career, and who could see it as it is now. I have just been there. There is the old mansion 'nestling at the end of the shady lane'; there to the left, is the new barn, one of his latest improvements; there is the old cattle shed I first saw when I was a happy boy at old master Beman's school; there is trusty old Mack still leading his fellow servants to field and labor; there's the faithful dog that was ever at his master's side when, with his broad-brimmed hat and long staff, he took his daily stroll; there's 'the gate on which the children used to swing'; there are the flowers and shrubs that shall never more receive care at the hands that planted them; then, there's the door through which has entered and departed so many welcome and happy guests; there is the instrument whose notes shall be waked no more as in days past; there are the ancestral pictures on the walls that have echoed sounds of gladness for almost forty unbroken years. . . . The void made in his loved ones' hearts and homes by his death can never be filled. . . . Yet they must remember that they can almost make him live with them again by cherishing and keeping vividly alive in the heart the memory of his favorite sayings, his maxims, his rules of life. Cherish even the memory of the little things in which he delighted in moments of leisure. Speak often and ever of what he said and did. Who can thus rob death of more than half his triumph, and keep the loved dead?"

CHAPTER TWENTY-TWO

SHERMAN TURNED HIS TROOPS northeast toward Fayetteville, North Carolina. Only a fringe of flankers brushed by Springfield, leaving it unharmed.

Making the railroads and bridges passable after the onslaught of Sherman's army was a gigantic task. Baxter worked day and night co-operating with the army. In return, Major John McCrady expressed his thanks and those of the Engineer Department of the Army for Baxter's "invaluable assistance to its officers in the execution of their work and the personal kindness and hospitality which gave them shelter during the recent severe weather."

Then the Major graciously added: "Were citizens in all parts of the country actuated by the same spirit as you, the work of the soldier would be more uniformly well done and much hardship and suffering saved those who in the service of their country are daily called upon to make the greatest sacrifices."

Confederate troops under General Joseph E. Johnston made their last stand against Sherman at Bentonville, North Carolina. With those troops was Baxter Springs' cousin Baxter Moore, who wrote: "Doubtless ere this you have heard of the drubbing Johnston gave Sherman at Bentonville. This *veritable* hero who has marched, you may say, almost unmolested through the state of Georgia and South Carolina has at last been compelled to halt his onward career to the Confederate capital by only 25 thousand Confederates hastily brought together. How crestfallen must this immortal hero feel with his 60 thousand veterans, to be thus brought to a standstill by a mere handfull of men and this too after all of his bluster and proclamations to the poor conquered people of Georgia and South Carolina. What unpleasant dreams must have been his on the night of the 20th. This, however, the duped North will not for a while know—for Sherman will, of course, try to make a victory out of a defeat. Had Gen'l Johnston, on the evening of the 20th, only had 15 thousand fresh troops to have followed up the routed columns of Sherman—how different would have been the result."

On April 3 Richmond fell. The ruins of the capital lay smouldering. The following day Abraham Lincoln rode into the city.

When Lee surrendered at Appomattox on April 9, "a more solemn scene was never witnessed. Tears were in every Confederate soldier's eyes and mortal man never received such enthusiastic cheers as General Lee and Gordon when they rode around their lines after the surrender. The Yankees had drawn their lines in near and witnessed the whole scene. They seemed more sad than rejoiced and said in the presence of the Southerners that it was no credit to Grant as he had been so long fighting Lee with nine to one."

Between Lee's surrender and that of Johnston's on April 26, soldiers were on the move everywhere, all hunting food, all hunting horses. Springfield was in the center of this activity. Blandie bore the full responsibility, because Baxter was called away in the emergency.

"The soldiers are pressing horses," she wrote to her husband. "When Harvey Wilson rode up from David White's on John White's horse, a Lieutenant came up to him and said, 'Sir, I must have that horse.' "

"Harvey said, 'You can't have it for 'tis Colonel White's* horse and you won't take a brother officer's horse!' Mr. Wilson, who had just passed General Ferguson said, 'I will ride back to the owner and to the General.' He went to the General and asked for a paper to protect the horse but the General would not give him one. When Harvey got back in a few minutes an officer came to the gate and said, "That horse I shall have.' Sam White said, 'If you come in that gate I will kill you.' And he went to speak to another officer. Then the soldier came in where David White had the horse and said 'Give me that horse,' and caught it by the bridle. David was armed and several went with him to the General and got papers to protect the horse. David said they cursed him and said they would be damned if they didn't

*Captain John White had received a promotion to Colonel.

intend to have one before they left. David thinks this was the same soldier who burned his gin house with 125 bags of cotton."

"There has been one jam and crowd here since you left," continued Blandie in her letter to Baxter. "We have cooked all day and last night until midnight. The soldiers seem starved. Three Brigades of Calvary passed yesterday at ten o'clock but before they could get to the river we saw the bridge on fire.* Oh, my dear husband, you don't know how it distresses me.

"After feeding soldiers I was worn out and at 3 o'clock I went over to Martin Kimbrel and Billy Bales. I saw that wounded Yankee soldier, a very young, pleasant, humble looking fellow. He thanked me for coming and begged me to come again, that he loved to hear me talk. Said he wished he could see a good physician. As I sat there I saw a car coming slowly down the tracks with a long white flag in front. I knew it meant something important. When I got home my house was crowded. About 10 o'clock a Captain came and said Johnston had surrendered and that the car was sent to stop hostilities. Everyone seems to think there is no doubt about it. Oh, you ought to hear a great many of them talk. They say they will go to another country. We are a subjugated people now and can do nothing. Grant and Sherman, they say, have sent a large force around to Georgia to head off Davis and any of our army to the Mississippi.

"Very few of the officers would sleep in the house. They are all watching their horses. Oh, Bac, five hundred soldiers were around me last night with not a piece of bread. I believe they will take all your corn. You will be in no danger of the enemy, so they say, but our own men will steal your horses. Jim has just sent for a lock to save some fodder. Yesterday a soldier came and said he would have your mare. The Negroes said he should not and sent for me. Then he left. Jim says he is afraid they will get her anyhow, but we will do all we can to protect her. I will try to get papers from a General."

The following day Blandie wrote again to her husband: "Captain Petegrew tells me that he was all day today with a son of General Breckinridge who told him that his father had sent a dispatch to President Davis, who is in Charlotte, that he thought there was no doubt about Lincoln's death. He was killed in Washington whilst

*General Stoneman burned the Catawba bridge at Nation Ford before the Confederate General Ferguson could reach it from Charlotte. When the latter arrived at the bridge it was already in flames. In the battle which followed the Yankees were driven off toward Yorkville.

going in the theatre and he was stabbed three times. Seward was wounded and his son was mortally wounded. But I guess you have heard all about it."

Blandie's next letter to Baxter was blue. She was showing the strain of her responsibilities. "Oh, our dear country," she lamented. "We are a ruined people, I am afraid. . . . Not a gentleman asked President Davis to enter his home in Charlotte. They thought if the enemy came it would be against them. Bates, the express man, had to ask him to his house. The officers who spoke to me about it, said it was a disgrace and seemed so hurt about it. President Davis, Gen. Gilmour, Cooper, Breckinridge and a score of others will pass here today. I will do the best I can. I wish you could be relieved so you could come home. . . . I will try to start the plowing with the oxen. I believe if we try to plow with a horse we would have to guard the horse while plowing."

President Davis and his Cabinet* had left Richmond by train April 2 and had set up temporary headquarters at Danville until the tenth of the month when word had reached them that Lee had surrendered. Then they boarded the southbound train, amid a great confusion of people, baggage, and mud. The President had previously sent Mrs. Davis and his children to Charlotte. Also he had sent the Confederate treasury of gold and silver there, where it was deposited in the Mint.

The Presidential party arrived in Greensboro April 11 and was shocked by the conduct of the people. It was only through the efforts of his aide and nephew,† Colonel Wood, that the President secured a room, while the Cabinet members slept in a leaky boxcar.

In the meantime, Stoneman had raided Salisbury, a town approximately halfway between Greensboro and Charlotte, and there his troopers had wrecked the railroad tracks. This made it necessary for Davis and his party to travel to Charlotte on horseback or in wagons and carriages. While all this was taking place, General Johnston was conferring with General Sherman on peace terms.

On the afternoon of April 16, Mr. Davis and his Cabinet rode into Charlotte. The town had been anticipating a raid from Stoneman

*General Breckinridge, as Secretary of War, remained in Richmond to supervise the evacuation.

†Colonel John Taylor Wood, grandson of General Zachary Taylor, was a nephew of Davis' first wife.

and Mrs. Davis had fled further south, accompanying the soldiers who were carrying the Confederate treasury to Abbeville, South Carolina. Stoneman had declared he would burn any house which sheltered the President. Only Mr. Bates, a bachelor employed by the Southern Express Company and whose home stood at the southwest corner of Tryon and Fourth Streets, had offered his home. The Cabinet members were quartered in other residences. With Sophia and William Myers was Attorney General George Davis, who resigned from the Cabinet while in Charlotte.

It was while President Davis was waiting to enter Bates' house* that he was approached by a gathering of soldiers and citizens, among them Colonel William Johnston, who welcomed the President to Charlotte. Davis was responding to this greeting when he was handed a telegram from General Breckinridge,† telling him of the assassination of Lincoln.

Davis, at this point, had not made up his mind whether to accept defeat for the Confederacy or whether to go west of the Mississippi and continue the struggle. It was while he was in Charlotte that he was forced to make this decision. He held a Cabinet meeting at a local bank and authorized Johnston's surrender to Sherman. When Sherman's lenient terms were vetoed by President Andrew Johnson, Davis directed Johnston to take his calvary to Alabama and Mississippi and fight on. But it was too late.

On April 26, after a Cabinet meeting at the Phifer home, Davis and five members of his Cabinet, guarded by a large cavalry escort and accompanied by the Confederate Archives, a tremendous wagon train of supplies, baggage and $35,000 in specie, left Charlotte in the direction of Springfield.

All the way through North Carolina, Colonel Francis Richard Lubboch (former Governor of Texas), embarrassed over Davis' cool reception, had boasted, "Wait, Sir, until you get to my native State, South Carolina." His boast was well justified. Blandie saw to that.

When the President neared the lane leading to the house, "a bevy of ladies approached the gate, strewing flowers before him and insisted on the President and his party dismounting." As Colonel Lubboch said, "They would not listen to us going further that day and we spent the night."‡

*Bates, thinking Davis would arrive by train, was waiting at the railroad station.
†Breckinridge had joined General Johnston in his peace negotiations with Sherman.
‡*Six Decades in Texas,* by F. R. Lubbock.

Baxter apparently hurried home just in time for the occasion, for Secretary of the Navy Stephan Mallory said: "In pursuing this route, the party met near the Catawba River a gentleman whose plantation and homestead lay about half a mile from its banks, and who had come out to meet Mr. Davis, and to offer him the hospitality of his house. His dwelling, beautifully situated and surrounded by ornate and cultivated grounds, was reached about 4 o'clock P.M. and the charming lady of the mansion with that earnest sympathy and generous kindness which Mr. Davis, in misfortune, never failed to receive from Southern women, soon made every man of the party forget his cares and feel for a time at least o'er all the ills of life victorious."*

Anyone peeking into the parlor of Springfield that evening would have seen a surprising sight. President Jefferson Davis and three members of his Cabinet were down on their knees. The Confederacy was in its death throes. Davis and his colleagues continued on their knees—laughing. They were playing a game of marbles with young Eli and Johnny. To the adults it represented relaxation and release from reality. To the two boys, one thirteen and one nearly twelve, it was a memory never to be forgotten.

Eli was teamed with President Davis and Postmaster General John H. Reagan, a forty-seven-year-old Tennessean turned Texan. John was even luckier in his partners. One, not named, was probably Secretary of State Judah P. Benjamin. The other, in any case, was John C. Breckinridge, the doughty Kentuckian and the best grown-up marble player in the Confederacy if not the world.

Mr. Mallory, standing above the competitors, joining in the general excitement and glee, later wrote:

"After such slight renovation and changes of their travel soiled toilets as circumstances permitted, and an hour of refreshing rest, it was a novel sight to see Mr. Davis and Mr. Reagan, with a little son of their kind host as their ally, playing an animated and well contested game of marbles against the second son, supported by General Breckinridge and another Cabinet officer. The game lasted nearly an hour; and withstanding the skill of his opponents, Breckinridge, who plays the best game of marbles of any public man since Judge Marshall,† and who had his usual good luck, came off victorious. The youngsters,

*Mr. Mallory's series of "Pen and Ink Sketches."
†Presumably Chief Justice John Marshall, of the United States Supreme Court (1775-1835).

two bright, intelligent Southern boys, will never forget that ardently disputed game of marbles with Mr. Davis, who to their infinite delight seemed as much at home with the words of caution and command, from 'knuckle down at taw' to 'roundings' as themselves."

The following morning, which was April 27, President Davis arose from the breakfast table and made his way to the front lawn. There he assembled the members of his Cabinet and high ranking military officers. Together they conferred as to their future actions and the most advantageous route for their retreat. Secretary of the Treasury Trenholm had spent the previous night a few miles away at the home of William E. White,* and so it was agreed that Davis and his party would proceed to White's and there have another meeting.

Mr. Trenholm had been ill for many days and while at the Whites' he decided to resign from the Cabinet. Postmaster General Reagan was appointed to fill the vacancy. Here on the lawn of Colonel White's was the last Cabinet meeting of the Confederate States of America.

The safety of the President and his party was being threatened every hour because the Secretary of War of the United States, Edwin M. Stanton, had issued orders to the Federal commanders "to intercept the rebel chiefs." The job of doing this was given to Stoneman and his cavalry who were at that very moment pressing in from the west. Therefore, the Confederates proceeded with caution.

When Davis and his party arrived at the river, the bridge having been burned, it was necessary for them to ferry across. The horses and wagons crossed in the water over the ford.

Here at the Nation Ford, this historic spot where the Catawbas of old had traded and where John Springs in 1840 had met with the Indians to work out a treaty, a ferry was fashioned from part of a pontoon bridge and on it stood President Jefferson Davis. One of the men in charge of the baggage wagons described the scene: "What a sight to see Jeff Davis and Breckinridge and the Cabinet standing on the pontoon. Dickinson and I thought of the Bruce and his retreat in the mountains surrounded by a few of his faithful followers. The cause has gone up. God only knows what will be the end of all this."†

Once across the river the Presidential party continued southward

---

*The home of William Elliott White is now the residence of the Elliott White Springs family, in Fort Mill, South Carolina.

†This was Col. Tench F. Tilghman speaking, as recorded in *Flight into Oblivion*, by Alfred J. Hanna. Col. Tilgham was an aide to Jefferson Davis and a descendant of George Washington's aide of the same name.

to a spot where the Nation Ford road forked, known as the "Old Crossroad." Branching off to the left was the road to Austin's Springsteen plantation. The road to the right led to Yorkville. It was the latter which the Confederates took, but they stopped long enough for Davis to review his troops. Their flight led them to Abbeville, then across the Savannah River into Georgia at Vienna. From that point, they went to Washington and Warrenton and Sandersville, passing within twenty-odd miles of Cornucopia. They were traversing a route which Eli Baxter had taken many times in court duties and in his campaigning. Maybe it was a blessing that Judge Baxter did not live to see his beloved land conquered and torn, without rights and privileges, a land in agony.

At Irwinville, Georgia, on May 10, Jefferson Davis was captured by Federal soldiers who had been ordered "to capture or kill him."

An era had ended. The fury was over. Now the South would have new enemies to fight, those of despair, defenselessness, defraudation, and deprivation.

CHAPTER TWENTY-THREE

To REBUILD THE SOUTH, men reared in luxury toiled as hard as their slaves had ever done, but with a difference. Their slaves had been well fed. Now nearly everyone, white and black, knew the agony of working with an empty stomach.

The broad acres of Springfield lay idle and waiting for fertilizer and the plow. The plantation was an agricultural organism that ran on cash. And Baxter needed cash. His Confederate money and bonds could be relegated to the attic as far as he was concerned. They were worthless. What to do? Where to turn?

It was Blandie who came to his aid. With flushed cheeks and a proud smile, she gave him an abundant hug and said: "This is for you. I saved them for years in case you should ever have need of them." She pressed something into his hand. It was a small suede bag bulging with gold coins.

This money, though not a tremendous sum, gave Baxter the impetus he needed. Immediately his spirits lifted and he began to reorganize Springfield as best he could under a new way of life.

Mr. Bales, the white overseer, continued on the job. And so did the Negroes Nathan, Jim, Caleb, Lucius, Mealy, Mary, and Ann. Old Aunt Betty, the children's nurse, was so much a part of the household that it never occurred to her to leave. Solomon tried to "get a house and part of a crop," but failing to do this, he drifted back to Springfield, sullen and disillusioned. Mr. Bales put him to work digging ditches, but "he said he could not go into another ditch as it was too damp and his shoes were too bad."

Blandie told Baxter, "I saw Solomon in the kitchen and told him if he needed shoes he should have told you. I did not like his manner. He said it was no time to dig ditches."

Negro Charles was difficult to handle, too. He came back to be hired but wanted to work only until Christmas. Mr. Bales told him he did not care to hire unless it was for a year. But Charles insisted that the "Yankees were going to fix him up after Christmas" and he was afraid to make a contract. Finally, the Negro said if "Mas Bac" paid as much as anyone else he would come back. When all was arranged, Charles asked for his provisions for another year and was completely taken aback when Mr. Bales told him he would have to buy his provisions out of the salary Mr. Springs paid him.

Negro George was not a problem. He was a lazy worker and Mr. Bales forthwith dispensed with his services.

Baxter sent for Plato and Jane to come back. "I am very much afraid," said Blandie, "you will have trouble by sending for them. They will expect you to take Winnie too. I can not and will not have her. The Negroes say she knows she never had to work in the house and that is why she is anxious to get back, but never with my consent can she get in this house."

Then Blandie added in an exasperated tone, "And I can't see why Gean will be any value to you. The room she takes is more than she is worth."

Thus it was. Planters who had felt duty-bound to retain, feed, clothe, and doctor shiftless, lazy Negroes now refused to hire the worthless ones. Therefore many Negroes, uprooted and thrown on their own resources, died of disease, overexposure, and starvation.

As a large landowner and one who had held a Confederate commission, Baxter was barred from a citizen's standing and could not hold a public office unless pardoned. He had to appeal directly to President Johnson in Washington. This he did, bearing a letter of introduction from the Provisional Governor of South Carolina:

Columbia, S. C.
September 21, 1865

His Excellency
President Johnson

My dear Sir,

I take the liberty of introducing to your Excellency Mr. A. B. Springs, a planter of York District, South Carolina, who goes to Washington to get his pardon and that of his brother, R. A. Springs, a planter also. They are both loyal citizens and disposed to act well their part as such in restoring the State to the Union. Their applications were forwarded some time since.

I am with great respect and esteem,

Yours truly,

B. F. Perry

The pardon came through just in time. Soon after Baxter returned from Washington, S. L. Love of Yorkville wrote him: "Your name has been put in nomination for the Legislature and you must run."

By the time Baxter decided to run, there was no time left to campaign. Nevertheless, he received a sufficient vote to elect him to South Carolina's first postwar legislature. In the same election, his friend James L. Orr was chosen governor.

Before this election could take place South Carolina had to comply with certain requirements of the United States Government. First, President Johnson had appointed a provisional governor. His choice of Benjamin Perry was based on the fact that Perry had always been a staunch, outspoken anti-secession man. A former state senator, a member of the Charleston Democratic Convention of 1860 who earnestly pled that a split in the Democratic party would be disastrous to the Union, he was adamant in his views until the day South Carolina seceded. Then he good-humoredly exclaimed: "You are going to the devil and I will go with you."

After Perry's appointment as provisional Governor, he had been instructed to call a State Convention to alter the State Constitution, accept the emancipation proclamation, declare secession invalid, and repudiate the war debts of the Confederacy. Baxter Springs had been one of the men appointed to this Convention. When all requirements had been met by the State and the new constitution had been approved, then a Governor and legislators could be elected by the people.

By this time "carpetbaggers"* had entered the South by the thousands. They came on the heels of the surrender and they stayed to defraud, steal from, and govern the Southern people. They were hated and despised. They joined hands with and exploited the Negroes. Any Southern white man who joined them was called a "scalawag."

---

*White men from the North arrived with only carpet bags in which they packed their belongings. Hence they were given the name "carpetbaggers."

Baxter and his fellow legislators were soon caught up in the problems of determining the status of Negro freedmen. He was showered with views from all directions. His old friend R. G. McCaw, in congratulating him on his election, gave his views:

"I trust you will receive these suggestions I have made kindly as I do not make them in a spirit of dictation. First, there should be a rigorous law against vagrancy, *irrespective* of color, for you have not only to contend with the idleness of the Negro but with a large number of white men who anticipate a subsistence off the industry of the industrious and provident. . . ."

Then McCaw went on to explain his second point: "I think it competent for the legislature to declare who shall and who shall not be citizens, and as a consequence the legislature should say that Negroes are not citizens. This has been done by three Yankee states, namely: Ohio, Indiana and Illinois. If they have the right thus to act, I think we might do likewise."

"My third point," McCaw explained, "is this: There should be strong preventatives against persons trading with the employees for anything raised on the plantation without the written permit of the employer. If this is not done the Negroes will continue to sell as they are now doing, both corn and cotton, to the many bad men who are growing rich in our country and who are demoralizing the Negroes and are their real enemies."

With the carpetbaggers encouraging the Negroes to be insolent, to plunder and steal, it became increasingly more difficult to employ Negroes. Blandie at times was so exasperated and weary of coping with the situation that she would have to write her husband in Columbia for advice—"Baxter, I don't know what you are to do with Lucius. Miss Pamelia* says she has made up her mind to leave if he remains. I have just told Eli to have Lucius black his shoes and Lucius told Eli, 'Confound it, you are big enough to black your own shoes.' If it were not that you need him for your work, he could not stay here, but we have to do a great deal now that we don't like and maybe could not do better. I try to make the best of everything."

Overriding all else, however, was the problem of making an agricultural economy operate with help that, in too many instances, did not really want to work. Blandie cited a prime case: "Nancy's son,

*Miss Pamelia Brown was the housekeeper.

Charles, is the last of creation. He will commence to cut a stick of wood and sit down two or three times to rest before he will get it cut. He has been spoiled."

The problem of securing efficient labor was not a local one. It was general throughout the South. From Clarksville, Tennessee, Baxter's lawyer friend, G. A. Henry, father of several Confederate officers and himself one, and owner of plantations in Tennessee and Arkansas, saw little hope for the South. He informed Baxter:

"The Negroes are idle and will not work, I believe without compulsion, and this is out of the question now. The worst of all is— they are nothing like as happy as they were and never will be. They now find it a difficult thing to support their families. . . . Now that the Negroes are free, my only wish about them is that they should be colonized somewhere and that there should be a separation of the white and the black races. They can not live together on terms of equality and such will be the judgment of posterity, I confidently predict."

Then Mr. Henry commented on an economic weakness of the South: "The most discouraging thing to me is that there is no productive industry in the country." This was all too true. There were no factories to take up the slack of unemployed white. Men took any jobs they could find. Even Baxter's deaf Uncle Richard Clark Springs,* now an aged man, wrote: "The Mute School has been closed since last spring and I see no prospects of it opening. I wish you would find a place of employment for me as a printer or something else. I feel very sad about the failure of our banks and hope some of my money will be saved."

White men were not the only ones faced with unemployment. Many widows were forced to seek employment as a means of living. General John A Young made a request of Baxter: "I have a friend who wishes to apply to you as a tutor or governess for your children. . . . She owned a large plantation and forty Negroes, but is now so much reduced by the present conditions of the country as to induce her to make this effort to support herself."

Springfield continued short-handed. Baxter searched for a solution. He wrote his cousin, Leonidas Springs, in Philadelphia, about employing foreign help. Leonidas replied: "You wished to know my

---

*Richard Clark Springs, half brother of John Springs, taught in the Mute School near Spartanburg, South Carolina.

views in regard to employing a German to take charge of your garden and orchard, and a Scotchman or Englishman to take charge of your cattle. I think it would be very desirable but such men can not be found here at the present time. Labor is scarce and high here. I trust you will be able to adopt some plan by which the Negro can be made useful to you."

There was a reason for labor being scarce in the North. The situation there was in complete reverse to the South. During the war many manufacturers prospered and expanded through government orders. When the Union soldiers returned, they found a prosperous economy with jobs for all.

Congress created, after the war was over, a Freedmen's Bureau which was supposed to watch over the Negroes and distribute relief to them. In apportioning supplies here and there, the agents of this Bureau caused the colored people to feel that it was unnecessary to work. Likewise, most of the agents who were sent South to administer this program taught the Negroes that the Southerners meant to oppress them. Therefore, the Negroes were suspicious of all white men's intentions toward them and were reluctant to take orders from them.

Colonel Cadwalder Jones, from across the river at Rock Hill, had foreseen that there would be difficulty and had written to Baxter: "I think it important that we should have an armed police organization. A large number of Negroes, having no homes and being dissatisfied with their pay and shares of crop, will become unruly. We can raise a company here whenever we are furnished with arms and authority to do so. We hope you will furnish us with that authority. We are not willing to raise a company to be subject to the orders of the U. S. forces as heretofore proposed."

The year 1866 came in accompanied by gloom, discouragement, and bad weather. Blandie had a house full of ill people. A sickness had put Johnnie, Alva, Brevard, and Baxter, Jr., to bed with chills and fever. Miss Pamelia and Aunt Betty soon came down with the same ailment. The proverbial doses of calomel, the medical standby of the South, had put them on their feet again—that is, all but Johnny, who suddenly became worse. Blandie quickly wrote to Baxter who was attending the legislature in Columbia: "Johnny has a burning fever. It is now 4 o'clock in the morning and he is no better. . . . The Doctor is now lying on the little bed and old Aunt Betty asleep. I am sitting in my large chair. Oh, my dear darling, come home to me. I trust and pray he may be better when you come, but it is to be a desperate case. God bless you, and may He in His wisdom and mercy spare our darling child is the prayer of your devoted wife."

Johnny was spared. Baxter, who had rushed to Springfield, did not immediately return to Columbia because it was time for Blandie to have her baby. On January 31 a boy was born; he was named for his uncle, William Myers.

It was during times like these that Blandie often wished for her mother. Many letters had been written to Texas, but for months no answer had come back, until the previous month when Julia Baxter's letter had arrived: "I have waited a long, long time to hear that the mails are running across the Mississippi and still there is no certainty of letters going to Georgia or Carolina. But I must write. I feel so anxious to commune with you and Baxter. . . . I feel as if the whole Southern country should wear mourning during the present generation. . . . The first months of this year were passed in grief and sorrow. My days were days of trouble; my nights were restless, disturbed and wretched. . . . Dear, dear Blandie, though far away I have lived a great deal this year *in thought* with my children. It is most prudent and advisable for Lizzie and me to remain on this place until Christmas. Eli is with us a good deal of the time. He is leaving for Georgia and when he returns Lizzie and I will go. He thinks it best for us to remain here until he returns from attending to business at Cornucopia. You will be astonished to see how old he looks. He was so much exposed and in such hard service during the war, was wounded in three different battles in one month. He says he intends settling himself in Houston in the future and Lizzie is anxious to live there too. . . . We have a very good man attending to our business here. Most of the Negroes are still on the plantation. The family of Louisiana Negroes I gave privilege to return with their former owner's Negroes. We had a very valuable and likely set of Negroes in this country. After we learn to do without them I think we will be a much happier people. There is no confidence or reliance to be placed in them. . . . We are anxiously expecting to hear from the trial of poor Mr. Davis.*

*President Johnson thought Jefferson Davis should be hanged and kept him imprisoned at Fortress Monroe, but never brought him to trial. Finally, Davis was released in May, 1867, on a bond of $100,000 signed by Cornelius Vanderbilt, Horace Greely, and others. Although Davis was eligible for pardon, he never asked Congress for it and therefore could never serve in public office.

Hope he will be acquitted and soon released, for the poor man has been tortured long enough."

Baxter at times was almost overwhelmed with thoughts of the future. There seemed to be no bright star of hope twinkling in the sky. February brought many perplexing questions. A letter to him from General A. C. Garlington of Newberry, South Carolina, summed up the political situation very well:

"Since our parting in Columbia, events have occurred which have materially affected my views as to our prospects in the future as a people. . . . I am inclined to think that the President did not properly estimate the strength of the opposition to his scheme of reconstruction which existed in the North. And hence those from our State who had conferred with him were unintentionally misled. The radical wing of the Republican party still maintains their ground. Sumner in the Senate and Thaddeus Stevens in the House appear to be the ruling spirits and to have the control of the party who are opposed to the President and who have with them a large majority in both Houses of Congress. Under these circumstances, what are we to hope for?

"I know your good judgment and I would be glad to have your views. I am aware that you have never aspired in the character of a politician and for that very reason I would have greater confidence in your opinion. Can you, from the lights before you, gather any comfort or consolation as to the future? I candidly say to you that I can not. If moderate counsel could prevail at Washington—if those who wield the powers of the Government would listen to the voice of reason and justice, our condition might be made tolerable. The white man would look upon the Negro in his true character as a freedman and accord him justice and full protection in all his civil rights. But this constant agitation in Congress as to his equality, the oppression heaped upon him, his right to land, and his elevation in the social and political scale, must inevitably lead to the worst consequences. There can be, under such circumstances, no regular system of labor, no government of these peoples, and no improvements in their condition. Their instincts, you well know, are against labor, especially under the control of the white man. The knowledge, therefore, that a dominant party in the Government is making every effort to elevate them to equality with the white man in civil and political rights will not only remove all inducement to labor, but will exasperate these people against the white race, and in the end will lead to a war of races which will deluge the country in blood.

"But this, as bad as it is, is not the darkest side of the picture. We have a still greater evil to fear. This party, which is now clearly in the ascendant, is actuated by the most malignant hatred of the people of the South. No harm, no injury, no degradation is too great, too revolting to all the finer sensibilities of our nature, to be inflicted upon us. The very air we breathe is looked upon by them as a privilege, as an act of mercy extended to us. What then are we to expect from them?"

Frank Sexton put the situation to Baxter in even stronger terms: "South Carolina and Texas have become territorial dependencies of a consolidated, centralized, immitigated despotism. Impoverished and humiliated, we are threatened with degradation even to a place below that occupied by our former slaves. May God have mercy on us!"

But then Sexton volunteered another thought which made Baxter smile. "I feel quite sure of one thing," declared this Texan, "that amid all the subjugation which the Yankees have affected, they have not subdued Cousin Blandie's cheerful spirit. That is worth everything in these times!"

The Treasury department was angering the South Carolina farmers by taking stock from them, which reduced the mule power, already too short. Also cotton, corn and wheat, which had been subscribed to the Confederate government and not delivered, was being hunted. The Treasury department was even taking over such things as iron works.

Spring, 1866, came with all its glory and the beauty of nature belied the fact that all was not well at Springfield. This time it was measles. The youngest children all came down with the disease. And as if Blandie did not have her hands full enough, on top of that the Governor called the legislature into session to amend the Negro code and to give relief to the people in the way of food—so Baxter had to go hurrying off to Columbia, leaving Blandie, Miss Pamelia, and Aunt Betty to nurse the sick children.

The young boys soon recovered, but little Fannie did not seem to pull out of it with as much vigor. According to Dr. Williamson's bill, he visited Springfield on April 6 to administer to Fannie. Three days later he was back again. Then his bill reads on and on, with visits listed for every day in May up to the 25th. That day Fannie died. The beautiful child, whom Baxter Connell had said was the prettiest child he had ever seen, was gone. For three short years, Blandie had petted, spoiled, and gloried in her only daughter. Now her sorrow was too deep to comprehend, too enormous to write about, too crushing even to endure.

Letters poured in to Springfield. One correspondent said, "You have so many disasters, but you could have stood them all without complaint had little Fannie been spared to you." Filed among the letters of condolence was a small slip of paper which read: "For one metallic burial case, $60." The finality of those few words was complete.

Julia Baxter came to Springfield, bringing with her comfort, understanding, and sympathy for her dear children. The summer passed quietly. It was not like the one the year before. That one was remembered by a friend in a letter to Baxter dated August 5: "A little more than a year ago I was at your house and received so much kindness from you and your good wife and children that I have often thought of it since with the liveliest feelings. The nice time I had there with your young folks, getting strawberries, etc., often comes to my recollections, and I ask myself the question—Are you and they all there yet, and well and happy now as you were then?"

A Congressional election was coming up that fall of 1866. The entire South, as well as President Johnson, was hoping for a triumph of a more conservative party, and the President was campaigning toward this end. But apparently his speeches did more harm than good, because the new Congress had more radical Republicans than before.

In the meantime, the Fourteenth Amendment had been agreed upon by Congress and offered to the States for ratification. It was a revolutionary amendment, as Baxter realized. Up until this time the States had had control over their citizens in order to protect them from the powers of the Federal Government. Now the Federal authorities claimed they were intervening to protect citizens from their State control. The amendment gave Negroes the right to vote. It also excluded from Federal or State office persons who had fought in the war against the Government until such time that Congress removed their disabilities. The Constitution of the United States had not undergone such a radical change since its beginning.

Due to the crisis, South Carolina called a special session of the legislature and Baxter left for Columbia. He had been in the capital slightly more than two weeks when a crisis developed at home concerning his infant son.

"Willie," Blandie wrote, "has been much worse since I last wrote, screaming with pain most of the time and sleeping neither day nor night, but we all think he is better today. I do trust and pray he may continue better. I hope your next letter will say when you will be home. It seems to me the Legislature is sitting a long time, considering you meet so soon again."

Willie, the seven-and-a-half-months-old baby, was dead a week later.

Baxter would always remember the heartaches and pain of that year of 1866. He would always remember the nausea he had experienced when he was told his baby was dead. He would always remember the evenings of the past several years when his exquisite little Fannie had said goodnight to him, throwing herself into his arms, kissing him in her affectionate way. But it only tormented him to remember.

Blandie's mother remained at Springfield through October, nursing and soothing her daughter, for by this time Blandie was ill and spent most of her time in bed. Then Julia Baxter went to Cornucopia to prepare it for sale. No longer was it painful for her to think of selling the old home. Her two Elis were in Texas, one dead and buried, the other waiting for her return. It was best that she go there. The era of Cornucopia, with its frolics, laughter, flowers, and wealth, was of the past now. So much had happened, so much had been drained out of her. She was resigned to what was ahead. And she was tired.

Before Julia Baxter left Cornucopia, she wrote to Baxter: "I can not go without telling you and Blandie goodbye, in fact your whole household, including the children, Miss Pamelia, not forgetting good old Aunt Betty, and Caroline too was an obedient servant to her mistress when she had not much help. Oh, I love everything in your 'surroundings.' My heart is tender now at the idea of soon leaving Cornucopia, this, to me, hallowed spot."

Baxter went back to Columbia in November after making arrangements to have someone stay with Blannie. The legislature was in session until nearly Christmas. This body of men, composed largely of Confederate veterans and scions of plantation aristocracy, voted overwhelmingly to reject the Fourteenth Amendment. So did every other Southern State except Tennessee with its Unionist mountaineer elements.

The radical Republicans in Congress, infuriated by the South's sharp rejection of the amendment, voted down moderates, overrode a veto by President Johnson, and on March 2, 1867, enacted the "Reconstruction Act." This branded Southern State governments as illegal, unseated Southern legislatures—although their previous ratification of the Thirteenth Amendment, abolishing slavery, went unquestioned—and declared martial law.

The former Confederacy, excluding Tennessee, was divided into five military districts ruled by Federal generals. Major General Daniel E. Sickles* became absolute governor of the Carolinas—"District Two."

The Freedman's Bureau now served as a political machine to enroll Negro voters. The carpetbaggers and scalawags, plus a few more intelligent Negroes, swayed the uneducated black multitude by this means. Federal aid became a vote-purchaser.

The days were growing increasingly more difficult for Baxter to get through. The tensions of the past year were beginning to take their toll. He was extremely weary. Then young Johnny came down with typhoid fever. After that, Baxter was ill.

In March, with Governor Orr's administration drawing to a close, the following letter arrived at Springfield:

Executive Department, South Carolina
Columbia, March 26, 1867

A. B. Springs, Esq.
Fort Mill
York Dist. of S. C.

My Dear Sir:

You have doubtless already received a communication from Lieut. J. M. Johnston, Lieutenant and Provost Marshal, from the Head Quarters Assistant Commissioner, Bureau of Refugees,

*Daniel E. Sickles had been involved in much scandal in 1859 when he killed Phil Barton Key, son of the "Star Spangled Banner" composer, because of jealousy over Mrs. Sickles.

Freedmen and Abandoned Lands in South Carolina, informing you that 200 sacks of corn had been forwarded to you for distribution among the suffering poor of your section, by the Southern Relief Commission, of the City of New York.

Upon its arrival, you will proceed to distribute the same among the destitute white and colored persons, according to their real wants and necessities, in such a manner as to give no cause of complaint.

When empty, please return the sacks to Lieut. Johnston, Charleston, S. C.

You will please keep a memoranda of the names of persons to whom the distribution is made, and the amounts they receive. And you will exercise your own discretion in the work—that being the only general guide. This is a bounty contributed to the suffering poor of our State, by charitable people in New York, and I have heretofore intimated to General Scott that its disbursement might, with safety, be confided to you.

As you are doubtless aware, your trouble will, likewise, be a gratuitous contribution to the suffering poor in your section, as no compensation attaches to the position assigned to you.

Very respectfully

Your ob't Servant

James L. Orr

Governor of So. Car.

Baxter was too sick to go about his regular business. The two hundred sacks of corn arrived. People were hungry. A note had come which read: "There are some families below Rock Hill who are almost at the point of starvation. We have written to Charleston, New York and Baltimore for aid. We did this before we were aware you had corn in view for the same purpose. Unless aid does come, *and that soon,* I can not say what will become of several poor families in this portion of the District. May the good Lord help us!"

Fearing to delay another day, Baxter sent a letter down on the morning train to Governor Orr, who replied promptly: "I have received your communication and regret extremely to hear of your indisposition. If sympathy will cure, I am sure you would have been a well man in half an hour after your letter reached me. Acting upon your suggestion, I have requested General Scott to designate Col. Cad. Jones at Rock Hill as a suitable person to distribute the corn sent to your address, and am glad to learn he is one of the parties whom you recommend for the trust."

But South Carolina was faced with problems other than starvation. Congress had passed laws which made it impossible for a person to vote, or help at the voting polls, who could not take an oath swearing that he had never borne arms against the United States, or given aid, countenance, counsel, or encouragement to persons engaged in armed hostility thereto or had never held or sought an office under any authority hostile to the United States or supported such an authority. This meant complete disfranchisement of the majority of Southern whites. And it was election time. Again, the Governor called on Baxter, requesting him to "furnish Major General Sickles the names of suitable persons who may act as registers of the voters in the several districts."

Baxter could find no such persons. Also his friend Cadwalder Jones said: "I have counseled with friends here as to the Registrars of voters. We know of no suitable persons who can take the oath."

South Carolina was now in a helpless condition, completely vulnerable to Yankee radicals, carpetbaggers, scalawags, and Negroes. With the coming of this group to power, a new era came to South Carolina. The Negroes controlled the elections which followed. The cause of the white man was forgotten. Historians would call it the "Tragic Era."

On May 14 (1867), Eli Baxter, Jr., wrote to Blandie and Baxter from Houston, Texas, where he was practicing law: "General Griffin, commanding the department of Texas, has issued an order that no one who cannot take the test oath can be a juror and that no distinction shall be made between the white and the black man. Hence, nearly all of our jurors are now composed of Negroes. If you were to drop into our Courthouse, you would find twelve Negro men as black as Erebus in the jury box. And with all the dignity and gravity imaginable we have to address these miserable ignoramuses as 'Gentlemen of the jury.' This is the severest blow I have felt. How awful the humiliation. I sometimes exclaim in my heart 'oh my poor country, my poor countrymen.' This last order forces us to quaff the dregs in the cup of degradation."

CHAPTER TWENTY-FOUR

BAXTER SPRINGS, NOW FREE from his duties in the State legislature, turned his thoughts to educating his seven sons, recouping his fortune, and tenderly caring for his wife, who was sick much of the time.

There were those who did not know how to take up life again following the war, but with Baxter it was different. He had a consuming determination to make money and to keep Springfield as it had always been.

He began to write letters to the companies in which he held stock. He evaluated his portfolio of investments. His Atlanta and West Point Railroad stock was paying a dividend of $4 a share. He would hold to that. The Mississippi Central Railroad Company owed him $3,360 in back dividends. He would contact a broker in Memphis to collect that sum for him and then as soon as possible he would sell those shares and put the money in stock and bonds of the Charlotte and Columbia Railroad, which was paying its dividends regularly, the bonds of which were selling for $65, the stock for $35. If he could just raise some money, there were excellent opportunities for investments. But how and where to raise it was the question. He did not wish to negotiate a loan because interest rates were 2½ per cent per month or higher. Cotton was selling at 25 cents a pound and he could realize a substantial sum from this if he could only hire more Negroes and plant a larger crop, but at that time he had only six field hands. Consequently, he was pushing daily to hire Negroes.

It was useless to try to raise money by selling land. Values were too low. And besides, the Springses were never people to sell land. They much preferred to buy it and hold it. But there were his acres and acres of woodland. With the tremendous amount of rebuilding to be done over the country, there was a demand for lumber. So he began to sell timber.

He scanned the newspapers for opportunities of buying or selling. He wrote to Cheraw, South Carolina, to see if he might sell what cattle he could spare. The answer came back: "You could not send your stock to a poorer market. There is literally no money here and no one who is able to buy on credit with any reasonable hope of payment. There are no planters in this section who will be able to meet the current expenses of the year. Our financial ruin is complete. I can see no light ahead."

Baxter kept working, planning and writing letters. *Industry,* his father had called it. There were times when his discouragement almost overwhelmed him, but he never gave up. He must make every attempt to recover his financial security. Men of dignity, integrity, and honor would have to stand up and fight this scourge of carpetbaggers and radical rule. How, Baxter was not certain. There had to be a beginning and he was ready, but to be of any help he had to keep his head above the waters of financial ruin.

He realized that he and Blandie faced many readjustments in their lives and in their way of thinking, and that it would not be easy. John Lyon, his nephew, expressed the situation aptly when he wrote: "The political revolution is complete; we have passed from a Confederation to Consolidated Nationality. Lincoln's Springfield speech has been fulfilled; and now the States bear pretty much the same relation to the Nation that counties bear to States. But the moral, social and intellectual revolution is still in progress; it has scarcely well begun. Opinions and passions and prejudices, the growth and fruit of two centuries and a half, are being eradicated, and new ideas and notions are being planted in their stead. Forms of government shape themselves to fit the body politic . . . and there will be no permanency in our government until public sentiment shall have got its growth, and its development, in accordance with (for want of a better phrase I will call) the spirit of the times. In a confederation the independent members may well be diverse; but under consolidation there must be homogeneity. . . . We will be *Yankeeised.* It will probably take twenty years to do it; but the middle aged men must die out; the young must outgrow the ideas and passions of their youth; the immigrant must come and make himself a social power; the habits of our people must be changed; the ladies, God bless them, must learn to love the Yankees, whom they now hate and despise so delightfully; the passions of this hour must be buried in oblivion, and our hearts engrossed in the development of the mighty resources and teeming wealth which Providence has spread so lavishly around us. Then and not until then will there be a permanent, healthy and desirable restoration of the Union; not to what it was, but to what it is to be."

It was to this "development of the mighty resources" that Baxter looked with an eager eye and a willing hand. And with every dollar that he could scrape up!

The education of his sons assumed great importance to Baxter now. The boys must be prepared to meet the challenges of the future. Young Eli was sent off to Bingham Military School in Mebanville, North Carolina. Johnny was placed in Sardis Academy, near the old Springs plantation in Mecklenburg County. Mr. Querry, an excellent tutor, was hired to live at Springfield and teach the children in a little school house down the road.

The younger boys were developing splendidly and each one had his duties on the plantation. Brevard was his father's "post boy" and brought the mail each evening. Leroy was the witty, mischievous one of the family. He would ride into Fort Mill and create quite a show in that little village, sitting atop his horse, Coleman, and wearing one boot and one shoe. He teased his older brothers incessantly. Austin, Alva, and Baxter, Jr., helped Mr. Bales to clear land for planting.

Baxter gave a great deal of thought to these boys. He remembered so vividly how his father had trained him, writing advice and encouragement, moulding his character, shaping his future. Maybe he should give his sons something to think about, a standard to set for themselves. He jotted down a few paragraphs of traits which he deemed important and mailed them to Johnny and Eli:

"Never forget that you have a Heavenly Father, that you are on your way to a world where you must answer for everything you have done. *Live so*, that you may give in your account with joy and not with dread.

"Remember your friends at home and how anxious they are for your welfare and improvement. If you will not take the trouble *to write* them, they can have no confidence in your affection.

"Be affectionate and faithful to your friends. Give up *your* inclinations when they interfere with theirs.

"Govern your passions firmly. You can be their master. Do not be their slave.

"*Always* attend to duties first, afterwards to pleasures.

"Ask of everything which you are disposed or tempted to do, *is it right?* If it is, *do it* however much it costs you. If it is not, *let nothing induce you to do it.*"

Young Eli was progressing nicely under Colonel Bingham and looked most handsome in his school uniform, which he said "consists of a velvet stripe on each side of my pants and a small stripe and one button on each side of my collar." He was a likeable young fellow and popular with the boys. Yes, and girls too. He was developing a trait which someday would make him famous throughout the South. He had a way with the ladies! In response to Colonel Bingham's request that he write a composition on politeness, he wrote: "How much more a young lady likes a polite fellow than she likes one that is not polite. The polite man can gain her love a great deal quicker than the other." Eli was learning fast. And he was a chip off the block of his grandfather, John Springs, when the time came for him to write his school paper on "Industry." He declared, "A man who works hard and keeps everything in good order and lets other people's business alone will be sure to get along in this world."

For a boy of fifteen, Johnny was intelligent and very cognizant of the political and economic affairs of the day. He wrote to his father: "When the President separated from the Radicals I believe he was doing everything in his power for the relief of the Southern people. But the Radicals have been determined to impeach him, right or wrong, and to hurl him from his position. Would it not be a strange coincidence if they would cashier President Johnson for insisting that the Southern States were in the Union and could not get out, and hang President Davis for insisting that they were out of the Union?"

It is plain to see that every person, young and old, was discussing the shocking predicament in which Congress had placed the President. In the spring of 1868, the House of Representatives in Washington impeached pro-Southern Johnson and the Senate came within one vote of convicting and ousting him. That same spring, a radical slate supported by Negro voters swept into power in South Carolina and Baxter advised Johnny: "We had a very close election in our District. The

Radicals whipped us by about sixty votes. If we had only commenced a little sooner, we could have converted to Democrats a sufficient number of Negroes to have turned the scale."

The election placed in the South Carolina legislature eighty-eight Negroes, many of them illiterate, and sixty-seven whites. This legislature, called into special session July 6, ratified the controversial Fourteenth Amendment in three days. During the session, it was virtually surrounded by bluecoats under Major General E. R. S. Canby.

"You had better tear yourself loose and leave South Carolina," wrote Baxter's cousin, E. P. Moore from Morganton, North Carolina. "I think we are far better off than you are or will be. Our Legislature will be very nearly evenly divided, but I believe two thirds of yours are Negroes."

From Virginia came another suggestion, this one from that former rider in Morgan's Cavalry, Tom Osborne: "I do wish you would effect a sale and come to our country to live. I am truly grieved to learn of the deplorable condition of our 'sister in distress.' I had gotten from the press some idea of the state of affairs in the states south of us, but had supposed they were exaggerated. Now, however, when I know them to be true my heart is aroused with pity, sympathy and grief. Our section has suffered but nothing, nothing to you."

Then Osborne went on to voice his opinion: "The wild fanaticism in the North is fast giving way to the 'sober second thought' of reason. They, the North, are beginning to feel a very acute nervous pain, *the taxes*—their most tender and delicate nerve is seriously affected. The tax collector has touched their *pockets*. You may do anything, say anything to a Yankee, but for god's sake don't touch his pocketbook!"

Baxter's pocketbook was fuller that summer because he had been most fortunate in selling his cotton crop at a top price. He had telegraphed his Charleston agent to sell at thirty cents. The order was executed and even though the crop was only fifty-three bales, it still produced the substantial sum of $7,159. However, by the time Baxter paid the Internal Revenue tax of $586, the freight and storage bill of $300, the insurance, the commission, and the United States tax on sales stamps he was left with $5,981. He was very pleased, though, because immediately after the sale the market dropped.

Racial tension produced a far different crop than cotton that year. It was something born out of desperation and destined to help protect

Southern society from the evils of menacing Negroes armed with rifles. The figurehead governor of South Carolina, an Ohio-born carpetbagger, R. K. Scott, asserted the white people of the State were only fit to be ruled by rifles and he used Negro militia to enforce his orders. Counter-action came quickly. It took the white-sheeted form of a new organization, the Ku Klux Klan, to suppress Negro unruliness and violence.

The earliest mention of such an organization in a letter to Baxter came from his uncle, Richard Clark Springs, written May 5, 1868, from Spartanburg: "The freedmen here have been agitated by the elections. The Democratic party won the day in Spartanburg by 549 votes. The colored and white Radicals are very much excited by the Secret Society called 'Ku-Klux-Klan' which has recently formed here at Spartanburg village."

White-robed riders moved in ghostly procession through the night in York District too. It has been said that the first Klan organized was in Yorkville. In June the Klan sent a threatening letter to Radical Governor Scott and in the fall they appeared at the voting place in Rock Hill.

In the meantime, Baxter had taken his wife north to Saratoga and Niagara Falls. There in the cool breezes of July and August, he hoped the color would come back to her pale cheeks and the sparkle back to her sad, sad eyes. He worried about her constantly. She was depressed. Her voice lacked the enthusiasm and ring it once had.

The color did come back to Blandie's cheeks, but it would be nine months before the sparkle would return to her eyes. She would have a baby girl! She would name her Bleecker.*

But tragedy was to strike again before that time came. Blandie's brother, Eli Baxter, Jr., died suddenly while on a business trip to Bellville, Texas, on December 13 (1868) . A telegram was sent to Jane and Dr. Connell, who were then living in Houston, telling them of the tragedy. It was their sad duty to get in their carriage and ride to the edge of town and break the news to Julia Baxter.

Blandie had once remarked that "Ma's whole life is Eli," so it was understandable that this shock was almost more than Julia could bear. Small wonder that every letter sent to Springfield by Dr. Connell after that declared "Mrs. Baxter seems to be failing rapidly."

*Bleecker Springs was born May 4, 1869.

The many editorials published in Texas newspapers concerning her son were small comfort to Julia Baxter. She knew the papers were correct when they called him a gallant, kind officer, the personification of honor, a chivalrous and magnanimous gentleman, a genial and social companion, a scholar and a good legal practitioner. Yes, she knew all these things, but she knew too that he was only thirty-one years old, her only son, the only Eli she had left. Jane and the Doctor gently took her to their home, closed her little cottage, and tenderly cared for her, just as Julia in years gone by had tenderly cared for her roses until they were full blown and quietly shedding their petals. Jane had once said, "I would rather please Ma than anyone in the world I know. She has done so much for me."

It was understandable that the atmosphere at Springfield during January matched the weather, which Baxter described as "gloomy in the extreme, dark rainy and lowering, fit only for indoors." Certainly, there was not much to be cheerful about.

"There is a great cry of the want of hands with everyone," Baxter lamented. "Many have left and gone to work on the many new railroads which are being constructed. Consequently, my crop is not as large as last year, but better than most of my friends. I hastened to send my forty one bales to Charleston as there is always risk in holding; the frequency of incendiary now through the country has largely increased the risk. Prices are not as high as I had hoped."

March brought changes in the Springs family. Johnny went off to Colonel Bingham's school, while Eli remained in Charlotte, clerking for the produce firm of Carson & Grier. "I like it very much," Eli commented. "I board at Aunt Sophia's, go with the girls a great deal and have a very good time."

March brought changes nationally. Ullyses S. Grant became President of the United States. Except that the word "united" was a mockery, thanks to the radical Republicans in Congress. The Southern States were set apart, not allowed to be out of the Union, but not declared worthy of being in it.

It was amid this gloom that Blandie's baby was born. But it was this little pink, yawning girl who brought joy to her parents. Blandie fondled her baby, holding the small, frail body close to hers, as if she dared not put her down for fear she might lose her. Baxter hovered over the child's cradle, looking in intense admiration at this tiny piece of humanity who would some day grow into a pampered, adored, vivacious, and extremely popular young lady.

That summer passed uneventfully, except for the fact that the Charlotte and South Carolina Railroad Company merged with the Columbia and Augusta line, with Baxter becoming one of the Directors. There was also time for fishing. "I went with the boys," Baxter said. "We caught nine perch and some small silver roach."

September brought Julia Baxter to Springfield, feeble and greatly aged, no longer the "host within herself" that Baxter had called her once upon a time, but still "Grandma" to her devoted little grandsons. Then it was school days. "But," said Blandie, "we kept all the little boys home for two days, with Eli as their Captain, to gather apples."

In October, Blandie explained to Johnny: "Your Grandma and Aunt Lizzie will leave the twentieth for Houston. It makes me feel very sad for she is so frail. I may never see her again for she is now 72 years old."

The rich splendor of blazing fall colors matched the splendor of a tournament and ball given in Fort Mill November 18. The impressive invitations announced that Colonel John White and Colonel A. Baxter Springs were managers of the affair and Eli Springs was one of the knights. To be specific, Eli was Knight of the Raven Black Plume, and he rode his brother Baxter's colt, the one "with the star on his forehead." The tournament was held in an open field, where an immense crowd had gathered by ten o'clock in the morning. A brass band from Charlotte played loudly and with much vigor. At eleven o'clock, the trumpet sounded and the knights rode onto the field. Half of them represented the west side of the Catawba River and the other the east side. Three knights out of the twenty-four tied the tournament for six times. Finally, the Knight of Indian Land won and he was allowed, as his reward, to crown the Queen of Love and Beauty. The runnerups, who were the Knight of Snowden, the Knight of Golden Fleece and the Knight of Golden Circle, ceremoniously crowned the Maids of Honor. As evening approached, the crowd assembled at the Academy where a grand supper was served, "equal to a wedding party," and then the elaborate ball commenced.

The following month, Eli dismissed tournaments from his mind and went north to attend the Eastman School of Business. His mother cautioned him: "Always answer every letter your Father writes for he is always overwhelmed with business, and if he takes time to write, you always answer."

Indeed, Baxter *was* overwhelmed with business. He was placing more and more emphasis on his outside interests and less on his farm, something that was happening all over the South. The plantation system had come to an end with the end of slavery. "We may pitch a crop," said Baxter, "for a certain number of hands and can have no certainty of their staying to work it."

Railroading was on the move. New lines were being built, while smaller ones were consolidating. Baxter was attempting to find a buyer for his Atlanta and West Point stock so he could increase his holdings in the Georgia Railroad and Banking Company. Then he was buying into a new business which had come into being in Charleston, the Wando Mining and Manufacturing Company. Phosphate had been discovered in South Carolina in 1867 and already it was creating a flourishing business. By February of 1870, he had bought into the Stono Phosphate Company and was made a Director.

Baxter Springs was not the only one busy with financial investments. The corrupt South Carolina legislature was in business for itself. Railroad companies were controlled and stolen by stock manipulations. State property was sold, the politicians dividing the money. Legislators attempted to enrich themselves by buying up State Bank notes at ten cents on the dollar, after which the legislature ordered the assets of the Bank turned over to the Governor who in turn planned to issue in place of the notes twenty year State bonds at six per cent. The Supreme Court stepped in, though, in this case and stopped the manipulation.

In vain, the better element of South Carolinians, white and black, banded together against the corrupt carpetbagger rule. Democratic editors, including W. B. Wilson and L. M. Grist of the Yorkville papers, held a caucus in Columbia in July, 1870. Baxter was invited to several such meetings. Out of them emerged the Union Reform Party, a bipartisan organization pledged to clean up the State government. A Republican, Circuit Judge R. B. Carpenter, was nominated for governor; M. C. Butler, a lawyer who had been a Confederate major general at the age of twenty-eight, received the nomination for lieutenant governor, and the Union Reform legislative slate was liberally sprinkled with Negroes.

Against this movement Governor Scott paraded his black militia. Baxter's friend R. B. McCaw warned from Yorkville, "Governor Scott has sent his gang here and to Rock Hill. The Negroes are exultant." In Yorkville they marched in broad columns that literally forced the whites off the streets. At nearby Chester, their phalanx of bayonets prevented Judge Carpenter from speaking.

The Radicals renominated Scott with a Negro running mate for lieutenant governor. The carpetbagger General Assembly, which Baxter described as "our vile and corrupt Legislature," passed a law that the ballots should be counted in secret at Columbia. Scott and his slate won. Baxter hastened to explain the situation to his son, Johnny, who took a great interest in politics: "Our election is over—a great relief. Freedmen were so absorbed by it for weeks that they worked to do no good. We carried the reform ticket at our box by about fifty three majority. We detected and *drove* back from the polls many illegal voters. I had Wiley Parks there for the purpose to detect and point out North Carolina Negroes. We shall gain considerable number of members of the Legislature. Scott, as we always concluded he would, was elected."

In the spring of 1871, politics boiled over. With Scott's victory had come more corrupt spending largely at the expense of white taxpayers and more arrogance and insults from the Negro militia. Outrages went unpunished. So the Klan began riding, sometimes five hundred strong. The Negro militia paraded and menaced by day. The Klan rode at night.

In answer to an appeal from Governor Scott, President Grant sent four companies of Federal regulars under Major Lewis Merrill to stamp out the Ku Klux Klan in York County.* They yanked suspects from their beds without warrants and made one hundred and ninety-five arrests in a few days. Most of those arrested were herded to Columbia without due process of law. Governor Scott, it seems, had promised Major Merrill a bonus of $200 for every arrest and conviction and the Major was out to make money.

As Baxter said, "Our District has especially had a hard time of it, in consequence of the malicious and partisan feeling which has actuated the officer in command at Yorkville .... They arrested upon any pretext, however unfounded, and no one who should fear arrest would

*The legislature had changed the word "District" to that of "County."

be willing to undergo the harsh treatment to which they were subjected, even though innocent they should be. It has, as you may imagine, proved very disastrous to the interest of the Country."

That October, Grant suspended habeas corpus in York and eight other South Carolina counties to crush out the "conspiracy." It left the population absolutely at the whim of the politicians and bluecoats. It also made headlines nationally.

From her home in Connecticut, Mrs. John Springs, who had recently visited Springfield for the first time since the war, wrote Baxter sympathetically: "Our papers are full of the troubles in South Carolina—of course it is all for political purposes, but I feel worried about you all, as the trouble seems to be in York District. How splendidly Grant has carried out his plan—'Let us have peace.' I could see him hanged on the gallows as high as Heaven. If money can get him out of office, A. T. Stewart's* will do it."

Mrs. John Springs entertained her grandson, Eli, for a few days after he completed his course at the business school in Poughkeepsie, New York. Then she saw him off on the cars for New York where his Uncle Austin's friend, Frank P. Waterhouse, took him under his wing. "But don't," Austin warned in a letter to Mr. Waterhouse, "suggest such places as *we used to visit* when we were boys! He is a good boy—doesn't drink, chew or smoke."

When Eli arrived in Charlotte, where he planned to resume his old job with Carson & Grier, he found the town in a flurry over the upcoming "Fair of the Carolinas." The tremendous sum of $10,000 was allotted for prizes. The young Springs boys were wild with excitement and each was competing. Brevard, assisted by Negro George, brought his heifers up and won a premium on one of them. Alva showed grain and won a premium on the rye and corn meal. All the family was present with the exception of young Austin, who was in his first year at Bingham's, and Johnny who was now a student at Davidson College. There was a circus and after that a concert. The only thing to mar the festivities was the weather. "When I saw how bad the weather was, I wished a thousand times I were home," exclaimed Blandie.

Baxter was pleased with the manner in which the boys assumed their duties on the plantation. The following month he wrote: "Hav-

*A. T. Stewart, a close friend of Mrs. John Springs and her sisters, was a behind-the-scenes political power.

ing worked so industriously through their entire vacation, hoeing cotton and lately in gathering it, I delighted each of the little fellows with a gun apiece and they are all out now rabitting."

It was amusing to Baxter to sit at the breakfast table, often before daylight, and listen to the conversation of his attractive sons. "Last evening," Alva said one morning, "I got a chance to plough. I ploughed Cheatham. As I was coming home, with my hands in my pockets, not thinking of Cheatham throwing me, he made three jumps and threw me. The first jump he set me on his side. The second jump he placed me on his hips. The third jump he set me right down on the ground. I was not at all hurt but could not help thinking how slick he threw me!"

"I am amused at them," laughed Blandie, "Alva calls Brevard 'Mr. Davidson' and says 'Mr. Davidson, it is time to start to school.' "

Leroy came to his father one morning and asked if he could cut down a certain hollow persimmon tree. There was a squirrel inside it. With permission granted, Leroy went hurrying off to enlist Alva's and Brevard's aid. When the tree was felled, the "squirrel" turned out to be a screech owl. "Brevard got him out," Alva later said, "but because it began to scratch his hand he set it on the stump, thinking it would sit there, but away it flew."

Brevard was the conscientious one. "He was cutting with Jim Meek's axe on a tree in the little orchard," said Alva to Austin, "and the axe cut from the toe of his boot toward his instep." This was serious enough, but what was even more important to twelve-year-old Brevard was the fact that he had been wearing his new boots when he should have had his old ones on. To avoid detection, and remembering that he was supposed to have only one pair of new boots a year, he carefully hid the damaged boots from the eyes of his mother and father. He wrapped and nursed his toes until they were well. Then he reported to one of his brothers: " My toes have grown together and are entirely well."

The year 1872 took its toll on the Springs family. First, "Grandma" Julia Baxter died in Houston, Texas, on February 2 while Blandie and Baxter were packing to go to her. Then Mrs. John Springs died in March en route to Springfield. She had stopped at Petersburg, Virginia, to visit the Lyons and while there developed pneumonia. The third death was Baxter's sister, Mary Davidson, who died in November, leaving a large family* and a devoted husband.

All the Springs boys were away from home that year except Brevard and Leroy. "How I have missed you boys," their father wrote, "especially since the beginning of the gathering of the crop and in other matters constantly requiring attention. Brevard and Leroy are too young. I have therefore been much confined when other, even more important matters, should have my attention."

The political clouds began to lift that year of 1872. The Democrats became powerful enough to get Congress to pass a general amnesty act which restored citizenship and officeholding privileges to nearly all white Southerners. Federal troops were withdrawn from all States except Louisiana and South Carolina. Scalawag Franklin J. Moses, Jr., was now governor of South Carolina and he was supported by a legislature that was two-thirds Negro and rapidly bankrupting the State. The Governor's constant appeal to the Federal Government for troops was only a safeguard to keep himself in office. The State University was turned over to Negroes. Even the Cedar Springs school for the deaf and blind, where Baxter's Uncle Richard Clark Springs had once taught, was forced to close because of the enforced regulations of integration. Responsible citizens sent a petition to Congress asking for relief. None was granted. An appeal was made to President Grant who practically insulted the petitioners and said South Carolina must help herself.

By 1874 the political scene was brighter. The power of the Radicals in Congress was broken with the election of a Democratic House of Representatives. This was good. But the economy was suffering, so there were still problems for Baxter. Every branch of industry was experiencing "gloomy times." And expenses were mounting in the Springs family. Baxter had sent Austin to Princeton. Baxter, Jr., and

---

*Mary and Brevard Davidson had sixteen children. Besides their plantation, Rural Hill, they owned a town house in Charlotte at the southeast corner of Tryon and Third Streets. Their sons, John Springs, Richard Austin, and Robert, fought in the Civil War. The latter was in a Yankee prison camp for two years and died shortly after his release. The oldest daughter, Sallie, grew into womanhood as an eccentric, well-loved, and respected person. Never having married, she traveled extensively abroad. Her manner of dress was always old-fashioned and peculiar, to say the least. One day she walked into Tiffany's, jewelers, in New York City, and asked to see diamond rings. The haughty clerk half-heartedly showed her what he had. When "Miss Sallie" made her choice, she wrote a check for the cost of the ring. The astonished clerk slipped into an inner office and telephoned Charlotte to see if the check was good. He was asked by the Charlotte banker to describe the lady's manner of dress and her appearance. The superior Tiffany clerk was astounded when the voice on the other end of the wire shouted, "Sell her the whole damn store if she likes it!"

Alva were at Bingham's. Brevard was now in Charlotte at the Carolina Military Institute. Johnny was taking a tour of the West. Eli was the only son working, and his mother admonished him: "Your Father thinks times are very hard. Do, my child, try to take care of your money."

Eli became a partner, the following year, in what was known as "Burwell and Springs, Grocers and Commission Merchants," of Charlotte. This was the beginning of a very remarkable business career for him. His father remarked, "Eli seems energetic in business and grows in popularity with the firm and the people."

Eli's popularity placed him in another position that year. He was asked to help engineer a celebration of the one hundredth anniversary of the Mecklenburg Declaration of Independence, to be held in Charlotte. For weeks during the spring, the town was a beehive of activity and Eli was right in the midst of it. The plans were advertised throughout the country. From Philadelphia a friend* wrote to the Springs family: "I feel interested in the 20th of May Centennial. I have often heard of Captain Jack† from Sussanah Alexander who remembered all about that matter. She died at ninety-six years of age. I used to love to hear her tell of old times."

Northern newspaper reporters took notice of the celebration and joined with the 30,000 people who jammed the streets of Charlotte May 19 when the program began at the square, where once had stood the small log courthouse. The Stars and Bars floated to the top of the flagpole as a score of Confederate Generals stood at attention, while the band played "The Old North State." Then the Mayor spoke and following this the Governor‡ of North Carolina addressed the enthusiastic crowds.

The following morning Charlotteans and their visitors were awakened by a one hundred gun salute. The day was off to an exciting start, and it was a beautiful day too, warm, sunny, and delightful. Flags flew from every window. The streets were soon filled with jubilant people, prancing horses, sleepy-eyed mules, elegant carriages, plain buggies and sturdy wagons. The most aristocratic stood side by side with the plainest backwoodsman to witness the parade which marched down the main street to the fair grounds where crowds

*Dr. Robert Gibbon of the U. S. Mint, Philadelphia, Pennsylvania.
†Captain James Jack carried the Mecklenburg Declaration to the Congress in Philadelphia.
‡Governor C. H. Brogden.

listened to speeches and band playing. There was more of the same at the square that night and then Charlotte's society turned out in all its finery for a grand ball at the Central Hotel, which stood on the southeast corner of the square.

Eli had worked diligently over every detail of the ball. The invitations had been printed in gold, displaying a hornet's nest and the American flag. On the inside of the folder were the names of the floor managers, Eli being one of them, and then came the honorary managers, among them General Joseph E. Johnston of Georgia, General M. W. Ransom of North Carolina, General H. W. Gary of South Carolina, Colonel H. M. Polk of Tennessee, General Johnston Haygood of South Carolina, General P. M. B. Young of Georgia, General T. W. Brevard of Florida, Captain J. Barron Hope of Virginia, and former North Carolina Governor Zebulon B. Vance.

The gentlemen bowed and the ladies smiled. Soon dancing began and continued into the small hours of the morning. If only John Springs could have seen this elegant affair he would not have said Charlotte was "poor," as he had once described the village. No, it was a town on the move, and progressing with it was Eli Springs.

But sometimes Baxter and Blandie had their doubts and worries about their oldest son. One such occasion came in August of that year while they were vacationing at White Sulphur Springs. One morning the *Charlotte Observer* arrived in the mail and, to their great surprise, Baxter and Blandie read of Eli's near drowning while rescuing a girl at the seashore. Blandie wrote immediately: "You can not conceive of our anxiety and distress in reading of your suffering at Beaufort. What in the world did you go in with girls without a sufficient number of gentlemen to assist in case of an accident and I thought you *did not approve of surf bathing*. It certainly looks fast for any girl to go in with a gentleman. I really don't know what the world is coming to and it seems you can't kill yourself fast enough. I feel very uneasy about you and think still you are far from safe. Do, my dear son, be prudent and take care of yourself. Don't run mad. Settle down and be a nice, dignified young man and save your money."

A few days later Blandie wrote to her son again. This time she was bubbling with news of the fashionables of White Sulphur. "I have never seen such a crowd as we have had the past few days. Wednesday and Friday nights were the dress balls and never in my life did I see anything like it. One lady had on a lace dress that cost twelve hundred dollars and there were four more from six to nine hundred, but still there were several dresses not costing near so much that were far prettier. This is a delightful place for those who have plenty of money. A young man from Memphis told your father that poor folks could not live here, that a poor woman came and the water killed her in two days! So you see *everybody is rich.* Your father says this is the busiest place doing nothing he has ever seen. Bleecker was very green at the beginning. When they had nuts one day she told some city children that she had lots of good things. A little boy called her a *pumpkin.* She called him a *green squash!"*

But because there was always that thought of money to be considered, Blandie added: "We are stationary here at White Sulphur until we leave for New York and Philadelphia—that is, if your father can stand the expense."

When the Springses arrived home in September, Baxter threw himself into the midst of a hot political contest. General Wade Hampton was running for Governor to unseat the corrupt Governor Chamberlain.*

It had all started back in the spring when on April 19 Baxter had received a letter marked *confidential:* "This is to notify you that at a meeting of the Democratic County Convention held at this place (York) you were elected as one of the delegates to the State Convention which meets in Columbia on May 4th." One of the leaders of the straight-out ticket at that convention was General H. W. Gary (the same gentleman who had participated in the Centennial celebrations at Charlotte), and he insisted that the issue of the campaign was race against race. However, Wade Hampton contended that good government was the issue and the Negro had a place in it. But race *was* the issue. At that time the Lieutenent-Governor, the Secretary of State, and the Attorney General were Negroes. The Treasurer and Adjutant-General were mulattoes. One of the associate justices of the Supreme Court was a Negro named Wright, or better known as "Tharsparilla Wright" because in his drunkenness in the Columbia saloons he, lisping, always ordered "tharsparilla and whiskey." A Negro gambler, a "notorious debauchee," was a circuit judge. It was all this that made

*Republican Daniel Chamberlain had taken scalawag Franklin J. Moses' place when the latter was indicted for stealing (but never convicted).

the people take drastic action. What took place was unprecedented and astounding. President Grant had said South Carolina must look after herself. She was determined to do just that!

A new organization, the Redshirts, open and above board, took the place of the secret and outlawed Ku Klux Klan. The Democrats formed rifle clubs (infantry) or saber clubs (cavalry). By the time Governor Chamberlain ordered them disbanded, they were too strong to be daunted. Their number had reportedly swelled to 100,000. They were made up of the well-to-do, the ordinary men, the farmers, the business men, all serious and determined that this time the carpet-bagger and scalawag would go. If a call to duty necessitated closing business, dropping plows, or rising from their beds in the middle of the night, it was cheerfully and willingly done. The white people of South Carolina had closed ranks. They were on the march. Nothing now would stop them short of their goal. Their red shirts were donned, their pistols were buckled on, their horses were ready and waiting. Between September and November they rode over the country thousands strong.

General Wade Hampton, often riding a spirited white horse, campaigned from county to county, accompanied by as many as 4,000 Redshirts at a time, all on horseback, all giving the rebel yell. The object was not bloodshed, but to show the Negroes and radicals that the Democrats were strong, they were serious, they meant business. When a radical meeting was held the Redshirts galloped to the spot, yelling and terrorizing the crowd.

Federal troops were sent to subdue the Redshirts, but the Federals were always outnumbered and overwhelmed, not with bullets but with cheering remarks, hospitable offers of whiskey, and in the end they were demoralized to such an extent that often the Negroes thought those troops were part of the Democratic group. In fact, it was afterwards reported that many Federal soldiers donned civilian clothes and helped the Redshirts.

No one will ever know how many votes were cast on election day. In lower South Carolina Negroes armed with guns and bayonets watched every Negro vote and threatened to kill him if he did not vote Republican. In some instances the Republicans dressed Negro women as men and sent them to the polls to vote. In other polling places the Negroes were afraid to vote because of the Redshirts, while some Negroes did vote and help campaign for Hampton, but it was reported there were only about 17,000 of these. However, it is said that Hampton never forgot that these law abiding colored people had helped with his election.

Hampton was declared elected. The Republicans threw out the entire vote of two counties, however, and declared Chamberlain the winner. Chamberlain occupied the State House in Columbia under Federal guard. Hampton and his body set up offices nearby. The Democrats met in legislative sessions, while the Republicans did the same. In one instance, when it was reported Federal troops were going to break up the white legislature, eight thousand Redshirts arrived in Columbia between ten o'clock on a Sunday night and noon the following day.

This went on for five months. Meanwhile, General Hampton went to Washington to confer with the new President, Rutherford B. Hayes, who finally ordered the Federal troops withdrawn from the Capitol in Columbia. The white legislature moved in. Chamberlain formally bowed out of the picture. The carpetbaggers and scalawags scurried to catch the first trains leaving South Carolina. The struggle was over.

When Wade Hampton returned from Washington he was met at every station by cheering crowds. His train was covered with flowers when it pulled out of Charlotte and as it crossed the South Carolina line it went under arches of flowers. The train stopped at each town to allow the people to welcome and cheer their new Governor.

Every Southerner living in the North applauded South Carolina in her victory over corruption. From Philadelphia Leonidas Springs wrote to Baxter: "A number of Southern gentlemen, now residents of this city, would like to show their appreciation of the noble fight made by General Wade Hampton for the down-trodden people of South Carolina. We think of having a fine portrait painted of the General and present it to Mrs. Hampton, provided you can furnish us with a good photograph likeness, giving color of eyes, hair and whiskers, etc."

Baxter informed his cousin that there was no longer a Mrs. Hampton. She had died the previous year.

But what was happening to the Springs family and to Springfield during all this cyclonic experience? A drastic change had taken place, a sad change, and yet a sensible one. Baxter rented a town house in Charlotte and moved his family there. To be sure, Springfield was kept open. The family used it for house parties, for week ends, and the boys spent most of their vacations there, but actually Springfield was never the same again. It was something that just had to be. Baxter was away from the plantation much of the time and he could not leave Blandie and Bleecker there with only servants. Besides, help was difficult to find. Once Blandie had written, "I have no servants but Caroline and Betty. I have very little time to sit down, am flying around from morning until night and when night comes I assure you I can sleep. I have taken two long carriage rides to see if I could muster a woman, but can hear of no one."

And another thing, Blandie was lonely at Springfield. Even young Leroy was now off at school. She wrote to one of the boys in 1875, "I miss you sorely." For many years the house had been filled with the sound of happy boys running through the halls, scuffling, playing, and teasing each other. Now the house was dreadfully quiet. She had only the boys' letters. "I am always glad," she said, "to hear from any of my children for it makes me feel that all my trials and anxieties about them are appreciated and I am not forgotten."

Bleecker was her mother's greatest comfort now. "I don't see how I could get along without her," exclaimed Blandie. "She is as bright and happy as a lark all day long." But then, because she always remembered her other little girls, she sadly said, "I try not to have my heart too much wrapped up in her for she is only loaned to me and may be taken."

Was it imagination, but did not the birds forget to sing the morning the last of the trunks moved down the avenue of Springfield, and did not the peacocks scream more furiously in protest that day? Maybe they felt like young Alva when he lamented: "The house seems desolate. I have felt lost."

In Charlotte there was an excellent school for Bleecker to attend. There was a dancing class for her to enjoy. There was a music teacher. There were playmates. In short, there was everything a little girl could desire. And that was the way Blandie wanted it.

That summer of 1876 Austin had come home from Princeton University telling of the great wonders of the Centennial at Philadelphia. Leroy, wide-eyed and listening intently, gloried in every word of the description. He imagined the great buildings which housed the exhibitions. He imagined himself walking up one aisle and then another seeing the woolens and china from England, the steel from Germany, the silks and laces from France, the ivories and carvings from China, India, and Japan, and the rugs from Persia and Turkey. He could almost see the fabulous exhibits of his own country, but he could not quite envision those new things, the typewriter, the telephone, and the air brake, which were creating such interest. And the art exhibits from abroad—why he had never had an opportunity to see anything like that before. Oh! if only he could go! He sat down one evening at Springfield and wrote a letter to his mother who had gone with Bleecker to White Sulphur Springs: "I asked Father about going to the Centennial and he said I better save my money for something else. I don't think so, for if I don't go I will spend it foolishly and never know what became of it. I came down here with no other intention than making money to go to the Centennial on. I have been busy making cider and vinegar for the last two weeks. The vinegar will bring at least $60. I have $35 besides that. I know I will enjoy the Centennial as much as a grown person. Austin says he is going back to school on the 8th and I could go along with him. I wish you would please write to Father and ask him to let me go and if he will I will study hard at school next session and I won't go out of the house after night and I will come down to the plantation every Saturday and pick cotton for nothing."

And so it was with a young boy when he had his heart set on something. And so it was with the Springs family at the close of reconstruction. This was the end of one era and the beginning of another, the beginning of a new South, a new generation.

Blandie had an inkling of the wonderful new age to come when she visited the Centennial that fall of 1876 and saw the marvelous new inventions and improvements. "It is beyond anything you can think of," she wrote enthusiasticly to Baxter. But because she was there without him, some of the joy was taken away. "I wish I had my old man to go around with me," she exclaimed. "I never pass a handsome man but what I sigh for my old fellow to be by my side."

Part Five
PRIDE AND PROGRESS

The new Springfield, Mecklenburg County, North Carolina.

CHAPTER TWENTY-FIVE

BREVARD DAVIDSON SPRINGS, the sixth son of Baxter and Blandie Springs, was twenty-four years old in 1884. He stood six feet tall and was large framed, of erect carriage, ruddy complexion, and dark, curly hair. He was impressive and full of dignity, but at the same time his kindliness shown from his handsome face and a twinkle brightened his blue eyes. The tone of his voice was rich, earnest, and persuasive. There was something in his appearance that made a stranger take a second look. He had the manners of a courtier. He loved nature and saw beauty in trees and flowers, which he planted with almost a tenderness. And everything he planted grew and flourished!

Yes, Brevard Springs was a very special man and Caroline Clarkson thought so, too. "The finest of the lot," she often said, in comparing him to his brothers. She was positive in her opinion, just as she had been positive during her courtship that she would marry Brevard, which she did on December 17, 1884.

Caroline Clarkson was a pretty girl of twenty-three. Her beautiful figure was well moulded, all the way from her blond, curly head to her very tiny feet. Her eyes were blue, her complexion clear and soft. Her way of laughing was spontaneous and charming. She was an aristocratic and spirited young lady, born in Charleston to parents who were accepted in the best circles because they were descended from Thomas Boston, the great Scottish Covenanter, from the Heriots of Scotland, and from the Simons.

Caroline's parents had been financially ruined during and after the war. When her father, Major William Clarkson, returned from battle with a severe wound in his hip and a rifle ball in his foot, he found his father's great mansion in Columbia lying in ashes, burned by Sherman's army. An account of the burning of Columbia describes how "the entire city was in flames, but the longest and grandest burned the Clarkson mansion. The building was surrounded by thirty arched colonnades which extended from the ground to the roof. They were of massive brick work and stood while the dwelling within was consumed. The fire encasing this imposing structure was grand beyond description. At 10 o'clock the building stood in all its beauty and symmetry, and at 12 o'clock it was in ashes, so complete was the work of destruction."*

With the family home gone and the 10,000-acre plantation ravaged and deserted, Major Clarkson and his young family first lived in Charleston and then for a year in Columbia. In 1874 they moved to Charlotte, renting the two-story white frame Irwin house in which Stonewall Jackson's family had dwelt during the war. It was here that Brevard spent many hours courting Caroline, or Carrie as he called her. Their entertainment consisted of buggy and tallyho rides, parties where their dance cards listed the quadrille, polka, waltz, lanciers, and military schottische; and there were evenings spent on the veranda when Brevard entertained the crowd playing his mouth harp. Often there were tableaus and plays at the Charlotte Female Institute where Carrie had received her education, and many times traveling stock companies would put on plays at the Opera House on Tryon Street.

When Brevard wished to make a date with Carrie, he would send a note by a little Negro boy who would wait for the answer. This was the accepted custom in Charlotte. Each day there would be dreamy-eyed young ladies all over town waiting expectantly to see into whose lane the colored boys would turn.

Carrie, however, did not wait languidly at home. On completing her education, she had become one of Charlotte's first public school teachers.† She taught until her marriage.

*From the account of Frank F. Whilden for *The State*, Columbia, S. C., February 17, 1900. Concerning the Clarkson house, which was built by Governor James H. Hammond and sold in 1851 to Thomas Boston Clarkson, it was said that General Sherman ordered his men not to destroy it because of its beauty, then he countermanded the order on learning that seven Clarkson sons were serving in the Confederate Army and said "Burn it to the ground." The house stood at the corner of Bull and Blanding streets.

†The first effort of public education was made in 1875 when Capt. R. P. Waring, State Senator from Mecklenburg County, submitted a bill in the legislature for levying a tax for educational purposes. In May of 1880 a levy of ten cents on the $100 worth of property and thirty cents on the poll was ratified by the voters of Charlotte and the first school superintendent, J. T. Mitchell of Ohio, was elected. Lucian Walker was elected principal with the following teachers: Carrie Clarkson, Sallie Bethune, Grace Dewey, Annie Davidson, Lucy Alexander, Fannie Brady, Mary Allen, Mrs. R. P. Waring and John W. Walker, Jr.

p: Lt. Leroy Springs, II, son of Colo-
and Mrs. Elliott White Springs, was
led in a plane crash in 1946. Right:
ptain Elliott Springs in France, fall of
8. He was a Colonel in World War II
d died in 1959.

Mrs. Elliott W. Springs with her daughter, Anne, and son-in-law, Hugh William
Close, the present president of the Springs Mills. With them are the Closes' eight
children, standing left to right: Patricia, Lillian Crandall, Frances Allison, Leroy
Springs. Seated, left to right: Elliott Springs, Katherine Anne, Derick Springsteen,
and Hugh William, Jr.

Mr. and Mrs. John M. Scott (Bleecker Springs) at White Sulphur Springs, West Virginia in the early thirties.

Mrs. Stuart W. Cramer, Jr. (Julia Ba×
Scott) with her children, left to right: J
Baxter (deceased in 1934), Stuart, III, ₂
John Scott Cramer. Charlotte, N. C., 1⚬

Mr. and Mrs. Stuart Warren Cramer, Jr., at Hot Springs, Virginia, 1945.

r. and Mrs. John Scott Cramer of Char-
tte, N. C. with their two daughters,
lia Baxter (left) and Alice. 1964. Mr.
amer is the son of Mr. and Mrs. Stuart
. Cramer, Jr.

Mr. and Mrs. Stuart Cramer, III, of Beverly Hills, California (in 1964), with
their sons, Stuart, IV, and Grant. Mrs.
Cramer is the talented and lovely Terry
Moore, popular movie and television ac-
tress.

daughters of Mr. and
. Muscoe Burnett, Jr. of
nnetka, Illinois (and
nddaughters of Bleecker
ings Scott), right to left:
ecker, now Mrs. Robert
m; Sally, now Mrs. Wil-
n Searle; and Calvine
v Mrs. Charles Bowen,
of Lake Forest, Illinois.

Richard Austin Springs, Jr. of Dagoden, Mt. Kisco, N. Y., 1964—fishing for blue marlin at Bimini. His children are, top left: Richard, III, quarterback on Princeton University football team, 1963. Top right: Clare, when she made her debut in 1962 at a supper dance at the Bedford, N. Y. Golf and Tennis Club. Bottom left: Bleecker and Orlando Weber Springs dancing at their sister's debut party. Their mother, the late Clare Weber Springs, was the daughter of the late Mr. and Mrs. Orlando Weber of New York City.

Mr. and Mrs. John Springs Myers of Columbia, South Carolina, in 1964 with their children, John, Jr., Sue (standing), and Margaret. Mr. Myers is the son of Mr. and Mrs. Richard Austin Myers.

Caroline Myers, daughter of Mr. and Mrs. Richard Austin Myers, died in 1947 at the age of 22.

(Top): Marguerite Springs who married Richard Austin Myers (bottom) in 1913.

Mr. and Mrs. Brevard Springs Myers with their children, Brevard, Jr. and Janet, of Charlotte, N. C., 1964. Mr. Myers is the son of Mr. and Mrs. Richard A. Myers.

Joseph Atkinson Jones, whose hobby is golfing, is a former champion of Havana Country Club. 1958.

Mr. and Mrs. Joseph A. Jones with their children, Blandina and Billy, in Havana, Cuba, 1920.

Brevard Springs Jones, second child of Blandina Springs and Joe Jones, died at the age of 20 months.

Blandina Jones Skilton, (Mrs. William Skilton) daughter of Blandina Springs and Joe Jones.

Captain William M. Jones (later Lt.-Colonel) in World War II is the son of Blandina Springs and Joseph A. Jones.

and Mrs. Harry Skilton skiing in Ne-
a, 1963. He is the son of the William
tons.

Standing: Mr. and Mrs. Joseph A. Jones in
Havana, Cuba, 1959, with their daughter and
son-in-law, Blandina and William Skilton.
Seated are Mr. and Mrs. William Jones with
their son, David, next to his mother, and Richard Skilton, son of the William Skiltons.

and Mrs. William Jones Skilton.
3. He is son of the William Skiltons.

Above: Daughters of Mr. and Mrs. William M.
Jones. (Left) Helen, (right) Nancy, Mrs. Richard Byrd. The Byrd children, Beverly, Bradford, and Bonnie are shown at left.

Mr. and Mrs. Eli Springs, II, and their family at Springfield, 1964. Standing, left to right: Eli, IV; Eli, III; Eli, II; Jack H. Shannon; Jack Shannon, Jr. Center, Mrs. Eli Springs, III, with little son, Brevard Davidson; Mrs. Eli Springs, II; Mrs. Jack Shannon with Lela Shannon. Seated on ground, left to right,

It was considered improper in the eighties for a bride-elect to be seen in public for a week before her marriage. But Carrie Clarkson was a determined young lady. She wished to have her picture taken with her maid-of-honor, Isabel Irwin (niece of Mrs. Stonewall Jackson), and so she defied social convention. On the morning of the wedding day, the two went in a closed carriage, with the shades lowered, to the photograph gallery of J. H. VanNess, where they had their picture taken.

Guests came from all over the South for the wedding. Among them was Governor Hugh Smith Thompson of South Carolina, the bride's uncle, who accepted Baxter's and Blandie's invitation to be their house guest. The ceremony was performed at 7:30 o'clock in the evening by the Reverend J. H. Thornwell, pastor of the Presbyterian Church of Fort Mill, with the bridal couple standing before a classic white marble mantel in the parlor of the Clarkson home. Surrounding the couple were ten bridesmaids and ten groomsmen. It was an impressive occasion, a beautiful tableau, and the bride was gorgeous!

Immediately following the ceremony the bridal party and guests were escorted to Baxter's and Blandie's house on Tryon Street for a reception and supper. "The spacious mansion," the *Charlotte Observer* recorded, "was lighted from top to bottom, and its doors were thrown open to admit the stream of friends who poured in to enjoy the festivities. At no wedding that we have witnessed in this city has there been such a large gathering of guests, old or young, or where the good cheer and old-fashioned hospitality of *ante-bellum* days was more vividly recalled. The newly wedded were the recipients of a large number of very elegant and costly presents from their friends, including silverware, china, diamonds, furniture, etc. Though the groom has been a *prima facie* resident of Charlotte during his courtship, his home is in Fort Mill and there he will take his bride." The correspondent of the hometown paper in Fort Mill waxed even more ecstatic about the wedding:

"The array of beauty from the two Carolinas on this festive occasion was so brilliant and angelic-like that visions of paradise passed before our minds as in admiration lost we beheld the scene. . . . Comus had visited the various marts where dealers in viands dwelt, the groves where fruits in abundance grew, and Bacchus from Reims and Bordeaux supplied the wines, nectar quaffs—such as the gods delighted to have on Mount Olympus—and in this department of the reception your correspondent, like all the others, *rejoiced* with exceeding joy!"

As he looked back over the preceding years that led up to his wedding, Brevard felt that time had been moving on at a rapid rate. Much had happened to him since his school days at Carolina Military Academy. Those days had been happy ones, he recollected, with many amusing incidents. He laughed when he remembered the time he and his roommate, constantly annoyed by dogs under their window at night, had dropped stove wood out of their window to end the annoyance of the growling canines. The next morning it had not been a dead dog lying under their window but the Major's prize hog, stretched out cold!

But there were sad things to remember too, like Uncle Austin Springs' death in 1876. Visiting Uncle Austin at Springsteen had always been exciting because he appreciated what young boys liked. His horses were superb, his hunting trips sporting and thrilling, his conversation sparkling.

As Brevard looked back on his school days, he could not help but feel admiration for his father. Undoubtedly, it must have been a financial burden to have kept Austin in Princeton, Alva and Baxter, Jr., in Davidson, and Brevard in the Academy. Then followed Leroy's entrance into the University of North Carolina and Alva's transferring to be with him. Austin had graduated from Princeton in 1877 and had immediately entered law school at Columbia University in New York. Bleecker was taking her schooling at the Charlotte Female Academy, preparing herself for Peace Institute in Raleigh. Yes, Brevard thought, his father had done well never to have complained when his sons' newsy, affectionate letters had usually ended in an apologetic request for money. Checks had always been forthcoming, of sufficient amount to supply the needs and the occasional extravagances of young fellows, even during the hard times of '77 when the railroads had experienced serious strikes all over the country and dividends were necessarily curtailed.

The railroads had returned to normal conditions with the ending of the strikes in 1878. Brevard remembered his father had felt safe in extending his Chicago, St. Louis and New Orleans Railroad bonds for another five years, through negotiations with the company's Secretary, Styvesant Fish. At that time Baxter Springs was a Director of the Charlotte, Columbia and Augusta Railroad, as well as the Danville,

North Carolina Railroad and the Atlantic, Tennessee and Ohio Road. Also speculations in cotton futures had proven profitable to Baxter that year. He was fortunate in selling at the right time, and his broker, Gwathmey and Company of 122 Pearl Street, New York, encouraged further speculation with a letter: "If you wish to make further purchases send along your order. We will not bother you about margins, if not entirely convenient, knowing, as we do, your standing and responsibility."

Brevard remembered how fascinated he, a small town boy, had been with the letters his brother Austin had written from New York. For instance, in February of 1878 there was this: "I have not been to see Mrs. Clinch or the Smiths lately, though I know I should have done so, for one cause or another, the principal one being, as Mr. Stewart's remains were stolen, there might be somewhat of a commotion in the family and the company might not be agreeable."* Now, there was a real scandal! Brevard had wondered when he had read that letter what his grandmother Springs would have thought of the great merchant prince's body being stolen from its grave.

In recalling his activities of 1878, Brevard mostly remembered it as the year he had made his first business venture. It was in October. He and S. P. Blankenship had taken the Alabama agency for "an improved cotton gin brush and wiper," an invention of a Mr. H. A. Walker. The world had gone mad over new inventions. Had not the phonograph, invented by Thomas Edison, been a miracle, and had not that great genius just the year before invented an incandescent electric light? Of course, a gin brush was nothing spectacular, but a better brush would be an asset to the hundreds of cotton gins throughout the South, especially Alabama, where he would make his fortune. And so December had found Brevard canvassing that delightful state by horse and buggy, carrying with him credentials of character which had been written by prominent business men and bankers of Charlotte, all properly notarized and stamped. Well, Brevard admitted, looking back on those days, making a living as a salesman had not been as easy as he had imagined. He had finally written his father: "I regret very much to have to call on you for money. I have not sold but one

---

*Mrs. Clinch, a sister of Mrs. John Springs, was a close friend of A. T. Stewart, who was one of the wealthiest men in the United States. He and his wife lived in a fabulous mansion on the northwest corner of Fifth Avenue at 34th Street, and where was housed the finest art collection in the country. Stewart died in 1876. After his corpse was stolen from its grave, it created such a furor that more than one wealthy man left instructions that his grave should be impregnable from robbers.

brush for cash since I came to Alabama. I hope I can collect for those I have sold on time, but it is better to sell on time than not at all."

Brevard, desperately wanting to make good, had later written his father: "I am in great hopes of success in my business and assure you I am grateful for the opportunity you have given me by purchasing and advancing the money for the Right." And so he plugged on, hoping that some of the business boom of the spring and summer of 1879 would come his way. Everyone else seemed to be making money. Speculation was rampant all over the country. His father and mother had even built a new house on Tryon Street in Charlotte and were busy furnishing it with marble mantels, expensive carpeting, draperies, bronze figurines, etc. The townspeople had said "it was about the prettiest place in Charlotte." Eli had written of his speculative successes. Austin had written: "I have finished law school. I have hung out my sign and am scattering my cards around—in other words, I am ready to receive clients and transact business." They had all seemed to be doing so well, while his first business venture was slowly going on the rocks. But what he had not known at the time was that Austin had written his father, "I now have my first case, but until I can become established I must call on you for funds." And Alva and Leroy, "sporting around at a rapid rate" at the University of North Carolina, had been calling on their father too for more money.*

Looking back on those hot August days when he had jogged along the dusty Alabama roads, Brevard could almost imagine the grit in his mouth and the dust in his nostrils. He remembered he had been actually envious when a letter had come from his parents in Saratoga saying: "It has never been more pleasant or gay. Racing is fine—elegant times." He had tried to picture what Eli was doing at White Sulphur, what they were all doing back home, while he was trying to sell those blasted gin brushes. But pride is a powerful thing and he had written his father, "Don't tell the boys that my business is not going well."

He had turned his horse homeward in September, reaching Charlotte in October. His hair had grown long and he had a beard. He

---

*Kemp Battle, President of the University of North Carolina, wrote to Baxter Springs: "I allowed your son Alva to go to Hillsboro to call on some ladies and he absented himself for two weeks. . . . The faculty passed a sentence of dismissal, but in consideration of Mr. Alva's good behavior generally the sentence was suspended. The leniency was caused in great part by the fact that the motive of Mr. Alva's absence was the desire to visit the ladies and not to engage in any bad conduct. . . . Your son expressed himself as truly regretting his course."

afterwards learned that Eli had written his parents: "You should see Brevard! He looks like a regular housier. He claims to have had a successful trip."

In reminiscing, Brevard was conscious of the tremendous change that one or two years can make in a person's life. As the old folks had often quoted, "What fleeting shadows we are." The years 1880 and 1881 had been years of change. He even dreaded to think of them. The only bright spot had been the hours he had spent with Carrie. Otherwise, it had been a grim time. It had all started in January of 1880 when Baxter, Jr., twenty-two years old, had come down with pneumonia. The boy had managed to survive the dread disease, but it had left him with a nagging cough. In March his mother had taken him to Palatka, Florida, accompanied by Eli. The trip had been pleasant enough, with sufficient excitement to amuse them, because "the St. James is a grand Yankee hotel. They dress magnificently and they all have their phaetons and horses." But Baxter, Jr., did not improve. Brevard could almost close his eyes and remember his mother's words when she arrived home, "I feel so anxious about Baxter. Oh! my children are ever in my mind, their welfare and success."

The following winter, it was the opinion of the doctors that Baxter, Jr., should go to Texas. He had tuberculosis. Each one of the boys had offered to go with him. Even Uncle William Myers said he would go. But neither his father nor his mother had been content to send their ill son away without one of them being with him, so his father had taken Baxter, Jr., to Boerne in Kendale County, Texas. That was in January, 1881. Shortly afterward, Eli had written his father: "I am ready at any moment to go to Baxter and relieve you as I know your business requires your attention so much. I have no idea I could fill your place with Baxter for I know from experience what a gentle nurse you are, but I think I could manage to take pretty good care of him. . . . I know you would have made money if you could have been here. Stocks have been booming. I am glad you are pleased with the sale of your A. W. R. R. stock. I should have sold it before for you but did not have your authority."

Brevard and the boys had tried to entertain their sick brother with frequent letters and gifts. Their mother had written to him of current events and various bits of town gossip, never giving way to her anxiety or fear. She even quoted the stock market to him. But Brevard had known how his mother had poured out her heart to his father in her letters. He had seen her at her desk, with tears running down her cheeks. Once he knew she had written: "My dearest old fellow, I have had the blues dreadfully. Oh! this parting with loved ones, 'tis so sad to stand. I feel so differently from what I did in the past years. I feel I am getting old and that every time we part it may be the last parting. . . . I trust and pray our Heavenly Father in mercy and wisdom may see fit to spare our son and restore him to health. I think of you morning and night." And to this letter his father had answered: "Blandie, how anxious I am to see you, no one can well conceive."

Brevard recollected that in April his Aunt Lizzie, en route to Europe, had arrived in Charlotte to spend a month with his mother and he also remembered that his father had written: "Blandie, it has been two months since I left you and I do not see that there is any improvement in Baxter's condition. Therefore, I have not been satisfied to leave him. . . . It is so lonely and monotonous here. I am getting very much fatigued and worn out. As soon as Baxter begins to strengthen I will leave."

But Baxter, Jr., did not strengthen. His father had brought him home a corpse in June. Eli had rushed to New Orleans to give what comfort he could to his father en route home. Brevard remembered the day the train pulled into Charlotte and came to a screeching stop. The man who stepped from the car—that thin, gaunt man with his shoulders drooping and his eyes sad—God, it was his father who had always been erect, alert, and smiling. What grief could do to a person!

Brevard and Alva had gone to the plantation after the funeral. Their father had asked the two of them to take over the management of Springfield with its 2,241 acres. Brevard had felt comforted being at the old homeplace. A quietness, an inner peace had come over him. And because he felt the need of comfort, he had had compassion on his dead brother's dog, Billy, and had taken him to Springfield. But the dog continued to mourn. "He lies around," Brevard had said, "and seems to grieve from one end of the day to the other. When I went to town he slipped down to the train behind me and slipped on board without my knowing it. When I did see him he looked as if he were afraid I was going to whip him. He went to the house and occupied his same bed in Baxter's room in the old broken rocking chair on the old red cushion. You have no idea how he misses Baxter. He seems to be lost and loafs around like he's lost his last friend."

And old Aunt Betty, the Negro nurse who had attended to Baxter,

Jr., during all of his childhood, who had washed his dirty little face, had dressed and undressed him, who had heard his prayers and watched his glistening eyes as he exclaimed over his rabbit runs or his 'possum hunts, that old, old woman was completely heartbroken. She had decided to go to her son's home. Her husband, Nathan, had passed on and she was lonely. Brevard remembered that he had agreed with Leroy when he said: "I think the old place much sadder now since Aunt Betty and Uncle Nathan are gone. It is unnatural not to see one or the other there."

Brevard could only think that his brother's death was truly a tragedy, but his grandfather had said many times, "misfortunes rarely come alone." Before Brevard had married Carrie Clarkson there had been another frightful blow to the Springs family. John, the second oldest son, was shot in a hunting accident. The bullet pierced his brain.

Frank Sexton, from far away Texas, had expressed it this way to Baxter and Blandie after losing one of his own sons: "It seems as if we are to outlive the young and vigorous—or at least those that seemed so. Why it is so, God only knows!"

Changes. Brevard had been living in a world of changes. He recollected the hours he had spent discussing it with his father. The family had changed, but the country was changing too. An industrial revolution had been taking place since the war. The many new inventions had brought rapid development of natural resources. Cities were becoming larger. The country's chief occupation was manufacturing instead of agriculture. Brevard had sensed this, thinking perhaps he should go into manufacturing as well as farming. He had been growing restless to make money. There was a business boom going on and he wanted to be a part of it. He remembered he had written from Springfield in 1882: "Freight is very heavy now on the railroad— always two up and two down each day. They consume wood faster than I can haul it. Passenger trains also seem to do a good business."

Yes, the country had certainly been on the move. And with the industrial growth had come a new society, a more colorful society which craved more display for its wealth. Houses had an oversupply of decoration, such as the cupolas and balustrades on the new Springs house. Stained glass windows, bright wallpapers, sentimental pictures and heavily carved furniture had come into vogue. The classic simplicity of the earlier years was disappearing. Soon the full skirts in which the ladies looked so elegant and which, according to Blandie's bills, took ten yards of material to make, would disappear for narrower ones.

Charlotte had changed too. It had adopted prohibition in a bitterly contested fight which had brought forth verbal abuses on both sides of the question. As Eli had expressed it, "The whiskey men had an injunction served on the Aldermen, restraining them from closing the saloons, but the Judge dissolved it and decided the city had a right to close them up."

After many consultations with their father, Brevard and Alva decided to postpone a venture into the manufacturing field and instead to open a business in Fort Mill, selling farm equipment and fertilizer, and acting as cotton brokers. Thus the firm of *Springs Brothers* came into being.

Meanwhile, up in New York, Austin had been looking into a new venture. A letter to his father in February, 1882, had stated: "I write you in regard to an article I saw in the *Charlotte Observer* in which the electric light is agitated. . . . I have an engagement with the President of the Brush Electric Light Company in the morning when he promised to give me all the information in regard to the cost of supplying light to a place the size of Charlotte. . . . I would like for you to advise me the present cost of lighting the streets of Charlotte by gas. If the city could be lit by electricity at the same cost it would be ten times better and be a great advantage to the town. . . . It would be all the better if 20 or 25 men would take up all the stock and run it on the same principle as the ordinary gas companies."

Brevard remembered how promptly his father had gone to work to secure this information for Austin. And he had also made other inquiries, one of which was to Leonidas Springs in Philadelphia, who had answered: "I called upon our great John Wanamaker to make inquiries into the comparative cost of the electric light. His experience was that the electric light cost 60 per cent less than gas. I think there will be great improvements made in operating the light. It will pay to wait a few months for developments."

The following month Austin made a decision concerning the establishing of an electric company in Charlotte which was no doubt a mistake. He said, "That the electric light has a bright future has already been demonstrated but that it can be introduced into smaller towns of the South at present is very doubtful."

In looking back to 1882, Brevard recalled that all talk of electricity had faded into the background when his Aunt Sophia Myers had become very ill. Two months later she had died. It was not only her husband and seven children who mourned her loss but all of Charlotte, because her influence had been felt in every circle in which she had ever moved. Even the Negro population mourned her loss because she had done much to promote their interests. She and William Myers had given the land on which the Negro Biddle University (now Johnson C. Smith University) had been built. With the passing of his Aunt Sophia, Brevard had realized that his father was the last of John Springs' children.

By now, Brevard's memory had carried him to the year previous to his marriage. He had been so deeply in love with Carrie that he had found it difficult to remain in Fort Mill and most of his summer had been spent at his father's house in Charlotte. His parents and Bleecker had gone to Rockbridge Alum Springs near Lexington, Virginia, and Eli was leading the gay social life in Newport and Saratoga, after a stopover in New York City to see the fabulous new Brooklyn Bridge, so Brevard had rattled around in the large house by himself. He had given Carrie a diamond engagement ring that summer and she had promised to marry him the following year. In comparison with that momentous event, most other memories seemed unimportant. Consequently, during the year which followed, Brevard and Carrie had spoken of the "sweet nothings" that make up the conversation of lovers.

But, meanwhile, the country's conversations were on a subject vastly different—politics. Grover Cleveland, a Democrat, was running for the Presidency of the United States against James G. Blaine, a Republican who was not entirely acceptable to all members of his own party.* The Democrats had not elected a President since Buchanan. Baxter Springs declared vehemently, "If the Democrats can't win this time they never will."

Economic conditions had been bad and the public, looking for a scapegoat, had pointed an accusing finger toward politics. Stocks, particularly those of the railroads,† had dropped in a panic decline, which

---

*Blaine was unacceptable to many influential and able Republicans who called themselves "Independent Republicans." Many of them advocated the election of Cleveland and were commonly known as "Mugwumps."

†Many stocks had been watered to two or three times their value. Poor's Manual recorded that in 1883 nearly all the capital stock of the railroads represented water. Jay Gould, a bold, successful speculator in railroads, had, following the Civil War, picked up small roads, manipulated their stocks and then unloaded on the public.

hit Baxter Springs' pocketbook. Millions had been lost in Wall Street. Financial giants had been pushed to the wall.

Austin Springs reported almost daily to his father, who was heavily involved in several railroad companies and President of the Atlantic, Tennessee and Ohio Railroad. By October, 1884, he reported: "I fully realize, with the hard times and the great depreciation, your resources are much reduced, but still I had hopes you and Mother would come to New York this fall. . . . Politics is really interfering with business. People are inclined to delay everything until after the election. Cleveland is growing in strength every day."

Yes, Brevard remembered all too well how tight money had been that fall. But he also remembered with deep appreciation that his mother and father had kept right on planning a fabulous reception for his wedding night.

Election day had come off with great excitement in Charlotte. Brevard had watched the returns with much interest. The whole affair had hinged on New York State's vote and there the outcome was so close and so doubtful that it had been several days after the election before the result was known. Consequently, Brevard and his family had expectantly awaited Austin's letter explaining the situation in New York:

"I feel that I can now write and exchange congratulations, as the election of Cleveland is fully assured beyond a doubt. It has been a bluff game with the Republicans for the past three days and they are dying very hard. Such excitement and wild uproar as has existed in this city for the past three days, I do not believe was ever witnessed before. The Republicans have been frantic and wild and loud, while the Democrats have had determination stamped on their faces. . . . I sat up until five o'clock in one of the hotels where returns were received and went home pretty well convinced Blaine had been elected, but later in the day better returns came in. . . . Cleveland's election was conceded by all the city papers today with the exception of the *Tribune.* . . . The Associated Press and the Western Union Telegraph, under control of Gould, has caused and continued this excitement by falsifying the returns and holding them back. That there has not been an outbreak or riot is to be wondered at. A crowd of several thousand gathered at the National Democratic Headquarters night before last and in an impromptu manner organized and marched up Fifth Avenue singing 'Hang Jay Gould to a Western Union Telegraph pole.'

It so frightened Gould that he left his home and went to the Windsor Hotel and slept there all night and the first news by 10 o'clock next morning was that Gould had telegraphed congratulations to Cleveland. It was certainly a narrow escape, there being only about 1500 majority for Cleveland in the state. I see in the morning paper there is a great rejoicing in the South. . . . We have an administration under which the South will have an equal showing with the rest of the country."

And so it had been in the fall of 1884. But the election had soon dropped from Brevard's mind. His wedding date was the seventeenth of December and as he looked back on those days he hardly remembered the details. One picture, though, would always be locked in his memory and heart and that was on their wedding night when he had presented Carrie with an exquisite pair of earrings. The light in her eyes had matched the sparkle of the brilliant diamonds!

CHAPTER TWENTY-SIX

LIFE GIVES AND LIFE TAKES AWAY. The cycle of living ends in its own completeness as each generation burns itself out. But in reality the cycle repeats itself over and over in a series of new generations. The study of a family, with personal details of succeeding generations, is a revealing experience. It seems to say that the length of life is not as important as the quality of life. The depth or impression or influence of one cycle appears to determine the strength and continuity of the next. There is a constant giving and taking.

And so it was with three generations of Springses in the fall of 1885. Brevard and Carrie became the parents of a baby son October 10. They named the child Andrew Baxter Springs II after his grandfather. Three and a half months after his grandson's birth, Baxter died.

When Baxter's health began to fail early in 1885, he rushed to New York to Dr. F. N. Otis, cancelling plans to join Austin in Washington for the inauguration of President Cleveland. He recovered sufficiently to take Blandie in April to New Orleans, where they joined Lizzie Baxter and Jane Connell, now a widow. In July, with Blandie and Bleecker, he vacationed at Saratoga and the Longfellow Cottage at Chatauqua, New York. Stopping in New York City to see Austin, they reported all the buildings draped in black, in mourning for General Grant's death. They also witnessed "the novel and unusual sight of cars running on Broadway below 14th Street."*

Late in August they hurried back to New York because Austin fell seriously ill with diptheria. In the fall they returned to Charlotte and

*These were New York's first electric cars. Horses had formerly pulled the street cars.

Blandie went on to Fort Mill for the birth of the first grandchild. When Jane Connell was notified of the baby's arrival, she sent Baxter a note: "So you and Blandie are Grandpa and Grandma. Old 'time' has not been slow in his strides."

Baxter became ill in November. The following month he went back to New York, where Austin reported to his brothers: "Father is beginning to show his sickness. He can't bear Mother being away from him and she hasn't left him for a week. I spend nearly all my time with him."

At one o'clock on the rainy afternoon of January 27, 1886, Baxter died following an operation. Dr. Otis reported to the family: "My own analysis was made at once during the operation and was fully confirmed by the Pathologist of the College of Physicians and Surgeons. The tumor was malignant. Recovery was out of the question. This it was impossible to know previous to the operation. . . . Your father's courage and his kindly appreciation of every effort on his behalf won my admiration and affectionate regard. . . . I can easily understand that such a man's influence does not cease with his life."

Messages by the hundreds poured in to Blandie and her children. Mr. H. Baruch, who had sat at the hospital with Eli and Austin, consoled: "When I parted with you last night I tried to appear calm, but God knows my heart was heavy. . . . Your father now rests with his beloved dead who have gone before him and probably have been teaching him through all these years the path which leads from life to a better and brighter sphere beyond the stars."

A cousin, writing from Augusta, Georgia, put it this way: "I feel that his spirit is revelling in the glories of heaven, that his ever questioning heart and brain are solving the great mysteries of redemption and creation. Think of his rapture!"

Blandie's friends stood abashed with a sense of helplessness. One said, "You looked so sad I felt as if I wanted to throw my arms around you." And Blandie felt helpless too. She wrote in her little note book, "The sun is going down while it is yet day."

Austin, upon his arrival in New York after the funeral, wrote to his brothers: "Let me hear from you often, if only a few lines. How thoughtful and kind father was in this respect."

Bleecker returned to Peace Institute in Raleigh. "It is hard," said Eli, "for Mother to give her up. It is quite lonely here. No one at home but Mother and myself, but Mother holds up remarkably well."

In front of her children and friends, Blandie did hold up. But she once told Eli: "I have cried many nights. How I miss your dear Father's thoughtful, tender love." Her children would always hold her interest, her pride, her love, but in the depths of her soul there was an emptiness, and her life from then on would be lonely. She vacated her house and rented it to the Baruchs, while she, Eli and Bleecker moved to the Central Hotel. She spent her summers at resorts, her winters either in Charlotte or traveling South. She watched her sons in their fantastic business adventures. She watched Bleecker in her courtships. She was always present when her children needed her. But she never ceased to long for Baxter.

In 1887 Brevard was having his business problems. The firm of *Springs Brothers* depended on farmers, who gave notes against their crop for the equipment and fertilizer they bought. But since 1882 there had been successively bad crops. There was a great cry of hard times and scarcity of money. The farmers were going deeper and deeper into debt. To offset the lack of cash income, Alva had indulged in a bit of cotton speculation which had proved disastrous. Conditions went from bad to worse until finally *Springs Brothers* was forced to close. Many of its debtors went to their graves still owing the firm.

Alva borrowed money and headed for Arkansas, where he would go on to bigger and better promotions which would eventually collapse into bigger and better failures. The Springs family was now waking up to the fact that Alva was impatient to make money and making it the slow way held no appeal for him. "He plays the grand gentleman," said Austin, "when he does not have the money to pay his own expenses. He can pick up a paperback novel at a minute's notice and cast off his troubles. As regards the transaction of business, he is as helpless as a child—so accustomed has he been to splurging." Alva's brothers dutifully paid his bills for years and years and showed nothing but patience and kindness toward him. Alva, in turn, wrote affectionate and apologetic letters.

Brevard, in that same year of 1887, turned to a new venture to recoup his losses. He took the lead with Captain Samuel E. White in founding a textile mill.* The Fort Mill *Weekly News* recorded:

"Captain Samuel E. White and Mr. B. D. Springs determined to build a factory in this place for the manufacturing of cotton plaids upon a joint stock company plan. With the assistance of Mr. J. M.

*This mill subsequently became Units 1 and 2 of the giant Springs Mills.

Spratt a sufficient amount of subscriptions were taken to justify a call for a meeting of the stockholders on the 26th of April, 1887, at which time the following officers were elected: Messrs Sam'l E. White, president; J. L. Watson, vice-president; J. M. Spratt, secretary and treasurer, and Messrs Sam'l E. White, B. D. Springs, J. L. Watson, J. W. White and J. M. Spratt, directors. The Directors were made the building committee, with the addition of Mr. J. C. Jones. The main building is to be 272 by 50 feet, equipped with about 2,500 spindles and 100 looms. The contract for the erection of the factory building was given to W. H. Stewart and the operatives cottages, 20 in number, to A. D. Haller and A. A. Bradford. The capital stock will be $75,000 with a probability of $100,000."

That same spring of 1887, on March 22, Brevard and Carrie had their second baby, a girl named Marguerite Clarkson for her maternal grandmother. Three months later their blonde, curly haired little son, Andrew Baxter Springs II, died after a very brief illness. Blandie went to them immediately, remembering the days of her own sorrows and remembering too what John Springs had once said to her, "It is an especially sore bereavement to lose a first born, the *pledge of mutual love.*"

After that sad experience, Blandie packed her trunks and went to Europe, taking Bleecker with her.

Leroy at this time headed the firm of Heath, Springs and Company of Lancaster and Camden, cotton buyers, bankers, and dealers in general merchandise. He was advertising that he still paid the highest price for cotton—and his boots and shoes were selling at prices to suit both the hard times and the cold weather! But he too was having his troubles when he said: "The Lancaster house makes a fair showing but both houses have entirely too much money owing them. I am afraid that Heath, Springs are accumulating too many notes and mortgages. If we attempt to close up our business at any time it would almost bankrupt the county. Cotton seems to have the black eye."

Eli was prospering more than any of the brothers. He was always ready to make a trade or invest in a new company if he thought it sounded promising. He was now the head of his own firm, *E. B. Springs and Company,* dealers in fertilizers. He had also gone into the utility field. He and Dr. R. J. Brevard formed a corporation which built the first municipal water plant. Eli financed it through a Boston bank and operated it privately for many years. Charlotte was growing and he continued to grow with it. The town now had such great conveniences as electric lights and horse-drawn street cars. A few telephones had been installed. Plans were being made to macadamize the dusty roads. The Charlotte Oil and Fertilizer Company, a plant to make oil and meal out of cottonseed, was built and Eli bought into it. He became a partner and president of the Piedmont Wagon Company, manufacturing and operating out of Hickory, North Carolina. This would not be all. He would go on to other adventures later, such as mining companies in the West; another cotton seed oil company, this time in Atlanta; president of the Atlantic, Tennessee and Ohio Railway; president of the Piedmont Fire Insurance Company; vice president of the Carolina Mutual Fire Insurance Company; and forty per cent owner of the Charlotte Consolidated Construction Company which developed Dilworth, the handsome new residential area, and which put electric street cars on the streets. Indeed, Eli was never idle. He worked hard and he played hard. And all the while he was buying and selling cotton, grain, sugar, and any other commodity which his speculative mind fancied.

Eli was adept at the art of "pleasuring himself" and giving pleasure to others. It has been said that bachelors are providential beings; God created them for the consolation of widows and the hope of maids! One friend expressed it thus, "Anyone who falls into Eli's hands will surely have a good time." While another said: "If there is a man on earth who knows how to make a woman have a good time that man is Eli." Having a great respect for all womankind, Eli's romantic adventures were discreet, never scandalous. Women were very important in his life. His love affairs had a touch of tenderness, kindness, and certainly generosity. Many a woman loved him dearly for these qualities, even when there was no hope of becoming his wife. He never felt disposed to marry.

The sight of Eli driving down the main street of Charlotte behind two spirited, magnificent horses, tipping his hat gallantly to his friends, sent the ladies into a flutter. Many a widow (for he was partial to widows), gaily courted at Saratoga, New York, White Sulphur, Asheville, or Hot Springs, held locked in her heart the memories of this handsome, fascinating man who had such a tremendous capacity to stimulate romance. He knew well the value of little things. A box of chocolates, a bouquet of flowers, a basket of grapes, accompanied by a pleasing, teasing note would usually open the hearts and doors of his ladies. As one of them expressed to him: "After being with you every other man seems tame. You have a very fascinating power." While another beautiful acquaintance declared: "I am convinced you have the most unselfish and kindest heart of any man I ever met."

One of his most flowery compliments came from the pen of a Northern widow who wrote enthusiastically: "My surprise was very great and my appreciation greater when I opened the box and found it was from you. It took me back to those halcyon days and I often dwell in them with pleasure. Oh, you Southerners! It would be my ideal life to have nothing to do but bask in the sunshine of some adorable and generous man's smile."

Next to the ladies, Eli loved handsome horses. He bought only the finest. Trainers all over the state bred and schooled his animals. In his files were pedigree records of the finest stallions and mares. Only perfectly trained horses were ever harnessed to his carriage. And he was very proficient in handling them, or so one young lady thought when she wrote him: "I tell my friends of the magnificent manner in which you managed those reins during our drive. But you are so accustomed to having everything your way in life I should not wonder at your management of *one* pair of horses."

In 1889, the Springs brothers were not daunted by the fact that markets were depressed. They kept right on going either long or short, making or losing money. There was a fascination about the markets which they could not resist. Particularly cotton. They could no more disregard that commodity than they could disregard their hunger for food. They sent their orders daily by Western Union telegraph to New York. Verification came back in code to keep other speculators from knowing their positions. They used a number of brokerage firms.

The following year Brevard started a second business. Since the railroads were besieged with freight and passengers, and contractors to build new lines were in demand, he decided to form a contracting company in partnership with his cousin, J. S. Moore. In the summer of 1890, they built railroad lines in Georgia. To supervise the work, Brevard moved to Elberton with his little family, which now had been increased by the addition of a beautiful little blonde girl, born June 9, 1889, and named for her grandmother, Blandina Baxter.

All summer Brevard complained that the railroad company was "certainly close" and he had never gotten his due. But he soon discovered that many railroads were hard up for cash despite the transportation boom. One crashed into bankruptcy without paying him and the firms that supplied material for constructing the lines were unpaid. Brevard was held liable for all bills. It took seven years of litigation to clear him of responsibility. "The crash cramped me very much," he commented, "but I hope everything will turn out all right."

The summer of 1892 found the Springs brothers exceedingly busy, all for different reasons. Leroy was in New York transacting business and outfitting himself in new clothes in preparation for his forthcoming marriage to Grace White, daughter of the family's good friend, Captain Samuel E. White. Brevard was in Fort Mill beaming with pride at another little daughter, blonde like the others, born June 25 and named Esther White for Captain Samuel White's wife.

Eli and Austin were being the gay sports at Saratoga where they were dancing every night and rubbing shoulders with the mighty financial barons. In the daytime they were attending the races and rubbing shoulders with colorful gamblers, or else they were promenading the avenues with beautiful ladies. Ah! this indeed was an atmosphere appealing to the Springs brothers.

There was an election that fall of 1892 and the country was in a turmoil of dissatisfaction, blaming, as usual, the government for all its ills. The Republicans under President Harrison had stood for high tariffs which the people now claimed made the industrialists rich while the poor suffered from the high cost of living. The farmers were distressed and threadbare. The politicians put the blame on overproduction. Former President Cleveland was blaming the Silver Purchase Act of 1890, saying the leading nations of the world were on the gold standard while America poured out her gold to buy silver. Anyway, whatever the cause, Cleveland went back to the White House on a tide of Democratic victory, and all the Springses went to Washington for the inauguration. Blandie was enthusiastic when she exclaimed: "We have rooms on Pennsylvania Avenue. The large window in my room will be worth the price of the bill on inauguration day. It will be a good place to see the procession."

By the time inauguration day arrived the country had been hurled into the worst panic of all times. The persistence of the repetition of cycles in business was beginning to be a wonder. Panics had been occurring through all the presidential terms, beginning with Jackson, even with the introduction of railroads, steamboats, and the electric telegraph. Now here it was again. Railroads were failing but along with them went hundreds of banks and thousands of business houses, crashing headlong in the onslaught of commercial ruin. Due to over-capitalization, 30,000 miles of railroad passed into receivership.

It was during these times that the South began to learn about the extraordinary genius, power, and wealth of J. Pierpont Morgan. More than thirty small Southern railroads, all weakened by bad times, banded together as the Richmond Terminal before the full impact of the panic. Looking for a way to reorganize, they approached Mr. Morgan, the giant of Wall Street. His terms were considered too severe, too dictatorial, and so the matter rested there. But the panic forced them to reconsider and accept. Morgan whipped the maze of leases and sub-leases, holding companies and plain bedlam into one big line, the Southern Railway Company. Among the railroads absorbed were two in which all the Springs brothers had inherited stock, the Atlantic, Tennessee and Ohio Railroad, which Eli headed, and the Charlotte, Columbia and Augusta.

Morgan placed H. C. Coster in charge of the reorganization and Eli dealt with him personally. Austin helped and on May 24, 1893, wrote to Eli: "The plan of the reorganization of Richmond Terminal is completed. It is very comprehensive and complicated and requires some study. . . . I talked with the elder Lehman today and he thinks well of the scheme."

It took time to work out a reorganization as complicated as this one and it would be two years before J. P. Morgan and Company would turn over to the Springs family preferred stock of Southern Railway Company in exchange for their Charlotte, Columbia and Augusta stock. Following this, Eli would add to his holdings, year by year, until he would become the second largest individual stock holder in Southern and a director of the company.

The Springs brothers were heavily involved that panic year of 1892. Brevard previously had bought a cotton mill in Alamance County, North Carolina, but had not been able to hold on to it and had sold it to Leroy. Now Leroy could not hold it and had sold it to Eli. Leroy was having his difficulties. Austin discussed this with Eli: "I have been afraid this squeeze would come and have warned you for the past two years. . . . Leroy would have gone up if you had not come to his rescue. . . . If he has been able to keep his head above water with the blows already received, it seems to me he ought to continue unless other mills fail."

The Fort Mill Manufacturing Company was suffering too but still producing ginghams, chambrays and twills. Brevard held his interest and Eli had come into the company as vice president and director to reinforce it.

During the summer of 1893, while the men attended to business, the women traveled. Carrie took her little girls and went to Catawba Springs, North Carolina. Blandie went to New York. The big city had always delighted her. It brought back so many happy memories. And also, she said, "I love to look around at the pretty things and buy gifts for Carrie and the children and go to the fine plays." But then she added, "I would not want to live there." When she had had her fill of seeing celebrities like Lillian Russell and Maxine Elliott, and dining at such glamorous restaurants as Delmonico's and Sherry's, she boarded the train for home, and Austin advised Brevard: "Mother left Thursday. She is getting old and I hated to see her start alone but she seemed to think she must go."

Later that summer Blandie and Bleecker went to Chicago to see the World's Fair. This splendid panorama of buildings, facing a formal court which displayed statues and flags, the first ferris wheel ever built, a midway where the men eyed the hootchy-kootchy girls who performed under the proper name of "The Egyptian Village"— all this was in celebration of the four hundredth anniversary of the discovery of America.* Bleecker was most enthusiastic about it, saying: "We have been so on the go that at night when we come in we fall on the bed and are not able to rise again. . . . Mama has been with us all of every day and I have begged her to rest, but she says she is so afraid we will do something that she won't!"

The country was in a panic, but the ladies (bless them!) could still enjoy the fun of a fair and exclaim over the fact that ladies were beginning to ride bicycles. The very idea!

---

*Chicago was unable to complete the preparations in 1892 and the Fair did not open until May 1, 1893.

CHAPTER TWENTY-SEVEN

"It's a boy! It's a boy!" The cry rang through the entire two-story white frame house that morning of July 19, 1894. Anyone passing along the street in Fort Mill surely must have heard the excitement. The house,* sitting back in a grove of trees, was the home of Brevard and Carrie Springs and she had just given birth to her fifth child. Blandie threw her arms about her son, congratulating him. Aunt Lizzie Baxter proclaimed, "I knew it would be a boy. I prophesied it!"

No one could have been prouder or more pleased than the baby's Uncle Eli when he was notified the child would be named for him. Another Eli Springs! He asked Austin to select a silver cup in New York for the baby. When the purchase was made, Austin wrote: "It is a heavy cup, quite handsome, and will take a lot of wear."

The three little sisters were enchanted with their baby brother and began to spoil him at an early age. The following spring, Blandina, then going on six, wrote: "Uncle Eli, our boy has a tooth. You had better come down Sunday and see him."

The "gay nineties" turned into busy nineties for all members of the Springs family. Those years were important because of decisions they saw made. This is what happened.

Bleecker was married in 1895 to John M. Scott, a popular young Charlotte man who was showing great capacity for business. The wedding was elaborate and beautiful, as anyone would know with Blandie engineering it. Eli made the Artillery punch which was consumed with great relish and extreme revelry! A year later the Springs home on Tryon Street was redecorated and the Scotts moved in. When Blandie was in Charlotte, she lived with them.

*The site of the present handsome office building of the Springs Mills.

Austin, in 1896, bought a seat on the New York Cotton Exchange and went into the brokerage business. "I know you have been averse to my making a change," he wrote to Eli, "and I realize the seriousness and importance of making such a decision, but I feel this is a great opportunity for me." He became a partner in the firm of J. H. Parker and Company.

That same year Leroy started operating the Lancaster Cotton Mills* which he had been building for a year. In 1899 he acquired the Eureka Mills at Chester. But his greatest acquisition was a son, born July 31, 1896, and named Elliott White Springs.

After a business misunderstanding with Leroy in 1896, Brevard sold out his interest in the Fort Mill Manufacturing Company and moved his family to Charlotte. This distressed Austin who wrote: "I think Brevard is too sensitive and made a mistake by getting out of the mill." That was the summer Brevard suffered a stroke. It came quickly, without warning, paralyzing one side and affecting his speech. However, in a few days he was better and he, with Carrie, left for New York to consult with a specialist. Aunt Lizzie Baxter wrote: "He has overworked himself. I don't wonder that his system gave way." But Brevard's answer to this was, "I ought to be home tending to my business." In a short time he was well enough to return to Charlotte and promptly entered into a partnership with S. S. McNinch to sell buggies, wagons, harness, fertilizers, and farm implements.

Eli, too, made a decision that year of 1896. He agreed to sell the waterworks, which he and Dr. Brevard owned, to the city of Charlotte. The negotiations were lengthy. Eli turned for advice to Austin, who wrote: "I want to see you get the full value, and I know you want nothing more, as you will get no credit for taking a cent less than you are entitled to, or for not making a stubborn fight for it. You must remember that the population of Charlotte has increased, and there have been great improvements since the original purchase was made and it was a speculation on your part, in as much as you had to finance the company, and if you had not been able to negotiate your bonds you might have been subjected to great inconvenience, and you are entitled to all the benefits and full value regardless of the original cash expense."

Having sold his waterworks to the city, Eli next sold himself to the

*This mill in 1914 was considered the largest cotton mill under one roof in the world.

voters. The incumbent mayor had not run the city's affairs and finances to suit most people. Eli consented to run against him on an independent ticket in 1897. One newspaper recorded: "The present Mayor, who is now the legally constituted head of the Democratic municipal ticket, had the very exclusive privilege of running Monday's primary all to himself, closed that day with 1,002 votes, about 30 per cent of which it is alleged were in the ballot box before the polls opened. . . . The boogy-boo of 'stick to the party' has frightened some, but this number is offset by those who are disgusted with the Mayor's attitude in not publishing a statement of the city's finances. As the days go by Mr. Eli Springs, the Independent candidate, gains in strength and popularity."

In a hot election, Eli was swept into office on a wave of reform votes. He cancelled plans for a long-deferred trip abroad and settled down to being a good mayor. One grateful citizen wrote him: "I regard the defeat of the present incumbent as meaning much for the prosperity and good name of Charlotte. Your actions insure your success, and for this God be praised!" And Eli's Boston banker, E. H. Gay, congratulated him in these words: "I will spare your modesty by omitting to detail the many sterling qualities I have found you to possess and which would ornament the office of chief executive of your city."

The most colorful experience of Eli's mayoralty was the 20th of May celebration of 1898. The speaker for the occasion was former Vice President Adlai Stevenson who delivered the address at the unveiling of a monument to the signers of the Mecklenburg Declaration of Independence.

Early on that Friday morning of May 20th, the various military organizations, bands, and groups began to assemble for a parade which proved the longest North Carolina had ever seen. "The arrival," the *Charlotte News* recorded, "of Governor Atkinson of Georgia and his staff on the 9 o'clock train was the signal for activity. He was escorted by a Drum Corps to the Manufacturers Club on Tryon Street where he and his party waited for the procession to be formed." That street, from the Buford Hotel to the railroad tracks, was lined with carriages of notables and elaborately decorated floats waiting to take their places in the procession.

Vice President Stevenson, accompanied by Mayor Springs, headed the parade which progressed to the yard of the First Presbyterian

Church where a speakers' stand had been erected in the grove. The *News* elaborated:

"The arrival of Hon. Adlai Stevenson was the signal for much cheering. As he mounted the stand, the first person to greet him was Mrs. Stonewall Jackson. The meeting was a most cordial one, Mr. Stevenson expressing much pleasure that Mrs. Jackson was present. . . . Before the ceremonies were well under way, a long line of Confederate veterans passed in review before the stand. Mrs. Jackson stood up and bowed to the old war-scarred veterans. With uncovered heads they acknowledged this recognition from the widow of the South's great general. It was a most touching sight."

The ceremonies soon commenced with a divine blessing invoked by Reverend Dr. J. R. Howerton of the First Presbyterian Church. Following this and the singing of "The Old North State," Mayor Eli Springs welcomed the visitors and crowds. The Mecklenburg Declaration of Independence was then read by Colonel Alexander Brevard and Colonel Hamilton C. Jones read a poem.

Adlai Stevenson's address was lengthy, sincere, and well received. "From my home to the westward," he said, "I gladly come to your bidding, to join with you in doing honor to the memory of the men who have made the name of 'Mecklenburg' immortal."

During the evening hours of that memorable day, Mr. Stevenson was Eli's guest at a concert. When the two took their places in the box of the theater, the audience applauded enthusiasticly.

It was during this year of 1898 that Brevard Springs moved his family into a beautiful new home which he had built in the fashionable suburb of Charlotte called Dilworth. The decorating and landscaping of this house and grounds took on more and more impetus as he made more and more money. At last he was really coming into his own, being heavily involved in the cotton and grain markets. His profits were doubling, redoubling. By 1903 he was approaching that much dreamed of state of being a millionaire.

His large, white, frame house had a wide veranda circling half way round. The entrance hall was graced at the far end with a handsome center staircase which rose imposingly and soon parted to the left and right, sweeping into a large upstairs sitting room, from which five bedrooms were entered. Downstairs was a spacious parlor, a sitting room, the Red room or library, dining room, pantry, and kitchen. In the latter could be found the Negro cook, Hattie, and puttering about the house was Rankin, the Negro butler.

The front lawn was planted beautifully in trees, shrubs, and flowers. In the rear was an exquisite rose and flower garden containing prize specimens which were Brevard's delight. Back of this was a large orchard that served not only to supply the most delicious fruit imaginable but also served as a place for the children to climb trees to their hearts' content. There was a barn where horses, ponies, and cows were kept.

It was in the rose garden here at Brevard's home that Blandie came one afternoon in February of 1902. She had ridden out alone on the street car and stood with Brevard for a long time inspecting his new rose bushes. How she loved roses! They always made her think of Cornucopia and her Ma. Dear Ma! When she was ready to leave, young Blandina walked with her to the car line. On the way, as she was accustomed to doing, Blandie pulled her voluminous black alpaca skirt to the front until she could find the pocket hidden in its folds and, pulling out a small purse, she gave the child a coin. This little purse sent Blandie's mind rushing back in memory to another purse she once had filled with gold. Ah, but that was a long, long time ago, she thought.

Blandie was taken with a cold the next day. Pneumonia developed. On February 27 she died, after having sent for her little granddaughters in the middle of the night. She wanted to give each one a gift. Eli and Austin, together with Brevard, Leroy, and Bleecker, were at her bedside. Only Alva was absent. They later found written in her little note book:

"The time in which I live is but a small moment in this world's history. It is a flight of a shadow; it is a dream of vanity; it is the rapid glance of a meteor; it is a flower which every breath of heaven can wither into decay; it is a tale which as a remembrance vanishes; it is a day which the silence of a long night will darken and overshadow. In a few years we will be laid in the grave. The children who come after us will weep for a few days; they will talk of us a few months; they will remember us for a few years—then our memory will disappear from the face of the earth and not a vapor shall be found to recall it."

Two years passed. Brevard and his family were very busy. The house was torn up to the extent of having beautiful new parquet floors laid down. Carrie had gone to New York to order furnishings for the house. Sloan and Company sent down the handsomest of velvet portierres, lace curtains, Persian rugs, etc. The finest of linens were bought. The children were dressed in New York's latest fashions. Brevard insisted that Carrie buy the handsomest fur coat she could find, which she did. But after reaching Charlotte she returned it. She was too modest to parade in front of her friends with it! The family was now summering each year at a large estate which Brevard had bought at Hackett's Point, Maryland. There they fished and crabbed and swam, while Brevard amused himself growing asparagus, and in hunting season he would go up to shoot duck. Marguerite and Blandina were sent to St. Mary's school in Raleigh. Esther would soon follow. Then there would be interesting times for them afterwards at Gunston Hall in Washington.

The tremendous cotton activity of 1904 challenged Brevard's talents for speculation. There was no question that two large operators by the names of McFadden and Sully were manipulating the markets. Leroy called it a dangerous market. But Brevard and his friend, O. P. Heath, kept on buying and selling, selling and buying.

With a booming economy, the exchanges were in frenzies with the avalanche of speculative orders. Money was being invested so rapidly that the rate for demand loans had gone over 100 per cent. Brevard was pyramiding his profits into a fortune. His trades became more daring. Cotton. Grain. Pork. Lard. Any commodity with an active market lured him into its midst. He was now the wealthiest of the Springs brothers. He had made his million. He would retire now from the market and take no more chances.

Eli, or Uncle Eli as everyone was then calling him, by this time had moved to New York. Even the offer of the Presidency of the First National Bank of Charlotte could not lure him back. He liked the big city. It was the business heart of the world. It thrilled him. He would never leave it.

The political outlook was the disturbing factor of 1906. Otherwise the country was progressing. When President McKinley had been shot in 1901, a man had come into the White House who held no love for the "divine right" of big business. That man was Teddy Roosevelt. He waged war on railroad trusts, steel trusts, and any other type of "malefactors of great wealth" which came to his attention. He swung his "big stick" and even the king of Wall Street, J. P. Morgan, had to duck many times. Whenever Roosevelt felt the public interest was at stake he was aroused, and the non-investors of the country, having already become aroused over monopolies, were now looking to him for action. Consequently, tremendous holding companies became Roosevelt's target. The Springs brothers, small investors as they were, looked on in fascination as the mighty giants of the country, Morgan, Harriman, Rockefeller, Carnegie, Armour, Mellon, all battled Teddy Roosevelt. The result of this great conflict was the closing of one era of high finance and the beginning of a new one.

Brevard, little by little, was getting back into the market. A few bales of cotton here, a few contracts of wheat there. Then the contracts grew larger and larger and larger. He was confident. He was assured. Success has a way of doing that to a man.

Then it happened. Like the roaring clap of thunder which warns of a storm, the markets began to tumble in February of 1907. But like lightning hitting often before a person can run for cover, just so the panic began to hit Brevard's interests in every commodity, every stock, before he could run for cover. The year 1907 was a never to be forgotten year. With the drop in the markets came a tightening of money. March brought another great decline. Pressure was put on Roosevelt to do something to stem the tide—stop hammering on business—reassure the public—anything—but for the country's sake take *some* action. He responded by saying the moneyed interests had brought this on themselves. Wall Street reiterated that Roosevelt had destroyed the people's confidence.

All summer Brevard was tense, worried, uneasy, and manipulating his holdings with a tremendous furiousness. It mattered not so much to him that many gigantic companies had gone under; all that mattered was the saving of his fortune. The markets continued to fall. Investors were panicky and turning their holdings into cash. There was no support to the market. Margins were being called. More. More. And still more. Five billion dollars had been wiped out in stock prices alone.

By September, Brevard was nearly crazy. During those frantic days the market was a veritable nightmare. Brokerage houses were suspending business. Corporation after corporation was going under. Banks were closing. October brought chaos and terror to investors as the wave of panic engulfed the entire country. Roosevelt opened the doors of the United States Treasury and gave J. P. Morgan authority to stem the tide by helping the national banks. Newspapers carried shocking stories of financial barons being wiped out.

On October 24 the New York Stock Exchange stopped all sales. The country stood horrified and bewildered. There was no money to borrow to cover losses. If it could be found the interest rate was 150 per cent.

It was all over with Brevard. He was wiped out, financially crushed. It was incredible that such a thing could happen. He emerged from the panic with nothing left but a handsomely furnished home which bore an unhandsomely large mortgage. And to think, only a short time ago he had owned, among his tremendous holdings—and he had figured it down to the last fraction just for the irony of it—enough lard to cover North and South Carolina three inches deep!

Brevard emerged from the panic with a singleness of purpose. He would pay every cent he owed! He hardly knew how he would manage it, but do it he would. Advice came to him from every hand and it was always the same. "Do like your friends have done. Declare bankruptcy. Make a new start." But Brevard did not do it. He could not do it. His pride expanded with his financial reverses. He had grown up imbibed with pride of integrity and honor. Now it assumed tremendous proportions. He loathed his indebtedness, but to shirk it, to hide behind bankruptcy, was unthinkable. All he asked was a chance to recoup his fortune and pay his debts. And so he worked and watched and paid and waited, remembering all the while the advice of his father: "Ask of everything which you are disposed to do, *is it right?* If it is, *do it* however much it costs you."

While all these tumultuous events were taking place in Brevard's and Carrie's lives, their little son, Eli, was developing into an attractive child with boundless energy. As a small boy he had been chubby, round faced, with hair that today's barber would term an "English cut." He was always laughing and his deep blue eyes, shaded with the most luxurious lashes imaginable, seemed to laugh with him. He was forever into merry mischief. At the age of two, his sister Marguerite recalled, "he went under the house and broke forty eggs that the hens were sitting on, just as they were ready to hatch. Father did not like it."

At five, Eli was hustled off to kindergarten. There he claims to have played hooky on his tricycle, accompanied by his good friend, Herschel Johnson.*

Eli grew up, as all young boys should, with a dog, a gun, a pony, and a bicycle. There were jaunts to Springfield, afternoon rides to the swimming hole, seining parties and camping trips to the mountains.

Brevard delighted in taking his son hunting at Springfield. The squirrel hunting, one frosty Saturday, proved so exhilarating that they stayed over Sunday and shot a bag that day. As their carriage horse trotted homeward, Brevard cautioned Eli not to mention to his mother that they had hunted on Sunday.

When a platter of stewed squirrel was served at dinner the next day, Carrie remarked, "I think I see Sunday written on each one of these squirrels." Little Eli jumped up and shouted, "Father, she's got you, she's got you!"

The next time Brevard prepared to go to Springfield, Eli tumbled into the carriage. His father sent him back into the house for something. When he returned, the carriage was gone. This was Brevard's quiet way of teaching his son not to tattle.

In the summer of 1909, Eli had a memorable experience. His father allowed the fifteen-year-old boy to go West alone. The railroads were then selling what they called "home-seeker tickets" to Texas and Oklahoma, the latter admitted to statehood only two years earlier. A special car ran via New Orleans to Corsicana, Texas, where Eli visited his Uncle Willie Clarkson for two weeks. Then he went to McAlester, Oklahoma, where his Uncle Alva Springs was in the real estate business. Alva took the boy to see the recently discovered oil wells around Tulsa, and then to Muskogee to see the Government paying off the Indians. Camped outside town were thousands of Indians in tribal costume. Could anything have thrilled a boy more?

A short time after Eli's arrival home, he walked into the sitting room while his father was talking to Joseph Atkinson Jones, formerly of Petersburg, Virginia, but then of Charlotte. Eli did not realize it,

*Herschel V. Johnson, grandson of Georgia's governor of the same name, has served his country in the diplomatic service for many years. He was Counselor of the Embassy in London, 1937-41; Minister to Sweden during World War II; Deputy Representative of the United States to the United Nations and on the Security Council; one of the chief delegates to the General Assembly of the United Nations, 1947; United States Ambassador to Brazil, 1948-1953.

but his sister Blandina's beau was asking for her hand in marriage. Brevard turned to Eli and asked, "Son, have you watered your chickens?" The reply was, "Yes, Sir." Pause. "Well, have you watered the pigeons?" "Yes, Sir." Impatient at the boy's failure to take the hint, Brevard stormed, *"Well, go do it again."*

This command sent Eli hustling out, but not to water the pigeons. Instead he went into the next room, where several of Blandina's friends* sat, all pretending to read, but in reality all listening to Joe's stammering attempt to ask for Blandina. So Eli sat down and listened too. Consequently, when Blandina and Joe announced their engagement to their friends, it came as no surprise. However, there was one person who still had to be told, Hattie the cook. So Joe rushed back to the kitchen. But his explanation had hardly begun before Hattie replied: "Lawsy, Missa Joe, you don't have to tell me nothin'. I wuz a-settin' de table and I'se heard evy word of it."

Blandina and Joe were married on November 17, 1909, and after living a few years in this country they moved to Havana, Cuba.

At sixteen, Eli was sent off to the Virginia Military Institute. With him went the following letter:

September 1, 1910

Gen. E. W. Nichols
V. M. I.
Lexington, Va.

Dear Sir:

This will be handed you by my son, Eli B. Springs II, who reports for duty. I trust that he will make a good cadet and the school will be a great benefit to him. He is young and this is his first school away from home. He has no bad habits, using tobacco in no form or intoxicant, but I fear you will find him very mischievous. He is our only son and we have raised him more as a companion with us and naturally he has had an easy berth and his own way.

I trust your school will bring him down to his "Knitting" and take the "Kinks" out of him as the military school did me when I was his age. I trust that he will be fortunate enough to have nice

*Ola Brown, who afterward married Martin Cannon, co-owner of Cannon Mills; Emma Drewry, who married Jim Hanes of Winston-Salem, North Carolina; and John Bass Brown of Charlotte.

gentlemanly room mates, as I think this is very important with a young boy leaving home and just forming his character.

Thanking you in advance for any attention that you give Eli I am

very respectfully yours,

Brevard D. Springs

P. S. If not inconsistent with your rules please allow Eli to attend the Presbyterian Church.

Eli found V.M.I. exciting. Even the penalties of being a "brother rat" did not dim his enthusiasm. The pain of having a broom handle broken over his *derrière* vanished in the pride of marching across the hallowed parade ground with the statue of General T. J. Jackson, once of V.M.I., standing "like a stone wall." For three years Eli studied hard, drilled and gloried in the gorgeous scenery of the valley of Virginia and the beauty of the girls attending the V.M.I. hops.

Eli's sister Marguerite was married January 29, 1913, but he did not get home for her wedding to her cousin, Richard Austin Myers, son of Jack Myers and grandson of Sophia Springs Myers. Dick, as he was called, was an engineer, surveying for the inland water route between Charleston and Savannah.

In June of 1913 Eli returned to Charlotte to stay. His father gave him a model T Ford so the two of them could drive together to the plantation. It has been said that the "Tin Lizzie" changed the face of the nation. Well, anyway, it changed Eli's way of life. He rode all over the state attending dances and calling on the ladies, using up more gas than he had money to pay for. Which brought him around to another point. It was time to go to work.

A group of Eli's friends, among them his cousin Joe Moore, had taken jobs at the Penns Grove, New Jersey, plant of the Dupont Powder Company which was then manufacturing powder for Russia. The boys wrote back, "Come on up. Everything's fine." So up Eli went, getting a job at a cutting machine. On night shifts when the air was humid, fumes from the ether-wetted powder made all the boys gaily drunk. It certainly was not the job Brevard had in mind for his son. Anyhow, it soon came to an end. Eli took leave to return home for a cousin's wedding. The following night, his section of the plant blew up. So that was that.

About this time, Henry Ford came out with a very astounding statement. He offered to pay five dollars a day to each of his employees. Industrialists prophesied that Ford would ruin the country by paying such prices. Having literally put the nation on wheels, he now proceeded to pad its pocketbook. If the Tin Lizzie was what the country wanted, the five dollars a day was what Eli wanted, and so he went to work for the Ford Motor Company in their Charlotte plant. He worked through every department, winning a number of promotions, and finally was traveling representative, calling on several hundred dealers in his territory.

Eli's experience with automotive engines soon stood him in good stead in another field. World War I had swept Europe. Now Germany declared unrestricted submarine warfare and sank the British liner *Lusitania*, queen of the Atlantic, with the loss of American lives. President Woodrow Wilson, re-elected in 1916 on the campaign slogan, "He kept us out of war," said sadly, "Right is more precious than peace," and America went to war.

Eli wanted to fly. He got recommendations from Henry Ford and from Secretary of the Navy Josephus Daniels, a fellow North Carolinian. But Army Aviation turned him down as underweight. Naval Aviation rejected him for a heart murmur. And Officers' Training Camp declined him for high blood pressure. So he and a group of friends, including Harry Dalton, Ben Hough, and Caldwell McDonald, decided to enlist. On December 13, 1917, they entered the recruiting office in the old Charlotte Mint building. Eli hesitantly took his physical. "Perfect!" He became a private on the spot.

At six that very evening, they were ordered to board a troop train. At two o'clock in the morning, the train finally pulled out of Charlotte in a blinding snowstorm. It laid over five hours in Spartanburg, South Carolina, and four in Asheville, North Carolina, arriving in Cincinnati fourteen hours late. In bitter, snowy cold, the recruits arrived at Fort Thomas, Kentucky. Again, Eli reported, "I passed a perfect physical examination, and have been put in Company 13, Platoon 4. . . . We have received our uniforms but I cannot hand them much. I am going to have a tailor cut mine up and make them fit me perfectly. . . ."

Private Springs spent most of his nights in Cincinnati at first because the overburdened Army had not supplied its recruits with mattresses. The family showered him with cakes and cash at Christmas. "I took the money and had a big time. Ran the risk, with six other fellows, and went to Cincinnati. . . . We went to three shows and slept in a good hotel and ate until I couldn't eat any more."

From Kentucky the unit went to Camp Hancock, Augusta, Georgia, only to find themselves freezing in tents with small inadequate wood stoves. The showers were outdoors and so frozen nobody bathed for weeks.

On the first night at Camp Hancock, Eli was designated sergeant of the guard. With his V.M.I. experience, he calmed and trained his green, nervous men. This so impressed his officers that he was appointed First Sergeant, 6th Company, 2nd Air Service Mechanics Regiment.

Camp Merritt, New Jersey, was Eli's next assignment. He wrote to his father on March 11, 1918: "Uncle Eli and Austin came out this evening to see me and Uncle Eli gave me a lot of French money—about a hundred dollars and also fifty dollars in cash."

Ten days later, Eli was in France, having crossed on the *Leviathan*, the largest ship afloat, with 14,000 others. This was the second trip the *Leviathan* made after having been commandeered from the Germans by the American Government. Her name had been the *Vaterland* and the Kaiser's picture which had hung in one of the lounges had been painted out. The stationery and linen still bore her original name. She was met some distance out from England and escorted to Southhampton. A rough trip across the Channel brought Eli to Le Havre.

On Good Friday Eli was in a truck train en route from Tours to Paris. "On Easter Sunday," he wrote, "we began to meet carts, autos, etc. fleeing from the city [Paris] with their belongings as we were about to enter. We finally arrived at our destination*. . . . I am now acting as post Sgt. Major. Have seen two air raids."

Then Eli's letters, eagerly awaited by his parents, came often:

"*Paris, May 19th, 1918*—I went up in a machine today. Flew all over Paris. Of course I was only a passenger. I expect to get a good many rides with Lieutenants who are stationed here for testing out the machines. I have about given up hopes of getting a commission. It is almost impossible over here from the way things look. . . . A German air raid was over Paris night before last but no damage was done. It is hard for the Germans to get to Paris now."

---

*Orly Field, 15 kilometers south of Paris. This company put up the first barracks and built the field. It was known as American Aviation Acceptance Park.

"*Paris, May 26th, 1918*—Last Sunday I did not go to Paris but went to walk in a little town on the edge of Paris. Through luck, I dropped into conversation (with as much French as I could speak) with an old man and lady. The old man runs an ammunition plant in Paris and to avoid the air raids leaves Paris at nights. I called to see them the next evening. The most pitiful sight was their son who returned from the war with both eyes out. This is only one of the many tragedies I have seen all over France. Everyone is in black. . . . Three more air raids last week. The big runs are certainly ruining some of the finest old buildings in Paris." Five days later Eli reported that the Germans' "Big Bertha" had been dropping shells on Paris about every seventeen minutes for three nights straight.

"*Paris, June 9th, 1918*—There has been heavy fighting going on at the front and we are increasing our output of machines every day. The death list must be very large on both sides. Two of our men brought down three German machines this week. The air raids have not been as numerous lately. I guess they are too busy else where and also our men make it too *hot* for them to reach us. Quentin Roosevelt is one of our pilots. You certainly would not know by the way he acts that he is the son of an ex-President. . . . The Red Cross and Y.M.C.A. are doing everything. If it were not for these two charity organizations I do not know what a soldier would do. We get all our pleasure and aid from them. . . . I received a letter from Elliott [Springs] who is now at the front. I have tried every where to go to the front or to get a commission. I have not succeeded at either. Of course I am leading an easier life than those at the front but there is not much excitement with just a few little air raids."

"*June 29, 1918*—We were greatly honored by a visit from General Pershing* today. He expressed his appreciation of the work that is being done at this field. He liked our place. I feel good over it as we were the first here and built it."

"*July 3, 1918*—Paris is all decorated for the 4th of July and those who get there will have a big time. The French, since the last drive, will do anything for an American. We ride or walk along the streets and they hollow, 'Vive l'Amérique.' I was in hopes of going but General Pershing, the Ambassador and several others are coming out here so I will have to stay and work."

*General John J. Pershing, Commander in Chief of the American Expeditionary Forces.

Eli, off and on, received letters from his cousin, Elliott Springs, who was making a very remarkable record for himself. Having received his preliminary training for the Royal Air Corps at Princeton University, Elliott had then sailed for England to attend a training school for flyers at Oxford University. Upon completion of this course, he had gone to Scotland to an aerial gunnery school. Then in May of 1918 he had had his first flight in aerial service. On the 25th of that month he wrote to Eli: "It's taken me long enough to get here, but thank God I'm at last flying over the lines so all is well. Hope you've fared as well as I have on this side. Best luck."

Elliott quickly won international recognition as an ace with the 85th R.A.F. Squadron and the 148th American Aero Squadron. Flying a little biplane fighter, he blazed through the skies with reckless daring and was nearly killed within a month. He wrote Eli on July 12, 1918: "I've just gotten out of the hospital after a little difficulty with a Hun several weeks ago, and won't be able to fly again for several days so I am lying around taking a rest. . . . However, I'm all O.K. now except for a slight damage to my face and hope to take over my flight any day. Glad to hear you are a Sergeant Major—Congratulations. I'm due for ten days leave in a month and may see you in Paris then. . . . I mopped up in a big crap game the other night so if you run short any time, as I usually do, remember I'm closer than home and have no use for it up here, so drop me a line. I don't mean to be vulgar about my winnings, but if you were on the line and I in Paris, I'd take all you had and swear at you for not having more. Throw a party for me some time, will you?"

Two weeks later, Eli reported: "I was to meet Elliott in Paris night before last but missed him so he came out here and we went about 15 kilometers to a cafe which is in front of one of Napoleon's old castles. It is one of the prettiest places I have ever seen. . . . Elliott is practically well now and has returned to his squadron at the front. . . . We are working hard trying to help those poor devils at the front during this wonderful drive."

"*August 15th, 1918*—We are working hard to keep planes at the front during this drive which started day before yesterday at five o'clock in the morning. We have the Germans on the run and are in hopes of keeping them going. The American Ambassador was out here today. Tomorrow we are expecting Baker, General Patrick (Chief of Air Service) and General Pershing."

"*August 29, 1918*—Sometime ago a pilot left this field and never returned. Today we received a note from him (written on scratch paper) which was dropped from an airplane with another letter written in German. The pilot stated that he was a prisoner in Germany and to take care of his effects. The German note requested information as to where two German pilots were and if alive. The information was dropped over the lines to the Germans that both their pilots were dead."

Among the American pilots who never returned was the handsome young Lieutenent whom Eli regarded so highly, Quentin Roosevelt. Having handed Quentin his orders assigning him to combat area, Eli naturally felt depressed at the news of his death and so expressed himself to his father. When Brevard received the letter, he wrote Teddy Roosevelt a note of sympathy, to which the ex-President replied with the hope that Eli would return safely.

While Eli was working on the ground to see that planes were kept in readiness for pilots, Elliott was having hair-raising experineces in the air. On August 3, while escorting a formation of De Haviland 9's, he drove off a strong attack of Fokker biplanes, shooting one down behind American lines.

On August 21, following an aerial battle, he crashed landed his shot up plane, minus one wheel. But he walked away from the wreck with only bruises. He had done this before. Once his superior officer had asked him if he were out to destroy the enemy or the allied planes!

Undaunted, Elliott was in the air the following day with a thirst for Fokkers. He found them—five, flying in close formation. Attacking, he sent one crashing to the ground south of Velu before the other four knew they were being pursued. He attacked again and drove a Fokker east, but his ammunition gave out and he made a run for home base.

Later that same day he went back into the air. Over Bapaume, he found three Fokkers attacking a British plane. Diving in, Elliott drove off two and sent the third hurtling to earth.

Many pilots died from flying over enemy lines, but, likewise, many died from accidents. Eli described one such case on September 6, 1918: "I acted as a body bearer at the funeral of a Captain Sanger who was killed on this field last week. He was thrown from his machine at a very high altitude while making a flight over this field. . . . It really was not much of a funeral—a small crowd. There were several prominent people there, Mrs. Vanderbilt and some of the Morgans who were kin to the Captain. Mrs. Sanger was a Vanderbilt."

Two weeks later, the Sangers dedicated a pilots' club in memory of the dead Captain. Eli had kept up from day to day in the colonel's offices a large map of the battle lines, marking off each Allied gain in colored pencil. "I think it pleases the Colonel and Major Jackson very much," he said, "as the first thing they do every morning is to look at the map to see what we did the day before." At Mrs. Sanger's request, Eli made a similar map for Sanger Hall.

Impatient to be a flyer, Eli again applied for pilot training, but was turned down. Discouraged, he wrote: "I will have to give up the idea of ever becoming a pilot as I had hoped. You need not say anything about me failing another physical exam as someone will begin to think there is something really wrong with my health. I can't feel or find it myself."

But Eli's spirits were higher on October 6. "The war news looks better every day but expect with even this proposal for peace which was in the paper this morning that it will continue for some time yet. Last night all lights were turned on in Paris for the first time in years. I think I will go in today and see her all *lit up*." Two weeks later, Eli met Elliott in Paris where they "did the town," and Eli commented: "Elliott is wearing a distinguished service badge and has to his credit twelve Boshe planes. It is a pity that he has not been attached to an American squadron because the British do not publish what their men do as the Americans and French do."*

On October 30th, Eli had other things beside Paris on his mind when he wrote, "We are working all night tonight putting planes in condition for the front tomorrow." The next day, he received the happy news that "Sgt. 1 cl. Eli Baxter Springs, 6th Company, 2nd Air Service Mechs. Regiment, Air Service," had been commissioned as "Second Lieutenant, Air Service (Aeronautics), non-flying status, per paragraph 29, S.O.299, 26th October, 1918."†

*Elliott Springs was officially credited with bringing down eleven German planes. He was awarded the American distinguished service cross and the British distinguished service cross. The latter was personally presented to him by the Prince of Wales at a ceremony in Washington, D. C.

†Lee Folger of Charlotte, N. C., Captain in World War I, wrote to Eli on Sept. 5, 1940: "It may be of interest to you and your family that I confirm the information discussed the other day to the effect that of the entire brigade of four regiments of motor mechanics sent to France during the World War, which brigade comprised 10,000 men, that you were the first enlisted man or non-commissioned officer to receive a promotion to a commissioned grade and not only this, but as far as I am able to determine, you are the only man to receive such recognition during our service in France."

Armistice brought great celebrations and in the midst of them was the new Lieutenant Eli Springs. "I have been in Paris," he wrote, "most of the time celebrating. Monday morning we all went to work as usual. Then about 11 o'clock the whistles and guns in Paris could be heard, letting everyone know that the armistice had been signed. It was a matter of only a few minutes before flags appeared in all windows and decorations everywhere. About 2 o'clock at the gates of this post a big crowd of war orphans with flowers, singing patriotic songs, assembled. They were allowed to enter and bring the flowers to Headquarters. One little fellow made a speech, saying they wanted to show their appreciation to the Americans. In Paris, the crowd began to gather. The streets, cafés, etc. were packed and jammed with shouting people. Pretty girls rushed to the soldiers, throwing their arms around them. (Of course I stayed away from this!) Parades marched through the streets and at this time—three days later—the celebration is still going on. Tomorrow is Wilson's day and we expect the biggest day yet. All who were lucky in being in Paris at this time will never forget such a celebration."

On November 16 Eli was ordered to St. Maixent, en route home, but, he later explained, "as luck would have it orders came to send me to HQ. S.O.S. and there I was assigned to Air Service Headquarters which is now at Tours. So I am here in the Personnel Office helping to send others home."

Christmas, the time that Eli expected to be home, was spent in Tours. "After leaving work Christmas eve," he wrote, "I took a Mademoiselle to dinner and a dance. About 12 o'clock she took me to a mid-night mass. Upon returning to my room, I found Joe Williamson in bed and he said Victor Shaw was at the hotel. . . . The next day we all loafed around the cafés all morning. About lunch time we ran into Lt. Paul Montegue, from Winston-Salem. He has just returned from Germany where he was a prisoner. He had been brought down while attacking a German plane. It was rather funny how the four of us, all having connection with the Ford Motor Company, should meet on Christmas morning in France. We all went out and had a big dinner. Capt. Lee Folger will be in town tonight."

New Year's eve was even more festive for the Americans in Tours. Eli explained: "I took a Mademoiselle out to dinner and afterwards we went to a soirée at the Hotel de Ville and did not get home until about 4 A.M. At the soirée I met Stuart Cramer, Howard Conway,

Stewart Gilchrest, Elliott Springs, Joe Williamson, George Munce and three V.M.I. friends. It was some crowd to get together in this country. And the Vouvrey certainly did flow!"

Elliott Springs was in Tours trying to get his orders back to the States. Most of his records had been lost and, for weeks previously, headquarters in Tours had been trying to locate him. Elliott was enjoying France!

During the first week of January, Eli was ordered to Angers, France, where he was the only Aviation officer on duty. On the 22nd of the month, his Christmas presents caught up with him. Among the gifts was candy, though slightly stale by that time, from Eli's cousins, Julia Baxter Scott, and Calvine Scott, daughters of Aunt Bleecker Springs Scott.

Angers, though larger than Tours, proved very dull. During February it snowed and the thermometer dipped. General Pershing dropped in but hurried away. And that was just what Eli wanted to do. But it was not until March 22 that orders came to "proceed to St. Nazaire, reporting upon arrival to Commanding General, for transportation to the United States." On April 3rd, he was ordered to "proceed at once on board the *U.S.S. Suriname.*"

The *Suriname* broke down when she was well out to sea and had to be towed back to St. Nazaire. When fully repaired, she started out again, only to meet heavy seas. It was twenty-eight days in all before she docked at Hoboken, New Jersey. Eli was given orders to report to the Air Service Depot at Garden City, Long Island. He was up bright and early the next morning and was the first in line at the depot to receive his discharge. No sooner had it been handed to him, signed, sealed, and delivered, than an officer laid orders on the desk for "Lieutenant Springs to proceed to the West." It was a narrow escape. He was out of the army and heading home!

But first, there was something he wished to do before leaving New York. To thank his Uncle Eli and Austin for all their letters and gifts sent to France was a pleasure he looked forward to with great enthusiasm. Uncle Austin was now married to a charming Canadian, Ethel Armitage, and they had a small son, Richard Austin, Junior.

When Eli boarded the train for Charlotte he was whistling a merry tune. It was good to be going home!

CHAPTER TWENTY-EIGHT

ELI SPRINGS II HURRIEDLY CROSSED the street at the corner of Broad and Wall in New York City on the morning of September 16, 1920. It was already nine o'clock. He was late for work. He did not notice a small wagon in front of the imposing office building of J. P. Morgan and Company. Nor did his close friend and fellow worker, Clarence Millner, notice it while rushing through the streets with securities at eleven o'clock. But at 11:59 A.M. lower Manhattan shook with a thunderous explosion. The wagon, crammed with dynamite and planted supposedly by the "Reds" to destroy the symbol of capitalism, had exploded with such fury that thirty-eight persons were killed, hundreds lay injured and bleeding. Automobiles were overturned, windows were shattered, and debris was everywhere.

With great haste, Eli left the offices of Bond, McEnany & Company, in the Cotton Exchange Building, and made his way through the excited crowds to the scene of the explosion. He stood watching the tremendous confusion with great consternation. New York was very new and spectacular to him, but the scene before his eyes was unbelievable. But for a stroke of luck, he or Clarence Millner could have been in the explosion.

He had recently come to New York at the insistence of his Uncle Eli to learn the cotton brokerage business. Immediately following the war, Eli had accepted a position with C. C. Coddington, a dynamic man who was bringing Buick automobiles into the two Carolinas by the trainload, and he was well contented there. But Uncle Eli said, "Just come up and talk it over with me. You do not have to make a hasty decision." The result had been Eli's acceptance of the job as clerk for Allen Bond and Elwood McEnany.

Within two years, Eli concluded he was not cut out to be a clerk. He disliked it intensely. And, as Clarence Millner said, "He was a darn poor clerk." So he called on his Uncle Eli in his brownstone house on West 47th Street off Fifth Avenue and announced he was going back to Charlotte. "No," Uncle Eli said, "I don't want to see you go back until you have made good." Eli then asked, "Will you finance a seat on the Cotton Exchange for me, as you once said you would?" His uncle replied, "Yes."

The seat was bought and from then on a glorious future was ahead for Eli. He was a natural born trader. He executed his orders quickly, with great discretionary judgment. His customers liked the way he did business and orders poured in. It was not long until Bond, McEnany invited him back as a partner. "I will join the firm and represent you on the floor of the Cotton Exchange," Eli agreed, "if after two years in which I make good, you will purchase a seat on the New York Stock Exchange."

Seats on the Stock Exchange came high even then. The firm was reluctant, but purchased a seat in April, 1927, and Eli went on the floor as a broker. He had insisted that the price would advance rapidly. In a short time it doubled, and later went up to $625,000.

Eli was intuitively a good broker. The mechanical and mathematical facts of the ticker tape were like a human pulse to him. He could sense the market trend from them just as a doctor senses his patient's condition. On the floor of the exchange, he never lacked self-confidence and the courage of his convictions. As an individual, he was well liked; as a broker, he was highly respected. He was a born speculator, but not a gambler. There is a difference. The science of the market was a challenge to him. Hot tips never appealed to him unless they were based on facts such as good earnings, growth potential, and general reliability. He was at his best when he was buffeted in a sea of market adventure.

I met Eli in the fall of 1926. Leaving Hollins College in Virginia with my parents' consent, I had come up to study at the New York School of Fine and Applied Arts because I wanted to become a commercial illustrator. I was completely fascinated by this suave young Wall Streeter. The college boys with whom I had been going did not wear derbies and spats and carry canes. Nor did they, on Sunday, wear cutaways and striped trousers. Hard as I tried to keep my mind on my work, because I felt obligated to my parents to become a good illustrator, my thoughts constantly strayed to Eli and the divine times we had been having. Those were exciting days in New York for they were truly the "roaring twenties." Jimmy Walker, while not the most efficient mayor, had certainly made the city the playground of the world. And he had done it to music. (According to some of his parties Eli would tell me about.) Those were the days when Richard Rogers was giving his first musicals to the public, the days of Texas Guinan's famous nightclub (she called Eli "Southerner"), the dark speakeasies on side streets, the Charleston, knee-length skirts, Peaches Browning, Charles Lindbergh's flight and Calvin Coolidge's bull market, with every man in the street buying stocks on margin.

Eli and I were married on December 10, 1927, in Charlotte. My mother and father, Lela and Frank Wooten, gave us a beautiful church wedding, followed by a reception and supper for nine hundred people at the Charlotte Country Club. The Orange Blossom Special sped us to Florida where we honeymooned in Palm Beach at the Breakers Hotel. From there we jaunted to Havana.

Springtime brought more bull markets and heavy trading on the exchange with busy days for Eli, while I kept house in our little apartment on University Place. Then there was a glorious summer in Europe for the two of us. Could anything have been more romantic than a rose covered balcony overlooking a Swiss lake in the moonlight? Or could anything have been more thrilling than to have had Chanel and Lanvin put on showings just for *me*?

But the greatest thrill of our lives came on December 27, 1928, when our daughter, Katherine, was born. She was an impatient baby and could not be bothered with the usual time requirements. Eli rushed me madly by taxi to Miss Lippincott's private sanitorium at 666 Madison Avenue at five o'clock in the morning. After a pat on the hand he hurried home (which was then on East 84th Street) to shave and breakfast. I remember vaguely being wheeled into the delivery room while the doctor, Harbeck Halstead, was pulling off his coat, saying with every step, "These Southern girls sure can fool you." And thus it was that I cheated my husband out of that much talked about experience of pacing the floor of the little room reserved for perspiring fathers. The baby was snugly tucked in cotton when Eli arrived. The nurse afterwards told me when he looked at the tiny bundle he exclaimed, "She's the most beautiful thing I've ever seen!" He still says it to this day.

Our summers were spent at East Hampton, Long Island, in those years, and Eli kept telling his friends during the summer of 1929 that the market was too high and bound to break. Very few agreed with him and stocks continued to rise. We returned to the city in September.

On the morning of Thursday, October 24, Eli left our apartment before nine o'clock and proceeded to the floor of the exchange. Large blocks of stock began to be sold soon after the opening gong. Eli and the other brokers raised their eyebrows in question. Selling increased. There were hurried conversations with customers by way of telephone. Eli advised Uncle Eli to sell some of his holdings. An hour passed and the market was still declining. Orders flooded in, "sell at the market." But there were no buyers, only sellers. Prices dropped drastically. The ticker tape was so far behind that no one knew the value of stocks. By noon, panic roared through the exchange. No one thought of lunch. Eli rushed frantically from post to post trying to sell his customers' stocks.

At 1:30 P.M. Richard Whitney, floor man for J. P. Morgan and Company, began buying large blocks of stocks. He bought millions and millions of dollars worth. (Actually, the leading New York banks had pooled $240,000,000 through Morgan to stem the declining market.) The market began to rally. When the exchange closed at three o'clock the situation was more encouraging. The ticker tape was running four hours late.

Eli went straight to his Uncle Eli's home and found the old gentleman sitting quietly in his magnificently paneled library on the second floor of his home. Here, surrounded by his first editions and paintings, Uncle Eli was waiting for Eli to recount the devastating happenings of the day and map a course of action. It was typical of Uncle Eli that he never raised his voice in excitement, just as it was typical of him never to appear nervous. That was why he had ulcers which gnawed and pained him excruciatingly at times.

The years had been kind to Uncle Eli. He had amassed a fortune to be counted in the millions. For a few years after moving to New York he had been in business with his brother, Austin, first in J. H. Parker and Company and then Springs and Company, but the brokerage business did not appeal to him and he retired from it in 1923. He preferred to invest and watch the markets and collect objects of art.

Uncle Eli surrounded himself with Corots, Gainsboroughs, Rousseaus, Daubignys, Dupres, painting after painting, all beautiful—for he bought only what was pleasing to the eye. Then there were his porcelains, ivories, jades, prints, miniatures, snuff boxes, bronzes and books—four floors of an amazing collection. Here in his home these objects were his friends. They took the place of the wife and children he never had. They were the background for the lavish parties he gave, for the exquisite intimate dinners he presided over and for the evenings he spent quietly with his books.

Sitting in his library on his plum colored sofa, smoking the mildest of cigars, Uncle Eli would give audience to his intimate friends and nod approvingly at their jovial conversation while the ashes of his cigar would drop down the front of his immaculate, well tailored suit. To the right and left of him, behind and in front of him, were rows of incredibly fine books. These were his jovial companions too. There were his first editions of the English and French romantic periods. There were his volumes illustrated by Henry Alken, his ornithological books, including the elephant edition of Audubon's *Birds of America,* his illuminated manuscripts, executed by Alberto Sangorski, and volumes containing miniatures in their bindings. All these remained after his other guests had departed.

This particular Thursday when the market was in a panic, Uncle Eli was extremely quiet. There was much on his mind. He was heavily involved in stocks. To what extent, his nephew did not know, because Uncle Eli never disclosed his holdings or positions, and used a number of brokerage houses. Actually, he had over twenty millions of dollars invested.

The following morning, Friday, sales on the exchange were heavy but prices held moderately well. The same was true of Saturday, which was always a half day on the exchange.

The market broke again on Monday and this time there were no large buying orders to save it. The following day, the well remembered October 29, there seemed to be no bottom to the market. Eli was so swamped with orders that he was giving them out to any broker who had time to execute them. Some stocks dropped as much as $60 a share. Outside on the streets newspaper boys were screaming extras. Wall Street had never seen anything like it.

On Wednesday, hope was given to investors when John D. Rockefeller, Sr. announced that he was buying stocks. Then the exchange
suspended business for two days to give the brokerage houses a chance
to clear their affairs and straighten their books. The clerks of Bond,
McEnany had been working day and night. Cots had been moved into
the office. Food was being sent in.

Eli and I took the train for Charlotte that Wednesday night to get
away from it all for a long weekend. He was exhausted and highly
nervous. When the Southern pulled into Charlotte the next morning,
the family greeted us. So did an urgent wire. It said that Eli had an
error of 7,000 shares of Skelly Oil with the brokerage firm of Fenner
and Beane. We ate lunch at the Springs home and boarded the afternoon train for New York. The error proved to have been made by
another broker. But Eli never got his badly needed rest.

Stocks fell for two weeks, hitting rock bottom for the year on November 13. The country's investors had lost fifty billion by then.

When all of Eli's trades were settled, he was slightly in the black.
We were lucky. Life could go on as usual with us, while many others
were wrecked. Our life was busy, happy and, as I look back on it,
certainly glamorous. There were our regular Saturday luncheons at
the Voisin, dances on the St. Regis roof, beautiful shows with haunt-
ing melodies like "Dancing in the Dark," superb dinners with Uncle
Austin and Aunt Ethel in their elegant apartment, sunny weeks at
East Hampton, the excitement of furnishing our new Park Avenue
apartment and bidding at the American and Anderson Art Galleries.
Then there were Sundays when we sat with Uncle Eli while he ate his
ten o'clock breakfast, surrounded by the beauty of exquisite porcelains and the talents of Diaz, Schreyer, Troyon, Ziem, and scores of
other painters. There were so many things to fill our days. But our life
was not complete until our son was born on April 7, 1931. Uncle Eli
called him "the General." We called him Eli Baxter Springs III.

The day that this new little Springs entered the world, an older one
departed. While Eli was trying to get his father by long-distance to
break the happy news, Brevard was calling his nephew Elliott to tell
him that Elliott's father, Leroy, was dying. Brevard, expecting to hear
Elliott's voice, instead got Eli. Leroy passed away later that day. Uncle
Eli, on being informed of his brother's death said sadly: "The family
chain has been broken. We will all go quickly now." He was correct.
The following year Alva died.

Leroy Springs* was head of five cotton mills when he died. His son, Elliott, put aside his career of writing, which included among his books *War Birds* and *Leave Me With a Smile*—and came home to Fort Mill to take over the mills which he had inherited.

To describe Elliott Springs and his tremendous accomplishments would fill a lengthy book. He has been the most widely publicized member of the Springs family. Many knew him as a playboy who could "feed his ulcers champagne and make them like it." Many knew him for his fancy sport cars and fast planes. The general public knew him only as the author of the shockingly funny Springmaid ads. Elliott was all this, but he was also the brilliant executive who engineered a chain of obsolete cotton mills, hard hit by the depression of the 1930's, into the giant Springs Cotton Mills, third largest textile organization in the country.

When Elliott took over the mills, he turned his writing technique to new targets. He launched a ribald advertising campaign for Springmaid products which opened eyes and mouths across the nation and shook up the advertising industry.

No one could ever accuse Elliott of being stuffy, nor his ads of being dull, but this was due to his own imagination and wit and not to his advertising agents who constantly cringed at Elliott's broad satire and brassy burlesque of conventional ad copy. He once told me that his agents never came up with what he wanted. "If I ask for a St. Bernard, they send me a poodle!" he declared.

While organizations like the National Better Business Bureau, Inc., protested Elliott's ads as "detrimental to the best interests of advertising," others proclaimed them as hilarious, clever and eye-catching. Whatever they were, they sold sheets. Soon Springmaid products were known from coast to coast, and Elliott was well on his way to reorganizing and modernizing his mills.

Elliott was a hard worker. He toiled early and late. He expected his employees to toil with the same sense of loyalty to Springs Mills. But, likewise, he saw to it that they played well on company golf courses and tennis courts, in company swimming pools, at company recrea-

---

*Leroy Springs' wife, Grace White, had died in 1907, and in 1914 he married a widow, Mrs. Lena Jones Wade of Pulaski, Tennessee, who was head of the English department of Queens College in Charlotte, N. C. She had the honor of being nominated for the Vice Presidency of the United States at the Democratic Convention in New York City in 1924. Leroy Springs was interred in a special crypt in the clock tower of the Lancaster plant, which he had made the largest in the world.

tional parks, bowling and youth centers, and at attractive company beach houses.

This strange, flamboyantly dressed man, who poked fun at conventional people and organizations, had a consuming desire to help create good citizenship in his community and state. He sent the sons and daughters of his employees to college. He took care of his 13,000 employees as if each one were his personal responsibility. His good deeds were never advertised. That would have embarrassed him. Few people ever realized Elliott Springs' gruff, eccentric manner was only a shield for a kindliness which was innate. He liked to appear indifferent. Once he was stopped by a traffic cop for speeding while on his way to Charlotte. "Ten dollars," the policeman said. "Here's twenty," Elliott replied. "I'll be in a hurry when I come back." His fun-loving, playboy traits only served to mask his genius and his industry.

Elliott showed his whimsy in his favorite plaything, the Lancaster and Chester Railway which, for its thirty miles of track, boasted fifteen vice presidents, all personal friends, among them Admiral William Halsey (in charge of White Horse supplies), Lowell Thomas (in charge of advertising) and Gypsy Rose Lee (in charge of unveiling).

In refusing through the years to join organizations which would tell him when to shut down or when to open up, and stubbornly resisting the unionization of his mills, Elliott reminds one of Uncle Eli Springs' teenage composition on "Industry:" "A man who works hard and lets other people's business alone will be sure to get along in this world."

In 1922, Elliott married Frances Hubbard Ley. They had two children, Leroy II and Anne.* They remodeled the ante-bellum home of William Elliott White and moved in, making it one of the show places of that section.

While Elliott was building his empire, Eli was doing a tremendous brokerage business on the stock exchange, even though the country was in the depths of a depression from the 1929 panic. In addition to his regular customers, Eli handled orders for several large speculators, among them Uncle Eli and Bert Castles, who were considered part of "the old Waldorf crowd." These two elderly gentlemen had

---

*Leroy Springs II was killed in an airplane crash in 1946. Anne Springs married Hugh William Close in 1946. At the death of Elliott Springs in 1959 his son-in-law became the president of the Springs Cotton Mills. Under Close's able leadership the organization continues to expand. In 1963, Springs Mills, Inc., the selling house for Springs Cotton Mills, moved into their new 21-story office building at 104 West 40th Street, New York City.

both started out in the brokerage firm of Springs and Company. They had much in common, being wealthy Southern bachelors and collectors of art. They lived only three doors apart. Mr. Castles' home was newer, handsomer, but his collection not as extensive as Uncle Eli's. Mr. Castles bought race horses, while Uncle Eli prefered fine gaited horses. Both invested heavily in New York real estate. Mr. Castles owned much of 52nd and 53rd Streets between Fifth and Madison Avenues. Uncle Eli owned four buildings on 47th Street between Fifth and Sixth Avenues.

Every New Year's day, the "Captain," as many called Uncle Eli, gave a huge eggnog party. It was a custom he had begun as a young man in Charlotte, copied from his father and grandfather. As the years rolled by these parties became more famous. Brokers would approach Eli on the Stock Exchange floor and say, "Can't you get me an invitation to your Uncle Eli's party?" The guest list usually included friends from Wall Street, that is, gentlemen friends. Wives were never invited. Ah yes, there were ladies present, but they were young, glamorous, and ravishing—New York's most charming models and actresses. A New York paper, as far back as 1912, had taken notice of these extraordinary parties. It published a cartoon or caricature showing Uncle Eli ladling eggnog into a cup, another of him riding horseback, and a third of him resting both arms on his New York skyscrapers.

In 1933, Eli and I took a house in Rye, in Westchester County on Long Island Sound. We wanted to get our children out of the city apartment. Christmas of that year we remained in Rye instead of going south as we usually did. We were reluctant to leave Uncle Eli because he was not well. His ulcers bothered him when the market sank and in those days stocks were exceedingly low. He came out to Rye Christmas eve, spending the night with us. He took his time in making and stirring the old fashioned toddies before dinner. He held "the General" on his lap while he talked to little Katherine. At dinner, we gave him the seat at the head of the table and he meticulously carved the turkey.

After dessert and coffee, we went into the living room where Uncle Eli was to watch us decorate the tree. In a few minutes he was down on the floor, not without effort because he was stout in his later years, and was helping us to distribute the toys. He shook his head and said in a nostalgic way, "I should have married and had twelve children."

The following morning after all the presents were opened, Uncle Eli left us to ourselves and returned to the city, where we joined him later in the day for a beautiful seven o'clock dinner party.

When the forty-pound turkey was brought to his dining room that evening, Uncle Eli stood at the head of the table, smiling with pride. "Brevard sent this to me," he announced. "It's the largest I have ever seen. He raised it on his farm. Neils had to have a special pan made to fit it." With that, he began to carve slowly, as though it were a ritual. When all the guests around the long banquet table were served, he sat down. He was tired, but he was still smiling. Neils, his Swedish major domo, supervised the serving of the meal, as he did everything else in the house for he was a very accomplished person, having been a valet to a prince at one time.

It was a lovely Christmas. It was filled with warmth, happiness and tenderness. It was Uncle Eli's last one. He died three and a half months later, on April 14, 1933. Despite increased pain during those last months, he was advised against risking surgery. The family agreed with the doctor. But the pains drove Uncle Eli to another doctor who decreed an operation.

The day before the operation Uncle Eli was a very discouraged old man of eighty-one. The market was at an all-time low for the depression. He had suffered the loss of millions. He did not wish to burden his family with his art collection, and thus it was that he did what he vowed he would never do. He ordered his entire collection liquidated at his death, along with all of his holdings.

Uncle Eli lived only thirty-six hours after his operation. It was in the small hours of Good Friday morning that he died. The Southern Railway brought him to Charlotte and there he was buried on Easter Sunday beside his mother and father.

The cataloging and sorting of his art collection took months. The American Art Association, Anderson Galleries, Inc.,* situated on East 57th Street, New York City, handled the sale. There were 2,196 items (not including furniture, linens, draperies, etc.) which went on exhibit in the velvet hung show rooms on Thursday, November 15, 1934.

As Eli and I wandered through the galleries, we were struck with the beauty of each item, even more than we had ever been before. It was difficult for us to decide what we wanted to bid on. We wanted

---

*These galleries were later known as Parke Bernet, Inc.

everything! Truly, here was the collection of a man who had bought for beauty and not for the dollars and cents value of an object. The restful, poetic quality of Corot's "La Charrette de Gres" might have been worth $50,000, but I daresay the monetary value was never considered when Uncle Eli feasted his eyes on its loveliness. Nor had he given a thought to the $1,100 he had paid for one volume, a book which displayed mementos of the ill-fated House of Stuart. It was only its magnificence that he gloried in, just as he loved to pick up his volume of Keats' poems and gaze upon its illuminated pages and its gorgeously jeweled binding, sparkling with nearly eight hundred semi-precious and precious stones. The night he had bought a very small K'ang-hsi vase from the collection of J. P. Morgan for nearly $1,000 he was not thinking of anything but the exquisite reds on this delicate white porcelain beauty. When he ran his fingers over his carved rock crystal, 16th century ink stand and felt the flowers and arabesques cut deeply into the crystal, it was a thing of loveliness, the work of the great Cellini, not an ink stand which had cost him $2,100. When he looked at his English and French prints he was thrilled with their reds, their blues, their shadows. He bought for the quality of their impression, the depth of their coloring.

We remembered how Uncle Eli's eyes had sparkled when he looked at his *Cries of London* by Wheatley. The thirteen engravings, bound in one folio volume, which cost him $10,000, were appealing to him because of their humanness and the expressions on the faces of the criers. He had once shown me a snuff box, only one of many, and he had not said, "This little two and a half inch box cost me nearly a thousand dollars and is a museum piece." No, he had shown me the translucent bleu du roi enamel as a background for the opals and rose diamonds which encircled the enameld portrait of the Grand Conde.

As we gazed and talked of all these things, Eli would remember the various sales that he had attended with Uncle Eli. There had been the C. K. G. Billings sale when that wealthy, unusual gentleman* and important collector had put thirty of his paintings up for sale at the American Art Association in 1926. The pictures had formerly hung

---

*C. K. G. Billings is probably the only person who ever entertained at a formal dinner in the grand Ballroom of Sherry's, in New York City, when all the guests attended on horseback. Dinner was served from small tables fastened to the saddles. The guests on their horses formed a circle around the elaborately decorated room.

at Billings' Fort Tryon Hall* until that estate was sold to John D. Rockefeller, Jr. The night of the sale, Eli had sat between Bert Castles and Uncle Eli on the front row in the auction room. His eyes had opened wide when Castles had purchased a painting for approximately $50,000, but he had been even more shocked when his uncle had totaled the cost of his purchases for the evening at $150,300.

Eli remembered how quiet Uncle Eli had been at auction sales. The old gentleman would sit reading his catalogue or gazing at the articles which took their turn on the platform, until something struck his fancy. Then he would raise his thumb or nod his head. That was all. The auctioneers all knew him, all watched him. He was an unpretentious buyer. He had been taught that way. Even as a boy his father had cautioned him, "Avoid the slightest appearance of egotism or bombast. Be simple."

There had been many exciting evenings, Eli recollected, when collectors had come from far and wide to bid on treasures and Uncle Eli had always been among them. There had been the A. E. Hippisley, the Samuel S. Laird, the Lee Van Ching, and the George T. Veitch collections when Uncle Eli had gone home from each richer in rare Chinese porcelains. Then from the Viscount Leverhulm, the Tom G. Cannon, and the Edith Kingdon Gould sales he had acquired delicate porcelains and Worcester. From the Nathan Kaplan collection had come some of Uncle Eli's finest miniatures and snuff boxes.

Each room, as we strolled through the gallery, brought forth new comments and old memories. We were seeing this collection in its entirety for the last time.

For one week, every afternoon and evening, the auction continued. Limousines lined up at the entrance to unload the fashionables of New York, and then returned to help them carry off their purchases. The gallery was packed to overflowing. The New York *Herald Tribune* carried a large picture of one of the paintings by Corot and it created a great deal of interest. During that week the newspapers carried daily reports of the sale. The Springs collection was being dispersed in the same exciting manner in which it had been purchased. Being the ardent devotee of the auction room that he was, it was fitting that Uncle Eli's possessions should be offered in this way to others who could find the same deep pleasure in their acquisition.

Two weeks after the sale, Eli and I left for Charlotte where all the

*Fort Tryon Hall, on the Hudson River, cost two million to build. It now houses The Cloisters, a branch of the Metropolitan Museum of Art.

family was gathering for the golden anniversary of Brevard and Carrie Springs. It proved to be a memorable affair. Blandina and Joe Jones came from Cuba, and joining them was their college daughter, Blandina.* Their son, William McPheeters Jones, was working in Haiti and did not get there. Marguerite and Dick Myers, who lived in Charlotte, were there with their two sons, John Springs Myers and Brevard Springs Myers and their little daughter, Caroline. Esther Springs was there. Everyone was there! There was a reception and hundreds came to congratulate this very remarkable couple. Carrie, just as she had done fifty years before, slipped off to the photographer's studio with Isabelle Irwin Graham and had her picture taken with her maid of honor at her side. Though fifty years away from being a bride, Carrie stood as erect and her figure was as beautiful as it had been the day she married.

Even in his seventies, Brevard's stride was that of a young man, alert and quick. He carried a cane, but he swung it more than he leaned on it. His hats were always broadbrimmed ones, black felt in winter, white Panama in summer. He smoked a long clay pipe when at home.

Once when Brevard was in New York, he went to the Stock Exchange with Eli. Visitors were allowed only in the gallery and so father and son stood looking down on the busy floor. Suddenly the members began booing and Eli realized his father was smoking a cigar. Smoking was not allowed. "Father," said Eli, "the brokers are booing you because you are smoking." Immediately, Brevard removed the cigar from his mouth, lifted his large white Panama and bowed deeply to the members. With one accord, a great shout of applause went up. Afterwards, one man said to Eli, "Your father is the only true Southern gentleman I have ever seen."

Brevard spent much of his time at the plantation. There he had the companionship of his dogs, his animals and his land. For his land was a part of him. Springfield, with its fields of cotton, appealed to him as no other place on earth. Here he remembered his boyhood days. In that field was where he and Alva had had a rabbit run. In that creek was where he had bathed and fished. In the pasture he had shot his first quail. There was the old rotted stump of the tree in which he had caught an owl. For hours he would walk over his fields, deep in thought, wrapped in a vale of contentment.

*Blandina Jones married William E. Skilton of Havana, Cuba, in 1937.

And on this land was where he died. Suddenly, it had been, with a heart that pained for a few minutes and then was still. It was on February 14, 1936.

The bell tolled a mournful knell that morning. Whiskers, an old-time Negro who had always worked for Brevard, upon being informed that Mister Brevard was dead, made his way slowly to the farm bell and, with tears streaming down his cheeks, began to pull the rope. For what seemed an interminable time, the Negro rang the bell until, finally, Murray Osborne, the overseer, led him away, a broken-hearted old darky who kept saying, "Misser Brevard said he'd ring de bell fo' me if I died an' I wants to ring it fo' him."

After the death of his father, Eli began to think of retiring from the brokerage business. His extreme activity on the exchange was gradually exhausting him. He had stomach ulcers and weighed 119 pounds. It would be better to retire, even though he had a brilliant future ahead, he reasoned, than to stay on and break in health. He confided this to his partners. They were shocked at first but soon came to understand. In September of 1936, Eli resigned from Bond, McEnany and Company. His partner, Elwood McEnany, did the same thing. The seat on the Stock Exchange was sold.

Clarence Millner, who had been a partner in the firm for a number of years, wrote a letter to Eli:

My dear Eli,

There comes a time in every man's life when he should pour out his heart to someone living who has done him great good. I'm going to choose this opportunity to tell you what I think of you. One of the most beautiful things that ever came my way has been my association with you. I say, profoundly, that without your help, that whatever success has befallen me might easily not have been mine. Henceforth, you could chuck me into the mire, but I say very definitely I would make every effort to leap from it to defend you against anyone. Would that I had the might of a Cicero to go on singing your praises. Suffice to say, you are the Prince of Princes to me and in severing our commercial contact January 1st next, I am not sad because of the fond memory I shall always have of the man whose partner I had the honor to be.

Much love to you,
Clarence

December 10, 1936

For one year Eli and I travelled, trying to make up our minds where we would settle permanently. We knew we wanted to go south and establish a farm, but *where* was another question. We took a house on the St. John's river out of Jacksonville, Florida, while we contemplated. We took the children and nurse and spent two months at the Princess Hotel in Bermuda while we contemplated. We relaxed in the luxurious atmosphere of Jekyll Island Club,* off the coast of Georgia, while we contemplated. Finally, we came up with the answer. What better place could we find than home? Where else but Charlotte?

In 1937 we began to build a plantation, located ten miles from Charlotte. It was in the same Providence section where John and Sophia Springs had settled in 1766. Eli and I decided that this would be a new Springfield.

Carrie Springs lived long enough to see us settled in our home, which she nicknamed "the woods." She died on October 11, 1938.

It was here at our new Springfield that our children grew up, among the beauty of stately oaks, green pastures, bubbling brooks, and fields of cotton. We had animals and fowl of every kind and description—all white, for Eli had a mania for everything white. In the evenings our white dog, our white cat, and our pet white peacock would sit beside us. At night our forty or fifty peacocks would thrill us with their piercing screams.

It was here at Springfield that I took over the management of the farm when World War II came and Eli went to work for the Navy in their shell loading plant on the outskirts of Charlotte. We strained to produce every ounce of food possible, even to our own cheese, and shared it with our friends and neighbors during those black days of rationing.

It was here that we turned on our radios the first thing every morning, eager, but half afraid, to hear the latest war news, because Marguerite's son John was a Major with Patton in Europe, while her son Brevard was a Captain on a B-29 in the Pacific. Blandina's son was a Colonel on foreign duty. Elliott Springs had returned to service as a Colonel in charge of the air field in Charlotte, while his son Leroy was a Lieutenant flying a B-17. Uncle Austin's son, Richard, was in the air flying planes back and forth to England and Europe. Each morning when the news was over I secretly thanked God my son was too young to go to war.

*Jekyll Island, a private club for members only, near Brunswick, Georgia, has since been taken over by the state of Georgia as a public park.

It was from Springfield that our children went off to prep school and college. And it was here that we were saddened by the telegram that told us Uncle Austin Springs had died on June 29, 1944. When Aunt Bleecker Scott* died in 1949 the chain was complete for Blandie's and Baxter's children, complete in that far off land.

It was here at Springfield that I saddled my horse on the morning of November 14, 1950, when our son, Eli, III, left the University of North Carolina and joined the United States Marine Corps. Those were the early days of the Korean War. I rode furiously across country for hours trying to ease the tension within me.

It was from here that a tall, handsome man by the name of Jack Shannon took our daughter to Birmingham, Alabama, as his bride in 1951, and it is here, only a stone's throw from our house that our son lives with his wife Rickey (Jennie Ann Sherrill) and his little family. It is the year 1964. The summer is warm. The gentle stillness of the day is broken by the sound of the locusts and the laughter of our eight grandchildren—three little Shannons—Jack, Jr., Katherine, and Lela—and five little Springses—Eli IV, Missy (Caroline), Sally, Amy, and Brevard Davidson II.

In a sense, my story is complete, and yet it will never be finished. It will go on and on—just as the world will go on and on, looking to its sons to give it spirit, heart, courage and devotion, with—God grant—the freedom to enjoy and express those qualities.

The Springs story to me is like a mighty trust fund placed, not in the vault of a bank, but in the hearts of the young. A fund, not of stocks, bonds, and dollars, but of character, example, honor, integrity, and faith. It, like a trust, was willed by those who have passed on, and inherited by generation after generation. Its dividends are paid in satisfaction and understanding. To this trust fund each new generation must look for its guidance and inspiration.

It was Blandie Springs who said, "Remember, my dear child, time passes swiftly and is precious."

---

*Bleecker Springs Scott was survived by two daughters, Julia Baxter and Calvine. Julia married Stuart Warren Cramer, Jr., head of Cramerton Mills, Cramerton, N. C. After the death of her husband in 1957, Julia Scott Cramer married Maurice R. Smith of Kansas City, Missouri, in 1959. Calvine Scott married Muscoe Burnett, an official with Union Carbide Company, and they live in Winnetka, Illinois.

THE SPRINGSTEEN-SPRINGS GENEALOGY

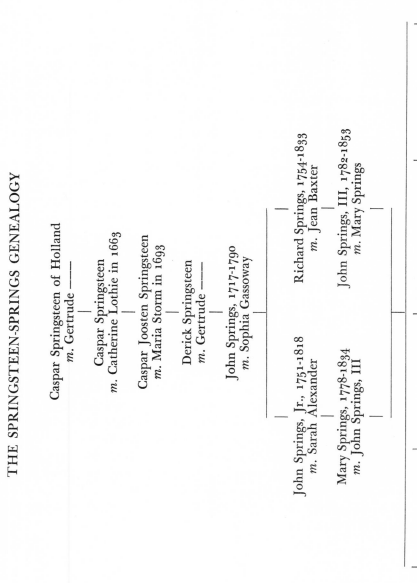

Caspar Springsteen of Holland
m. Gertrude ———

Caspar Springsteen
m. Catherine Lothie in 1663

Caspar Joosten Springsteen
m. Maria Storm in 1693

Derick Springsteen
m. Gertrude ———

John Springs, 1717-1790
m. Sophia Gassoway

Richard Springs, 1754-1833
m. Jean Baxter

John Springs, III, 1782-1853
m. Mary Springs

John Springs, Jr., 1751-1818
m. Sarah Alexander

Mary Springs, 1778-1834
m. John Springs, III

Andrew Baxter Springs
1819-1886

Richard Austin Springs
1807-1876

Leroy Springs
1811-1863

Mary Springs
1813-1872

Sophia Springs
1821-1883

Alva
Springs
1859-1932
m.
Miriam Seltzer

A. Baxter
Springs, Jr.
1857-1881

John
Springs
1853-1882

Eli Baxter
Springs
1852-1933

Brevard Davidson Springs
1860-1936
m.
Caroline Clarkson

Richard Austin
Springs, II
1856-1934
m.
Ethel Armitage

Leroy
Springs, II
1861-1931
m.
Grace White

Bleecker
Springs
1869-1949
m.
John M. Scott

Esther Springs
1892-

Eli Baxter Springs, II
1894-
m.
Katherine Wooten

Marguerite Springs
1887-1960
m.
Richard A. Myers

Blandina Springs
1889-
m.
Joseph A. Jones

Katherine Wooten Springs
1928-
m.
Jack H. Shannon

Eli Baxter Springs, III
1931-
m.
Jennie Ann Sherrill

Jack H. Shannon, Jr.
Katherine Shannon
Lela Shannon

Eli Baxter Springs, IV
Caroline Springs
Sally Springs
Amy Springs
Brevard Davidson Springs, II

INDEX

NOTES

NOTES

NOTES

NOTES

NOTES

NOTES